The *Star Wars*
Phenomenon in Britain

The *Star Wars* Phenomenon in Britain

The Blockbuster Impact and the Galaxy of Merchandise, 1977–1983

CRAIG STEVENS

Foreword by Tom Berges

McFarland & Company, Inc., Publishers
Jefferson, North Carolina

All photographs are from the author's collection unless otherwise indicated.

Library of Congress Cataloguing-in-Publication Data

Names: Stevens, Craig, 1970– author.
Title: The Star Wars phenomenon in Britain : the blockbuster impact and the galaxy of merchandise, 1977–1983 / Craig Stevens ; foreword by Tom Berges.
Description: Jefferson, North Carolina : McFarland & Company, Inc., Publishers, 2018. | Includes bibliographical references and index.
Identifiers: LCCN 2018001215 | ISBN 9781476666082 (softcover : acid free paper) ∞
Subjects: LCSH: Star Wars films—History and criticism. | Star Wars films—Collectibles. | Motion pictures—Social aspects—Great Britain—History—20th century.
Classification: LCC PN1995.9.S695 S885 2018 | DDC 791.43/75—dc23
LC record available at https://lccn.loc.gov/2018001215

British Library cataloguing data are available

ISBN (print) 978-1-4766-6608-2
ISBN (ebook) 978-1-4766-2850-9

Front cover image of hyperspace © 2018 Rost-9D/iStock

Printed in the United States of America

McFarland & Company, Inc., Publishers
Box 611, Jefferson, North Carolina 28640
www.mcfarlandpub.com

For my wonderful wife, Karen.

And for Paul and Gary.

Table of Contents

Acknowledgments

A large number of people made a contribution to this book by sharing memories, providing information, donating materials and offering support.

My deepest thanks to those who took the time to answer my incessant questions: Sarah Baker-Saunders, Dave Barnacle, Peter Beale, Robert Beecham, Ian Boyce, Bob Brechin, Nicholas Broome, Laurie Calvert, Bob Cole, Les Cooke, Grant Criddle, Gerald Crotty, Peter Davis, Shaun Dawkins, David Day, Carole Deighton, Derek Dorking, Tim Drummond, Pete Dummer, Robin Edmonds, Jackie Ferguson, Bob Fischer, Anthony Fredrickson, David Giddings, Jason Grant, Tim Hampson, Richard Harris, Gary "Tich" Harvey, Philip Heeks, John Higgins, Jane High, John Holmes, Robin Kennedy, Charles Lippincott, Andrew Maconie, Geoff Maisey, Lorraine Malby, Glen Maloney, John May, Declan McCafferty, Frank Mewes, Craig Miller, Roger Morrison, Graham Ogle, Marc Pevers, Allan Rosser, Jordan Royce, Joe Sales, James Simmonds, Andrew Skilleter, Dez Skinn, Darren Slade, Barry Smith, Jason Smith, Craig Spivey, Brian Turner, Louise Turner and Ian Whitlock.

I'd like to thank many other people I have spoken to over the years regarding *Star Wars*, including Scott Bradley, Mark Daniels, Stephen Danley, Peter Davis, Andy Dukes, Anthony Fagan, Matt Fox, Andrew Gerino, Jonathan Hart, Rob Holmes, Mark Howard, Richard Hutchinson, Duncan Jenkins, Jason Joiner, Gus Lopez, James Martin, Richard McClean, Dave Moore, Chris Muncke, David Oliver, Andy Preston, David Raider, Jamie Richards, Mark Richards, Darren Simpson, Derek Tate, Pete Vilmur, Jon Ware, Ross Williams, and my fellow collectors at starwarsforum.co.uk.

Special thanks to Joe Sales for proofreading and fact-checking. To Bob Brechin for arranging many of my interviews. Special thanks also to Jordan Royce for granting me permission to use extended quotations from *Starburst* magazine and sharing his memories. John May deserves a special mention for allowing the use of some of the content of his Generalist blog, for sharing his memories and for his advice and support. Also special thanks to Dez Skinn for his kind assistance. Nick Symes, Sarah Baker-Saunders, Darren Simpson, Craig Spivey and Derek Dorking for supplying so many wonderful photographs from their extensive collections. Peter Beale deserves a special mention for providing so much information and sharing his contacts. My thanks to the staff of Vectis Auctioneers, Stockton-on-Tees, for putting me in touch with many of my interviewees. Thanks to Grant Criddle for his advice and support. Thanks to Robin Kennedy for supplying me with a DVD full of classic Palitoy television advertisements and to David Tree for creating it. To Bob Miller for checking my sources. Finally, to Tom Berges for writing the foreword.

My greatest appreciation to Hilary Bliss, the archivist of Dennis Publishing, who was incredibly generous in arranging for me to comb through the company archives. Also to the late Felix Dennis, who granted me access. Thanks to the staff of the British Newspaper Archive, the British Film Institute Library, the British Library News Room, the *Southend Echo*, the *Star Wars* Magazines Encyclopedia and ceraloffers.com.

My endless love and affection to my gorgeous, patient wife, Karen, for all of her support. My greatest thanks to Christine and Charlie Stevens. My love also to my mother, Rosemary, for being so supportive and for storing my *Star Wars* junk for so long.

Foreword

by Tom Berges

As a Yank from the other side of the Pond, I was delighted to read this wonderful book which lovingly captures *Star Wars* fever in the UK. What better way to celebrate the Original Trilogy than a book documenting the mad yet methodical dash for merchandising and promotion that would reach fever pitch well before the British release of *Star Wars*, and forward through *The Empire Strikes Back* and finally *Return of the Jedi*? Fevered fans owe much to the unsung heroes who brought us many products we purchased. From bubble bath, to the very first collector magazines and comics, to the UK's Palitoy for action figures and the like, the list goes on and on.

Star Wars was an undisputed, absolute powerhouse of fun, and no one was spared the magic. Nor would we want to be. The UK, along with the United States, was blessed with an equal amount of *Star Wars* mania enjoyed by myself, and apparently the rest of the free world. The book you are about to enjoy is filled with accounts from people who were there on the front lines. The creators, the marketers, the manufacturers and last but not least the fans who voraciously ate it all up and begged for more. This book is a love letter to the creation and consumption of everything that made my childhood a magical and memorable time. *Star Wars* is forever, no matter what galaxy, or side of the Atlantic you're from! *Bravo!*

Tom Berges is curator of igrewupstarwars.com and mygalacticchildhood.com.

Preface

Finding a new angle on a story that has been told many times over is far from easy. And on the subject of *Star Wars*, it would on the surface seem a thankless task. There are countless books on the subject—each successive author seeking to burrow ever deeper into the same story, to delve deeper into the mind of George Lucas. No matter what the precise details may be, the fact that the *Star Wars* trilogy was a success and that the accompanying merchandise was also successful nowadays seems not even worth repeating. Reading the various accounts of the *Star Wars* story, I was struck that all of them are written from the point of view of the financiers, the filmmakers, the actors and the behind-the-scenes boffins. The success of the *Star Wars* trilogy depended not only on these people but to a great degree on those concerned with the promotions, of creating the merchandise—and of course the fans who lifted the films to exalted heights. I realized that the story of these individuals has not been told before and the fact is that the British story of *Star Wars* has not yet been told. Britain had its own unique release schedule of the films, received unique promotions, enjoyed exclusive merchandise and underwent a special kind of craziness restricted to the country. Great Britain, too, made its own mark on the *Star Wars* trilogy that has not been fully recognized to date.

Beginning in October 2012 with only a page or two of basic information about *Star Wars* in Britain, of the kind that can be derived from an Internet search and from previously published *Star Wars* books, I have been astonished by the information that I have been able to glean. Physically searching through newspaper and magazine archives. Sending countless begging emails and letters. One clue leads to another. One person knows someone else. In time, the overall picture began to flower and the result has been far greater than I dared to imagine. I have met colorful individuals along the way, and it is my pleasure to introduce them to this book's readers. *Star Wars* in Britain is a story of initiative, of making the best of slender resources, of grasping opportunities when they arise and having a great deal of fun in the process.

Introduction

"I remember queuing up to see *Star Wars* in the summer of 1977." This is how many a conversation on *Star Wars* will begin in Britain. It has become part of the culture, a collective memory. The problem is that it never happened. Great Britain did not receive the film until December 27, 1977. The trouble is that Britain has adopted the American story of *Star Wars*. Many people in Britain have memorized and embraced the tales of queues forming around the block at Mann's Chinese Theatre in Hollywood on May 25, 1977—the remarkable story of how the Kenner "early Bird" kit was sent to shops in December 1977 (it was simply a voucher that entitled the purchaser to be mailed the *Star Wars* figures in the new year); how the *Star Wars* characters placed their footprints in wet cement in the street; and how, if collectors were very lucky, they might have got their hands on a rocket-firing Boba Fett. Such things are certainly worth noting but they have nothing whatsoever to do with the British story of *Star Wars*. Britain has its own remarkable *Star Wars* history that has simply never before been recorded.

I have not focused too heavily on the impact of *Star Wars* on the film industry, on special effects technology, on toy manufacturers and on world culture because these are subjects that are mulled over and debated everywhere. And too, George Lucas' inspiration for *Star Wars* and how it was brought to the screen has been given sufficient coverage elsewhere, to the point that most people now must be aware of the basic story. This book is the dark side of the "Making of Star Wars" moon. For people living outside of Britain, the story of *Star Wars* within its shores will come as a total surprise. Preconceived ideas may be challenged, and I hope there will be smiles and chuckles along the way.

The story is all the more personal, as I was one of the people who saw *Star Wars* upon its original release. I immersed myself in the *Star Wars* universe, read the comics, collected the merchandise and even got Darth Vader's autograph. In the period of time beyond the scope of this book, I joined with other fans to form the UK *Star Wars* fan Club when the official *Star Wars* fan club closed down. My writing odyssey began when I became the fanzine editor and later the club chairman. Years later, after traveling to conventions as far as Australia, being involved in fandom, being part of the delegation invited to the Lucasfilm relaunch of *Star Wars* in Britain, writing for blogs and magazines, running several collector's shops and displaying my *Star Wars* Lego models far and wide, the next logical step was to write a book. During the writing, I took time to auction my mint condition Palitoy Boba Fett for a record-breaking £17,000.

Some fans in Britain are old enough to have seen *Star Wars* at the cinema but their memories are foggy at best. There was once a radio show, a *Star Wars* special on *The Muppets* and a television screening of the film. The fans who were around during this time are the lucky ones for they at least have some inkling as to what happened. A way for them to relive the past, to finally connect the dots, is overdue. People who came later to *Star Wars* have only the barest idea of what came before the current *Star Wars* age, and if they grew up with instant internet communication and movies on demand, the story this book tells will be all the more surprising. It is set in an age when childhood and adolescence required a lot more effort in seeking out things of interest and staving off boredom. There were only three television channels, no videos, no computers, and no internet. There were no mobile phones and the family had just one phone with a dial attached to a wire. There was a single television in the living room that often screened in black and white. Even if a child-friendly television program such as *Star Trek* or *Doctor Who* provided an hour of respite, they did not remain in the mind for very long. A trip to the cinema was a special treat but producers did not place a great deal of emphasis on family-oriented films.

The *Star Wars* films did not appear everywhere at once in Britain as films do today via the wonders of digital technology. Movies were released on actual film and their slow march across the country was agonizing, especially for those who had a great interest in them. The majority of fans had the opportunity to read the entire story, watch the "Making of" documentary on television and collect all of the memorabilia before *Star Wars* appeared anywhere near their area. In between the release of the films, it was down to the ingenuity of fans to keep themselves occupied. The question of when the films landed in individual cities and towns has barely been approached before. The release of the *Star Wars* films required a strategy and promotional ideas with which to inspire the general public to attend en masse. The people who wracked their brains, used the talents they had and drew in others for the struggle for promotions are featured in this book. Another important aspect is that so many items of memorabilia are often regarded as being commonplace, lacking in value and not even worth putting on the shelf alongside the rocket firing Boba Fett. The fact is that every piece of merchandise has a story to tell—its own creator and path through *Star Wars* history. While it would be impossible to focus on every piece of *Star Wars* memorabilia in one book, I hope that I have been able to record some of the most entertaining examples. At the very least, I hope that collectors will be able to look upon their items with fresh eyes. The range of Kenner/Palitoy *Star Wars* toys has become so familiar that it has been eclipsed to some eyes by better, more detailed modern examples.

I have focused on the *Star Wars* comics from Marvel because they are looked upon by modern eyes as being quirky, often ridiculous and certainly as far away from the official storyline as they could be. From 1977 to 1983, fans considered the Marvel comic saga and the newspaper comic strip that ran alongside it to be the actual continuation of the *Star Wars* storyline in between the films. The stories were considered to be as real as the onscreen universe and they were a vital aspect of keeping the saga alive considering that the films were released three years apart. Even though the writers of the comics were entirely in the dark regarding the content of an upcoming *Star Wars* film, they managed somehow to segue their storylines into the films almost seamlessly. Of course, there were many stories that were not part of the ongoing storyline and the fans reading them could discard them if they wished, or adopt them accordingly.

The official Poster Monthly publications of the *Star Wars* trilogy were extremely important, not only in keeping interest going between films but also in laying down the foundations of the *Star Wars* expanded universe. Whether it was the tale of Darth Vader's past, what lay behind the mask of Stormtroopers, Han Solo's indebtedness to Jabba, or Chewbacca's life debt to Han, it was the Poster Monthly that brought all of the facts together in one source. The writers filled in many of the blanks themselves and their ideas were extremely influential. It may be all the more surprising that the official Poster Monthly was created and written in Britain.

Finally, the people who saw *Star Wars* have stories to tell—how they experienced the films for the first time, coveted the merchandise, grew up alongside the trilogy and how, in many cases, the course of their lives was changed. I consider myself fortunate to be part of this clan.

It was my intention from the outset to make this book accessible to everyone. It will not please those expecting panache in the text. I made a conscious decision to tell the story in simple (but hopefully entertaining) prose, for the amount of information I wished to convey is so great, so detailed, that it did not leave a great deal of wiggle room on the page. I hope that the average reader will appreciate that I have stuck to the facts, for there is a great deal of information to absorb in the process of travelling back in time. If the reader experiences a similar journey of discovery as I did while writing this book, I will consider myself well satisfied.

May the force be with us all.

Chapter 1

A Beginning Beyond Belief

On a fresh sunny morning in June 1977, Peter Beale had a bounce in his step as he walked down Kensington High Street, located in one of London's most affluent areas. A film called *Star Wars*, which he had been an intimate part of, had opened big on May 25 in America and was proving to be a massive success. "I received reports from America on a daily basis," says Beale. "Each day it became increasingly exciting seeing the reaction grow and grow." As managing director of 20th Century-Fox Productions Ltd. in the UK, Beale had been producer Gary Kurtz and director George Lucas' first point of contact for the *Star Wars* production based at EMI Elstree Studios:

> In *Star Wars* we had a film that was full of advanced special effects. It was very sophisticated to make and other studios having turned it down, so the first challenge I had faced was finding out if it could be made and how it could be made. Vice-president for creative affairs Alan Ladd Jr., working at the 20th Century-Fox offices in Los Angeles, used to send me scripts on a regular basis, *The Omen* for instance, to see if they could be filmed in the U.K. within a certain budget. Not all scripts could be made for the budget the studio wanted. I received *Star Wars* as a script and six paintings by the conceptual artist Ralph McQuarrie that George Lucas had hired. It was a major deal to put it together, especially to make the film on what was a relatively low budget in those days. I insisted on a year's preparation which everyone said was crazy but it wasn't. I recommended two or three people for each head of department and from that George and Gary put together the most amazing British crew. When we started making the film, we were really prepared for it.

Having shepherded the film through its production, Beale had a fresh challenge: handling the *Star Wars* merchandising. "The thought of tie-in merchandise for Britain had not been seen as a high priority," says Beale. "But as soon as *Star Wars* began to be such a success in America, Alan Ladd Jr. called me and we agreed that I should handle the merchandising in Britain and Europe." Visiting every shop along Kensington High Street, Beale looked out for products that could easily be adapted to bearing the *Star Wars* image:

> I looked at what was the most prominent product on the shelf and I made a list and decided that these were the things that I wanted there to be merchandising on. I had my wife Francesca with me as I wanted a woman's perspective as to what merchandising would be successful. My main interest was the publicity point of view rather than making a profit. To have an identity for the film everywhere people went. I then took out to lunch someone from Disney, because they were the only ones doing merchandising in those days. He was very generous and gave me a briefing on how to go about it. I then systematically began calling up all of the major companies.

Thirty-two years old in 1975, Beale had the youthful energy and approach that the *Star Wars* production required. Now he would turn his zeal to the matter of *Star Wars* licensing.

The British media had been kept well briefed on *Star Wars* via its publicist Brian Doyle since it had entered production on March 22, 1976. Journalists from all over the world had been invited to tour EMI Elstree Studios, and depending on their status, they had the opportunity interview the stars, Gary Kurtz and George Lucas. The media had plenty of excuses to become excited as the *Star Wars* presskit further emphasized the British connection, with its listing of the actors and the film crew being mostly Britons. The fact that Alec Guinness was appearing in a science fiction film made headlines because it was a far cry from his more serious film roles. *Variety* had profiled George Lucas, who was not well known in Britain, revealing that he was an independent filmmaker working from his partially restored Parkhouse mansion in San Anselmo, California, purchased with his *American Graffiti* profits. The building was reportedly fitted out with a screening room, offices, work rooms and a ton of equipment.[1] A graduate of the University of Southern California Film School, Lucas was keen to point out the benefits of enrolling. "Think of it. In two years, you can learn the basic technology and actually put it into practice."[2]

Reporter Sue Summers secured an interview with Gary Kurtz for *Screen International*. A photograph of an exhausted-looking Kurtz and Lucas, sitting on the Elstree set, revealed both men to be very young-looking, despite their beards. Kurtz described *Star Wars* as "a blend of the ideal of all American children of the Space Era; of *James Bond* and action adventure."[3] The article shed light on how esteemed film director Francis Ford Coppola had been instrumental in shaping the careers of Lucas and Kurtz. During the production of *The Terror* (1963) for legendary B-movie producer Roger Corman, Kurtz met Coppola, as production assistant and second unit director respectively. Lucas came onto the scene later, when as a film student he arrived as an observer on the set of director Coppola's *Finian's Rainbow* (1968). Lucas soon met Kurtz and they embarked (with Lucas as director and Kurtz as producer) on the science fiction film *THX 1138* in 1971 and *American Graffiti* in 1973. In those pre–Internet days, the British press pored over *Variety* and *Screen International* for this kind of information and the most noteworthy reports filtered through to the general public via newspaper and magazine articles. Both publications were used by film companies to place advertisements for their films and to make announcements.

The success of *Star Wars* in America was immediately picked up upon by the national newspapers in Britain. The film's British connection was well-known within the media, so it was a dream story for any newspaper editor. "If you haven't heard of it yet, you soon will," wrote New York–based reporter Lesley Hinton, for the *Sun* newspaper. The film was reportedly taking £1,300,00 at the box office every week and was on course to overtake *Jaws* as the biggest money spinner in film history. "*Star Wars* is all good clean fun. No sex, no sadistic violence. Only the merest trickle of blood. Yet outside the cinema two blocks from my office, the queues each day stretch 200 yards."[4] David Lewin sent a report from Hollywood for *The Daily Mail*: "Every morning as I drive through to my office, queues are forming for *Star Wars* at one of the cinemas in Westwood, the University suburb of Los Angeles. And at night, right until midnight, the queues are still there, waiting to see one of the six daily performances. The lines—mostly young people between 18 and 22 move slowly, if at all, and there is a party atmosphere as people wait to see the film which has been the phenomenon of 1977. For this is happening not just in Los Angeles but right across America." Lewin explained how in the six weeks since *Star Wars*'s opening, it had taken more than $12 million at 409 cinemas and how the price of 20th Century-Fox shares had reportedly doubled, adding nearly £50 million to the company's stock value. British cinemagoers hoping to see the film would no doubt have been disappointed by Lewin stating, "England will have to wait until Christmas."[5]

It was reported in the press that two cinemas—the Dominion Theatre Tottenham Court Road and the Odeon Theatre Leicester Square—in London would premiere *Star Wars* on Tuesday, December 27, 1977. The run in Ireland and Northern Ireland also began on the 27th, at the Savoy Dublin and Curzon Belfast. The scheduled United Kingdom opening of *Star Wars* was evocative of the standard pattern of family-oriented films opening at Christmas in Britain, taking advantage of the holiday season, as Peter Beale explains:

> In those days, films opened in America first and then based on the success there the different countries around the world would pick their best dates for release. Typically summer in England is not very good for cinema. Europeans have historically have gone to the cinema more in the winter than they have in the summer. So it would be unlikely, at least in those days, that you would have brought out a film at that time of year. The investment in promotions and the release involved was such that you would see how it goes in the American market and go from there.

The British press continued to print updates on the Stateside success of *Star Wars*. It was beginning to build into a major news story. "The total gross through June 2nd is three million dollars," John Austin wrote from his Hollywood office for *Screen International*:

> Albert Szafbo, manager of Avco Embassy cinema in Westwood, told me, "I have never seen anything like this. They are filling the theater for every single performance—six a day. This is not a snowball, it's an avalanche." One woman was in line for the fifth time, another for the third. One half of the people in a two-block line, it was estimated, had seen the film more than once. The people in the queues exchange bits of dialogue and talk constantly about the Laurel and Hardyesque of Artoo Detoo and See-Threepio.

John Austin described how 20th Century-Fox had had to send maintenance crews to clean up the debris from the food consumed by people in the queues:

> [The Avco Embassy cinema] turned away 5000 people last weekend and several hundred a day during the week. As a sidelight, Fox records cannot press enough LPs to satisfy the demand for a soundtrack. Over 10,000 were sold in Los Angeles in three days alone, and the record plant is working around the clock to keep up with the demand. The studio is also negotiating with an additional avalanche of merchandising requests from toy manufacturers."[6]

Star Wars *Everything*

The interest in *Star Wars* tie-in merchandising was certainly something George Lucas approved of. Before production had begun, he had been buzzing with ideas of how *Star Wars* could generate tie-in products—even Wookiee cookies. In his childhood years, a merchandise boom had built up around the character Davy Crockett, so the potential clearly existed. Lucas' friend Steven Spielberg had been frustrated that despite his *Jaws* (1975) becoming the most successful film in history, its merchandise potential had not been fully realized. There had been dull items such as board games and beach towels but he had wanted *Jaws* ice creams where you bit into them and red liquid would spill out. Lucas had studied how Disney promoted and merchandised its films and wanted to up the ante further, with visions of dedicated shops selling *Star Wars* memorabilia. Marc Pevers, director of business affairs at 20th Century-Fox, had spent months attempting to drum up enthusiasm, writing over 200 letters to potential licensee companies without receiving a single positive response. Ordinarily his job involved looking after the film and television licensing deals that were already in place at 20th Century-Fox but for *Star Wars* he had been charged with making deals well in advance of the film opening at the cinema. "At one stage, I started telling the potential licensees 'if this film doesn't make $30 million, I'll give you your money back.' Back then, $30 million was a lot of money. That figure turned out to be way off as *Star Wars* really began to hit the big time." Now that *Star Wars* had opened, Pevers' telephone barely stopped ringing. "I began to receive phone calls from companies that had spurned our offers before. 'Whatever's still available, I'll take,' one company said. 'I was in Hong Kong when your letter came,' read one excuse. 'My secretary didn't give me the letter,' wrote another company's spokesperson."[7] Pevers was used to anonymity in his role but so great was the reaction to *Star Wars*, that a light was even shone into his corner of 20th Century-Fox: a photographer from *People* magazine arrived at his desk wanting to do a story, which was a startling reversal of the situation he had previously faced when nobody had been interested. Pevers was pictured in the magazine on the telephone at his desk, wearing a Darth Vader mask, surrounded by *Star Wars* merchandise.

Charles Lippincott, the Lucasfilm vice-president of advertising, publicity, promotion and merchandising for the *Star Wars* Corporation, had covered much of the same ground as Marc Pevers, in contacting potential merchandise producing companies for *Star Wars* well in advance of the cinema release. But Lippincott's brief was wider, having been charged with finding ways to promote the film outside of the standard channels that were being covered by the 20th Century-Fox publicity machine. Lippincott based his campaign on the world of sci-fi fandom and magazines amateur fanzines, and he also traveled city to city in America, presenting slide shows at science fiction and comic conventions. "I was working out of an office that George still had at Universal Studios but he and Gary weren't there," says Lippincott,

> so I had the Los Angeles office to myself. When *Star Wars* happened, there was talk of hiring a licensing agent from outside the company but I told Fox I didn't want to do it that way. We were all overwhelmed by the success of *Star Wars* and George decided after about three weeks that we should be able to hire some people. It was a little late [*laughs*]. All I had was my former girlfriend Carol Wikarska [later Titelman] as my secretary. …Marc Pevers didn't get an awful lot of assistance with the merchandising at Fox either. So I hired a crew of people and a new secretary so Carol could go and work on *Star Wars* publishing.

Lippincott had made frequent visits to Elstree Studios during the filming of *Star Wars*. According to Peter Beale,

> Charles Lippincott was the one that created the concept of going to comic fairs and developing the underground for *Star Wars* before it opened. The fact that there was a queue for the preview of the film in San Francisco was down to Charles Lippincott. He had generated this enormous excitement. I must say that I have enormous admiration for him and he was a pleasure to work with.

Factors Ltd. was a major company to jump aboard to produce *Star Wars* merchandise including T-shirts, buttons (called badges in the UK) and a host of other items. Another company that was granted a license early on was high-class mask producer Don Post Studios. It had the full cooperation of Lucasfilm, which lent the original masks to base copies on. Fans could obtain exceptionally accurate full-head masks of Darth Vader, C-3PO and the Stormtrooper. Topps Ltd. was interested in producing the first of five sets of *Star Wars* trading cards but the deal that Marc Pevers struck was not as generous as the one he had previously offered. According to Pevers,

I originally proposed standard deal of $5000 vs. .5 percent. Their initial lack of enthusiasm meant they had to pay $100,000 vs. ten percent after *Star Wars* opened. I solicited all of the licensing deals but they would be mutually approved between 20th Century-Fox and Lucasfilm. The merchandising provisions gave either side reciprocal right of first refusal with each simultaneously seeking to make deals with licensee companies.

Pevers' approach to merchandising was innovative. From the outset, he had sought to award Master Licenses to a select number of companies. Traditionally, licenses were offered to as many companies as possible but if over-saturation occurred and retailers marked down the merchandise, it could kill off any future merchandising potential. "I believed that *Star Wars* had the potential to be this generation's Mickey Mouse and Donald Duck," says Pevers. "The traditional strategy would have been disastrous for *Star Wars* because retailers, having gotten burned, would never have wanted to carry new merchandise."[8]

The Toy Story

The spirit of satisfying George Lucas' desire for *Star Wars* toys led to Pevers and Lippincott teaming to attend the New York Toy Fair staged at 23rd and Broadway from February 21 to 25, 1977. They set up showings of the *Star Wars* teaser trailer and Lippincott's slide show at the Dorset Motel where they were staying. Pevers prepared a speech emphasizing the marketing potential of the film. He was essential to the mission to the fair, as he had the clout not only to gain entry the trade-only event but to approach with authority the promotional stands piled high with toys and games of every description. It would not be a cold pitch, as Pevers had sent letters of introduction to all of the main toy companies in advance informing them of the *Star Wars* presentation. "Despite our efforts, very few companies responded," says Pevers. "Mego International, which was a successful 20th Century-Fox licensee with its *Planet of the Apes* action figure line, wouldn't even attend the presentation."[9] Pevers and Lippincott entered the company's display area of the Toy Fair, but even with his heavyweight companion beside him, Lippincott found himself ejected as soon as his identity had been established, "trade-only" being the criterion for entry. The chief buyer dampened the mood further by telling Pevers that he was not interested. Mego already had a top-selling sci-fi toy line called Micronauts and the most they wanted was information on 20th Century-Fox's next television series that had merchandising potential.

A smaller toy company was displaying at the show however: Kenner Parker (made up from two affiliated but separate companies) dealt with licenses and had done very well with toys based on the *Six Million Dollar Man* television show; the latest selection was there, shining resplendently under bright lights. Action figures, playsets and accessories—all seemed to be precisely the products that could be produced for *Star Wars*. Although Kenner Parker attended the *Star Wars* presentation and was buoyed by Pevers suggesting that *Star Wars* could be turned into a television show, where traditionally profits could be made, they did not make a commitment. Pevers recalled, "Other than some small toy companies' offers, we had no commitments. I was depressed. Here I felt we had the hottest property in the world and I couldn't get anyone interested. The depression faded quickly however after a phone call from Craig Stokely, the vice-president of product planning for Kenner toys. Kenner, he reported, wanted the worldwide toy, game and craft rights to *Star Wars*!"[10]

When it came down to the final negotiations for the *Star Wars* license, Pevers was determined to strike as hard a bargain as possible. Bernie Loomis, then the president of Kenner Parker, recalled, "Marc Pevers added one condition. 'George says, "If you do *Star Wars*, you can't do *Close Encounters* [*of the Third Kind*].' When someone tells me I can't have something, I want to know why." Bernie Loomis arranged an appointment to sign the *Star Wars* deal at the Century Plaza Hotel in Los Angeles, a few minutes away from the Fox Studio. Earlier in the week however Loomis traveled to Columbia to meet with Julia Philips the producer of *Close Encounters* and its director Steven Spielberg. Bernie Loomis recalled his conversation with the director: "I remarked that it sounded like a great movie but it didn't seem 'toyetic' to which he said 'What is toyetic?' and I said 'The property of being expressible in playable figures and hardware.' To which he said, 'Well, it's not *Star Wars*.'" Spielberg revealed that he had seen *Star Wars* and admitted that it was quite "toyetic." Having realized that a toy deal had slipped through his fingers, he told Loomis that he was not too upset. "George was his best friend and they had traded pieces," said Loomis. "In other words, George owned a piece of Steven's share of *Close Encounters* and Steven a piece of *Star Wars*. When the toys went into production, George had us send one of each new toy to Steven."[11] When the eventual contract was signed by representatives of 20th Century-Fox, the *Star Wars* Corporation and General Mills Fun Group, the rights extended to all of the GM international affiliates, which placed restrictions on merchandise being developed by other licensee companies elsewhere in the world, including Britain. "I was required to sign off on all of the merchandise in Britain," says Pevers. "But I could not approve every deal that Peter Beale sent to me, as many of his proposals conflicted with worldwide merchandise arrangements I had made such as toys, games and crafts with General Mills Fun Group." The toy license having already been taken by Kenner Parker, other manufacturers could only look on with envy.

The challenge remained to turn George Lucas' sweeping saga into a toy range. Kenner design manager Ed Schifman recalls, "Bernie called me into his office and said, 'I want you to take your staff to a movie this weekend,' and I said, 'Bernie, it's a holiday weekend.' And he said, 'So what? We just bought the rights to this movie. I want your staff to see this.' He didn't tell me anything about the movie. He didn't tell me what the name of the movie was. At least they paid for the tickets."[12]

Tom Beaumont, a designer at Kenner, picks up the story. "They took the whole department, all of the development people and we all hauled in cameras in there so we could take pictures of the screen looking for all of the elements in that movie we could create into toys. Everybody was just blown away at the number of machines and all of the fighters and the robots."[13] The *Star Wars* figures were prototyped by Jim Swearingen at Kenner. "It came into the office as a script and a series of black and white photographs," Swearingen recalled. "There were different vehicles, there were different characters waiting to be turned into a toy."[14] Swearingen used Fisher Price Adventure toys, among others, to create the prototype action figures. However, when it came to finalizing the look of the *Star Wars* figures to be produced, fellow Kenner designer Steve Hodges started with a clean sheet, apart from the Fisher Price scale and general design.

Fisher Price incidentally did not invent this style of toy. The 3¾-inch action figure can be traced back to companies which produced 1:18 scale metal toy vehicles in the early 1970s such as the Nylint Corporation, which occasionally included a posable action figure driver or rider as an accessory. Later, companies such as Fisher Price based toy lines around the same style of 1:18 scale figure, which Kenner picked upon. The design and production of a new line of toys was far from an instant process and Kenner would not be able to produce *Star Wars* action figures and vehicles until early 1978.

The *Star Wars* toy range was to be released in Britain by Palitoy Incorporated, which in effect was Kenner's sister company. Based at Coalville, Leicestershire, Palitoy began in 1919 as Cascelloid Ltd., which produced a variety of celluloid and plastic products. Cascelloid's toy division became Palitoy in 1935 after the company was sold to British Xylonite. In 1968, Palitoy was sold to the American company General Mills, which also owned Kenner and Parker Bros. Palitoy formed part of the General Mills UK Toy Group. British toy companies Denys Fisher and Chad Valley were acquired and added to the group in 1970 and 1978. General Mills also purchased the French division of Meccano in 1971 along with its factory in Calais, which was handed the responsibility for the distribution of *Star Wars* products in France. Palitoy's marketing director Les Cooke recalls how he was initially less than enthusiastic to receive the news of the upcoming *Star Wars* range:

> I was made aware that our sister company in the USA, Kenner, had the rights to two properties, a TV show called *The Six Million Dollar Man* and a film called *Star Wars*. Kenner had decided that our U.K. sister company Denys Fisher would have the rights to the TV show and we would get *Star Wars*. Without having any knowledge about *Star Wars* whatsoever, I thought Palitoy had drawn the short straw here. TV licensed products had a good record for toy merchandise unlike films, which produced a limited amount of products, which traditionally didn't last long. Palitoy was the U.K.'s largest toy company after all so I questioned the logic of this product allocation.

At the time, Palitoy commonly distributed products derived from overseas companies such as Mego's *Starsky and Hutch* and *Planet of the Apes* figures via its Bradgate division: It sold direct to wholesale companies, which would in turn sell to retailers. Les Cooke continues:

> I learned that the core *Star Wars* line was to be an action figure range, so my thoughts were to allocate it to Bradgate. Palitoy, our retail division (that sold direct to retailers), after all contained Action Man, the dominant force in the action figure market. Bernie however was not happy with this plan and said, "Put *Star Wars* in your retail division, and it will outsell Action Man and be a major force for the next 20 years." He really did say that and something about flying pigs came to my mind! Although I crossed swords with Bernie at times, I had a lot of respect for him. I consequently saw the film and the Kenner range on a visit to America, so I could see that this was going to be a very major toy category and should obviously go into our main retail division.

Palitoy brand manager Geoff Maisey says,

> Les first wanted Bradgate to handle *Star Wars*, on the premise that Palitoy had Action Man, which would be its key competitor. However, Bernie Loomis persuaded Les to leave it with Palitoy. His strong view, shared by most of the other marketing team at the time, was that Bradgate did not have any experience of handling a complex and fast-moving line like *Star Wars*. Further, Bradgate had no relationship with retailers, reaching them instead through wholesale and cash-and-carry operations. Also, most major retail customers would not deal with Bradgate, only Palitoy, as they felt that would be the highest corporate level for them to negotiate terms.

Chief designer at Palitoy Bob Brechin recalls, "It wasn't long before I was informed that Palitoy was going to be producing the *Star Wars* toy range and as chief designer, I would be in the thick of it. Geoff Maisey called me aside one day. 'You must go and see this *Star Wars* film, Bob. You may be involved in some design work on the toy line.' He told me that there would be a special preview performance ahead of the U.K. release date, so I waited in anticipation." A long-standing member of Palitoy staff, Brechin's responsibilities ordinarily were centered upon the company's Action Man toy range. "When I joined, Palitoy was officially known as the Toy Division of Bakelite Xylonite Ltd. I joined Palitoy during the second year of Action Man, which was marketed by Palitoy under license from Hassenfeld Brothers [later Hasbro]. One of my main jobs was to help turn Action Man into a truly British brand."

The British Campaign Begins

As the reaction in America spiraled out of all proportions, the delay in the British release of *Star Wars* appeared to be an act of genius, for the promotional campaign would have time to build momentum and the merchandise could become fully fledged. "A lot of the signing up in the USA happened after the film opened, so there was a lot of interest from possible licensees in Britain to get on board for *Star Wars*," says Charles Lippincott. "We had to be careful as we had some worldwide licenses like the toy companies and we also had to interface with stuff that was going on in the United States and make sure things didn't go too far." Peter Beale has strong memories of the time: "Fortunately, *Star Wars* opened in the States six months before we got it, so happily we had a large window to get things going."

The countdown had begun, so a relaxed attitude was not in order. Much of the strategy for releasing *Star Wars* was down to Percy Livingstone, head of 20th Century-Fox UK Distribution. Fox's promotional department, headed by Colin Hankins, was springing into action with the promotion of *Star Wars*. Palitoy too had an in-house marketing department led by brand manager Geoff Maisey based at the Coalville building.

Stanley Bielecki is not a name widely known outside of the filmmaking world but he too made a considerable contribution to the *Star Wars* promotional campaign. Beginning as a photographer with the *Sunday Times*, Bielecki went on to be an expert on using stills in the marketing of films, including the use of high-quality books of photos. Gary Kurtz met Bielecki when he visited London on 1975 to begin the *Star Wars* production: "He made some suggestions about photographers and how we should go about a kind of concept of selling the film before we started shooting."[15] Following the meeting, Bielecki at his London studio put together a book of images that aided with the promotion of *Star Wars* in America. Now that it was a hit, he concentrated his efforts on selling the British press on the merits of *Star Wars*. "Other than producing beautiful books of photographs, his other skill was getting photos into the weekend press, especially the *Sunday Times*," says Peter Beale. According to Andrew Harvey, photo editor of the *Evening Standard*, "I remember that he had no doubts about its potential and did a very hard sell with me with a series of images that quite frankly seemed bizarre but you know, you learn to trust Stanley. *Star Wars* may have been born great but it certainly had great marketing thrust upon it."[16]

Adding their considerable weight to the *Star Wars* promotions was Palitoy's public relations agency Munro/Deighton. "We began handling p.r. for *Star Wars* Toys as soon as Palitoy knew they would be producing some of the *Star Wars* products at Coalville," says Carole Deighton. "We worked closely with Palitoy's marketing team and 20th Century-Fox. It was an exciting time because we were well aware of the tight deadlines and the countdown to the release of the film. Even at that early stage, we had a feeling it was going to be something pretty special."

Star Wars would not be as hard a sell in Britain as other territories, as the country in 1977 was already a place with a healthy interest in science fiction, especially in the realm of television. Programs such as *Doctor Who, Space 1999* and *Star Trek* were broadcast regularly. Classic programs *Thunderbirds, Quatermass* and many others were fondly remembered. Writer Tony Crawley had noted that unlike America, where science fiction television programs were shown late in the evening, television stations in Britain used "the family-viewing period of 5:30–6:30 p.m. Why family viewing? Well, it works. The U.S. shows are usually juvenile enough to appeal to children, but tend to require an elder around in case of monsters (*à la Doctor Who*); the adults always get hooked on anything even slightly reminiscent of *Star Trek* and they make sure the kids don't miss an episode—because they'd feel embarrassed watching it alone. No kidding!"[17]

Newspapers were quick to print stories about the latest science fiction fad, especially regarding the Doctor of *Doctor Who* and his nemeses, the Daleks. Newspaper editors eagerly sought the latest craze or mania. British television, radio and newspapers reached the entire population, so the public enjoyed a shared experience of the media. The small number of sci-fi films that had been produced in the late 1960s and the 1970s had been very popular in Britain, including *2001: A Space Odyssey* (1968), *The Planet of the Apes* (1968) and the fantasy adventure films of Ray Harryhausen. Kevin Connor's British-produced *At the Earth's Core* (1976) had been a recent hit at the cinema. Starved of new science fiction, fans often looked back to previous decades for films such as *The Forbidden Planet* (1956) becoming staples of the sci-fi fan scene.

Spreading the Word on Star Wars

One group of people in Britain who were certainly aware of *Star Wars* were the science fiction fans. Mail order businesses, market stalls and comic shops such as London's Dark They Were and Golden Eyed were an outlet for American science fiction and horror magazines. Titles such as *Analog, Starlog* and *Mediascene* were keenly scrutinized by science fiction aficionados seeking the very latest news. One of the earliest reports appeared in the November/December 1976 issue of *Mediascene*, which featured a cover with Ralph McQuarrie's artwork of a space pilot firing at the Millennium Falcon, with the Death Star looming in the background. Inside, there was a whole page of storyboards from the upcoming *Star Wars* and a fantastic double spread painting of a pair of masked individuals—one of them Darth Vader, the epitome of evil—fighting with lightsabers.

The news spread very quickly among fans—word of mouth being perhaps the greatest promotional tool. "My first news of *Star Wars* was when a friend of mine mentioned a new science fiction film that America was going crazy for," says Laurie Calvert. "He'd seen a scene that looked really great where a guy and a girl swing across a chasm. I wasn't all that impressed and told my friend that I'd make up my mind when I eventually got to see it. At 16, I was a big fan of science fiction. *Forbidden Planet, The War of the Worlds* and *The Day the Earth Stood Still* were among my favorites. It was those kinds of movies that I grew up on and that was really down to my dad who brought me up on science fiction."

Gerald Crotty also has strong memories of the time. "I was 14, 15 years old in 1977. I was a big fan of all Gerry Anderson's stuff, *Lost in Space* and *The Prisoner*. Sci-fi movies seemed rare though and were often disappointing. Someone I knew had an issue of *Starlog* that featured *Star Wars*. I remember thinking that the movie wouldn't live up to the pictures, that there'd be very few effects shots, etc. They always seemed to promise more than they delivered back then." Sarah Baker-Saunders says:

> As a 13-year-old in 1977, I used to watch TV shows like *Planet of the Apes, Star Trek, Logan's Run* and *The Six Million Dollar Man*, along with reruns in the school holidays of *Flash Gordon*. There wasn't a great deal of choice on the television so you watched whatever there was, but I guess I loved all of it. I also went to a Saturday cinema club that used to run old movie serials and the occasional sci-fi film. My local news agents stocked *Starlog* magazine that showed all the exciting developments in the sci-fi universe. I remember reading about *Star Wars* and I was really quite interested.

British science fiction fans were also well served by homegrown publications. *House of Hammer* magazine had been published since 1976 and although its mainstay coverage was horror film-based, it covered science fiction too. Its editor Dez Skinn was aware of *Star Wars* as soon as the news broke. "Being responsible for *House of Hammer* and *Mad* [magazine] with its film spoofs, plus whatever film-related one-shots [one-off magazines] I could dream up, forthcoming movies were an important part of my role. So naturally enough, I got the film trade magazines *Variety* and *Screen International* every week. I'd always been as big a fan of science fiction as I was of horror, so I was ecstatic when I saw the *Variety* June 1, 1977, cover headline '*Star Wars* Best Start Since *Jaws*.'" This news was enough to get Skinn's entrepreneurial juices flowing. "*Jaws* had of course, been the biggest-ever box office hit at that time and I'd long wanted to produce a science fiction sister title to *House of Hammer*, so now was my best chance! I knew that *Star Wars* wasn't due to open in Britain until Christmas, six months after its U.S. premiere, so I had plenty of time to get together what I anticipated would be a surefire hit!"

A new magazine of course needs a snazzy title but the choice was far from an easy process. Skinn continues: "With the perennial popularity of *Star Trek* on the small screen and the forthcoming *Star Wars*, the first part of the title was obvious. But what to put with it? *Starfall* was the popular choice for about a week, but I didn't really like the connotations of -*fall*. Then I hit on -*burst*. Positive and exciting, so *Starburst* it was."[18]

Another British-produced title, *TV Sci-Fi Monthly*, published by Bunch Associates, focused on popular TV series such as *The Six Million Dollar Man*. The owner of Bunch Associates, Felix Dennis, was extremely well-known in the print industry and the media. He had achieved notoriety at a national level due to his activities with the underground magazine *Oz* before founding the *Kung Fu Monthly* poster magazine, which proved to be exceptionally popular. Dennis had established a working relationship with fellow Briton Peter Godfrey, who ran (with his business partner Bob Bartner) the American printing company Paradise Press, which printed Bunch Associates titles in America. Mark Williams explains how Godfrey secured the rights to create the company's first movie tie-in, a poster magazine based on *Jaws*: "Peter was delegated to fly to California to negotiate with Universal Studios, and Felix would create the product back in the U.K. As this was before the licensing of movie products had really begun, it wasn't too difficult to get a deal to publish a poster magazine."[19] However, it transpired that Universal did not have the rights to use the images of any of the actors, which left the publication short of material. "We were left with the

adventure film is released in the U.K. later this year and on these pages, you can see a fore-taste of the thrills coming your way!"[28] Michael Rogers, writing in the July 28 *Rolling Stone*, reported that the American reaction to *Star Wars* was nothing short of phenomenal. "For the past few weeks, on my way to the office, I have been passing the San Francisco theater where George Lucas' remarkable movie is being shown. By 11 a.m. every day, the line for the one o'clock show has already begun to form. Each day as I drive past and as I wait at the stoplight I'm starting to recognize some of the same faces."[29] Richard Roud, writing for the *Guardian* newspaper, said, "So why all the fuss? Why have there been these tremendous long queues? The answer, I suggest, has to be found in the fact that the film corresponds to some deep need for mindless heroism in American youth today.... It's also a reaction against the excessive American belief in the power of rational thought, a notion which is proving itself bankrupt with each passing year."[30] In the *Sun* newspaper on July 27, there was a profile of David Prowse (Darth *Vader) and Peter Mayhew (Chewbacca), "Mask Force,"* in which both actors expressed their intention to make the most of their *Star Wars* exposure, even though their faces were not seen on film. "I would really like to make it successfully as an actor but I'm keeping what else I've got," said Prowse, referring to his gym and other business activities. "I don't intend ever to be in the position of staying at home waiting for the phone to ring"[31]

The enthusiasm for *Star Wars* in America was further emphasized when on August 3, Darth Vader, C-3PO and R2-D2 immortalized their footprints at Mann's Chinese Theatre on Hollywood Boulevard in front of a huge crowd. Gary Kurtz helped Anthony Daniels write "C3PO" in the wet cement. Charles Lippincott was in attendance to look after Daniels, along with *Star Wars* special effects crew member Peter Kuran, who was the body double of C-3PO when Daniels was unavailable. R2-D2 was moved by radio control. The Darth Vader costume was filled by the sizable form of Kermit Eller, a Don Post Studios mask company employee who had been contracted to make appearances as the Dark Lord throughout the country. Daniels could not resist sneaking back after the ceremony and adding his own name in the cement. The actor also traveled to America to appear alongside Peter Mayhew on *Donny & Marie* in a star-studded musical parody of *Star Wars*. Although Dave Prowse was not employed to appear in the Darth Vader costume in America, he did make appearances in his earthly guise. "I did a personal appearance outside San Francisco, in Union City.... I sat down at 1 p.m. to sign autographs and didn't stop until seven o'clock."[32] Even those in minor roles, such as Alex McCrindle who played General Dodonna, were in demand. The elderly Scottish actor was flown to New York for a promotional event and was surprised to discover that a Topps trading card featured his image. "Now that is *really* fame," he told *Screen International.*[33]

John May gained an insight into the phenomenal American reaction to *Star Wars* when he visited a London pub with some of his colleagues. "A journalist I knew had just come back from New York, where he had seen *Star Wars*. He had been in a queue for something like two hours and he was absolutely raving about it."

Charles Lippincott made the journey to London to attend the British Comic Art Convention Comicon, held at the Bloomsbury Center on September 3 and 4. "My first point of contact on my arrival was the Dark They Were, and Golden Eyed comic shop in London. I became friends of the owners and they became my major outlet. I also became friends with Nick Landau, the future owner of the *Forbidden Planet* shop and Titan Publishing. At

Comicon I put on my regular slide show that I took to conventions. I had Ralph McQuarrie paintings and also production photographs so I could tell this exciting story but I never told the *whole* story. I told it up to a point where I would keep it in suspense." Lippincott's stay in Britain was fairly brief, however:

> There wasn't much time for me to do things in London after the Comicon convention because I was getting the promotions ready for Europe. In October 1977, I traveled around the world with Mark Hamill visiting 20th Century–Fox offices on the way. Anthony Daniels did some of the promotions too. We took R2-D2 but there wasn't anyone inside it. We went to Rome and Paris and to the book fair in Frankfurt, where *Star Wars* had a lot of activity because of the success of the books in the United States. From there I went to Tokyo and ended back in Los Angeles which finally ended my *Star Wars* promotional tour.

John May and his colleagues were working flat out to produce the first issue of *Official Star Wars Poster Monthly*, which by that time was a huge priority at Bunch Associates considering the storm that was being whipped up in America. "We had no editorial contact between with Lucasfilm, or anyone in the States," says May. "We were all pretty serious journalists. The content was based on anything we could get our hands on, including American sci-fi magazines and the *Star Wars* novel." *Star Wars Official Poster Monthly* #1 began with "Birth of a Space Legend," which provided a round-up of the story of how the film had opened to incredible success. "Not since *Star Trek* has a science fiction event gotten into the hearts and minds of so many people. In a few short months, the epic fantasy that is *Star Wars* has rocketed into the consciousness of the crew of Spaceship Earth." Even though the publication was being prepared in London, far from Lucasfilm, the article declared, "We don't want to give away all of our secrets…"[34] thus making it appear is if it was coming from the *Star Wars* people themselves. This issue also included a profile and photograph of each of the main characters. Mark Williams recalls that the Bunch Associates art room was "stuffed with arcane equipment that most designers today have scarcely heard of, let alone used."[35] Since computer technology in publishing had yet to be developed, magazines were assembled in a labor-intensive way. The text was produced in columns on an IBM golfball typesetter, the illustrations and photos were sized up on a large process camera, headlines were produced using Letraset, and all these elements were pasted down with Cow Gum on art boards that had several cover sheets attached, carrying detailed instructions about color separations for the printers. Another Bunch Associates staffer, Dick Pountain, recalls that the *Star Wars* poster magazine was being prepared right up to the last minute and that he had to race on his motorbike to deliver the prototype of the magazine to Heathrow Airport. A scheduled mail service would deliver the precious package to the American publisher Peter Godfrey of Paradise Press. "I got from the office in Goodge Street to Heathrow in something like 18 minutes, admittedly on a Sunday night. All the lights were green on the Westway…. I was doing 125 mph most of the way, some of it on the Euston Road, and caught the plane by five minutes."[36] This first issue went on sale in America in October and according to Peter Godfrey it became "a gargantuan success and along with Bruce Lee fueled our publishing ventures with Felix (and Bunch Associates) for some years."[37] There could be no pause for the *Star Wars* poster magazine staff, as there was a monthly schedule in the U.S. to adhere to. According to John May, "We began knocking out profiles of the main characters, articles on the science of *Star Wars* and anything else we could think of."

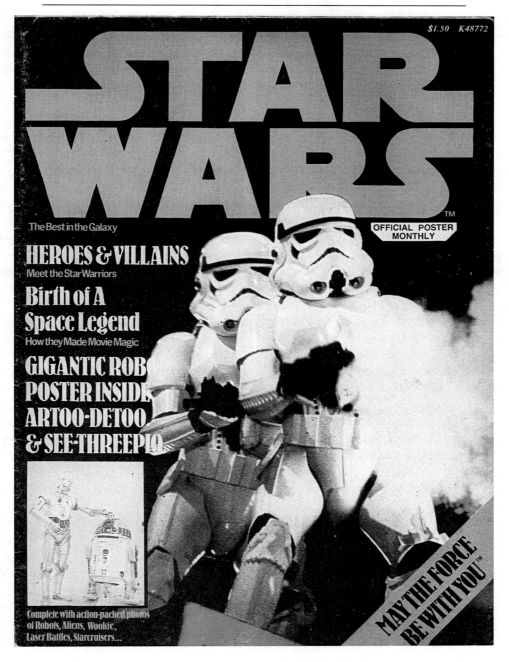

The Official *Star Wars* Poster Monthly was produced in Britain and dispatched to America for printing and distribution.

The Media Storm

By the late summer, newspaper and magazine stories about *Star Wars* became even more frequent in Britain. The cover of the August edition of *Films and Filming* magazine featured a black-and-white photograph of R2-D2 and C-3PO on the cover and contained a two-page photo preview. The names and the images of Darth Vader, Luke Skywalker, R2-D2 and C-3PO were becoming extremely familiar among the public, although their precise roles in the film were not widely known. That August, the highly influential *Rolling Stone* magazine featured a *Star Wars* article that had been arranged by Charles Lippincott. The cover was a photograph of the main cast which has since become a classic: Han Solo and Luke Skywalker with their weapons drawn with Princess Leia shielded by a snarling Chewbacca. At the time, the very fact of being featured on a *Rolling Stone* cover was a major event in itself and a real coup for *Star Wars*. *Rolling Stone* was published all over the globe, including Britain, and had a huge readership. George Lucas had been interviewed for the magazine on his return from his holiday in Hawaii, to recoup from the immense task of bringing *Star Wars* to the screen. Despite the overwhelmingly positive reaction to the film, Lucas did not talk up his creation. "It is not as good by a long shot as it should have been," said Lucas. "I take half the responsibility myself and the other half is some of the unfortunate decisions I made in hiring people, but I could have written a better script, I could have done a lot of things; I could have directed it better." While audiences viewed *Star Wars* as a seamless viewing experience, which seemed to be technically perfect, its maker's view could not have been further away. "I can see nothing but seams."[38]

The September issue of *Photoplay* magazine included an article on *Star Wars* under the heading "Why you will queue to see the most fantastic film of the year." John Austin was quoted as saying *Star Wars* is "...a space western, it is a space historical drama, it is every motion picture ever made rolled into one. It is timeless; it is what motion pictures are all about." The article finished with the statement "*Star Wars* is coming. You must not miss it!"[39]

There was soon another factoid for the newspapers to report upon, with the September 21 edition of *Variety* including a double-page advertisement proclaiming, "20th Century-Fox is proud to announce that *Star Wars* has become the most successful motion picture in the history of the company. We thank all of those people who have made this possible."[40] The ad included a full-page list of people who according to Fox were due thanks for the film. It seems that whoever compiled the list had no special knowledge of the making of *Star Wars* and went through the credits of the film and in the process left out many of the key individuals that had not been named there.

On September 28, an edition of the BBC1 program *Tomorrow's World* presented by Michael Rodd, William Woolard and James Burke featured *Star Wars*. The program lived up to its title, with an exclusive clip from the film of Luke and Han shooting at TIE Fighters from the Millennium Falcon. The same clip was later shown on the ITV Saturday morning TV program *Tiswas*. Derek Dorking reminisces:

> I was at Southend College of Technology studying art when I saw what I believe was the first clip of *Star Wars* on shown on British television. It was the TIE Fighters attacking the Millennium Falcon. As I watched C-3PO walking down the corridor of the ship, I thought to myself, "Is that animation? Is it a puppet? This looks good." This was my first awareness of *Star Wars*. I was a fan of science fiction and of Gerry Anderson productions especially, but this looked like something else entirely. Gradually more coverage appeared in the press and I learned that the film would be opening at Christmas. I thought that R2-D2 looked really good and in casual conversation with my college friends, I said that I could probably make a model of it. They reckoned that I couldn't and jokingly taunted me about it, so I went ahead and started on R2-D2 basically as a dare. Just to get one up on my mates. The only reference I

could find was a poster of R2-D2 and C-3PO in the desert and later, the Collector's Edition book. The scale I chose for the model was one-third and I was determined to pack in as many working features as possible. It ended up a bit wide in the shoulders but it helped because it didn't fall over when it was moving around on two legs.

The Kids in the Know

Star Wars' target audience, young people, became quickly infatuated with the film. "I remember there being a lot of interest for the original movie starting in late '77," says Sarah Baker-Saunders. "Newspaper reports, other children at school talking about the movie and creating a buzz." Shaun Dawkins has similar memories. "I read some news reports at this time about a new magical film about robots and a princess in it. I was as much of a fan of science fiction as young people were; anything with spaceships, robots and the like in it. I had seen a lot of the '50s and '60s stuff. Later I saw Barry Norman present a preview of *Star Wars* on *Film 77*, which I believe featured R2-D2. That was it—my first love. I was a very excited 11-year-old at this stage."

Darren Slade says, "I remember being aware of *Star Wars* some time before it arrived. I was ten years old at the time and I was skeptical about the film at first. They showed the scene where the Millennium Falcon escapes from Tatooine on the *Pebble Mill at One* television show and seeing Chewbacca, I said to my brother that it was nothing compared to *Planet of the Apes*, which was my favorite film at that time. I'm not sure why I was determined not to be impressed. Maybe because there had been so much hype about it already." Jordan Royce says, "The first image I remember seeing was of a Stormtrooper and I just freaked out. I thought it looked so cool and so amazing. Being ten years old, I had been able to see sci-fi films on television and at the cinema such as *Logan's Run* and they just didn't look like that. This was something entirely different. I remember being so excited. Then I saw that iconic picture of R2-D2 and C-3PO in the desert. People take the characters for granted now but the iconography and the visual impact of seeing the characters for the first time was very, very strong." Gerald Crotty says, "I began to become more excited in the autumn, when a piece on the BBC program *Newsnight* (that was an entirely different show to the one that begun in 1980 and has run to the present day) reported on *Star Wars* breaking all box office records in America. They showed the clip where the Death Star destroys Alderaan. I don't know why but I was convinced at that point that it was going to be the best film ever. I bought the novel around August 1977, I read it in two days which was the fastest I'd ever read a book back then. I was amazed by it. This is what really got me hooked on *Star Wars*. I thought if the movie could capture 50 percent of what was in the book, it would be amazing."

Even young children were able to pick up on the new film. "Although I was only five in the autumn of 1977, I was still aware of the hype surrounding *Star Wars*," remembers Craig Spivey. "My earliest *Star Wars* memory was seeing a clip of the film on the children's quiz show *Screen Test*. I distinctly remember the Millennium Falcon escaping Mos Eisley and C-3PO falling over and being extinguished by R2-D2. I also have recollections of TV news reports about 'Star Wars fever' and footage of people disco dancing in *Star Wars* T-shirts and shiny hot pants. I later did a slapstick 'Look-at-me-I'm-the-copper-colored-robot' impression for my mum. I imagine the reference was lost on her!"

I was seven years old in 1977. I grew up in the small Greater London town of Collier Row, which was roughly a mile from bustling Romford and roughly 14 miles to the north of London's city center. In fact, Collier Row is only deemed to be part of London because the expansion of the capital drew to a halt at its leafy gates. A short walk to the north of Collier Row will bring you to the farmers' fields. In common with many schoolboys at the time, I had a strong interest in Action Man, model soldiers and all things military. There was science fiction in my life too, which in Britain was difficult to avoid, since it seemed to be everywhere. The toys in the shops were of the coolest looking sci-fi hardware—Dinky die-cast Space 1999 Eagles, Daleks and Thunderbird craft. *The Six Million Dollar Man* and *Doctor Who* were favorites of mine on television and also the Adam West *Batman* television show, which appeared much more realistic on my family's black and white television set than in its overbearing color palette. A new science fiction show on television, *Blake's 7*, had me captivated. My parents did not buy a daily newspaper and I don't recall ever watching the news at that age, or much television at all. I was aware of *Star Wars* in any case, not as anything specific but as a happening.

The October issue of *The House of Hammer* magazine was the source of many young people's knowledge of *Star Wars*. It stretched its horror-based format considerably to include a detailed five-page preview of the film. The article had a genuine sense of excitement and left the reader in no doubt that something very special was on the way:

> "*Star Wars* looks like becoming the biggest-ever box-office film success [sic]. In its first six days on release in only 41 cinemas in the United States it has grossed a staggering $2.5 million. Judging from ecstatic audience reaction, that experience is likely to be repeated when the film goes on general release and *Star Wars* will probably replace *Jaws* as the most profitable movie ever. Which is pretty good for a film that was once nearly scrapped by 20th Century-Fox executives who feared that *Star Wars* would not even cover its costs! Now a jubilant Fox executive is quoted as saying: "It's madness. The queues at the cinemas are unbelievable."[41]

The article stressed that readers of *House of Hammer* would be familiar with *Star Wars* actors Peter Cushing and David Prowse, as they had both appeared in many horror films. The Cantina sequence was pointed out as a highlight of the film, with its many monsters.

Star Wars *Hits the Charts*

Meco's disco style version of the film's theme was played constantly on the radio and sold enough singles to spend nine weeks in the British official national music charts. It peaked at #7 on October 1. This provided the record's distributor Chappell & Co. the hit they did not get with the *Star Wars* theme single. New York City resident Meco Monardo was already an established musician, co-producing hits for Gloria Gaynor and Carol Douglas, when a viewing of *Star Wars* inspired him to produce a disco version of the soundtrack. Meco said, "Because I was an avid science fiction fan, I saw the first ten o'clock showing the first day and was so impressed I went back the next day to see it three times in a row. I absolutely loved the music. I was aware of the many great and beautiful themes John Williams had written and bought the soundtrack. I got my inspiration when I played the soundtrack and realized that I could not recreate the visuals from listening to it. I wanted to hear the space ships, R2D2, the lightsabers, the creature sounds, etc."[42] Such was the success of *Star Wars* that Neil Bogart at Casablanca Records agreed to the idea of a record without hearing a demo or even listening to any of Meco's other music. Bogart's decision paid off, as Meco's *Star Wars Theme/Cantina Band* entered America's Hot 100 on August 1 and hit the #1 position on October 1, staying there for two weeks. Remarkably, it was the same day the single reached its highest position in the UK chart. Although the record did not hit the #1 spot in Britain, it was an indispensable part of the soundtrack of 1977 and 1978.

Another version of the *Star Wars* theme by Maynard Ferguson and his band was released for the British market by Chappell & Co. on August 25. Utilizing a big band disco sound, this single may have edged the Meco version in the opinion of some fans. Chasing another hit, Chappell & Co. released a snowstorm of British produced *Star Wars* singles including a big band swing version of the main theme by The Rainbow Dance Orchestra by hugely prolific producer Ray Horricks on the PYE label, a disco style version by Cook County produced by Barak Records, *Star Wars Disco* by The Force from Splash Records and a version of *Princess Leia's Theme* from Manuel and the Music of the Mountains for EMI, which was the occasional recording name of the well-known band leader Geoff Love. Also new was a funk/soul version by the Graffiti Orchestra produced in America by Prodigal (Motown). Ambassador Records released *Living in These Star Warz* by soft-rockers The Rebel Force Band, which incorporated elements of the *Star Wars* theme. The band released an album of the same title in America on Bonwhit Records but there is no evidence of it being released in Britain. The public missed out on classic tracks such as *Don't Fall in Love with an Android, Chewie the Rookie Wookie, Respirator for Darth Vader* and *The Ballad of Obi Wan*. This was a pity because the album seems to have been produced with genuine enthusiasm for *Star Wars* and it would have appealed to younger fans especially. Adding to the bewildering array of singles available, British-based musician Rico Rodriguez released "Ska Wars" on a 12-inch record (Island Records), which presented the main theme in a laid-back ska sound. Prolific producer for the PYE label Robin Blanchflower had scored top ten British singles with Carl Douglas' *Kung Fu Fighting* and Johnny Wakelin's *Black Superman (Muhammad Ali)*, and he teamed up with arranger Barry Guard to score another hit via latching on to a popular theme. However, their record *May the Force be With You* under the name Skywalker, along with all of the other *Star Wars* themed records, did not make any impact on the nation's top 40 singles.

Advertisements began appearing in newspapers for short breaks in Paris that would include tickets to see *Star Wars*. The film had opened on October 19 in France but the adverts failed to mention that it was dubbed into French! Unwilling to wait for *Star Wars* to appear in Britain, Jon Smallwood decided to make the journey to France with his friend John Kaye. Smallwood says,

> Looking back on it, we took a few risks. No advance tickets and nowhere to spend the night! On a Thursday, we drove from Gloucester down to Dover early morning for the ferry to Calais. We drove straight to Paris. We parked in the northern suburb of St. Denis, took the Metro to the Champs Elysees and bought tickets with schoolboy French. "Avez vous deux billets pour *Les Guerres des les Etoils*?' and yes, they did! We loved the film even though it was dubbed into French. We didn't understand a word and didn't understand the story at all but the special effects were brilliant so we didn't care! Annoyingly, no one really believed we went. We never thought to take any pictures."[43]

Star Wars *in the Home*

It would not be allowed in the copyright-conscious world of today but *Star Wars* itself was also available to buy in Britain well in advance of it being shown at the cinema. "The British premiere of the blockbusting film *Star Wars* has already been held," wrote Fred Wehner for the November 10 edition of the *Daily Mail*. "It took place in my living room a couple of days ago. The only first-night celebrities in attendance were my seven-year-old daughter and a friend's two toddlers. At the same time, a thousand similar first showings are taking place in sitting rooms around the country. True, my screening was only an eight-minute excerpt of the two-hour epic. But my first night audience experienced the seat-gripping attack by four inter-galactic spaceships"[44] This was the familiar 1970s experience of watching short clips of a feature film at home. Since home video technology was only beginning to reach high street shops and even then with an extremely high price tag, movies in the late 1970s were primarily released in shortened form on actual film that could be shown in the home on 8mm projectors. The Super 8 film format was first introduced in 1965 and had become extremely popular as a medium for showing and making films. Amazingly, *Star Wars* had been legally available in a shortened form on Super 8 in the U.S. almost as soon as it appeared at the cinema. The British company Mountain Films was a major supplier of the Super 8 *Star Wars* clips that had been imported from the U.S. for the British market. It had not been signed up as a British licensee but was simply acting in its usual capacity of distributing Super 8 reels via Ken Films, which had the American license. Mountain Films produced a poster featuring R2-D2 and C-3PO and A4 sized leaflet containing various glowing headlines and reviews to promote the release. Peter Burt, co-director of Mountain Films said in November 1977, "The demand is fantastic. We got 1000 prints of the movie in and sold them in 48 hours, it's unheard of. Personally, I think its bloody crazy."[45] Mountain Films sent for 3000 abbreviated six-minute versions in quick order, plus 3000 copies if the 400-foot version. "*Star Wars* fever is spreading," said Ralph Payne-Gill, proprietor of another 8mm film dealership, PM films. "When it starts in the U.S. it usually comes over here. Also the fact that many of the special effects were made in this country has a lot to do with it." Payne-Gill, who ran his Super 8 home movie business from Beaconsfield, Buckinghamshire, had also found himself unable to keep up with demand. "I've sold 50 copies this week. I'm down to my last three copies. Today I ordered three dozen more. I wish I had the rights to the movie, I could retire."[46] Projection equipment was very expensive, so 8mm films were commonly shown in community halls and working men's clubs. The experience of seeing a short version of *Star Wars* on a small projection screen with often dodgy sound was a long way from the experience of the cinema. "The 8mm version of *Star Wars* went back to a license that Fox already had with *Planet of the Apes*," recalls Charles Lippincott. "At the time, since there was no video market, there would be these short versions of successful films that would come out on 8mm. We weren't aware in the States that *Star Wars* had come out in England. It certainly wouldn't have hurt us at all, it was just a promotional thing. Stores could get kids excited show the film in parts so to me it's just another way of promoting the film."

Star Wars *Fever Hits the UK*

There was another *Star Wars* preview screening at the Dominion Tottenham Court Road on Wednesday, September 28, at 10:30 a.m. This event also incorporated a trade show, for companies interested in producing *Star Wars* merchandise. The strategy of inviting *selected* members of the press and others to a series of private *Star Wars* screenings could not have worked better. The film was kept firmly in the headlines, while the interest from the general public kept ballooning. Much of the publicity stressed that *Star Wars* had been filmed in Britain and that the special effects had been created there too, in the most part by Englishman John Stears. Even though the miniature spacecraft effects and the fantastic backgrounds utilizing matte painting techniques had been completed in America, the misconception that *all* of the movie's visual wonders were British became widespread. The actual homegrown technical achievements included Luke Skywalker's Landspeeder, R2-D2 and the lightsabers. The majority of the press were not technically minded, and adding to the confusion was that special effects had become a short hand in the film industry for effects of every kind. Whatever the truth was behind the source of the *Star Wars* effects, the reportedly fantastic visuals remained one of the film's key selling points.

By the time October came around, *Star Wars* fever had begun to grip the nation, although the release was still months away. Peter Beale recalls, "We had so many people applying for licenses and trying to decide which was the one that would be the appropriate image and trying to keep some kind of reasonable creative control on the quality." The press kept tabs on the vibe from America, which was showing no signs of weakening, with the film enjoying an extended run all over the country. Charles Lippincott says,

> When *Star Wars* opened at Mann's Chinese it only stayed there a month because that was all the theater would give us. Billy Friedkin's film *Sorcerer* was due to open after our month there. Well, Friedkin's film wasn't ready and we had moved *Star Wars* over to the Egyptian, also on Hollywood Boulevard. It turned out that *Star Wars* was still doing fantastic business so after it ran at the Egyptian we moved it back over to Mann's Chinese, which was the key theater to be in on Hollywood Boulevard, and we stayed there right up to Thanksgiving. I don't think they'd had ever had an opening like that.

On October 1, the *Daily Express* reported that Carrie Fisher had arrived in London to promote *Star Wars*, with the headline "Carrie, the *Star Wars* Princess." Speaking to the *Observer*, Fisher said, "I've moved back to New York because the selection of films you can see there is better. My one extravagance (from the *Star Wars* profits) was buying a 16mm projector and a screen and showing old movies to friends every Thursday night."[47] On October 27, the newspaper *The Sun* printed a four-page feature which told the story of *Star Wars*, illustrated with photographs. The headline was "The film that everyone is talking about." According to the article, "*Star Wars* is simply the most successful film ever made. *Jaws, The Godfather, Gone with The Wind*—they're also-rans in comparison." The article focused on the attention the young actor Mark Hamill had been receiving from female fans. "At first I didn't mind the fans too much—the love letters and the cakes left on my doorstep every morning. Then the girls got more aggressive. I began finding that they had left photos of me with arrows and knives drawn through my heart. Finally, the police asked me to move out. They said that they couldn't spare men to protect me from the fans any more."[48] Hamill also mentioned his latest starring role in the film *Corvette Summer* but that seemed a light year away from the upcoming *Star Wars*.

On October 14, the *Sun* article "Meet the Stars of the biggest movie hit ever made" profiled Anthony Daniels and Kenny Baker. "So far it has taken about £95 million at box offices around the world and it won't even get to British cinemas until Christmas," wrote Judy Wade. Daniels said, "Working under those bright lights in the studio almost finished me. Every time I moved, my suit pinched me somewhere." Baker had his own challenges. "When the director said 'cut' I couldn't hear him and just kept on tootling across the set." Referring to the growing amount of *Star Wars* merchandise, Wade wrote, "As one of the executives of 20th Century–Fox put it, it's not so much a film, more an industry. It's going to make Walt Disney look like small time."[49] The press reports of *Star Wars* became more frequent and the hype was reaching a fever pitch. "People had of course heard all about *Star Wars* by then," says Peter Beale. "They knew that it had been filmed over here and understandably the excitement just grew and grew."

Bob's Mission

There was another *Star Wars* preview screening at the Dominion Theatre on Sunday, October 16, at 10:30 a.m. A highly enthusiastic attendee was Palitoy chief designer Bob Brechin:

> With my ticket for the preview performance in my hand, I arrived at the Dominion Theatre in great anticipation of this much-hyped movie. I arrived early so that I could get a seat in the middle of the auditorium about two-thirds back from the screen. As I sat there, I saw various celebrities arriving to take their seats, some trailing a gaggle of excited and animated kids. The opening scene was stunning! As the story scanned across, and the Imperial ship appeared and began to fill the screen, I realized that this film was going to be something special and memorable. It had a great story and was extremely well-paced; the excitement did not relent. At the end, you also knew that this was not just a one-off. You felt, and you hoped, that it was not the end of the saga. I returned to Palitoy the next morning with thoughts of the potential *Star Wars* toys spinning through my mind.

Brechin's involvement in *Star Wars* was about to take him further than he had envisioned:

> Shortly after seeing the film, my boss at Palitoy, Bill Pugh, sent a message from Hong Kong, where he was chasing up production of new Action Man designs and other doll and toy products, to tell me to arrange a trip to the States. As second-in-command to Bill at that time, I would be running the Palitoy design and development department in his absence which would be for about a month twice a year. His instruction was to arrange visits for me and the tooling manager Roger Morrison to visit Kenner and also Hasbro, which was the manufacturer of G.I. Joe from which Action Man was derived. Process engineers Les Codrington and Dave Eames were to go also, but their main reason was to visit Parker Games which was producing *Star Wars* board games and jigsaws.

Fay Taylor, Pugh's secretary, duly arranged all the flights and itinerary for a date in November. According to Brechin,

> We visited Kenner at Cincinnati on the 9th, 10th and 11th of November to see what they were doing as regards all the toys for *Star Wars*. During the visit, we were shown the development of the Landspeeder, X-Wing Fighter and TIE Fighter. The engineers at Kenner were at the stage of making the models and patterns of the vehicles prior to manufacturing the injection molding tools. I was able to take photographs of the models and patterns. We were well-entertained by those designated to care for us during the visit. Jack Holland, who was the manager of model-making, kindly entertained us at his home. He was so proud to show us his E-type Jaguar he had restored. Roger Morrison hadn't seen *Star Wars*, so we arranged to go to see it at a very big shopping mall some way out of town. The mall itself was a highlight of the trip as it was the first time we had experienced one of these shopping experiences.
>
> We then made a trip to the Fundimensions company, which was also part of the General Mills toy group, in Detroit, who were producing the die-cast *Star Wars* toys. The intention was for Fundimensions

to produce the die-cast toys for Palitoy, which would simply distribute them in Britain. We completed the trip with a visit to Hasbro in Pawtucket, Rhode Island, to meet all the G.I. Joe designers and engineers. When I returned to my desk at Palitoy, it was all go for the *Star Wars* range.

Display manager Brian Turner was another key member of Palitoy staff. Approaching in January were the toy fairs in Birmingham and Harrogate where the *Star Wars* line would be displayed to industry buyers. According to Turner:

> As display manager, my main job was to design the stands for the toy fairs at Harrogate, Brighton and Nuremberg followed by eight provincial shows around the country. Each year after Easter, I was responsible for in-store and window displays. When *Star Wars* arrived at Palitoy, I was coming to the end of my time in display and was soon to move over as a designer with the design and development team under Bob Brechin. The upcoming January, Harrogate toy fair in Yorkshire would be my last. As per my usual brief, I would have to include within the Palitoy stand offices, storerooms, a reception area, etc., and also have a visually imposing entrance to attract visitors to the stand. Areas for product ranges such as *Star Wars*, Action Man, Mainline, dolls, etc., would have to be integrated so that Sales and Marketing personnel would have a natural flow around the stand when showing their customers the product range. *Star Wars* was a big new thing, so I was determined to make it something special.

Star Wars *Frenzy*

On November 10, the *Evening Standard* newspaper contained Alexander Walker's two-page article in "The Wonderful Wizardry of *Star Wars*," which began with a sentiment that would resonate with many. "Even before it's opened outside America, so much has been said about *Star Wars* that a lot of people may already be thinking that they've seen it." According to Walker,

> Lucas' film relies heavily and successfully on the magnified, mind-blowing special effects which wrap up one's critical faculty in a lush package of "Let's pretend" and stow it away for the duration of the experience. It also casts its fantasy net wider than any TV series can do. Every character in the film suggests fantasies that some time or other, but probably when most of us were between 11 and 12, set our imaginations lighting up like a pinball machine.[50]

One person whose imagination lit up was Gerald Crotty:

> It's hard to explain why but once I started seeing clips from the movie, I was amazed, the look of it was so fantastic, like a huge leap in imagination. Usually movies would have maybe two or three cool, spectacular aspects: a car, a robot, a spaceship. But with *Star Wars*, with each new photo I saw there was just so much cool stuff. R2-D2 and C-3PO were fantastic enough, but there were other robots, and the Stormtroopers—great design and they were just henchmen! Darth Vader, Chewbacca, loads of aliens, then all the fantastic spaceships, etc. By the end of the year, I knew a lot about the movie including its genesis. I was amazed that Lucas wanted to do *Flash Gordon* (a name that would inspire giggles amongst my school friends and rightly so!). I'd seen the *Flash Gordon* serial and thought it was awful.

Jordan Royce has similar memories: "I couldn't wait to see what this was all about. There was no escaping it at the time. By the time the first clips started appearing on television, I was at a fever pitch, along with all my friends at school. It was all everyone was talking about."

TV coverage continued on October 27 with ITV's *Time for Business*, which featured topical business-related stories. Host Eamonn Andrews interviewed Peter Beale and Cliro Perfumeries manager Robert Beecham about *Star Wars* merchandising. Robert Beecham recalls,

Peter phoned me and said, "You and I are going to go on television. Eamonn Andrews wants to do a spot on *Star Wars*," and I said, "Great." So we went down to the studio in this red and silver 1952 vintage Bentley that Peter used to use. The agreement we came to before the interview began was that under no circumstances should the figure of five percent I was paying for the rights to *Star Wars* be discussed. That was private. So when Peter and I were sitting there on set, the first question Eamonn Andrews asked was, "Robert, how much are you paying for the rights to *Star Wars*?" I was taken aback but fortunately Peter interceded and managed the situation perfectly!

Peter Beale recalls, "Eamonn Andrews was saying that we were exploiting children and was very critical. I pointed out to him that children had to have baths. Typically, the weekly bath that one had in those days. So if you could make it easier for the child to play and enjoy the bath, it was of benefit to the mother. If the soap did the same job and didn't cost any more money, what was the ethical problem? At the time, there was an attitude of anti-business instead of celebrating it."

Television coverage was only one part of *Star Wars* promotions. Every effort was being made to keep the film in the public eye by 20th Century Fox UK's publicity department.

A *Star Wars* advert was played on the radio; the London underground and buses sported eye-catching posters. By mid–November, the Leicester Square Theatre and the Dominion Theatre were being swamped with inquires about *Star Wars*, with hundreds of calls and literally bags of mail arriving daily. Leicester Square Theatre house manager Phil Logan was left stunned. "We've never had anything quite like it. We've never opened the box office three months in advance, as we did for *Star Wars*. Normally, it would be a month to eight weeks in advance maximum." *Star Wars* was booked to run for three months at the Leicester Square Theatre. "Hopefully it will be six months," said Logan.[51] The release of *Star Wars* in the U.S. was still going strong. The November 19 *Variety* reported that the box office total had reached $186,000,000.

Enter Starburst

Dez Skinn achieved his aim with the November launch of his magazine *Starburst*, just as the *Star Wars* phenomenon in Britain was beginning to peak. But the process had not been entirely straightforward. "20th Century-Fox put an embargo on releasing any visuals from *Star Wars*," explains Skinn. "They had realized how valuable this new film was to them and refused to hand out any photos to new cash-in titles." Behind the scenes at 20th Century-Fox, it was Marvel that had secured the rights to produce a regular British *Star Wars* publication. "When we asked, we were told we had to have an interview with Fox, to show them the dummy magazine and see if was approved. When the day for such came at 20th Century-Fox's Soho Square offices, there was a bunch of us waiting to be heard, outside the MD's office, with titles such as *Starfall, Space Wars, Star Sci-Fi* and so on. I could tell by their faces that everybody before me had been turned down. When my turn came, I found myself being grilled by a very heavy lawyer, with the Fox head of *Star Wars* licensing Peter Beale just sitting there silently. Then Peter touched the lawyer's shoulder in the middle of my grilling and said; "This guy's okay. He's covered a lot of our poorer efforts in another magazine [*House of Hammer*] he does and given them good write-ups." He then turned to me and said, "Just put something else on the cover as well as *Star Wars* or we'll have official licensee Marvel Comics breathing down our necks!"[52]

Someone who received *Starburst* #1 very warmly was Jordan Royce. "I picked up the first issue in a shop and I re-read it time and time again. It was my bible, almost, on *Star Wars*. This was the first extensive coverage that us kids had seen and it was a real driver for the excitement surrounding the film. I actually became editor of *Starburst* in 2011 and I subsequently learned that the first issue was reprinted three times and sold over a quarter of a million copies. The success of *Starburst* was tied completely to *Star Wars*." Despite 20th Century-Fox's apparent misgivings regarding "cash-in titles," *Starburst* appeared ahead of a whole slew of new science fiction magazines. Titles such as *Outer Space Magazine*, *Future* and *Starforce* crowded the shelves at news agents, all with full-color *Star Wars* front covers and competing claims of fantastic coverage. *Starburst* was the only one to have to have anything approaching longevity, with all of the others fading very quickly. The threat by 20th Century-Fox of prosecuting magazines that used *Star Wars* photographs was a very real one. *Screen International* reported how *Starforce* magazine had been taken to the High Court in London over copyright infringement. Hugh Laddie, appearing for 20th Century-Fox, said of the case; "The warfare, unfortunately, will not be restricted to deep space. There are going to be conflicts in the courts and this is the first."[53]

The UK Merchandise Picks Up Pace

Additional *Star Wars* printed material began to appear in British shops, such as a hardback edition of the novel by Book Club Associates and *The Star Wars Storybook* from Armada, which consisted of a digest of the film's story illustrated with photographs. Part one of a large format version of Marvel's *Star Wars* comic also arrived with a cover price of 50 pence. Posters from Scandecor International arrived too. Letraset Ltd., based in Ashford, Kent, was extremely quick to respond to the wave of interest in *Star Wars*, becoming a licensed manufacturer even before Peter Beale had begun to sign up British companies. "I was not involved in the Letraset license at all," says Beale. "That was an entirely U.S. deal." The company was used to producing rub-down transfers and background scenes based on children's favorites, which could be produced quickly and relatively cheaply. Children certainly did not mind Letraset cranking up the action in the first two sets, *Battle at Mos Eisley* and *Escape from the Death Star*, with the characters depicted with guns blazing and lightsabers swinging. The third set *Rebel Air Attack* was more sedate and actually resembled the scene it was depicting. Transfer sets were the 1970s version of computer games, where everything needed to be 100 percent correct to make them work. The different sized characters demanded a sense of perspective and the laser beams, explosions and unfortunate Stormtroopers in various dying positions had to be lined up perfectly. The transfers were permanent, so there was only one chance of getting it right. "It was a good deal of fun working out where to put the heroes with their blasters drawn," recalls Darren Slade. "So that they matched up with Stormtroopers who looked like they were being hit; or finding the right spots for the droids and the Jawas to be running away from the gunfire." With the novelty of creating *Star Wars* scenes from scratch and the advantage of being one of the few items available connected to the film, Letraset transfer sets sold phenomenally well, especially in the buildup to Christmas. The Letraset sets also served to promote the film among children, who took their completed scenes to school to show their friends.

Letraset rub-down transfer sets helped spread the word about *Star Wars* among children and sold a million in the process (*right:* courtesy Craig Spivey).

The *Star Wars* toiletries from Robert Beecham's Cliro Perfumeries arrived in shops in time for Christmas and the range seemed tailor-made for wrapping up as presents. There was a set of four 300ml bottles of bubble bath: R2-D2, C-3PO, Darth Vader and Chewbacca. Then too, there were molded soap models of R2-D2 and C-3PO and an Imperial Cruiser box containing 140ml bottles of shampoo and bubble bath. The standout items from the range were a pair of molded plastic bubble bath containers in the shape of R2-D2 and Darth Vader, the screw-off top of which had been injection-molded into

the shape of the villain's helmet. Both products had been sitting on Robert Beecham's desk when he was interviewed for the *Sunday Times*. "Can you believe Darth Vader in a bubble bath!" Beecham exclaimed, barely able to contain himself, beating his chest for effect. "Darth Vader *is* the bubble bath! A sculptured bottle! Can you believe that? His head will screw on and off!"[54] In his column for the December 22 edition of the *Daily Mirror*, Keith Waterhouse said, "As for your mania for buying bath salts for all and sundry year after year, I suggest for once that you get on the ball and invest in *Star Wars* bath salts." Even though evidence of this particular item has yet to emerge, as is the case with the aftershave lotion, roll-on deodorant and talcum powder he described, Waterhouse's advice was sound when he said, "Be guided by me; you can get *Star Wars* everything"[55]

As large as it seemed, the current range of *Star Wars* merchandise had not even scratched the surface, as Philip Norman was able to explain in the *Sunday Times*:

R2-D2 Bath Bubbles was part of the range from Cliro Perfumeries.

> Next year as the film reaches more and more cinemas, British shops will be bombarded with *Star Wars* goods in a quantity that may still not satiate our newly awakened craving for interstellar fantasy. *Star Wars* merchandising is directed for 20th Century-Fox by a stern-faced young English executive named Peter Beale. Beale's chief concern is that no British licensee shall besmear the film's moral purpose. Those who can resist the Force and its by-
> products are in for a trying experience. The cinemas will soon be full of hurriedly made rivals to *Star Wars*, whose official sequel is due to begin filming in January 1979. As one Fox executive said: "It's with us for our lifetime."[56]

The growing amount of *Star Wars* merchandise also caught the attention of Suzy Menkes, who addressed the subject in the *Daily Express* on December 21. "There are a few days before *Star Wars* opens," said Menkes "…but spin-offs have already conquered the shops and there's no sign of an armistice." Interviewed for the article, Peter Beale said, "There's a risk overdoing things but for every license we have granted, 50 have been rejected. We have tried to spread the merchandise so that each type of shop has one or two things." The article described how *Star Wars* sweet cigarettes had been rejected because of concerns that children might be encouraged to smoke. A range of 3D posters did not print well enough and a collection of cheap jewelry looked shoddy. "We're not just in it for the money," explained Beale. "We reckon we can get an enormous amount of publicity from this"[57] Despite all of the fuss surrounding the impending *Star Wars* merchandise blitz, many of the license-holding companies were waiting until the film opened in the New Year to launch their products. For them, January would be their Christmas. Perhaps all of the planned merchandise would have appeared before Christmas, however, if the demand had been fully realized.

On November 15, BBC1's early evening show *The Tonight Programme* featured Barry Norman interviewing Gary Kurtz. The program explored how *Star Wars* was filmed, the reasons for its enormous appeal and the use of British technicians. The preparations of the upcoming sequel were also covered, which seemed amazing. There were reports of *Star Wars II*, when the *first* film had not arrived yet! On November 21, Norman presented a preview of *Star Wars* on his TV program *Film 77*. On December 5, the ITV television program *Clapperboard*, presented by Chris Kelly, featured *Star Wars* and an interview with Kurtz. The *Star Wars* trailer began playing at cinemas before films including *Return to Witch Mountain* and a re-release of *Snow White and the Seven Dwarfs*. Mitch Franks has memories of that time. "I was at the Wood Green Odeon watching a Saturday morning double-bill of *Candleshoe* and *Escape to Witch Mountain* when a trailer for *Star Wars* hit the screen. I was 11 and thought what I was seeing was just not possible."[58] on December 13, *The Sun* printed a two-page article describing *Star Wars* as "[a] science fiction fantasy which, since it opened in America, has already become the most successful film ever made. It's a star spangled adventure which will make a cosmic Christmas holiday treat for the kids and grown-ups too"[59] On December 19, *The London Evening News* printed a full-page advertisement, with the tag line "Tickets to see *Star Wars*.... The Best Christmas Present in the Galaxy." For the uninitiated, the advert confirmed the release date of the film as December 27, where it would be shown at two of London's premier cinemas, the Leicester Square Theatre and the Dominion Tottenham Court Road, in 70mm. This edition of the newspaper began a five-part serialization of *Star Wars*, complete with photographs. Also on December 13, the *Daily Mirror* included an update on *Star Wars* under the heading "Here at last— The space-age movie that's blasting into cinema history, Out of this world!"

Mark Hamill arrived in London again on the 13th with his girlfriend Marylou York, which was another large news story. He brought some of the masks that had been used in *Star Wars* to his interview appointments, which were photographed by the press. Mark Hamill appeared on the BBC1 children's television program *Blue Peter* on the 15th December. One of the hosts, John Noakes, arrived on the set wearing a TIE Fighter pilot mask, which seemed huge on his small frame. Earlier in the day on the 15th, Hamill had been interviewed at the Imperial College, London. 20th Century-Fox had arranged a frenetic schedule of interviews, even one with a German pop magazine.

It was not just Hamill who was making headlines. Jenny Rees had managed to arrange a rare interview with Harrison Ford for the 16th December edition of *The Daily Mail*, while the actor was at Britain's Shepperton Studios filming *Force Ten from Navarone*. The article "The Galactic Cowboy Comes Down to Earth" was aptly titled for it neatly summed up Ford's attitude towards his newfound fame: "As you can see, there's none of my personality that you see there in Solo. He's no one I know. What George Lucas did in *Star Wars* was ensemble casting, and most of Solo is in the script. You won't find me walking around advertising the fact that I'm the guy from *Star Wars*. *Star Wars* has offered me more things in the way of work. I'm not ambitious. I don't have a plan of what I want to do. Now I'd like to be surprised about the parts that are offered to me. I'd like someone to offer me something I'd never imagine myself doing"[60]

There was a further boost to the publicity when a display of *Star Wars* props and costumes opened on December 16 at London's Science Museum. There were huge crowds and a lot of interest from the press. Interviewed for the *Daily Mail* on the 19th December, 20th

Century-Fox UK marketing director Colin Hankins said, "One morning at my office, I was told that there were some people waiting for me at reception. I came downstairs and there were these two [R2-D2 and C-3PO] in crates. They're both exceedingly precious properties as both robots will be used in the sequel to *Star Wars*, which is being made in 1979."[61]

The Reviews Arrive

With the release of *Star Wars* imminent, the reviews arrived en masse. "I was kept wondering up until last week if I was actually going to get a ticket to see the damn thing,"[62] John Coleman wrote in the *New Statesman* on December 19; he went on to give *Star Wars* a positive review. Derek Malcolm's review in the *Guardian* newspaper on the 19th read:

> [T]here is a space-age saloon, there's swashbuckling with laser beams, there's slapstick which reminds one of Laurel and Hardy and sentiment which reeks of *The Wizard of Oz*. There are lines which are almost, if not quite, taken from old movies and direct allusions whipped from everything from *The Searchers* to *Triumph of the Will*. It's an incredibly knowing movie. But the filching is so affectionate that you can't resist it. The entirely mindless could go and see it with pleasure. But it plays enough games to satisfy the most sophisticated.[63]

Gordon Gow's review in *Films and Filming* magazine was similar: "[George Lucas] must have either Fairbanks or Flynn, or both, in mind when he made Luke grab the princess and go rope-swinging with her to safety—a joyous fragment of affection amid the profusion of events that constitutes this energetic outsize romp."[64] For the *Times* newspaper, David Robinson wrote, "*Star Wars* unashamedly restores all those qualities which filmmakers and audiences have almost forgotten in their chase after illusory sophistication—brightly defined characters; a story which hurtles along at such a pace that it leaves no time for questions; a world of fantasy so confidently portrayed (in *Star Wars* special effects achieve new heights of technical expertise) that there is no thought of disbelief; a genuine escapism that obliges you to make no connections at all with real worlds."[65] In *House of Hammer* magazine, John Brosnan wrote,

> The first and inevitable question one is going to ask about *Star Wars* is—"Is it as amazing as all of the overkill pre-release suggests?" Well, the answer to that, for once, is *yes*. It *is* an amazing movie. Whether it is a great movie is debatable, but it is definitely a visual masterpiece, full of moments that had me gaping with astonishment—scenes that I've pictured in my mind's eye while reading science fiction but I never expected to see on the screen. I must admit that *Star Wars* had me enthralled for most of its running time of 2 hours and 1 minute, it was only afterwards that quibbles and doubts began to percolate through my mind. For me the main problem was the story itself ... the plot could have been lifted from a low quality, science fiction pulp magazine of the 1930s or from a comic strip of the same period—and the whole thing is really on the level of the old *Flash Gordon* serials. But that isn't surprising as that was the *intention* of *Star Wars'* writer and director George Lucas... "It's the flotsam and jetsam from the period from when I was 12," he said. "The plot is simple—good against evil—and the film is designed to be all of the fun things and fantasy things I remember. The word for *Star Wars* in fun." A statement like this from a filmmaker practically disarms all serious criticism beforehand—one can't, for instance, accuse him of writing banal dialogue when that is exactly what he set out to do.[66]

A number of reviewers did not enter into the same kind of spirit regarding the film. "3–2–1, Rip Off!" was the heading of Michael Moorcock's piece in *The New Statesman*, where he cited many alleged sources that Lucas had drawn from. "None of that would matter if the script and conception (both by Lucas) had an ounce of original flair. The script has one or two good jokes but is otherwise feeble. The film depends entirely on its 'visuals' and to me those are breathtaking only because they are so completely second-hand. He has no suitable actors. The main characters are TV smoothies who would look happier in aftershave ads. Guinness and Cushing are wasted."[67] In a lengthy dissection of *Star Wars*, *Sight and Sound*'s Jonathan Rosenbaum described *Star Wars* as having a plot "that any well behaved computer fed with the right amount of pulp could probably regurgitate.... Westerns, samurai sagas, Arthurian legends, Disney bestiaries, DeMille spectaculars and World War II epics have been borrowed from as liberally as earlier SF. The climactic Death Star attack is modeled directly after a compilation of air battle clips from over 50 war films.... But the point of this approach is to make all the myths it plunders equally trivial and 'usable' as plot fodder, even if most of the emotions are absent."[68]

Perhaps the greatest of the film's detractors was Margaret Hinxman. Her December 13 *Daily Mail* review was printed under the banner "The woman's view": "The thrills, it goes without saying, are spectacular. But the people are just ciphers... [I]n fact, the roles might just as well have been played by robots too. For me (and I know I'm in the minority) the film is a mechanical wonder and nothing else. *Star Wars* is a superior junk movie, to be equated with junk food (hot dogs and milk shakes) and junk junk (the knick-knacks grandma chucked out because they were dust traps)."[69] Roderick Gilchrist's positive review, printed next to Hinxman's under the banner "The Man's View," contained an update on the American reaction to *Star Wars*:

> The Arctic blasts cut right through the muffled and overcoated queue, winding from Loew's Astor Plaza cinema off 44th Street all the way into Times Square, New York City, on a Saturday night. It was America's coldest day of the year, and even though those at the end of the queue guessed they wouldn't get to see the movie, no one left. They were mostly young, holding mittened hands and laughing a lot, and some had seen the film they were queuing for three or four times already. But they couldn't wait to get into the warmth of the movie house again so they could cheer and jeer with everyone else when the heroes and villains came on the screen. Terrific fun. It sounds extraordinary but once you've seen the film for yourself, you'll understand.[70]

Star Wars *Finally on the Horizon*

With there being seemingly as many negative reviews in December as positive ones, the question remained if the British reaction to *Star Wars* would be as meteoric as it was in the U.S., where according to the December 7 *Variety* the box office total had soared to $192,899,264. To provide an extra boost for the release, 20th Century-Fox sent out posters, T-shirts and foyer displays to cinemas in readiness for the individual releases of *Star Wars*. The T-shirts were very eye-catching with the words "*Star Wars* is coming." An exploitation brochure was also supplied to cinemas. It was in the style of the presskit but on the cover was "Advertising. Publicity. Promotion." The contents included "Editorial Blocks": photographs with accompanying text which could be supplied to local newspapers. Also competition templates and ideas of how the excitement surrounding *Star Wars* could be ramped up.

Incidentally, "exploitation" is a word that can have unpleasant connotations but within the film industry it simply refers to making the most of a publicity campaign surrounding a release. It is actually the film that is being "exploited," not the general public. Local newspapers in the large towns and cities which would open *Star Wars* in January began to include front page headlines excitedly proclaiming that the film was on its way. Photo serializations and competitions helped generate the spirit of a very special cinematic and cultural event.

Barry Norman in his *Film 77* review program (BBC1, 10:55 p.m., Saturday, December 17) praised *Star Wars* highly: "For total entertainment, one can do no better than to recommend *Star Wars* which, for those who might approach it in the right mood, is two hours of sheer bliss—the ultimate in space-age fairy tales"[71] Also on the 17th, Alec Guinness appeared on ITV's *Parkinson* at 10:15. Michael Parkinson wanted to clear up the rumors in the press concerning Guinness' fee for *Star Wars*, with the actor revealing that he would be receiving 2¼ percent of the profits. Guinness admitted that he asked for a percentage on all of his movies but *Star Wars* was the first one to actually pay off. A clip from the film was shown where Ben Kenobi explains to Luke Skywalker the truth about his father, after which the studio audience applauded. Parkinson said that had enjoyed the film greatly. Guinness too was full of praise: "It has a marvelous healthy innocence. Great pace, wonderful to look at. Full of guts, nothing unpleasant. I mean, people go 'bang, bang' and people fall over and are dead. No horrors ... no sex at all and a wonderful freshness about it like a wonderful fresh air."[72]

Guinness was also interviewed by Paul Gambaccini as part of a *Star Wars* feature on the BBC Radio 4 program *Kaleidoscope*, at the hardly child-friendly hour of 9.30 p.m. London's *Time Out* magazine published a "Christmas Double Issue" (December 16–29) with a fantastic cover painting of C-3PO with a tray of drinks, with Robert Mitchum with his arm around his shoulder. The merging of the magazine's two lead stories (*Star Wars* and Mitchum's apparent alcoholism) into one image seemed bizarre. On the center pages was a double-page *Star Wars* advertisement, with a London underground map on the reverse. The idea was that readers could pull out the center pages and use the map to find their way to the cinemas showing *Star Wars*. This could prove to be extremely useful to cinemagoers, especially if a journey to see the film was their first visit to London. *Time* reported:

> *Star Wars* opens this week in London but the Force is already there. Discotheques have been playing the music for months and London papers don't look complete these days without a *Star Wars* cartoon, joke or picture. The two giant theaters where the film will play have already racked up $320,000 in advance ticket sales—more than three times the previous record. Said a theater spokesman, "It's easier to get knighted than to buy *Star Wars* tickets." "I've been in this business for 45 years, and I've never seen anything like it," says John Fairbairn, the film's publicity director at 20th Century-Fox. "It's an eruption."[73]

On December 24, issue #44 of *2000AD* featured *Star Wars* on the cover and a two-page photo feature with the message in capital letters: "Go out and see *Star Wars*—It is the best film of all time!"[74]

On Christmas Day, some children woke to find *Star Wars* presents waiting for them. A set of Letraset transfers perhaps, a large format comic book, a pair of soap models, or the soundtrack even. The ultimate *Star Wars* present, of course, was the all-important tickets to see the film at the cinema.

As Christmas celebrations drew to a close and the release date loomed, *Star Wars* had been promoted to an unprecedented degree. In one last bid to make the opening of the film as spectacular as possible, 20th Century-Fox had reportedly arranged for a powerful laser to be installed on the roof of its Soho Square headquarters to shine a light show incorporating the *Star Wars* logo and characters onto surrounding high rise buildings such as the towering Centre Point every evening from December 27 until New Year's Eve. This was genuine cutting edge technology from Shepperton Studios-based company Holoco, which had regular collaborations with *The Who* pop group and later provided the laser covering for the egg chamber in the film *Alien*. It seems unlikely that the laser show took place; the press does not seem to have reported on it. "I'd be surprised if that happened," says Peter Beale. "My office was on the very top floor of the Soho Square headquarters and they would have had to have come by me to install and operate it." Real-life lasers or not, with every promotional effort finally expended, all that remained was to wait and see if Britain's cinemagoing public would actually respond and join a queue to see *Star Wars*.

Star Wars *Arrives—at Last!*

When *Star Wars* opened in London on December 27, the exteriors of both the Leicester Square Theatre and the Dominion Theatre featured giant photographic blow-up hoardings of the *Star Wars* poster by Greg and Tim Hildebrandt which attracted a great deal of attention. The Leicester Square Theatre's hoarding featured moving lights which was very effective. At the Dominion Theatre, queues started forming at seven a.m. for the 10:50 a.m. performance (that time slot had been added due to the phenomenal demand). All of the regular showings were booked until March but people were content to queue to book for later dates. Representatives from 20th Century-Fox hurried giddily between the two cinemas, delighted at the reaction from the public. A BBC1 news team was on hand to cover the occasion for the main evening news program. "The first of what the makers of *Star Wars* hope will be thousands of queues started at seven a.m. outside London's Dominion cinema," began the reporter. "Brought out by a publicity campaign of unprecedented proportions, the audience knew what they were after." A microphone was thrust in the face of the teenager who was first in the queue. "We wanted to see it at six p.m. but it's booked until March," he said. "We couldn't afford to wait *that* long. The prestige of being able to say you've seen *Star Wars* is something akin to royalty." The report continued as a voiceover, while a clip of the Millennium Falcon taking off from Mos Eisley was shown. "The film which has already outstripped the legendary *Jaws* as a money spinner in America tells an outer space war story with strange monsters, robots and special effects *all* made in British studios. Here the ruthless Imperial guards are beaten and a rebel ship escapes."

The reporter interviewed people as they emerged from the cinema. "Everything was fantastic! Whoever wrote it had a fantastic imagination," said an elated young woman. "I think it was good," said a young boy. "Just good?" countered the reporter. "No, fantastic," said the boy, to which the reporter said, "That's better." Another boy gave an indignant response: "It was exciting but I didn't like the bit where the man chopped off the person's arm." When asked why, he replied, "Because there was blood!"[75]

An ITV news crew was there too. During the report, a coach arrived with a *Star Wars* party on board, and the passengers had stuck drawings and photographs from the film on the windows. The ITV report followed much the same format as the BBC and even interviewed the same teenager waiting in line. As the audience emerged from the cinema, a woman exclaimed, "I thought it was stupid! You need to be an eight-year-old to enjoy it." Fortunately, an eight-year-old boy was next in front of the camera and said, "I liked all of the monsters and how they placed it in outer space." A teenage boy was full of praise too: "It makes you laugh. It makes you feel like you want to get up at the baddies and all that"[76]

Among the advertisements shown before *Star Wars* during its initial release, was one which began with an automated production line manufacturing golden robots very reminiscent of C-3PO. As the advert progressed, one of the robots had his head put on backwards. To compensate for his misfortune, the robot smoked a Hamlet cigar as he disappeared from the shot. The similarity of the robot to C-3PO and the *Star Wars*-like quality of the ad were hardly surprising, as it had been

Advertisements for the opening of *Star Wars* in London were difficult to miss.

filmed with the assistance of *Star Wars* crew members including John Stears and Brian Muir. There was also an advert for Smash, a brand of instant mashed potato, with a group of manic robot aliens making fun of human being who still make mash in the traditional way. The advert began by copying the opening of *Star Wars*, by showing the words "A long time ago in a galaxy far, far away."

"Those ads were fantastic," remembers David Day. "It was hilarious to see C-3PO having his head put on backwards and it seemed as if *Star Wars* had begun, only to have the Smash Robots come on. The whole audience laughed and it really added to the atmosphere in the cinema." The Smash ad campaign had been running since 1974 but the release of *Star Wars* provided the Smash Robots with a new lease on life and made the product seem bang up-to-date.

The trend during the 1970s was to release a film in London before gradually distributing it to the rest of the country. At that time, a trip to London to see a film was a special journey, especially if that film was *Star Wars*. Shaun Dawkins noticed that *Star Wars* was being shown in London while on a day out with his parents. "I remember begging them, literally begging them, and telling them that I would sell my soul if we could stop and let me see the film. They said 'no' and dragged me back to my little town by the sea, Folkestone—the equivalent of Tatooine. I then started counting the days until *Star Wars* would open."

Peter Beale explains the rationale behind the slow release of films:

> In Britain, you didn't open the country all in one go. You opened in London and then you had 50 or 100 prints and on Thursday evening vans came and collected the prints from the cinemas showing them and they moved them north. In that way you slowly distributed the film and they were done in areas based on the local newspaper distribution. Remember in those days, television advertising was not so common for films, so the distribution was based much more on newspaper zones. Prints were a large cost so you would make them work as long as possible, so if you were unfortunate to be an audience member towards the end of the life of the print it could often be very scratchy.

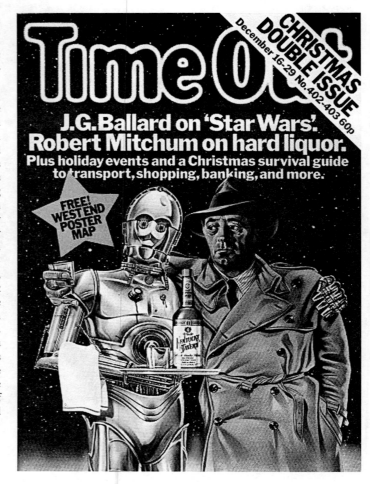

The December 16–29, 1977, *Time Out* had a bizarre *Star Wars* cover (*Star Wars* Magazines Encyclopaedia).

Star Wars: *Worth the Wait?*

After all of the buildup, the release of *Star Wars* certainly did not disappoint, with audiences leaving the cinema with a huge sense of euphoria. They had been promised "The best film of all time"[77] and for many, that was just what they got. Despite the hard-nosed response from some reviewers, the reaction to *Star Wars* on both sides of the Atlantic remained absolutely phenomenal. Film publicist Alan Arnold described how he received reports of the tremendous reaction in America while working on a film production in Greece, alongside some of the technicians who had made *Star Wars*. To them, the reports of people queuing around the block to see it was unfathomable. Visiting London in December 1977, Arnold was able to soak up the atmosphere himself:

> It was also apparent that publicity's most potent agent, word of mouth, was spreading the film's fame more effectively than a whole army of publicists could ever hope to do. When I talked with 20th Cen-

tury-Fox, they told me that no film in living memory had launched itself with such meteoric thrust. Far from being concerned as how to promote it, they had the unique problem of appeasing exhibitors outside of London who, reflecting public interest, were demanding the right to show it concurrently with the capital.[78]

For once, the views of reviewers were irrelevant. This was a young person's film or for those who were young at heart. The fact that *Star Wars* had been largely *made* by young people was not lost on the audience either and it seemed that the makers were tuned exactly to their wavelength. Audiences received *Star Wars* in exactly the kind of spirit that was intended when the film was made and that translated into huge numbers of tickets sold. The Dominion Theatre alone garnered £117,690 in the first week, breaking the record set by *Jaws*, which is all the more surprising considering tickets were priced at £2.20.

The success of *Star Wars* could not have come at a better time for the film industry and cinema chains on both sides of the Atlantic. The 1970s had produced a string of critically acclaimed films but few which attracted audiences in droves. S. Schoenbaum's article "Another Part of the Galaxy" for the August 5 edition of the *Times Literary Supplement* contrasted the success of *Star Wars* to the reported failure at the American box office of seemingly surefire big-budget 1977 movies such as John Boorman's *Exorcist II: The Heretic*, Martin Scorsese's *New York, New York* and William Friedkin's *Sorcerer*. "They no doubt looked profitable on the drawing board," said Schoenbaum. "These proven directors seemed to be taking little risks. Film enthusiasts may quietly (however) relish the apparent failure of these big-budget epics based on crassly inhibiting formulae. Meanwhile we have *Star Wars* with a couple of unglamorous veterans and the rest of the cast mostly nobodies. The movie has gone into orbit."[79] Becoming desperate to attract cinemagoers in the numbers that would keep the moviemaking machine going, cinema had resorted to offering content which was not available on television, leading to a constant stream of disaster films, violent police dramas, soft porn flicks and car chase films. *Star Wars*, along with *Jaws*, provided an alternative blueprint where films were returned to their origins as popular entertainment that appealed to an extremely wide demographic. Summer *blockbusters* would allow film companies to return to profit once more and be able to invest in the more thoughtful films so cherished by the cinemagoing elite. *Star Wars* was assisting in reviving the fortunes of 20th Century-Fox, and the future of another studio, Columbia, largely depended on the success of another film from the blockbuster stable: *Close Encounters of the Third Kind*.

Howard Rankin and Martin Raw of London's Institute of Psychology put forward a theory of *Star Wars'* success in the January 1978 edition of *Psychology Today*, that the film was part of a trend of people seeking to understand and interpret life via science fiction, in place of religious teaching. In America, the general public had been lifted from a national cloud of gloom generated by the Vietnam War and scandals such as Watergate. *Star Wars* had been flagwaving without any direct connections to American nationalism and had featured a sense of unashamed euphoria almost completely missing from the current trend in filmmaking. *Star Wars* even had the novelty of a happy ending. "It's easy to forget how downbeat many movies of the 1970s were," says Darren Slade. "There were a slew of films in which the heroes were not easily distinguished from the villains and in which endings were at best ambiguous. There was clearly a feeling that being downbeat was the same as being sophisticated. Then along came *Star Wars*. A movie in which the good guys were good, the bad guys were bad, and the little band of democratic heroes defeated the evil Empire. No wonder the public loved it."

"*Star Wars* lifted us out of our sort of depression of the seventies," Walter Cronkite recalled. "Into an awareness and focus of space and a possible future."[80] American journalist Bill Moyers said, "Timing is everything in art. Bring out *Star Wars* too early and it's Buck Rogers. Bring it out too late and it doesn't fit our imaginations. Bring it out just as the war in Vietnam is ending, when America feels unsure of itself … and suddenly it's a new game. It's also a lot of fun to see *Star Wars*."[81]

Britain had its own woes based on the winding down of the British Empire, the seemingly never-ending series of union strikes and soaring prices at the gas pumps and in the shops. The country was apparently broke, down on its luck, and had a bleak future ahead. It could be argued that *Star Wars* was an antidote to Britain's malaise. At the very least, as George Lucas had said of the audience, "for two hours they could forget."[82] The thought that for once something made in Britain was a phenomenon in America, in a reverse of the cultural tide, was intoxicating. Half of the heroes too and all of the villains, depending on what side people preferred, were also British.

So as 1977 came to a close, a relatively small number of people finally got the chance to see *Star Wars*. The media were still reporting excitedly about the film, with even the queues to see *Star Wars* being a news feature. In America the film was still showing and had reached $195,666,111.[83] The December 31 issue of the youth magazine *Look-In* sported a fantastic cover depicting the movie's main cast. Inside there was a special feature, a free poster and a competition. In December, the *Star Wars* merchandise had gone completely off of the charts, with the paperback alone selling over 700,000 copies. Letraset Ltd. Was on the way to selling a million transfer sets, more than justifying the company's early leap into the world of *Star Wars*

The first *Star Wars Look-in* cover, December 31, 1977.

Early morning at the Leicester Square Theatre (courtesy Derek Dorking).

marketing. Robert Beecham's hard work had paid dividends as the Cliro Perfumeries *Star Wars* range had sold phenomenally well. The London Symphony Orchestra soundtrack album sold over 150,000 copies, being awarded Silver status by the British Phonographic Institute. Even through all of the hype, some young children did not understand exactly what *Star Wars* was but they already knew it was cool. If those in the know thought that they had seen and heard enough about the film over the course of the year, they had not seen anything yet.

Chapter 2

Star Wars on the Home Front

The year 1978 began well for 20th Century-Fox, with the news that *Star Wars* had passed the £250,000 mark at the Odeon Leicester Square Theatre and Dominion Tottenham Court Road. "As all seats are booked until March, those who have seen the film can score prestigious points over those who have not," the *Evening Standard* reported on January 3. "Now the only way to get in is to queue for the unbookable first performance at 10:50 each morning, or to see the film in the middle of the night. Today hopeful queuers wound themselves all the way round the Dominion Cinema, jogging fitfully as icy winds swept around the corners."[1] Many young people used the Christmas holiday to travel into central London to see *Star Wars*, while adults often combined attending the performances with visiting the New Year sales.

Derek Dorking had another reason for heading for the capital. He had decided to take his R2-D2 model to the very heart of *Star Wars* in Britain:

> Although I hadn't got the mechanics inside the head working, I went to 20th Century-Fox headquarters in Soho Square to show them my model. I met Colin Hankins there and I showed him and his colleagues how the model could project an image of Princess Leia's hologram. They asked me how I had done it and I described how a local cinema had cut a frame out of the *Star Wars* trailer for me and I'd mounted it behind a lens in the robot's head. I mentioned that I was having trouble with the head mechanism but I was told that no photographs or blueprints of R2-D2 were available. Instead, I was led downstairs to find an American man in a jersey looking very cold. He said, "Wait until you see this, Derek," and led me to the main foyer of the Fox building where the real-life radio controlled R2-D2 was in a packing crate. The C-3PO costume was there too, in what looked like a packing crate coffin. Someone said that Anthony Daniels was due to appear on television that evening, on a news program.
>
> The American introduced himself as Brian Haines and said that he was the operator of R2-D2. "Wherever he goes, I go." He unpacked the robot and began driving it around the foyer and there were people coming into the building wondering what on earth it was. Brian Haines wouldn't reveal how the head of the robot worked but I was allowed to take photographs and I was even lent the cassette tape containing the bleeps and bloops for me to record for my own use. Considering how new I was to *Star Wars*, the welcome I received at 20th Century-Fox and actually seeing the real R2-D2 spurred me on to make my model even better. Before long I had it doing forward and reverse, turn left, turn right, turn on a sixpence and speak. The head could turn, the blue light on the head lit up, as well as projecting an image of Princess Leia's hologram. All on a two-channel proportional system radio control. A few days later, I got a letter from Peter Beale thanking me for bringing along the model and clarifying what kind of promotional work that I could do.

A major rival to the London Symphony Orchestra's *Star Wars* soundtrack album was still present in the form of the Damont *Star Wars* soundtrack album by the London Philharmonic Orchestra. On January 12, a High Court Judge awarded a temporary injunction to Pye, who in conjunction with 20th Century-Fox Records and 20th Century-Fox Films

Corp. was preparing a "passing off" action against Damont which prevents a company from selling items which purport to be associated with another. The judge prevented Damont from pressing any more albums but allowed the company to sell the stock that it already held, as long as they included a sticker stating that the records did not contain the original soundtrack. The *Star Wars*–like sleeve was the point of contention. Cover versions of previously recorded music were in fact completely legal, and rights were being issued without any barriers. "It doesn't break copyright to produce a recording of a piece of music," explains Marc Pevers. "As long as the rights have been paid for, anyone could have released a version of the *Star Wars* tune, on a mouthorgan or whatever."

The Birmingham Gaumont cinema put on a special premiere on the 13th January in conjunction with Palitoy, who wanted its sales force to see the film in the evening after close of business at the Birmingham NEC Toy Fair. A report from the show was filmed for ITV news in the Midlands that was broadcast the same evening. Reporter Derek Hobson interviewed TV celebrities Alfred Marks, Terry Scott, Frank Williams and Richard O'Sullivan, who each gave their reaction after seeing the film. The large crowd behind the camera crew roared with laughter as Marks impersonated a malfunctioning computer, spluttering that the film was fantastic. Talking naturally again, Marks said, "I'm a bit too tall. I wanted to be inside that little robot thing. I think it's wonderful." Asked why he thought *Star Wars* got the reaction it did, he replied, "Well, it's a technical masterpiece. It's a technician's film."

Bouncing into frame, a beaming Terry Scott said, "And it was made in England. That's the super thing!" He then jokingly added, "The only thing that bothered me was the amount of bullets they missed!" Marks said dryly, "Yes, the other side were terrible marksmen, weren't they?" Frank Williams, best known for his role as the vicar on the *Dad's Army* TV series, was grinning like a small boy. "I thought it was marvelous. It was so funny as well as everything else. It was very exciting. I loved it."

Richard O'Sullivan was apparently suffering from the effects of a late night the previous day. "Well, it's very good for a hangover," he said, bleary-eyed. "I thought it was terrific; there are a lot of new faces in it and I thought the presentation was terrific." Marks had the last word: "I'd see it again," he deadpanned. "I might even pay next time," causing the crowd to roar with laughter again.[2] On January 24, there was a similar advance performance of *Star Wars* at the Leeds Odeon, where the press, television and radio were invited.

Star Wars *Unleashed*

Star Wars went into general release in 12 cities and large towns on Sunday, January 29: the Gaumont cinemas in Birmingham and Sheffield and the Odeon cinemas in Manchester, Glasgow, Liverpool, Southampton, Cardiff, Newcastle, Bristol, Bradford and Leeds. The Nottingham Odeon jumped in early on Thursday the 26th. The choice of venues was undoubtedly influenced by *Screen International* using the same towns and cities in its UK provincial box office chart. The results from each venue could be tracked in this way free of charge, simply by buying the magazine; then the next steps in releasing *Star Wars* to smaller venues could be planned in detail. The Savoy Dublin and Curzon Belfast were not included on the provincial chart, so their release of *Star Wars* on December 27 could not be tracked. The same scenes of long queues seen in London were repeated nationwide as people finally had the opportunity to see the film in their area. Cinemas gave away free car window stickers with the words "I've seen *Star Wars*," which was a considerable boast. A *Star Wars* program book was on sale at cinemas for the princely sum of 50p, with T-shirts at £3.00, the *Star Wars Soundtrack Album* at £5.00 and the novel at 95p. The Hilderbrandt *Star Wars* poster was changed to an action-packed design by English artist Tom Chantrell, both for use at cinemas and for advertising in the press. Chantrell had worked in film posters and commercial illustration since 1946, most notably for Hammer and the *Carry On* series. Despite the change in the poster, the London cinemas retained their Hildebrandt-styled frontages.

"I went to see the film as a treat for my eighth birthday at the Odeon in Cardiff's Queen Street," says *Star Wars* fan Richard Harris. He continues:

> I can vividly remember staring at the lobby cards in the grand entrance hall while my parents paid for the tickets at the kiosk. Before going to our seats, my parents bought me a *Star Wars* book at the sweet counter, which I clutched firmly in my hands as I watched in amazement as the film unfolded. I felt as if I was with Luke every step of his incredible journey, and after the ceremony at the end of the film, we left the cinema to go to the Wimpy burger restaurant next door. I had no interest in the food that was laid before me, only the book that I was now eagerly flicking through trying to recapture every scene in the film that I had just seen. I know now that 'the book' was the movie program and it holds the greatest memory for me about my first *Star Wars* visit to the cinema.

Jordan Royce recalls that it was not just children who were excited:

> Even parents who are usually disinterested were very up for seeing what this film was all about. I was raised by my grandparents and they were very excited about coming along with me when we saw it at the Odeon Manchester. I remember thinking, "Wow, normally I was having to badger them to take me to see a film." I got the impression they were looking forward to it just as much as I was. We lived in Stockport, which wouldn't be receiving the film for a few months.
>
> My grandparents lied to me in a nice way. They said that we'd be doing some shopping in Manchester but when we got there I found that the trip was actually to see *Star Wars*. I just couldn't believe it. I

Star Wars finally opens all over Britain.

was so excited. My grandparents didn't appreciate having to queue for hours; for me it was just part of the excitement. When we got in and the film began, it was far, far greater than my expectations.

Gerald Crotty says:

I saw *Star Wars* at the Gaumont in Birmingham City Center. Even though I knew the story inside out when I saw it, the film still blew me away and what happened was, I really fell in love with the characters. I liked them from the book but the movie really takes it to another level. I thought the performances were so great, especially Mark Hamill. This was the first time I'd ever really related to a movie hero. In the past, movie heroes were like James Bond—they were already mature and cool and knew what they were doing, there wasn't really any emotion involved. But with *Star Wars* it was about Luke, who was someone who yearned for adventure. He was a different type of hero. Usually heroes were already mature and confident (James Bond, the Saint, etc.) but Luke was a teenager still trying to find his way, so he was much more relatable. Luke met up

Mark Hamill, Kenny Baker and Anthony Daniels visit Birmingham January 25, 1978 (Mirrorpix).

with these other characters who were similar in that they were young and un-cool too. The bickering and the comedy made them all so relatable, it's an element of "realism" in characters that behave like us, they make dumb mistakes, they're alive, they were so much more human than other movie heroes.

All over the country, children and young people were ready for the upcoming release, wondering eagerly if the film would match the pictures in their mind. Ian Whitlock's memories:

I don't remember ever hearing about *Star Wars*. I just seemed to know about it for some reason and bugged my father endlessly to see it from late 1977 to when the film came out at the Odeon Bristol, when he finally gave in. It was extremely cold outside and there was a huge queue going around the corner, so I wasn't sure we were going to get in. I was thinking that my father would not wait much longer when we finally reached the doors of the cinema and stumbled inside. We walked into the auditorium just as the opening crawl had finished. When the star destroyer flew over my head, the sound

David Prowse poses with model Val Robinson at the Palitoy stand at the Toy Fair at the Birmingham NEC Arena (Mirrorpix). The Birmingham Evening Mail reported that the Darth Vader costume failed to turn up.

nearly knocked me over! After the film had finished, I was just so excited about it. I met Darth Vader not long after that at Martins toyshop in Kingswood, Bristol. I kept his autograph in a scrapbook I made, consisting of sheets of paper taped together. We didn't have much money back then.

Derek Dorking was still working on his R2-D2 model. "Although it wasn't 100 percent finished, I approached the manager of the Southend Odeon, Arthur Levinson, to inquire if he would like to display my R2-D2 when the film opened in a few weeks' time. He was one of the most important local cinema managers because in the '60s they had all of the big pop groups, including the Beatles, at the cinema. He asked how long it would take to finish and I said, 'Long before you get the film, easily.' The pressure was on then because he was seen as being the big man in town and I couldn't let him down."

Taking a fresh approach to her complaints about *Star Wars*, Margaret Hinxman (in a piece for the February 7 *Daily Mail*) sought to warn her readers that the much-publicized box office results of the film had not taken into account ticket price inflation, even though its success could have been judged against other films released concurrently and shortly before. "Don't get conned because so many pounds and pence on the balance sheet insist that a film must be good and therefore you'd be mad to miss it. Make your own judgment. I wonder in 1980 who will remember *Star Wars*?"[3]

Birmingham was one of the areas that enjoyed an extended run of *Star Wars*.

The wider distribution of *Star Wars* was preceded on January 28 at 2:40 p.m. by the BBC2 television program *Arena*. The segment "Cinema: The Force Is with Us?" presented by Gavin Millar, featured interviews with Gary Kurtz and Mark Hamill in London. Another presenter reported on how the robots had been made; viewers also saw footage of Alec Guinness and George Lucas speaking on the *Star Wars* set.

On Sunday, January 1, Carrie Fisher appeared in the Anglo-American television drama *Come Back, Little Sheba*, which aired on ITV. She played the part of Marie alongside fellow *Star Wars* actor William Hootkins, who played Red Six Porkins. Bruce Boa, also featured in the drama, went on to play General Rieekan in the *Star Wars* sequel. The appearance of Hootkins and Boa was not as coincidental as it seems, because both actors were based in

Britain, where *Come Back, Little Sheba* was filmed. The powerful actors' union Equity lobbied heavily for supporting roles, demanding an American to be offered to the fairly small pool of American actors living in Britain who were Equity card holders. A number of Canadian actors based in the country too could pass for Americans, at least to British ears. Eagle-eyed viewers are able to spot the Americans and Canadians who filled minor parts in the *Star Wars* films in countless British television and film productions that required that distinctive yawl.

The Mighty Poster Magazine

The Official Star Wars Poster Monthly became available in Britain with a variation of the American cover, the price having been changed to 35 pence. The printing in the UK was credited to Fleet Litho Ltd., but the magazine was still written and assembled by Bunch Associates and Oley Press Ltd. In common with its American counterpart, the magazine was a folded A2-sized poster, with the reverse side containing detailed articles. This issue began with John May's article "Birth of a Space Legend," which was an entirely different piece to the one printed in the American version. "*Star Wars* is the most spectacular sci-fi film ever made, an epic of a movie. Excitement lurks behind every doorway. There are duels with laser swords; flying cars and robots; immense space stations and giant hairy aliens. This is a galactic tale of heroes and villains, a special effects extravaganza which actually gives you the feeling of being in deep space." The gap between the release of the American and British publications had enabled May to report on the success of the film in America. "Now *Star Wars* is invading the rest of the world. And it is only a beginning; George Lucas recently announced that there will be many more *Star Wars* films, the first in about two years' time. In the meantime, sit back and enjoy one of the most exiting motion pictures ever made."[4] This issue also included the profile of the main characters from the American version, which was very useful information considering that by far the majority of the magazine's British readership had not yet had an opportunity to see the film. According to May, "The mag sold well because, in a world without Internet, every piece of information about the film had to be sought out by fans and was harder to find."

Jordan Royce was an enthusiastic purchaser of the poster magazine and *Starburst*, the second issue of which contained yet more *Star Wars* coverage. "There was no Internet back then. It was either television or magazines that children got their information from. It was titles like *Starburst* and the poster magazine that got us kids just freaking out and begging our parents to [take] us to see the film." Sarah Baker-Saunders also purchased the *Official Star Wars Poster Monthly*. "There were articles on behind-the-scenes and technical processes of making the movie, as well as character articles. All of the things that I had an interest in, as well as talk of sequel films. I believed them to be completely authentic. It said 'official' on the cover. The other draw for these magazines was the large fold-out posters, always a favorite. The magazines also offered a mail order page with a T-shirt, patches and badges. All exciting stuff for a fan."

Bunch Associates/Paradise Press also produced a one-off *Star Wars* publication for the American market; it was imported back into Britain by comic shops and dealers. *Star Wars the Full Story* featured fantastic illustrations from British-based artists Dave Gibbons and American-born Joe Petagno, a very well-established name in rock music album covers and science fiction novels. The publication went on to become a million-plus seller.

For a time, it seemed as if nearly every magazine for sale in the shops had *Star Wars* on the cover. The January edition of the film magazine *Photoplay* covered the film heavily,

It seemed as if every magazine had *Star Wars* on the cover in early 1978.

as did *The House of Hammer*. The January *Film Review* had a *Star Wars* calendar centerfold and the February issue was a "bumper colorful *Star Wars* edition." The February issue of *Photoplay* had Harrison Ford on the cover and included yet more *Star Wars* coverage. *Star Wars* became a regular feature in *Look-In*. The fantastic covers of the magazine were painted by Arnaldo Putzo, an Italian film poster artist working in London; they were treasured by *Star Wars* fans. *Look-In* #11, published on March 11, was the most *Star Wars*-packed issue of them all with a competition to win a set of *Star Wars* figures, a free strip of Letraset transfers and a rare interview with Harrison Ford. Richard Tippet had caught up with the actor in London at the time that *Hanover Street* was being filmed. Asked about his original expectations for *Star Wars*' success, Ford said. "I thought that it would probably be successful. But to anticipate the kind of success it's had, I would have had to be a madman. If you went around saying, 'This picture's going to make $200,000,000 in America alone,' they would have taken you away with your hands behind your back. No one really had any idea that it was going to catch on in the way it has, except perhaps George Lucas."[5] Also in this issue of *Look-In*, Gerry Anderson praised *Star Wars* in his regular column "The Worlds of Gerry Anderson." "I for one would be very surprised if there were a single boy or girl in the country who wouldn't like to see this truly entertaining film!" was his closing statement.[6] This issue of *Look-In* had been advertised on television; the ad included crude animation, making the Palitoy action figures appear to move.

Fans seeking to learn more about *Star Wars* and the design process behind some of its fantastic imagery would have been fascinated by *The Star Wars Sketchbook* from Ballantine Books, first released in America in September 1977. Written by Joe Johnston, who was credited as "Effects Illustrator and Designer: Miniature and Optical Effects Unit," the book contained a wealth of original design sketches and blueprints. Princess Leia's ship, described as a galactic cruiser in the novel, was in fact a Rebel Blockade Runner, an antiquated craft with multiple fuel-burning engines from an era when spacecraft were commissioned and handcrafted. Imperial Cruiser had been the name for the Imperial capital ships in the film and novelization and other surrounding media but Johnston provided the craft with the much more sinister moniker Star Destroyer. The vehicle seen parked in the background in the Lars homestead garage scenes was revealed to be Luke Skywalker's *Skyhopper* craft (Luke played with a miniature version in the same scene). Johnston explained that Luke did not use the *Skyhopper* to search for R2-D2 in the film as the craft was being overhauled at the time. It also explained that the *Millennium Falcon* begun its existence as a stock light utility freighter before extensive modification by Han Solo. The shapes that protruded from the front of the ship were described by Johnston as freight-loading *arms*. X-Wing Fighters had apparently been acquired decades before the events in the film, at a discount, and had been made to last by Rebel technicians. The smooth Grand Prix Car shape of the Y-Wing cockpit originally covered the entire fuselage but Rebel mechanics had "left the hood off," being tired of frequent breakdowns. TIE Fighters were described in the *Sketchbook* as having been designed by the Empire to instill terror into its victims, with T.I.E being an acronym for Twin Ion Engine.

Ballantine Books also released *The Star Wars Blueprints*, a selection of the original designs for many of the incredible sets and models. This was soon followed by *The Star Wars Portfolio*, a fantastic selection of beautiful pre-production paintings by Ralph McQuarrie which had influenced a great deal of the *Star Wars* imagery and had been used to great effect in promoting the film.

Meanwhile at Palitoy

With the film blazing a trail across the country, Palitoy was striving to produce the *Star Wars* range on time. The production line was not the only challenge to the company, as Geoff Maisey was still working to secure orders. "To try to overcome the toy trade resistance, we began linking the ranging of the *Star Wars* line to additional incentives off Action Man, based on cooperation on number of products listed and an agreement to keep the line on display through the Christmas 1978 period. We also offered key retailers the opportunity of 'tagging' a *Star Wars* toy ad to be run before the movie in a cinema local to their nominated store with displays in the cinema foyer for selected major retailer outlets."

Palitoy received a great deal of support from Kenner, even though it had its own *Star Wars* production schedule looming in America. Thousands of children across the Atlantic too had *Star Wars* appetites to satisfy. "As a subsidiary of General Mills, Palitoy had strong links to Kenner through their president of International Sales, Bernie Loomis," Maisey says. He continues:

> Loomis was a very well-known and powerful figure within the industry, with very strong views on how the *Star Wars* concept should be marketed. He was supported by vice-president Ed Thelan, and a very able department charged with helping us to obtain samples, marketing materials and production allocations. The arrangement between Palitoy and Kenner was that we had access to all sales and marketing data, including trade presentation films, TV commercials, product samples, manufacturing tooling and production sites. We were able to place orders on Kenner Hong Kong for our merchandise, including *Star Wars*, and we bought it at cost plus design-tooling royalty."

Geoff Maisey describes an occasion when it came time for Palitoy to play the host. "We had access and good contact across the U.S. marketing group and, most important, the Kenner president, Joe Mendelsohn. He would make an annual visit to us at Palitoy, along with the General Mills board, to review product and financial plans prior to each fiscal year." Palitoy had taken great care to organize a special presentation for their guests and was anxious to impress. "It was due to take place in the Palitoy building where we had taken over the design studio recently vacated by Palitoy design group. It was converted into showrooms and a presentation theater. Bear in mind that in those days, everything was committed to slide projection, so the whole presentation involved a bank of around ten projectors. The presentation involved the whole Palitoy range and business plan, of which *Star Wars* was only a part. The trouble was that the flights that the GM board members were booked on were severely delayed, so only one of them arrived on time. We decided to run the presentation for him anyway but immediately it started he fell asleep from exhaustion, waking at the closing address and congratulating us on a good review!"

On January 17, ITV news in the Midlands included a report by presenter Chris Tarrant from the Toy Fair, The National Exhibition Center, Birmingham. Tarrant did not mention *Star Wars*, but there was a short clip of the Palitoy display being guarded by a Stormtrooper who did his best to ignore the attention of a large group of fascinated children crowding around attempting to peek under his mask. Palitoy display manager Brian Turner says,

I had come up with the idea of emulating the *Star Wars* packaging by integrating a mirror surround on each of the boards that displayed the products. I also included some dioramas that were created by Nick Farmer and Greg Hughes. There was an area that featured life-size models of Stormtroopers, R2-D2, C-3PO and other principal characters. Also on the stand, arranged by Munro/Deighton, we had actors dressed as characters from the film. The *Star Wars* section of the Palitoy stand proved to be a huge success. The costumed characters especially; [they] attracted the attention of the television news reporters.

Robert Beecham was at the show and set out an eye-catching stall for Cliro Perfumeries *Star Wars* products.

I was approached by an American who was the greatest salesman I had met in my entire life. He did not have any connection with *Star Wars* at all but he had a great lightsaber—or "Force Beam," as it was sold. The salesman wanted to come onto the Cliro stand and show off his lightsaber and we let him. The place virtually came to a standstill. They hadn't seen a lightsaber in the flesh before but they knew what it was. Containers of these things were sold all over the place.

The toy show later in January at Harrogate, North Yorkshire presented a worrying situation for Brian Turner.

When I arrived at the Harrogate Center, I found to my horror that I had mislaid the X-Wing fighter. I thought it had been left behind at Coalville so had to make a long return twilight journey by car from Harrogate to Coalville, a round trip of over 200 miles, only to find out, when I got back to the Toy Fair, that it was hidden behind a door on the stand!

The Stars Go on the Campaign Trail

Mark Hamill arrived in London again in January and included a visit to Birmingham to his hurried schedule. He was in the company of Anthony Daniels and Kenny Baker, who had been contracted to tour regional cinemas showing *Star Wars*. Birmingham was considered to be an extremely important venue. The sole purpose of the visit was to engage with and be photographed by the local press. Hamill was pictured in the *Birmingham Evening Mail* posed cheek to cheek with lucky female fan Janet Bridge, a worker at the local Holiday Inn where the actor was staying. In an interview for the *Birmingham Evening Mail*, Hamill revealed to reporter Maurice Rotheroe, "If I had really been given my choice of parts in *Star Wars*, it would not have been Luke. But it might well have been See-Threepio. Now my biggest problem is convincing people that I am not just a simple guy who says dumb things like, 'Gosh, we're being followed!' True, I have been made offers of money a mile high but not always to the kind of thing that I want. I want to do the kind of movies I want to see myself."

Rotheroe, a very well-known reporter in his own right, was hoping to receive a sample of C-3PO's voice (which of course few people in Britain had heard) from Anthony Daniels during his interview with the actor. Rotheroe recalled: "For some reason which he declined to explain, Anthony is very coy about his screen 'droid' voice. He refused to give us a sample of it." Daniels seemed happy to provide a description, however. "As See-Threepio, I sound like an upper-class English butler—half an octave higher than normal—who has lived in Hollywood for a couple of years. I speak very clearly and precisely, a sort of gold-plated cross between Jeeves and Noel Coward—terribly correct."

Although his R2-D2 character had achieved worldwide recognition, Kenny Baker explained how he would still be performing at the seaside resort of Margate in his double act "The Minitones," with fellow *Star Wars* actor Jack Purvis. "Despite people thinking that

I must have made a packet from the film and that it has changed my life. The fact is that Jack and I are still working as hard as usual in our musical-comedy act around the clubs and in cabaret. It's our bread and butter."[7]

The upcoming *Star Wars* opening at the Hanley (Stoke-on-Trent) Odeon was promoted by a visit by Hamill, Daniels and Baker. The cinema was close to Birmingham so the trio could probably have visited both venues on the same day. The local paper featured a photograph of the three stars, with a homespun Darth Vader looming in the background (the reporter claimed in error that it was actually David Prowse). The Manchester release had been also provided a boost by a visit by Mark Hamill, Kenny Baker and Anthony Daniels. Only the droid actors were interviewed by the *Manchester Evening News,* however. After Manchester, Baker continued the promotional tour by himself, taking in geographically close Monkseaton before moving on to other towns including Lowestoft and Leicester.

The Empire Strikes Local Areas

Numerous incarnations of "Darth Vader" and "Stormtroopers" made appearances along with the release of *Star Wars* around the country. Mainly it was a batch of twelve professional looking Stormtrooper costumes that had been organised by the Rank Organisation, that had been announced in *Screen International* in December. In addition there were a number of Darth Vader costumes that were more of a mixed bag of quality. Cinemas would receive the costumes for use in their promotions and then forward them to the next venue on the list. One of the cinemas to take advantage of the costumes was the Birmingham Gaumont cinema, who had Darth Vader and a Stormtrooper on hand to assist in the promotion of *Star Wars.* One of the stunts arranged was an "invasion" of the local newspaper, the *Birmingham Evening Gazette* that practically guaranteed a front-page story. If however the Rank Organisation costumes were unavailable, it would be down to local talent to construct the outfits.

The authentic Vader and Stormtrooper masks from Don Post Studios were frequently used, if the individual people charged with creating the costumes wanted to go to that kind of expense. The general public was not familiar with the finer details of the Darth Vader and Stormtrooper characters, so the promotional versions did not need to be perfect replicas. Considering that the manufacture of some of the Vader and Stormtrooper costumes had been arranged by local cinemas, the results were generally very good. The occasionally dubious nature of the costumes did not seem to matter to adoring fans.

Charles Lippincott was not aware this activity was going on in Britain and had actually made an attempt, months earlier to rein in the more outlandish promotional ideas. "Things looked like they were going to get out of hand with the British promotions because I don't think that Marc Pevers and I got it across to U.K. promotions people that you couldn't have a whole bunch of people dressing up. In the United States, we had just one troupe of people because we had a bad time with a major toy store trying to do promotions dressing up in the masks, so we wanted to put a limit on that. I had one guy in the United States, Kermit Eller, who was allowed to dress up as Darth Vader." In common with so many other cinemas, the Odeon Exeter had Rank Organisation Odeon Darth Vader and Stormtrooper costumes on hand to promote its showing of *Star Wars* from Sunday, February 19, but the concept was taken to a higher level. The staff of the local Caroline Design Disco suggested to the Odeon

Exeter Cinema manager Tony Wadey that they could appear on stage at the local premiere. A deal was struck where a banner for the Caroline Design Disco was placed in front of the stage, upon which the dance troupe—dressed as Vader, Stormtrooper and a range of home-made space costumes—boogied before the film began. The Caroline Design Disco troupe helped promote *Star Wars* in the surrounding towns, dressing up for the part as Vader, Stormtrooper, space princesses, etc., and plastering their van with *Star Wars* pictures and logos. The Exeter campaign is a fine example of how people came together with huge exuberance to promote *Star Wars*, using their own initiative and individual talents.

Going Star Wars *Loco*

Local newspapers all over the country covered *Star Wars* very heavily in the weeks leading up to the film opening in their area. The *Leicester Chronicle* covered the entire front page with pictures from *Star Wars* to advertise that the serialization of the film was due to begin in the next issue. It was not simply a film that was on the way, it was a national phenomenon. The *Star Wars* serializations printed weekly in many newspapers were often designed so that they formed a pamphlet that people could keep as a souvenir of the film. Local businesses were encouraged to place advertisements crammed onto a *Star Wars*-themed page, a separate pull-out section or even a color poster. Businesses showed a sense of humor in attempting to link their services to the film, including many tenuous examples. John Rhodes men's outfitters placed an ad stating: "Space suits? Sorry not in this century! Many STAR bargains for your WARdrobe." Wadeham Stringer used cars had a very special offer: "Yes, we'll take your spaceship in part exchange!" Rich's Ice Cream Parlor offered a "star spangled banana flavored ice cream" created to celebrate the film.

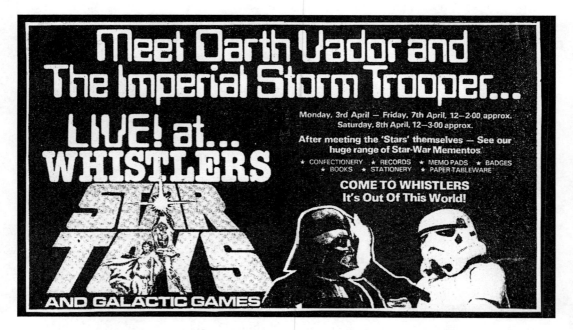

Darth Vader and Stormtrooper appeared all over the country courtesy of Rank Cinemas.

Above: **Darth Vader and Stormtrooper hit the streets of Southend-on-Sea (*Southend Echo*).**
Right: **Darth Vader and Stormtrooper meet Derek Dorking's R2-D2 at Keddies department store, Southend-on-Sea (courtesy Derek Dorking).**

Cinema managers used their own initiative to promote the arrival of *Star Wars* in their area, employing some extremely innovative ideas. Jimmy Brandon, manager of the Granada Clapham Junction, Greater London, employed the talents of local model-maker Bob Ballan to scratch-build an X-Wing Fighter, Y-Wing Fighter and Star Destroyer for a display in the cinema foyer. Considering that reference photographs were not easy to come by, the models were exceptional. Ballan went on to be a professional model-maker in the British special effects industry. The Kilburn Gaumont State manager Bill Weir arranged for the construction of a large roof rack sign for his car and for a woman to dress up as Princess Leia to make the most of the Darth Vader and Stormtrooper costumes he had been sent. The manager of the Oxford ABC Malcolm Bickley worked hard in the weeks leading up to his cinema's showing of *Star Wars*, with a large foyer display of ephemera and a double window display in conjunction with the local WH Smith, Harlequin Records and the Paperback Bookshop. Bickley also arranged for David Prowse to make an appearance at the cinema and take part in a question-and-answer session. Finally, he sat for an interview with Radio Oxford, no doubt glad to take a couple of hours' rest from all of the excitement surrounding the imminent release of *Star Wars*.

Responding to the exploitation pamphlet sent by 20th Century-Fox, many cinemas teamed with local newspapers to run identical quizzes and "spot the differences" competitions. The *Southend Evening Echo* went to the extreme of buying all of the opening day's *Star Wars* tickets as prizes. The winners still had to pay the newspaper for the tickets, though!

The Force Spreads

Sunday, February 5, was the beginning of a wider release of *Star Wars* to a great many additional venues: In Greater London, the Odeon Cinemas in Bromley, Barking, Barnet, Ealing, East Ham, Guildford, Ilford, Lewisham, Streatham, Twickenham, Elephant & Castle, Watford, Woolwich and Wood Green. Also the Finchley Gamont, Kingston Granada, Clapham Junction Granada, Staines ABC and Enfield ABC. Coastal towns were included. On the South Coast, the Southsea Salon, Worthing Odeon, Clacton-on-Sea Mecca, Margate Dreamland, Eastbourne Curzon, Hastings Classic, Brighton Odeon Film Center, Bournemouth Gaumont, the Portsmouth Odeon and the Southend Odeon. In Cornwall, the Bude Picturehouse. On the North Sea coast, the Lowestoft Odeon. In Devon, the Torquay Odeon and Plymouth Drake Film Centre. In the North, the Scarborough Odeon and the Blackpool Odeon. Some seaside towns published a weekly newspaper on a Wednesday, so a great many coastal venues began their film showings on Thursday the 9th. At one such venue, the Bournemouth Gaumont, its showing of *Star Wars* was the first time both screens had shown the same film. Darth Vader was present for the opening along with the Bournemouth Lottery Robot, a hulking static model that dwarfed the Dark Lord. The model had not been used for some time and had stood in its creator Dick Shepherd's porch. A local pensioner had previously written to the paper, declaring herself to be Bertie's greatest fan and expressing concern as to where he had gone. She was invited to the opening of *Star Wars* to meet Bertie and Vader. Her name was very apt: Mrs. Kenner.

Darren Slade finally had the chance to find out if his initial doubts had been well-founded:

> The Gaumont in Bournemouth was one of those cinemas that had had an enormous auditorium that had been turned into a twin screen a few years previously but the screens were still pretty big. As far as I'm aware, it was the first time a film had been on both screens simultaneously. I remember looking at the lobby cards outside the cinema endlessly as we waited in line with my uncle. When we eventually got in, there was a film about scrambler bikes which took forever and when the main title march began, I was surprised that it wasn't the Meco version of the theme! As the film progressed, I wondered what had happened to the scenes featuring Luke's friend Biggs Darklighter that I'd read in the comic. When they escaped the Death Star, I thought to myself that that had been a really good film but it was a shame

that it didn't go on longer. Then as the film continued to the rebel attack on the Death Star, it was a real bonus. I had never before seen anything as intensely exciting as this film. The sheer exoticism of the galaxy George Lucas created—its aliens, its scenery, its robots—was unlike anything depicted on screen before. After we came out of the cinema that afternoon, the ordinary world seemed unreal and sort of smaller. We had spent the afternoon in another universe. I knew that I'd had a profound experience.

The February releases also included the Odeon cinema in Edinburgh, which began its run on Saturday the 4th. The trend of opening films on a Saturday instead of Sunday in Scotland was based around the *Glasgow Times* publishing cinema listings on a Saturday. The Scottish release continued with openings at the Odeon cinemas in Perth, Aberdeen and Dundee on Saturday the 11th. The campaign in Wales began on Sunday the 12th at the Swansea Odeon and Bangor Odeon and would go on to the Colwyn Bay Princess and Rhyl Plaza. Later in February *Star Wars* began premiering in additional large venues including the Odeon Leicester, ABC Oxford, ABC Wolverhampton, Hanley Odeon (Stoke-on-Trent), Gloucester ABC, Cambridge Victoria, Derby Odeon, Cheltenham Odeon, Norwich Odeon, Salisbury Odeon, Ipswich Odeon, Exeter Odeon, King's Lynn Magestic, Tunbridge Wells Classic and the Lincoln Odeon. In the North, the York Odeon, Hull Dorchester, Bolton Odeon and Sunderland Odeon. In Cornwall at the Truro Plaza, on the Isle of Man at the Douglas Picture House and in Cumbria at the Carlisle 123.

"When *Star Wars* opened on the 5th February at the Southend Odeon, there were queues around the block," says Derek Dorking. He continues:

As promised, I had lent my R2-D2 to the cinema and there were press people taking photographs. I had fully completed the radio control movement and had finished the head, although it couldn't turn. I thought that the film was fantastic, especially compared to the dreadful films that had come out in

Queues such as this at Southend-on-Sea Odeon were happening all across England (*Southend Echo*).

the '70s that were supposed to be science fiction. I was bowled over. I wanted to know more about it, who was behind it, how they made these things—I was really in deep with it. Later, the biggest department store in town, Keddies, put my R2-D2 in their toy department as part of their *Star Wars* display. There was a Rank Organisation Darth Vader and Stormtrooper doing the rounds in the store and they posed for photographs with the model, although they completely dwarfed it. Having a good knowledge of materials and how things are made, I could see that the Stormtrooper outfit was constructed of off-white cream Fiberglas and seemed to have been molded off of an original costume. The Vader, though, was wearing silky black leggings. The helmet wasn't too bad a copy and the shoulders were fairly good but the control panel was actually a Kellogg's Cornflakes packet painted black with bits of cardboard glued on to it, tied on with black insulation tape! What looked really strange was that the tall guy was wearing the Stormtrooper and the short one was Vader. The guys inside were employees of the Southend Odeon, so it's clear that the outfits had been sent to the cinema. The best thing was, the cinema put my R2-D2 in a glass case in the Bar foyer for the remainder of the run and they let me in free to see *Star Wars* whenever I wanted, so I saw it well over 12 times that month.

Silver Jet shared strong memories at thedigifax.com of the excitement that had built up by the time *Star Wars* finally arrived:

All the kids at my junior school were talking about it for weeks before the film came out. One kid was lucky enough to be taken to Leicester Square during the first week. He became the star of the playground because he had a *Star Wars* program that his parents had bought him and everybody squeezed him for every detail of the film he could remember. My dad took me and my younger brother and sister on the first Saturday *Star Wars* was shown at the Odeon in Gants Hill [Ilford]. I remember the massive queue as there was no pre-booking tickets in those days. We had to queue for about an hour and the thing I most remember was, as the audience for the previous showing was leaving, a dad with his kids walked past us making laser gun noises and pointing his fingers at his children as if they were laser guns. He looked more thrilled than his kids and I'll never forget that moment.[8]

Star Wars became a shared experience of children all over Britain, with many finding that making new friendships was much easier. "Just before my tenth birthday, our family had just moved house to Stoke-on-Trent and I had to start at a new school," says Graham Ogle. "I was terrified. On my first day, one kid asked me if I had seen *Star Wars*, which I had never heard of. By the end of that day, I had made a new friend, but more importantly I knew that *Star Wars* featured spaceships, a tall gold robot, laser swords, an old man called Ben with a weird surname and 'really good special effects.'"

I first saw Star Wars *at an evening show at the Odeon Gants Hill, Ilford with my dad and my only sibling, my younger brother Paul. We had not asked to see it. It was my dad who had responded to the hype rather than his two young sons, which says a lot about the marketing campaign, especially as this was the first film we had seen at the cinema. I thought it was a very long drive but as I later learned, the local cinema in Romford had yet to begin showing it, so it meant a longer trip to the adjacent town of Ilford. I left the cinema quite literally dazzled. What I had witnessed had been burned into my mind. Being only eight years old, I was not able to take it all in. It was the highlights that Paul and I were buzzing about afterwards: the cantina, the swing across the chasm, the fantastic robots. Paul and I kept talking about the film all the way home, in case we forgot anything.*

After that, I wanted to find out everything that I could about the fantastic universe I had seen, which (considering my small pocket money budget) consisted of reading any printed material owned by friends and studying the backs of action figure backing cards in order to learn all of the character names. I can appreciate how other people's Star Wars *experience centered on Luke Skywalker but for me, the film was not about Luke but Han Solo. His brash, cocky attitude and bravery made him the star of the film. I have since learned that viewing* Star Wars *following Luke Skywalker's journey (in the way that George Lucas had intended) is a completely different experience. Personally I had no interest in Luke, who I saw as a very weak character compared to Han, who was intended by Lucas to be the sidekick.*

Soon after seeing Star Wars, *I became friends with another fan at school, Gary Harvey, who was nicknamed "Tich" (his spelling) due to his extreme height at such a young age. "Titch" means small in colloquial British and his nickname was typical of British humour, where someone who is extra tall can be ironically called "shorty." It was handy that we had* Star Wars *in common because we didn't have any interest in football, cars or the usual schoolboy pursuits. Gary had* Star Wars *wallpaper in his bedroom, which was cool beyond imagination. I had chosen Action Man wallpaper the previous year and it wouldn't have been reasonable to expect my parents to redecorate my room all over again! The most important thing was that I had a best friend who I could share my passion for* Star Wars *with.*

Meanwhile, the main regional cinemas that had opened *Star Wars* on January 29 were still being inundated. House records were broken in the first week at all 12 venues, with an incredible total of £138,340. The second week saw even greater attendances. "Full house signs mark the start of the third week of *Star Wars*, the space fantasy which is breaking all box office records at the Odeon 1," reported the *Manchester Evening News*. "Cinemagoers leaving the theatre often ask to book a seat for a second visit, but there's no advance booking. The only surefire way is to get there early and join the queue. It's a long time since the cinema had a hit like this on their hands."[9]

Sarah Baker-Saunders was one of the fans who saw the film at this time:

I first saw *Star Wars* on the 14th of February as a birthday treat. It was just my mum and me, as my older sister was not really interested. We lived in the outskirts of Manchester so it meant taking a bus to the big Odeon in town. I remember the huge queues all the way round the corner and down a side street and all the people were giddy with excitement and anticipation on that cold February evening. When the queue started to move and we reached the foyer, there was a buzz of people buying badges and the *Star Wars* program. I begged my mum for a copy and it was my first piece of merchandise, and yes I still have it! I remember the excitement of finally getting in the cinema and getting two seats together. This was an adventure in itself. It was late on a Tuesday evening, a school night, and we were at the cinema as a special birthday treat, and this before the movie had even started! When the lights finally went down and the 20th Century-Fox music started, we were all silent. The opening crawl and the Star Destroyer going overhead is imprinted in my memory. The film went past so quickly with new, exciting, never-before-seen images and the fun adventure in another galaxy. It was over far too quickly. I chatted constantly on the way home on the bus, reading the program, remembering scenes, learning characters names and reliving the adventure. When I got to school, my classmates were jealous as I recalled the previous evening's adventures.

Killer Bs

The age-old practice of showing a "B" movie before the main feature was still followed in the 1970s and *Star Wars* was no different. In some areas *Fast Company* was shown, a 15-minute-long documentary about motor biking in Britain. Some cinemas received the Warner Bros. cartoon short *Duck Dodgers in the 24½ Century* which starred Daffy Duck,

Porky Pig and Marvin the Martian. *Variety* reported that the choice to show the film as a "B" was actually made by George Lucas. He had long been a fan and had requested in December 1977 that 20th Century-Fox sales managers Ashley Boone and Peter Myers negotiate a deal for the rights for distribution. Warner Bros. domestic sales manager Terry Semel was willing to rent the cartoon short for a reported weekly fee of $250 (probably per print). Lucas had shown *Duck Dodgers* at a cast-and-crew screening of *Star Wars* and it had gone over so well, he decided that the public should have a chance of seeing it too.

The Unlikely Stars

There was a great deal of coverage of the leading players in *Star Wars* but the media spotlight too was shone on the small army of technicians who created the film's visual wonders. On January 25, *The Sun* ran the story "*Star Wars* Secrets." *The Daily Mail* followed suit on March 29 with a Making of feature. Everyone, it seemed, had been confounded by the special effects and wanted to know how it had all been done. The popular *Planet of the Apes* series and *Jaws* had been the subject of documentaries, books and magazine articles which explained the behind-the-scenes processes but the coverage had been fairly limited. With the event of blockbuster movies, the "Making of" became part of the overall package. In the case of *Star Wars,* the few writers who understood the effects process involved took a deep breath and attempted to squeeze information that was very nearly rocket science into a format that could be understood by everyone, in the few pages that had been assigned to the subject. John Brosnan wrote insightful overviews of the effects processes for *Starburst* #1 and the January issue of *House of Hammer.* He explained that John Dykstra (who had previously worked with Douglas Trumbull on *Silent Running* and *The Andromeda Strain*) headed the young team put together by Lucas to create the *Star Wars* effects. Dubbed Industrial Light and Magic, the team worked from a warehouse in California and completed 365 effects shots, some of them involving up to ten different image components, augmented using a revolutionary computer-assisted effects system. Readers attempted to wrap their minds around processes previously only heard of within the effects industry such as matting, motion control, rotoscoping and the essential blue screen.

John Stears was permanently based at Elstree Studios and much more accessible to the British press than the California effects crew. He was one of the unsung heroes of the film industry, most notably devising James Bond's gadgets (many of which worked practically). Stears appeared to be more than pleased to share some of his secrets. Another key member of the production team highlighted by Brosnan in *House of Hammer* was production designer John Barry. "Also very impressive are the enormous and spectacular sets in the film, all of which were designed by John Barry and were built at Elstree Studios (one particularly large set was constructed within the big 'H' stage at Shepperton Studios). It was up to Lucas to combine all of these different components, shot in different parts of the world at different times, into one complete and apparently seamless movie."[10] The American magazines *Starlog* and *Fantascene* featured every *Star Wars* effects process imaginable, from the traditional techniques used to create the background matte paintings to the cutting-edge computer graphics for the Rebel pilot briefing scene. Never before had a film been picked over in such detail.

The articles just kept on coming. Although *Star Wars* had ushered in a new generation of special effects technology, fans may have been surprised that many of the shots had been achieved using decades-old methods, such as the use of matte paintings. The only difference was that for the first time, a camera was now being pointed in the opposite direction, revealing the techniques that had been used and the people behind them.

The Star Wars Collector's Edition published by Marvel contained a digest of the film plot and various features on the origin and the making of *Star Wars*. Among the features was a profile of Ralph McQuarrie, the artist responsible for the beautiful pre-production paintings that had been published in newspapers and magazines since *Star Wars* had been announced to the world at large. The article revealed that McQuarrie had attended trade school to study technical illustration before joining the army. He had worked for the Boeing Company and produced animated segments for the NBC coverage of the Apollo space program before being hired by Lucas to work on *Star Wars*. McQuarrie produced a series of paintings based on Lucas' ideas, creating much of the look of the film in the process. Among his designs were R2-D2, C-3PO, the Sand People, Jawa Sandcrawler and Darth Vader's armor. McQuarrie had also been called upon to produce many of the film's matte paintings; despite a complete lack of prior experience in this area, he did a magnificent job. "One of the geniuses of the film was Ralph McQuarrie," says Peter Beale. "He doesn't in my mind get anywhere near the credit that he should. The whole visual look of the film came from him. We set the art department up to visualize his vision. We brought him across to be part of the art department. We gave him a studio in the art department at Elstree and I said 'Just paint' because his work was so fantastic."

The Poster Magazine *Continues*

Issue #2 of the *Star Wars Official Poster Monthly* became available in February, the cover featuring an X-Wing Fighter instead of Luke Skywalker and Darth Vader as on the American version (published the previous December). Inside it retained the fairly basic look of the premiere British issue, while in contrast the American #2 had been given a much more professional looking makeover. The poster that the reader could unfold in America was Darth Vader aboard the Blockade Runner, while the British version was the *Star Wars* heroes in the cockpit of the Millennium Falcon. The articles were identical on both sides of the Atlantic however; Jon Trux focused on the special effects, describing how dogfight scenes from war films had been used to help plan each shot. "Space fighters replace aircraft, lasers replace machine guns and the horizon and sky of earth becomes the Death Star and deep space."[11] This footage had subsequently been edited into early versions of *Star Wars* to provide an impression of how the eventual film would look. People who are knowledgeable about the movies can spot whole sequences from films such as *The Dam Busters*, which are almost identical to *Star Wars*, including some of the dialogue.

This issue of the *Star Wars Official Poster Monthly* also included the article "The History of Tatooine." Michael Marten, calling himself Dr. M.F. Marten, used his journalistic skills to gather all of the known facts on the subject from diverse sources and extrapolate them further. His vivid description of life on Tatooine included this fact: "The harvested food-plants from the moisture farms are shipped off-planet from the Mos Eisley Spaceport and fetch high prices in the galaxy's overpopulated urban worlds." Regarding the Jawas: "Their faces are surrounded by small clouds of insects with which they apparently live in some weird symbiosis."[12]

In that same issue, the article "Darth Vader Lives! But Will He Return?" had an unexpected impact. John May, on his own initiative, used Lucas' explanation of Darth Vader's past from the August 25, 1977, *Rolling Stone* interview. The director had stated that Vader had fought Ben Kenobi and fallen into a volcanic pit, causing him to wear the black armor as a mobile iron lung. May also drew upon the novelization and the film to limn an in-depth picture of the Darth Vader character:

> His face, now too horrible to behold, remains permanently hidden behind the sinister metal breath screen from which his red eyes glint unmercifully. Only his heavy, rasping breath reveals the suit's true function. There was no hope of Vader ever returning to the path of light after this. A fallen angel with his control of the Force intact, Vader turned against his former brethren and everything they stood for, aiding successive evil Emperors in their task of destroying the republic.[13]

The mention of "successive Emperors" and of Darth Vader killing Luke Skywalker's father "in a fierce battle" would eventually be contradicted by the ebb and flow of the *Star Wars* story but initially it was May's version that held sway.

The *Star Wars Official Poster Monthly* was of huge benefit to the embryonic Lucasfilm, as the company did not have the staff available to rake through diverse sources of information and bring them together in an official guide to the film. A *Star Wars* bible had begun to take shape at Lucasfilm but it did not go far beyond keeping tabs on particulars such as how many toes Chewbacca had and the spelling of names. It was the poster magazine that writers could use as a reference for their own *Star Wars* publications and articles, assuming that the information had come directly from Lucasfilm. In that way, the *Star Wars Official Poster Monthly*'s facts and figures help to shape a *Star Wars* universe based on every known source. In the case of the story of Darth Vader's past, even if Lucas had forgotten about his *Rolling Stone* interview, or had changed his mind, the Sith Lord's past had been etched into *Star Wars* lore and into the minds of fans.

C-3PO Takes to the Stage

On Thursday, February 16, there was a concert performance by the London Symphony Orchestra at the Royal Albert Hall, "The LSO in Space," conducted by John Williams. The program book had a *Star Wars* theme and included an advert for the release of the film at selected cinemas in Greater London. The *Star Wars* segment of the concert was introduced by Gary Kurtz. There was a surprise for the audience as Anthony Daniels, in the C-3PO costume, strode onto the stage, took up the baton and proceeded to conduct the orchestra. R2-D2 stood silent in one of the aisles, with just his lights blinking. This was the hollow version of R2-D2 into which Kenny Baker could be installed, but he was not present. The concert was a very high-profile event, with C-3PO's stint as a conductor reported by the press. "The highlight of the evening was when the tall gold colored Robot with an awkward walking style moved out in front and conducted the orchestra,"[14] wrote Tony Berry for the *Gloucester Journal*. According to John Jones of the *Daily Express*, "Clever things these robots, equally at home outwitting galactic Stormtroopers or putting 140 musicians through their paces. After a few lessons from *Star Wars* composer John Williams yesterday, C-3PO stepped jerkily onto the rostrum to be the first robot to conduct the famous orchestra. Anthony Daniels, C-3PO's inner man, admitted to having little knowledge of classical music and besides he can hear very little inside the robot."[15] A mannequin was later dressed in the C-3PO costume and displayed in a window display at Liberties of London department store on Regent Street, along with the hollow R2-D2 prop.

Star Wars soon permeated the world of television comedy. An episode of the BBC program *The Goodies*, "U–Friend or UFO?," broadcast on February 4, had a distinctly sci-fi theme. A very authentic-looking R2-D2 clone named EB-GB (Electronic Brain of Great Britain), built by the BBC Special Effects Department, appeared on the show. It was so convincing that viewers could be forgiven for believing it was genuine. This droid displayed yet unseen characteristics such as being used a vacuum cleaner, a washing machine and a trash can—with hilarious results. A children's series produced by BBC1 Manchester, *Potter's Picture Palace*, was about a down-and-out cinema and starred John Comer, Angela Crow, Mark Dempsey, Colin Edwynn, Melvyn Hayes, Eden Philips and Reg Thompson. The actors would frequently dress up and spoof various films. The April 28, 1978, episode "One of Our Spaceships Is Missing" was based on *Star Wars*. Hayes played Luke Skywalker and Comer the villain. A greenhouse was the setting for the final confrontation, where Hayes asked, "Are you Darth Vader, Lord of the Sith?" and Comer replied, "No! I'm Fred. Bloke what looks after the vegetables."[16] Comer then produced a pocket-sized umbrella which he extended in the manner of a lightsaber and the duel began!

Although *Star Wars* had been in release a short time, it was already becoming part of popular culture in Britain. Trebor mints used the slogan "May the Fizz Be with You" in a national advertising campaign. The Northern England food company Sutherland had their own take on the slogan, issuing badges with the words "May the Taste Be with You." An article in the *Observer* newspaper focusing on automated robotic car manufacture was titled "Artoo Detoo's big brothers." Reviewing the newly released Citroen CX2400 for the *Observer*, Philip Llewellin likened the instrument panel to something from *Star Wars*.

The Merchandise Charge

In February, the merchandising of *Star Wars* had begun to pick up pace. Waddingons had released a set of four jigsaws unique to the UK Random House produced *The Star Wars Punch Out and Make It Book*, designed by Ib Penick and illustrated by Patricia Wynne. Available at 5p per pack was a blue-bordered set of "movie photo cards plus bubble gum" from Topps Ireland (distributed by Trebor Sharps Ltd.) that was identical to the set that had been released in America except that the set of stickers were not included. There was an R2-D2 bedside lamp from Northlight; it illuminated a hollow plastic shell of the droid. Bennett Associates of Glasgow produced a range of badges, stickers, T-shirts and bags which were derived from the range produced in America by Factors Ltd, apart from a set of badges of its own design. A wristwatch from Ingersoll with R2-D2 and C-3PO on the face became available. Letraset Ltd. released a range of notebooks, jotter pads, exercise books and a scrapbook, all of which had *Star Wars* covers but were plain inside. A major licensee, Helix International, produced pencil cases, sets of math tools and individual items such as pencils and rulers, all with *Star Wars* photographs and graphics. Helix was canny enough to reissue its globe pencil sharpener as a Death Star pencil sharpener; it remained the only exterior model of the battle station available to buy until the 1990s. "It was our company that made the approach to produce a *Star Wars* line," says Helix sales manager David Giddings. "It was a big risk for us at the time, as this was the first time we had ventured into character merchandise. We presold at the Harrogate Toy Fair in February and the trade was extremely excited. We managed to sell on the basis of a split order to the wholesale trade, with one-third delivery March, and two-thirds delivery for Back to School in June [ready for children returning from their summer holiday]." Helix stationery items complimented the Letraset *Star Wars* stationery range perfectly, with Helix producing items to write and draw *with* and Letraset producing the items to write and draw *on*, although this was simply a fortunate coincidence. *Star Wars* party paper wear from Deko consisted of cups, table coverings and two sizes of plates. According to Peter Beale,

> That is a deal that I recall. Two companies came in to my office on the same day regarding the party wear license. The first one was Deko, which was a small company, but the artwork they presented was very good. The other was a big company and they were really quite arrogant. They acted as if they were doing me a favor but their artwork was terrible. I said, "Your artwork isn't very good" and the salesman barked back, "Well, that's what we do." I replied, "Well, you can do it for someone else." They were not very happy, as you can imagine. I thought in the end that Deko did a really good job.

The tie-in blitz did not stop here. Heinz launched a "Spectacular *Star Wars* school set by Helix" offer on its cans of baked beans with eight grilled pork sausages. Walls advertised a *Star Wars* painting competition in the national press on February 22, with the prize of a family holiday in America (or £1000) awarded for the best child's *Star Wars* painting. For every specially printed *Star Wars* wrapper of Wall's sausages wrapper sent in, the company would mail a strip of Letraset transfers. Although it was hardly summer, Lyons Maid produced a range of *Star Wars* ice cream lollies, along with paper masks that could be handed out by the retailer with each lolly sold. Also in the food department: *Star Wars* marshmallow shapes from Travenor Rutledge and chew sweets from Trebor Sharps Ltd. "I have a rather personal story surrounding the *Star Wars* chews," says Beale. "People may notice that I have a broken nose. That happened when I was 12 years old, when I had a fight with a chap who I had been friends with. As I recall, his passion had been drawing airplanes. When it came to my meeting with Trebor Sharps, regarding the sweets license, who should their art director be, who walked into my

Marshmallow shapes from Liverpool-based Travenor Rutledge were released two days before the city received Star Wars on 27th January 1978 (photograph courtesy Darren Simpson).

office? It was that very same chap. Well, I thought. I'd learned a lot from the experience and I kind of owed him, even though he broke my nose!"

Some products were aimed at an adult market and were sold in upmarket shops or department stores. Silver-plated *Star Wars* mirrors were produced by Cosalt Exports. Greville Silver (some listings say Pastahurst) released its own brand of *Star Wars* jewelry in silver gilt, solid silver and, on request, solid gold. "These premium items were important

Stationery from Helix and stationery from Letraset (courtesy Craig Spivey).

as the merchandise aimed at children," says Beale. "My philosophy was, wherever we could get visibility for *Star Wars,* it would help to sell the movie." Marks and Spencer had been announced in the presskit as a licensee. Peter Beale is able to explain however that the company had been unable to produce *Star Wars* T-shirts due a clash of interest with another licensee company. "They were very put out and said to me, 'Don't you understand? Every family comes into a Marks and Spencer store at least once a week.' I said, 'I'm sorry but you just can't sell T-shirts.' And then I suggested, 'What about pajama tops?' which was basically the same thing, and that's what they ended up selling." With *Star Wars* product ranges such as Marks and Spencer collectors need to take an archaeological approach. There are not any catalogues, advertisements or other paperwork to use as reference, and when memories of the time have faded, all collectors can do is judge the situation from what they find. The *Star Wars* press kit lists Marks and Spencer pajamas, corduroy trousers, aprons, t-shirts, bed linen and slippers. A *Star Wars* apron and a pajama top have been found but they are not labeled as being from Marks and Spencer, although they may have been produced by the company. A set of bedroom ware was available but it was from the British company the House of Ratcliffe, and some of the products came with a cardboard sheet printed with photographs and artwork images of the *Star Wars* heroes and villains, the intention being that children could cut them out and decorate their bedrooms or stick the images into scrapbooks. *Star Wars* slippers were made available in Britain by Pirelli.

The massive success of the Cliro Perfumeries *Star Wars* line had been due in part to Robert Beecham putting together what he describes as the ultimate business plan. "I made a list; who is it that I want to talk to? Who is going to be interested in talking to me? What countries in the world do I want to export to?" Peter Beale was able to make a print of *Star Wars* available to aid in the launch of the Cliro Perfumeries *Star Wars* line in 1977. "Peter said to me, 'I want to you to work out where you want to show it, the venue you're going hire. Make it proper, because I won't accept some cheap solution,'" says Beecham. He continues:

So I rang up the British Academy of Film and Television Arts [BAFTA] and inquired how much it would cost to hire their first-rate cinema venue at 195 Piccadilly, in the heart of London. I agreed on the price and booked it. I phoned Peter and he said, "Perfect." On the day, there were about 350 people in the cinema. There were buyers from Boots, Tesco, Woolworths, Bon Mache Paris; every store and shop chain I wanted to sell my products were invited. There were journalists from *Vogue, Tatler, News of the World,* the *Times* and so many others. Everybody I had spoken to, without exception, had wanted to see *Star Wars.*

I got up onto the stage and introduced my products. I said, "I don't know if you're aware of what's going on in America but the strapline for *Star Wars* is 'May the Force Be with You.' Well, my strapline is 'May the Goods Be With You.' I want you to buy my goods. Please come and speak to me after the film." During the two hours of the film, I had no idea what the reaction would be but as the end credits rolled, people began to clap. They stood up. They cheered. The reaction was phenomenal. The buyer from Boots came up to me and said, "You're Robert Beecham, aren't you? I want to see you in my office at nine o'clock tomorrow morning." Tesco came up to me and said, "How many of these products can you make?" and I replied, "As many as you could possibly desire." Another buyer came up to me and said, "I want to buy all of your production for the next six weeks." I reached the end of the evening and I realized that my entire life was going to change. And it did, because that evening triggered an avalanche. I exported all over Europe, Australia, New Zealand. I sold millions upon millions of pieces of *Star Wars* soap and bubble bath. I traveled the world with R2-D2 and Darth Vader in my pocket. It was sensational and best of all, it was fun. And I had a good guy called Peter Beale supporting me.

The boxes that were supplied to retailers containing Cliro Perfumeries *Star Wars* products doubled as counter displays, brightly printed with imagery from the film and with lids that could be folded to create an eye-catching sign. Topps photo cards, Trebor chews, Travenor Rutledge marshmallow shapes, Letraset transfer packs and Helix stationery were also displayed in this manner on shop counters and shelves. There seemed to be posters and standees advertising *Star Wars*-related products everywhere you looked, many of them having been arranged by the individual shop chains or manufacturers. Electrical goods store chain Curry's created promotional material to highlight the *Star Wars* digital watch from Texas Instruments, one of the more expensive items at £9.99. The nationwide burger restaurant chain Wimpy, which preceded McDonald's in Britain, created a *Star Wars* theme for its restaurants, with posters and table standees, and they gave away free packs of Letraset transfers with every children's meal. W.H. Smith stocked a wide range of *Star Wars* products and produced its own shopping vouchers which were popular as gifts. The vouchers came with specially printed gift cards, one of which featured a photograph of R2-D2 and C-3PO. By this time, Mountain Films was being listed as an official licensee and had produced its own promotional posters featuring R2-D2 and C-3PO.

Journalist Berry Ritchie collected every *Star Wars* item he could find for a *Sunday Times* article, printed February 12, 1978. "If you thought you had already heard about *Star Wars*," he began, "let me tell you, you ain't seen anything yet. The spin-off marketing products are only just beginning to gather momentum in this country. As they say in the trade, 'Let the selling force be with you.' Let me warn you. Keep a tight grip on your wallet or you will find your children will be the proud owners of the most amazing collection of trivia you have ever seen." Ritchie was photographed, surrounded by a huge mass of *Star Wars* merchandise. His point was that the *Star Wars* merchandise blitz had already far outstripped the pocket of the average person, if they wished to collect everything. "Call it a round £100," said Ritchie. "Of course I forgot to add in the cost of going to the film itself. I went last Tuesday, to the Leicester Square Theatre, where I paid out £2.20 each for myself and my family for the fourth row of the dress circle. Do you know the place was three-quarters empty? Perhaps it is a good thing that the much-vaunted super film is soon going on general release, so enthusiasm can once again be whipped up, this time at a local level."[17]

Ritchie was correct in saying that the merchandising of *Star Wars* had hardly begun. The coming months saw wallpaper from ICI, an offer of a *Star Wars* kite on KP Outer Spacer crisp packets, a C-3PO costume from Cheryl Playthings and a second set of Topps photo bubble gum cards manufactured by its Ireland branch, this time with a red border. The cards differed from the American versions in that the numbers started with no. 1A, when the American set began with no. 67, following on from the blue set.

Understanding that that children's *Star Wars* addiction was based on the family shopping budget, the individual manufacturers had the good sense to make their tie-in products no more expensive than they would have been ordinarily. The thinking was more of a grab of the market share than a rip off. Craig Spivey remembers the time with a great deal of clarity.

The first-ever *Star Wars* item I owned was a Helix Stormtrooper ruler. Later I was bought a wooden Helix pencil box but for all its bulk and weight it didn't actually hold very much. The pencils would clatter around inside and all the leads would break. I saved the Outer Spacers crisp packs and sent off for the *Star Wars* kite. When the kite arrived, it wasn't much more than a printed sheet of polythene and some plastic sticks. It didn't survive much beyond its maiden flight and, as such, was pretty disposable. My dad and I would drive to the big Asda in Scunthorpe to do the big shop every Friday night. Thinking back, it was probably as much a chore for him as it was for me and we'd always dwell in the non-food aisles. While he'd browse sci-fi novels with lurid covers, I'd flick through the children's books.

I have very vivid memories of encountering the Letraset *Star Wars* stationery on the shelves for the first time. It just looked incredible. The entire range was priced in pence so Dad let me put a Princess Leia Rebel Jotter in the trolley. Over the coming weeks, I pretty much collected all the Letraset exercise books and drawing pads and filled them full of epic space battles and robots. I would bike to the other end of the village to a shop because they sold *Star Wars* Trebor chews. You couldn't get as many for your 10p as the shops nearer to my home, but hey, it said "*Star Wars*" on them.

Ian Whitlock has strong memories too. "Both the blue and red *Star Wars* card sets were something that I really coveted and as there was no way of seeing the film except at the cinema, the cards were a great way of reliving it. The packs were something that I could afford with my ten pence pocket money and it meant that I could get two packs. I would always be disappointed if I had a double but swapping the cards in the playground was a good way of getting to know children with a common interest." Richard Harris has similar recollections: "My favorite memories are of the *Star Wars* trading cards. Me and my friends would swap doubles and I eagerly wanted certain numbers to complete the jigsaws that were on the back of certain cards."

Darren Slade recalls the *Star Wars* merchandising boom: "The ubiquity of *Star Wars* merchandising seemed astonishing. Record stores gave their windows over to the double LP of the film's soundtrack, its gatefold sleeve pinned open to display a host of color pictures. Stores everywhere displayed the official posters. Ice cream vans were soon selling a *Star Wars* lolly. Clothing stores had *Star Wars* T-shirts depicting Han and Chewie with blasters poised."

Star Wars Weekly *Lands*

Outside of the film, the biggest contributor by far to the British *Star Wars* scene was the homegrown Marvel weekly comic, which had a cover date of February 8. Other comic titles published by Marvel carried advertisements proclaiming the title's launch, telling readers: "Hurry before they are all sold out!" There was also television advertising as remembered by Phil Heeks. "The evening of February 8, 1978, I saw a TV commercial, maybe the most

The *Star Wars* connection continued with Topps bubble gum cards (courtesy Darren Simpson).

exciting of my life, certainly up until that point. *Star Wars Weekly* was on sale. Even R2-D2 was bowled over (the commercial showed the clip of R2, post-zapping). I had to have this comic!"[18] Darren Slade has similar memories. "I remember the TV ad for *Star Wars Weekly* which I saw the week before the first comic came out. C-3PO spoke to the camera, telling you how fabulous the comic was, and shots of the comic were intercut with moments from the film, including R2-D2's fall when the Jawas zapped him. I remember this because it was the moment I decided to abandon my cynicism about this *Star Wars* thing and accept that it was right up my street." Sarah Baker-Saunders was another enthusiastic purchaser. "I bought the first issue of *Star Wars Weekly* from a local news agent shop the day after seeing the film. It had a free gift! (Yes, I still have it!) From then on there was no turning back. I was a dedicated fan of *Star Wars*."

Star Wars Weekly contained the comic strip adaptation of the film, along with competitions, readers' letters and adverts for *Star Wars* merchandise. A cardboard X-Wing Fighter was supplied with

A promotional table decoration from the Wimpy burger bar chain.

#1 and a TIE Fighter with #2. The letters page generated a genuine sense of community, with many long-running discussions and fans writing about their *Star Wars* experiences. The in-house computer, a Class Y Readers Inquiry Logistical Computer C.Y.R.I.L (in reality the sitting editor), held court and attempted to answer queries sent in by readers. Unlike the monthly *Star Wars* comic in America, the British *Weekly* was printed in black and white, perhaps lending the artwork a more realistic feel. As all of the *Star Wars Weekly* stories were derived from the monthly American comic, additional material was needed to pad out the pages of comic. Several back-up comic science fiction stories were included each issue; they were hardly kiddie fare and provided the title with a more a mature tone. Previously printed in America by *Marvel Preview*, "The UFO Connection" was a dark tale of alien invasion where a father and daughter's victory came at the cost of their own lives. "War Toy" told of an intelligent android developed as a soldier for the U.S. Army that fought on the front line against an alien invasion, but was left to fend for itself and eventually committed suicide. While the robot's remains lay smoking, news came that the aliens had invaded again.

Star Wars Weekly represented the final filtering-down of information on *Star Wars*. Younger children who did not read youth-orientated magazines such as *2000AD* or *Look-In* encountered the comic at news agents, or had it bought for them by their parents. Joe Sales had such an experience:

> I was only vaguely aware of films as a six-year-old and it was when I visited a local newspaper shop with my parents I spotted a copy of *Star Wars Weekly*. I was already aware of *Star Wars*. There was something in the zeitgeist that told me that this was something of interest. I started getting the comic every issue from then on, as you do with comics—you want to find out what happens next week.

Craig Spivey was another *Star Wars Weekly* reader.

> My Grandma would always have a comic on subscription on the go for me and my sister. We'd go round most weeks and it gave us something to do whenever we visited. I was strictly a Beano guy until *Star Wars* came along and my Gran informed the news agent of my maturing tastes. To be honest, the best things about *Star Wars Weekly* for me were the covers and the adverts inside. I found the black-and-white strips themselves a bit dense and hard to follow (especially compared to something like the Beano). The further away it got from the core story, the less interested I got. The accompanying strips, like "Guardians of the Galaxy," left me completely cold.

I had a similar experience as a child. An aunt had sent two comics in the post for my brother Paul and me. While mine was a Disney comic, Paul's was issue #21 of Star Wars Weekly. *I had a strong interest in the film but this was the first time I had seen the comic and I was glad that Paul was happy to swap gifts!* Star Wars Weekly *became an instant must, although I did not realize that comics could be reserved in shops, so I often missed out on buying it due to there being no copies left. I considered the comic to be the actual continuation of the* Star Wars *story which was just as valid as the film. The comic was something that could be read time and time again while the film was almost akin to a distant dream.*

Star Wars Weekly was a welcome shot in the arm for Marvel UK, just as the monthly version had been with the American parent company. Marvel's American editor-in-chief Jim Shooter later commented, "We had been losing money for several years. If we hadn't done *Star Wars,* we would have gone out of business. *Star Wars* single-handedly saved Marvel."[19] Dez Skinn has similar memories: "Marvel acquired the license to *Star Wars* because George Lucas felt it would help promote the film, little realizing the impact it would have. But it was a far greater benefit to the publisher than the producer as it proved so viable that, at a time when comics sales were plummeting, it became their best seller and actually saved the company on *both* sides of the Atlantic with its variant editions."[20]

Skinn's contribution to the world of *Star Wars* became greater: "Seeing a sliding balance sheet despite Lucasfilm's input, the [Marvel] U.S. parent company offered their British imprint [Marvel UK] up for sale to existing comic publishers, but only the monolithic IPC Magazines expressed any interest. At that, their only desire was to acquire *Star Wars Weekly*, which at the time was outselling their own originated *2000AD*. Perhaps the full depth of their desperation can best be seen by U.S. head honcho Stan Lee eventually offering me the publisher role to totally revitalize the U.K. company!" Dez's *Starburst* work had paid dividends far greater than he imagined. "I think they really noticed me when *Starburst* #1 scooped them, coming out with lots of *Star Wars* coverage a full three months before their official licensed *Star Wars* souvenir magazine."

Star Wars Weekly from Marvel UK hits the shops.

Star Wars Weekly #1 contained an advertisement for the Official *Star Wars* Fan Club, which could be joined for relatively expensive sum of £2.95. Members would receive a color poster, a heat transfer for a T-shirt, embroidered jacket patch, self-stick color decal, a *Star Wars* book cover, a membership card, a color photograph, a wallet-sized photo and four issues of the quarterly newsletter. Although the mailing address was in London, the club was run in America by Craig Miller, who had been recruited by Charles Lippincott to work for Lucasfilm to help deal with the explosion of interest in *Star Wars*. According to Miller, "I was involved with licensing and promotions. I also created and ran the Official *Star Wars* Fan Club back in '77. I wrote most of the newsletters that we used to send out quarterly and did all of the interviews with the cast. Initially, Factors was awarded a license on the fulfillment of the fan club. We at Lucasfilm produced all of the material and Factors took over the physical production and mailing. They only had the license for a year or so, for the first four issues of the club newsletter, after which Lucasfilm brought it back in house."

Miller explains the rationale of Lucasfilm seeking to keep in touch with the *Star Wars* fan base: "The purpose of the club was to keep the fans happy, involved and interested. It wasn't just a business decision. We felt an obligation to fans everywhere." The first issue of the *Star Wars Fan Club Newsletter*, printed in March, contained an update on the *Star Wars* sequel, which stated that production would begin in early 1979, with a tentative release date of the first quarter of 1980. There was also a feature on how Mark Hamill, Carrie Fisher and George Lucas were apparently all comic book fans. In an interview printed in *Star Wars Weekly* #2, Hamill revealed more about his hobby. "Spider-Man, Hulk, Silver Surfer…. I couldn't get enough of them. My parents were against me buying them because they said they were a waste of money, but somehow I built up a large collection." Hamill had even had time to read the *Star Wars* comic. "The parts of the film I liked best were eventually edited from the film. They were scenes that showed the relationships of Luke Skywalker with Biggs, and his friends on Tatooine, who thought Luke to be a fool. These scenes enlarged upon Luke's character. Marvel comics kept these parts of the story, I see."[21]

The Missing Scenes

The scenes that had been excluded from *Star Wars* were extremely familiar to fans, as they had been included in the novel, storybook and the comic. A great number of people had read these publications before seeing the film, so the missing scenes were seen as legitimate sections of the *Star Wars* story, which had not survived the final cut of the film. There were a number of large scenes which fans could see in their own minds, if not the film itself. The first section was the one that Hamill referenced, where Luke met up with his friends Deak, Windy, Camie and Fixer at the Tosche Station near his Tatooine home. Luke's best friend Biggs Darklighter had arrived fresh from his Space Academy graduation, kitted out in uniform, ready to take up his commission aboard the spaceship *Rand Ecliptic*. Luke had rushed to the Tosche Station because a glint in the sky had led to him witnessing (through his macrobinoculars) the capture of Princess Leia's ship. In the excitement of meeting Biggs, Luke almost forgot his reason for being there. When he finally mentioned the "space battle" in orbit, the skepticism of Windy and the others seemed to be confirmed by Biggs when he located the orbiting spacecraft with the macrobinoculars and theorized that they were simply re-fueling.

The next major missing scene took place after C-3PO had spotted the glint of a transport on the horizon and shouted "Over here!" Luke and Biggs spoke privately outside the Tosche Station in the bright sunlight. Biggs revealed to Luke that he was going to jump ship and attempt to join the rebellion. Luke had clearly heard about the rebel movement and was stunned by his friend's admission. Luke explained that he would not be going to the Space Academy that year as planned, much to Biggs' consternation. Before they parted, Luke promised Biggs that he would someday make it off of the planet.

In another missing scene, the pair met again while the Rebels were preparing their ships to attack the Death Star. Red Leader questioned if Luke had been tested out in an X-Wing Fighter; Biggs vouched for Luke, calling him "the best bush pilot in the outer rim territories." It transpired that the controls of Luke's Incom Company T-16 Skyhopper craft on Tatooine were very similar to the Incom Company T-65 X-Wing Fighter that the Rebels flew. The exclusion of this scene led to some people claiming that it was unrealistic that Luke turned up at the Rebel base and was instantly given a fighter ship to fly. "I had bought the novel before seeing the film and read it over and over again," says Jordan Royce. "That book was really important to me as I felt that it was the authoritative version of the story. It contained the parts of the film that were cut and so when I saw *Star Wars*, I was a little disappointed. I was thinking, 'Where's Biggs gone?' I thought that Biggs Darklighter was an important part of Luke's journey." The missing scenes of *Star Wars* rapidly took on a mythical status among fans, with many people claiming that they had seen an early version of the film with the scenes included. The truth is that these scenes were *not* included in any print of the film released to the public.

Although children's annuals were traditionally published towards the end of the year to take advantage of the Christmas market, W.H. Smith began advertising in children's publications that *Star Wars Annual No.1* was available from its shops priced at £1.50. This was more of a souvenir edition than a traditional annual. Published by Brown Watson, it contained the Marvel adaptation of the film and was packed with additional material. "*Star Wars*! A conflict so vast it spans an entire galaxy," began the editorial. "Fought out by interstellar ships at faster-than-light speeds, ranging through the stars from planet to planet. And the planets are inhabited … some by humans like you and me, others by aliens of stunning diversity … hairy, slimy, small and tall. It may be lying ahead of us, it may have taken place long ago … who can say? One world's past is another world's future."[22] There was a profile of each of the film's stars containing various facts and a list of their previous roles. "*Star Wars*—the evolution of an epic!" described the development of the film from a George Lucas idea, through to the creation of the special effects. The annual neatly brought together all of the key facts about *Star Wars* and its stars in a condensed form. Fans who had not delved through a diverse number of publications had all the core information at their fingertips, which was especially important for younger fans. "The annual was a common gift across the country, being read and re-read by ravenous fans who had a limited amount of product to devour," Mark Newbold recalls. "I know that when I got to the final page I would often go right back to the beginning and start again."[23]

The first items from Palitoy began arriving in shops. These were not the action figure toys but other kinds of paraphernalia: a Dip Dots painting set, a Keel Kite, poster painting set and Escape the Death Star Game had been derived from the Kenner products selection but a selection of *Star Wars* masks were of Palitoy's own design.

One of the Kenner-designed products released by Palitoy was a lightsaber, or Light Saber as it was spelled on the box. It did not feature a solid plastic blade but instead had to be inflated before use, which did not get the seal of approval from every fan. "This was an item that I was very disappointed in as a child," says Graham Ogle. "As anyone who owned it can testify, the tube bent and flopped all over the place and fighting with it was impossible. The actual lightsaber light effect was weak also. My friend had *a Force Beam* lightsaber that was much better. It had a solid plastic tube that held its shape and the light-up effect was pretty good. Trust me to buy 'official.'" The unofficial version of the lightsaber had not escaped the attention of Berry Ritchie; he said, "The Force Beam is that phallic goosing stick in *Star Wars*, and comprises a plastic torch with a long polythene tube which lights up in red, white or green. More than a million sold in the U.S. in the two months before Christmas and it is now going on sale in the U.K. for about £3.50. Heaven knows what 20th Century-Fox will do to Force Beam Marketing when it finally catches up with it."[24]

The Force Beam was an essential item for fans my age in 1978. It was built ruggedly and could stand up to the fiercest lightsaber battle. Even as a child, I was curious as to why it wasn't an official Star Wars *product. It was produced in America by Jack A. Levin & Associates and distributed in Britain by Loydale Ltd., which placed full-color adverts in* Star Wars Weekly, *complete with the* Star Wars *logo and characters. The story that was told among collectors during my youth, that I cannot substantiate, was that the Force Beam was invented and copyrighted by an American businessman before* Star Wars *arrived and that Lucasfilm could therefore not develop their own solid, light up lightsaber toy.*

Not Quite Star Wars II

The Alan Dean Foster novel *Splinter of the Mind's Eye* added a great deal to the continuing *Star Wars* phenomenon. The author's brief had been to write a sequel to *Star Wars*, based on story notes by Lucas, which could be filmed cheaply, using the existing *Star Wars* sets. The predominantly ground-based story featured Princess Leia, Luke Skywalker, R2-D2 and C-3PO crash-landing on the strange jungle planet of Mimban. Reaching a human settlement, Luke and Leia became embroiled in a brawl in a bar with some miners and arrested by Stormtroopers. A local woman, Halla, who was a Force sensitive, helped the pair escape the Imperial prison in a Landspeeder, along with the droids and two fellow prisoners, the powerful Yuzzum aliens Hin and Kee. Halla was in possession of a shard of the Kaiburr Crystal, a gem that magnifies the owner's power with the Force, and she had made locating the entire gem her life's pursuit. The Imperials set out after the rebels in an armored Landspeeder; they were led by Captain-Supervisor Grammel, who had recognized the true identity of the rebels and had sent a message to Darth Vader. In the midst of the jungle, the rebels were chased by a gigantic worm creature which caused Luke and Leia to become separated from the rest of the group. Luke and Leia encountered a primitive tribe called the Coway who joined the rebel cause after Luke fought their chief warrior. Grammel, the Imperials and the newly arrived Darth Vader invaded the Coways' underground home, where they were ambushed and all but wiped out by the Coway and the rebels. Vader, disgusted with his subordinate, put an end to Grammel. Then there came a final confrontation at the Temple of Pomojema where the Kaiburr Crystal was housed. Vader apparently killed Hin and Key; Luke, trapped under a large boulder, was unable to intervene. Leia took up Luke's Lightsaber but Darth Vader merely toyed with her, parrying with his own saber. Hin, dying from his wounds, managed to free Luke, allowing him to fight Vader. Using the power of the Kaiburr Crystal, Luke eventually defeated Vader, sending the Dark Lord tumbling into a bottomless pit. Sophisticated fans questioned the depiction of Luke and Leia, including the obvious error of Luke being a strong swimmer despite living all of his life on a desert planet. Young fans received *Splinter of the Mind's Eye* as a rip-roaring adventure which saw Darth Vader defeated once more.

Available in March, *Star Wars Official Poster Monthly* #3 was another variation on the American title, sporting R2-D2 and C-3PO on the cover instead of Han Solo. The poster was Darth Vader and Stormtroopers posing in front of a silver foil background. The back page was packed with items that could be purchased by mail order including the recently published *Splinter of the Mind's Eye*. There was also an offer to subscribe to the magazine, with the promise of future issues extending to #6. Inside this issue, the format had been increased in quality dramatically. There was a profile of every fan's favorite smuggler, "Han Solo—Rogue Spacer," which stated, "Han Solo may still be fairly young but in his time he's traveled from one end of the galaxy to the other with illicit cargo, in the process earning himself a reputation as one of the best smugglers in the business." This was John May, again squeezing every drop from the scant information available. May elaborated further: "There he was, deep in debt to Jabba the Hut for a cargo of spices he'd had to jettison while under attack from Imperial Forces, when two complete strangers offer him seventeen thousand to get them to Alderaan as fast as possible with no questions asked."[25] Fans who were not familiar with the *Star Wars* novel would have been introduced to the full name of the Tatooine crime lord, with "Hut" being the correct spelling at that time. They would also have learned of the true state of Han's plight. The situation of Han being indebted to Jabba the Hut subsequently became a major subplot in the Marvel *Star Wars* saga. Darren Slade was collecting the poster magazine. He recalls, "It included what I took to be the official backstory to the film, including how Darth Vader killed Luke's father and how he fell into a volcanic pit. At the time it seemed like the gospel according to George Lucas. I bought issue #2 belatedly because my local bookshop had it on the wall for some time before they took it down and put it on sale on the magazine rack. I didn't mind that it had pinholes in the corners!"

The Action Figures Invasion

Star Wars action figures from Palitoy were announced to *Star Wars Weekly* readers via a competition to win a whole set of 12 in February. In March, Palitoy placed in the comic a double-page spread advertisement which contained a gallery of other toys connected to the film, among them the much anticipated action figures. Geoff Maisey recalls that despite their initial reluctance the previous autumn, retailers were now more than interested in stocking *Star Wars*. "There was a strong up-take by the trade in general during the early part of 1978, hoping to exploit the *Star Wars* fever that, in their opinion, would almost certainly die by the end of spring. Even so, there was strong resistance to taking the entire range of action figures, just the very key ones, together with the lower-priced accessories."

The action figures were not manufactured by Palitoy but were produced and packaged at Kader Industries, which was owned by the Palitoy (Far East) Company Ltd. "The figures were imported by Palitoy fully packaged," says Bob Brechin. "The packaging was specially tailored with Palitoy branding." The *Star Wars* figures were placed inside a clear plastic bubble (sometimes referred to as a blister), sealed against a backing card printed with a photograph of the character. In March, issue #5 of *Star Wars Weekly* contained an advert proclaiming that the figures were finally available in shops. "All of a sudden, the kids in my area started coming out to play with these colorful plastic figures," remembers Gary Harvey. "These were *Star Wars* figures and it seemed like everyone wanted to get hold of them."

But Palitoy had been beaten to the punch, albeit on a relatively small scale. Market stall sellers had obtained *Star Wars* figures and were doing a roaring trade. Silver Jet remembers back to when he was eight: "We were shopping in Romford town center when we saw a kid walking past with a C-3PO figure in his hand and I was almost giddy with excitement. My mum asked his mum where they got it, and she was told a fly-pitcher was selling them out of a suitcase in Romford market. My mum bought me a Chewbacca. I was the first kid from my school with a *Star Wars* figure."[26]

Geoff Maisey explains the source of the illicit trade in *Star Wars* toys: "This stock did not come from Palitoy but instead was purchased opportunistically in bulk by distributors in the U.S. and Hong Kong and shipped to the U.K., their next biggest market outside the U.S. In many cases, their U.S. distribution agreements did not permit this but these were largely ignored. Don't forget that *Star Wars* did not really sell in Europe in anything like the U.K. volumes, so every piece of surplus stock came our way, legally or otherwise!"

As a frequent visitor to Romford, I can recall how the town's thriving open air market had an abundance of Star Wars *toys, with the action figures almost exclusively Kenner-packaged. The Kenner version of the Landspeeder is quite commonplace in Britain, which is probably due to the illegal shipments that Geoff Maisey describes. The Landspeeder would have been cheaper to ship in quantity to Britain than the much bigger-boxed TIE Fighter or X-Wing.*

The recommended retail price for *Star Wars* figures was 99 pence, which matched other toys available at the time. But independent toy shops inevitably hiked up the price, giving *Star Wars* toys a reputation for being expensive. There were 12 action figure characters available, Han Solo, Luke Skywalker, Princess Leia Organa, Ben (Obi-Wan) Kenobi, Artoo-Detoo (R2-D2), See-Threepio (C-3PO), Darth Vader, Death Squad Commander, Jawa, Stormtrooper and Sand People. In America, early versions of the figures' lightsabers included a double-extending feature; they were molded in one piece in Britain. A rarity which Palitoy did release was an early version of the Jawa, which was dressed in a plastic cape rather than one made of cloth (that appeared later). No matter how it was dressed, the Jawa figure was very difficult to find. This was because initially it was not released with the rest of the set. "I had 11 of the 12 *Star Wars* figures but couldn't find the Jawa anywhere," says Ian Whitlock. "My mother finally brought it home for me out of the blue one day and it was a vinyl (plastic)-caped one. Talk about lucky!" Jason Smith has similar memories:

> I grew up in the Highlands of Scotland where it was very difficult to get hold of *Star Wars* figures when they came out. My grandparents and other family were from the Midlands and when we used to visit them in the school holidays, I would get to visit the big toy shops in Nottingham and the surrounding area. Soon I had 11 out of the 12 in the set, all except for the Jawa. I remember dragging my dad around every toy shop in Nottingham but none of them had one. Finally, in a toy shop in Beeston, outside Nottingham, the owner went out the back and brought out a couple of unopened boxes. I got to open a shipping case of original *Star Wars* figures! I rummaged through and found a Jawa at long last. It was a cloth-caped one (rather than the rarer vinyl-plastic cape version) but I was so pleased to have completed the set of figures.

Jordan Royce was collecting *Star Wars* figures too. "We weren't well off and I must have almost bankrupted my poor grandparents because I just had to have these figures. My grandfather would phone the local toy shop and get him to put some aside. He even located a Jawa which was very difficult to get hold of." The vast majority of buyers opened their *Star Wars* figures with little regard for the packaging, which of course is the normal behavior with toys. Some however sought to preserve the packaging of their figures by carefully opening the protective plastic bubble. The ultimate in collecting *Star Wars* figures, although it must have appeared foolish at the time, was to leave the package unopened.

Personally, I was in the second camp of collectors although I sincerely wish I had been in the third. The packaging to me was almost as precious as the figure itself with the large color photograph of the character and pictures of the rest of the set on the reverse. To me, every Star Wars *item was akin to gold dust, so I opted to open the bubbles at the top, like a trap door, but of course the packaging today is not worth a fraction of unopened examples. My brother and I only managed to gather a handful of figures—Darth Vader, Chewbacca, R2-D2 and C-3PO—but they turned into our most precious possessions. My parents did not have a large budget for toys and if* Star Wars *figures were unavailable on a shopping trip, Action Man, toy soldiers or Micronauts would be bought instead. I don't think that I ever saw my dream toy: a Han Solo figure. Childhood has many distractions of course and it was relatively unusual for children to be solely dedicated to* Star Wars.

The Star Wars Album Blitz

The February 18 issue of *Billboard* reported that court action over the Damont London Philharmonic Orchestra *Star Wars* soundtrack album had been concluded by amicable agreement. Damont had not admitted liability but had agreed to change the cover of the album, and went on to make good on their promise with a version that contained only text over a star field background. However, a stylized X-Wing fighter was featured on the reverse. Woolworths soon began placing national newspaper adverts for the album for the incredibly low price of 65 pence. The London Philharmonic Orchestra soundtrack was never destined to register on the national album chart but it may have had an effect on the sales of the London Symphony Orchestra version which, by February 18, had sunk to #44 after debuting on January 21 at #37. (Orchestral soundtracks have not traditionally sold in huge numbers in Britain.)

The LSO *Star Wars* album bounced back up to its highest position of #21 on March 4, the same day that another *Star Wars*-related record debuted at a lofty #12. "Disco Stars,"

The arrival of Palitoy *Star Wars* figures was announced in an advertisement in *Star Wars Weekly*.

complete with a *Star Wars*-inspired sleeve, was from K-tel, based in the U.S. state of Minnesota. It was a compilation of original recordings of various disco-style songs including "Star Wars/Cantina Band" from Meco. As the tune was still being played constantly on the radio, the album may have presented a very attractive purchase. "Disco Stars" rose to its highest position, #6, on March 11, while the LSO record began its slide down the chart, making its last mark on April 22 at #49.

It was little wonder that the London Symphony Orchestra struggled to make an impact on the album chart, as rival *Star Wars* soundtrack albums arrived in record shops in droves. Surprisingly, many of the competing albums had been recorded in Britain. The cover of "*Star Wars* and Other Space Themes" by Geoff Love and His Orchestra, available at £1.25 on the Music for Pleasure label, featured artwork depicting lookalikes to the *Star Wars* characters on the very edge of infringing copyright. Although Love's ensemble of musicians was well known for pop recordings, its unique versions of the "Main Title" and "Princess Leia's Theme" were fully orchestral. "The Sounds of *Star Wars*" by the Sonic All-Stars conducted by Bruce Baxter, from Pickwick Records, graced many a fan's collection and was also good value at £1.15. A well-known British music producer, Baxter was responsible for Pickwick's successful "Top of the Pops" series of albums, which in common with "The Sounds of *Star Wars*" were performed by uncredited session artists. Also recorded in Britain was the album "*Star Wars* Dub" by Jamaican-born Phil Pratt, released on the Burning Sounds label, complete with a stylized image of Darth Vader on the sleeve.

Owning a *Star Wars* record was a must for fans, as Peter Davis can testify. "I had both the "Sounds of *Star Wars*" record and Geoff Love's "Other Space Themes," the cover of which had a crossover of Luke and Han which I loved. The *Star Wars* theme got played hundreds of times by my brother and me at our house to the point of driving my father mad and restricting our time on the record player!" Graham Ogle was another fan who owned a cash-in soundtrack. "My aunt bought me "*Star Wars*" by Bruce Baxter and the Sonic All Stars. It sounded like it was all composed on a Casio keyboard, but it was close enough to the actual music for my purposes and I played it to death!"

Also for sale in Britain: *Star Wars* albums imported from the U.S. Zubin Mehta and the Los Angeles Philharmonic was the highest profile American orchestra to record *Star Wars* music and the result was a high-quality version of all five of the soundtrack movements and also the Cantina theme. Patrick Gleeson attempted to create with "The World's Most Sophisticated Synthesizer" what John Williams had achieved with the London Symphony Orchestra. His strange electronic sound may have provided a glimpse of what the *Star Wars* soundtrack would have been like if George Lucas had chosen to go in that direction instead of an orchestral score. Electronic music pioneer Isao Tomita released via RCA the album "Tomita: Kosmos," which included the *Star Wars* theme. Don Ellis and his band Survival released a *Star Wars* album, but it had been at the record company's request rather than a matter of choice for Ellis. Ellis had been in the middle of preparations for a performance at the 1978 Montreux Festival when Atlantic Records requested that he record a version of *Star Wars* to capitalize on the film's success. It was originally intended as a single, with Princess Leia's theme on the B-side, but Atlantic suddenly requested that the recording be expanded to a whole album. Ellis completed the entirely original material for the album in a matter of days, without duplicating any of the material he was about to play at the upcoming Montreux festival because that too would be recorded for an album. Ellis had only recently returned to his music career after a hiatus due to a severe heart condition. It had been worth the effort because the album "Music from Other Galaxies and Planets Featuring the Main Theme from *Star Wars*" went on to become the most successful of Ellis' career.

Other albums from the U.S. vying for attention at record shops included the Electric Moog Orchestra's "Music from *Star Wars*" and Meco's "*Star Wars* and other Galactic Funk," which expanded upon his successful single. Meco recalls that he was short of inspiration for the B-side of the record, which was not based on *Star Wars* themes:

> I went strolling through Central Park. And then just like in the movies, I heard—*it*! There was this wonderful percussive beat coming from over the hill in the park. I ran over there to find six kids dressed in their drum corps uniforms playing beats—just beats—no music! When they finally took a break, I spoke to them about my *Star Wars* recording and asked if they would like to participate. I rushed them into the studio the next day and recorded about an hour of drum beats. Harold Wheeler took those beats and created three songs. I'm happy today that the royalties they received put them through college![27]

K-tel made use of Meco's "*Star Wars*/Cantina Band" single for another compilation, "Disco Double," which reached #10 on the album chart on June 17, 1978. Despite all of the competition from other albums, the British Phonographic Industry awarded John Williams and the London Symphony Orchestra Gold status in February, for more than 400,000 units sold for *Star Wars*.

The Cinema Release Marches On

On March 4, the Leicester Square Theatre ceased showing *Star Wars* after ten weeks; it had accrued a highly impressive £320,000. The Dominion Theatre continued with its run. The Odeon Marble Arch took up the *Star Wars* mantle from March 12. That theater was able to boast of being Europe's biggest screen and only Dimension 150 venue, so the public had the chance to see an even more impressive version of the film. In addition to the screen's incredible size, its

Above and opposite page: **There were plenty of *Star Wars* records to choose from in 1978.**

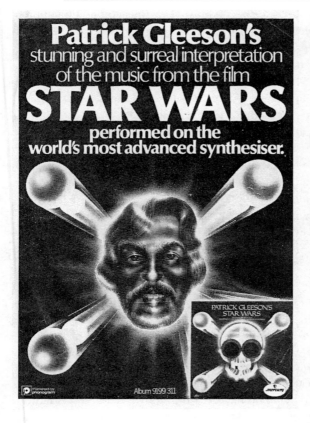

Patrick Gleeson's stunning and surreal interpretation of the music from the film **STAR WARS** performed on the world's most advanced synthesiser.

curvature provided the audience with a much more immersive experience. Dimension 150 had been in existence since the 1950s but been almost completely abandoned; *Star Wars* was the last film to be shown at the Odeon Marble Arch in that format. On March 5, *Star Wars* began to reach additional areas of Greater London such the Well Hall Odeon, Gerrards Cross Classic, Golders Green Iconic, Hendon Odeon, Holloway Odeon, Orpington Commodore, Hounslow Odeon, Rayners Lane Odeon, Sidcup ABC, Sutton Studio, Swiss Cottage Odeon, Uxbridge Odeon, Walthamstow Granada, Walton-on-Thames Odeon, Wimbledon Odeon and the Purley Astoria. Large towns continued to open *Star Wars* including the Odeon Stoke-on-Trent, Odeon Colchester, Odeon Romford, Odeon Croydon, Odeon St. Albans, Sevenoaks Focus, Oxted Plaza, Burton-on-Trent Odeon and the Kings's Lynn Pilot. *Star Wars* debuted on the Channel Islands at the Odeon Guernsey and Odeon Jersey. Laurie Calvert has strong memories of the Romford showing:

I saw *Star Wars* on March 18 at the Romford Odeon. Despite all of the publicity surrounding *Star Wars* in the press and on television, I thought, "I'm not going to be taken in by all of the hype. It had better be good." So when I finally got to see the film a full ten months after it had opened in America, there was a massive queue around the Romford Odeon. There was excitement in the line, with the front-of-house stills providing a glimpse of the film to come. The program book I bought promised even more, so by now I was thinking that it was going to be something special. When I came out of the cinema, I knew I had just seen the most fantastic film of my life. I was blown away. I went back three times within the end of the month. There was a huge increase in quality to anything that had been seen before. Everything looked so good and very realistic. It wasn't just the special effects. It was great music, great characters and storyline. It really won me over.

Graham Ogle also saw *Star Wars* at this time:

My parents took me to see it in early March at the Odeon Stoke-on-Trent. First came the endless wait outside in the huge queue, then a boring short film [*Fast Company*] about bikers, and then it began. I remember little about that first showing; the Star Destroyer looming overhead, the Blockade Runner shootout, the droids in the desert, the cantina are what I remember most. Also the shock at seeing the smoldering skeletons of Owen and Beru, the most gruesome thing I had ever seen up to that point. It's become a cliché, but I left that cinema changed somehow.

The Odeon cinemas in Colchester, Romford and Croydon arranged the familiar appearances by Darth Vader and his Stormtrooper accomplice, with varying degrees of costume accuracy. Their appearance in Croydon was typical of various goings-on nation-wide. The pair arrived at the local cinema in the morning, attracting a great deal of attention; made a pre-arranged "invasion" of a *Star Wars* promotion at a large local high street store; signed autographs for a huge crowd; and finished the day by visiting the local hospital's maternity unit and holding a newborn. Photographers were on hand at each stage to capture the action, which was covered in the local newspapers. Reynolds Motors in New Road, Dagenham, organized a competition in conjunction with the *Romford Recorder,* the winner of which could meet Vader in person at a special *Star Wars* event in the car dealership's showroom. In Colchester, the Dark Lord was the star attraction at an event at the Co-Op Fiveways Superstore timed to coincide with the release of the film. He distributed free tickets, posters, car stickers, T-shirts and badges and also signed autographs for crowds of fans. *Focus,* the in-house magazine of the Colchester and East Sussex Co-operative Society, featured the event but with a distinctly cynical tone. "The stars of this intergalactic extravaganza bear more resemblance to animated dustbins and recycled Cybermen (from *Doctor Who*), and yet overnight they have become as celebrated as any Hollywood stalwart. Signs are, however, that the phenomenon of *Star Wars* could be short-lived. Another film entitled *Close Encounters of the Third Kind* is poised to receive a greater reaction."[28]

Jonathan Johnson has a memory of another incarnation of Darth Vader: Dave Prowse minus his costume. "I saw him opening a fete. He gave away important information about the film and the films to come. In 6 or 7, Darth Vader gets unmasked and you see what lurks behind it, and he eventually dies."[29]

On March 7, the Ideal Home Exhibition at London's Olympia exhibition center opened; it included a considerable *Star Wars* display. There was a section dedicated to how the film had been made, C-3PO and R2-D2 and mannequins dressed in movie costumes. A clutch of Stormtroopers patrolled to help entertain the crowds. *Star Wars* began to reach additional towns in April via the Odeon Peterborough, Odeon Canterbury, Odeon Taunton, Odeon Yeovil, Classic Redditch, Classic Herne Bay, Classic Deal, Classic Cannock, ABC Dover, Folkestone Curzon, the Regal Leamington Spa, the Birmingham Quinton Classic and the Odeon Queensway Birmingham in 70mm (transferred from the Gaumont which had begun showing *Close Encounters of the Third Kind*). The northerly release was expanded by openings at the Odeon Southport, Odeon Sutton Coldfield, Odeon Bolton, Odeon Bury, Classic Durham, Classic Stockport, ABC Rochdale and the Gatley Talton Luxury Cinema (Greater Manchester). The Scottish release continued with the ABC cinemas in Dumfries, Falkirk, Ayr, Kilmarnock and the Greenock Gaumont. On the Isle of Wight, the Newport Empire. In London, the Odeon Marble Arch finished with *Star Wars* on May 20 after an 11-week £131,435 run.

"I was three and a half when *Star Wars* finally reached Leamington Spa," recalls Peter Davis. He continues,

> My five-year-old brother had picked upon the hype from school and his friends' older siblings. My mother took us both one afternoon, skipping school for my brother because often we would go to the cinema and give up with the queue seemingly miles long. My mum thought the film was about a music group instead of outer space stuff. The Leamington Regal Cinema was an enormous cinema with red seats and if you didn't smoke, you had to sit in the aisles. My only memory of the film was the X-Wing fighters. Apparently I fell asleep after that but I was hooked. I loved the robots but I had little memory of their names. We never got to the cinema twice to see to see the same film again, so that was my *Star Wars* experience for quite some time to come.

Being a slightly older fan, Shaun Dawkins did not have to rely on his parents to take him along to the Folkestone Curzon:

> It had taken so long to come down to us that it had already smashed all the box office records. It had already got massive press in the U.K. so it was a very large story locally. My friend and I were determined to be the first ones in and we thought that there wouldn't be many people. How wrong we were. The queue started at ten a.m. and there was a genuine buzz in the line. The local press turned up and there was even a Darth Vader and a Stormtrooper there, which we were totally convinced by, being at that impressionable age. At the end of it, it felt like we'd just run a marathon and we needed to recover. There was a wonderful sense was that this was amazing—and then I went back. We saw *Star Wars* every day after school, which we could just afford due to there being a special discount. Of course, in those days you could sit in the cinema all day and watch a film, with the toilets being very useful. I hope that they didn't notice! We pooled our pocket money and begged our families a lot. *Star Wars* ran at the local cinema for something like 16 weeks and I made sure I saw it as much as I could.

Jordan Royce says, "When *Star Wars* opened in Stockport, me and my two friends saw it as much as we could. At least ten times. We just kept on going on Saturday and Sunday afternoons. *Star Wars* really took over. It was everything for us three: buying the weekly comic, the toys and anything we could find."

The Oscars Triumph

On April 3, the Oscar ceremony was broadcast on television. *Star Wars* won Best Art Direction-Set Direction (John Barry, Norman Reynolds, Leslie Dilley and Roger Christian), Best Costume Design (John Mollo), Best Sound (Don MacDougall, Ray West, Bob Minkler and Derek Ball), Best Effects, Visual Effects (John Stears, John Dykstra, Richard Edlund, Grant McCune and Robert Blalack), Best Music, Original Score (John Williams) and a Special Achievement Award for Sound Effects: Voices of C-3PO and R2-D2 (Ben Burtt) and Best Film Editing (Paul Hirsch, Marcia Lucas and Richard Chew). John Jympson was not included in the nomination as he had been replaced as editor during the production. *Star Wars* was nominated for Best Picture (Gary Kurtz), Best Director (Lucas), Best Actor in a Supporting Role (Alec Guinness) and Best Original Screenplay (Lucas), but did not win. During the event, there was a fashion show by the nominees for Best Costume Design, which took a bizarre turn when Kermit Eller as Darth Vader and Susan George as Princess Leia strode onto the stage ahead of a troupe of costumed *Star Wars* characters. Mark Hamill in the company of R2-D2 and Anthony Daniels dressed as C-3PO in a bow tie presented a Special Achievement Award for Sound Effects to Frank E. Warner for *Close Encounters of the Third Kind* and to Ben Burtt for *Star Wars*.

In the wake of the Oscars, a new version of the *Star Wars* poster was issued to British cinemas, with the addition of the Oscars logo and the statement that the film had won seven Academy Awards including Best Visual Effects and Best Original Score. Peter Beale, along with special guest Kenny Baker, hosted a London party which Leslie Dilley, Roger Christian, Norman Reynolds, John Mollo, John Stears and their wives attended, to celebrate their Oscar success. The group were also presented with awards from the American Academy of SF, Fantasy and Horror Films.

Star Wars II *News*

Star Wars' Oscars were covered by *Star Wars Fan Club Newsletter #2*, which also provided an update on *Star Wars II*: "On February 23rd, it was announced that Star Wars Corporation will begin production on the sequel to *Star Wars* this summer. The title has not been selected yet but it will not be *Star Wars II*. George Lucas' company, Lucasfilm Ltd., will finance the production, currently budgeted for 10 million dollars, with 20th Century-Fox acting as distributors. Based on the second of twelve stories in George Lucas' Adventures of Luke Skywalker series." The article revealed that the first draft of the screenplay had been written by Leigh Brackett, who had extensive credits in both motion pictures and science fiction, having written the scripts for such films as the 1946 version of *The Big Sleep*, *Rio Bravo, Hatari!* and *The Long Goodbye*, and the science fiction books *Sword of Rhiannon, The Ginger Star, Starmen of Llyrids* and *The Long Tomorrow*. Assigned to director was Irvin Kershner, whose most recent film was *The Eyes of Laura Mars*. His directorial credits also included *The Flim-Flam Man, A Fine Madness, Loving, The Return of a Man Called Horse*, the telefilm *Raid on Entebbe* and episodes of the TV series *The Rebel* and *Naked City*. Mark Hamill, Harrison Ford and Carrie Fisher were confirmed to have been signed to continue their roles. There was also a *Name the Newsletter Contest,* where members were invited to send in suggestions, with *Star Wars* character mugs and R2-D2 cookie jars offered as prizes. The subject of Chewbacca not receiving a medal in *Star Wars* was addressed in the Q&A column: "The Rebel forces wanted to give Chewbacca a medal for his part in saving Princess Leia and in the destruction of the Death Star, but Wookiees don't approve of medals. So, respecting Chewbacca's wishes, they didn't give him one. They didn't want Chewie to go totally unrewarded, however. So, after the ceremony at the Rebel base, they flew to the Wookiee planet for a celebration."[30]

Derek Dorking was finding that his R2-D2 model was becoming more widely known than he had ever imagined:

> It was pictured in the local newspapers. *The Evening London News* got hold of the story, then *The Daily Mail* and then I was written to by the BBC asking me if I could appear on the *Blue Peter* television program on the 3rd of April. I was aware that it went out live, nationally, so the prospect was quite nerve-wracking. I agreed and on the day, me and my brother Philip drove to London as we had to get to the studio at 10.30 a.m., as they would be rehearsing the show all day. The director decided just to feature the R2-D2 being driven by John Noakes, who would describe it and mention my name. Philip, who is a professional photographer, took some shots. We then went around the corner to get the pictures processed and sped back to get them signed by the *Blue Peter* presenters.
>
> By that time, *Star Wars* was turning into more of an explosion. The toys were selling out in the shops. If you saw something *Star Wars* that you wanted, you bought it because you wouldn't see it again. Things were literally flying off of the shelves. *Star Wars* was everywhere—you couldn't get away from it.

In May, Nabisco's Shreddies cereal became available with a free set of Letraset transfers and a *Star Wars* scene on the back of the packet. "My sister had got to the free *Star Wars* transfers in packs of Shreddies, and had put them in all the wrong places on the back," remembers Nicholas Denny. "She ruined the perspective and even put some of them upside down. I didn't mess with her stuff."[31] Some parents may have reached their spending limit on memorabilia for their *Star Wars*-obsessed kiddies. Writing to *Star Wars Weekly,* John Marriott had clearly had enough, although his tongue was probably firmly in his cheek:

If I tell you that I am old enough to have one foot in the grave, yet have a fanatical sci-fi son coming up to the tender age of five, you can probably understand why I hate you, *Star Wars* and *Star Wars Weekly*!!! Being old and un-imaginative, who cut the competition coupons from his beloved *Star Wars Weekly*, who got most of the answers wrong and who as punishment had to take him to see *Star Wars* YET AGAIN. What with sweets, car parking and entrance price it's costing me a fortune! Let's hope the Force stays with Darth Vader, he sure made the film, let alone the planet go with a bang. Jamie keeps asking me what will happen when *Star Wars Weekly* gets to the end of the film story and I keep telling him that Darth Vader lives! Luke and Leia will get married and live miserably ever after, the sickening goody-goodies and Chewbacca will become the editor of *Star Wars Weekly*! Six weeks of *Star Wars*, I just can't afford it.[32]

The *Star Wars Official Poster Monthly* #4 was identical to the American edition, except for Darth Vader featuring on the cover and small variations in the layout of the pages. "Luke Skywalker—From Youth to Man" was the lead article. John May described Luke having feelings for Princess Leia that would eventually jar with the eventual revelation of their true relationship, but at the time, those emotions seemed perfectly logical. May wrote, "Right from the very first moment that Luke set eyes on the fragile projection carried by Artoo, he felt a strange stirring within him. Never before had he seen such a beautiful girl, let alone a princess. It did not need much persuading for him to make her struggle his own. His love for her—that's what it was, even though he would be embarrassed to admit it—received little encouragement from the Princess."[33] At this point in time, Luke Skywalker was seen as being every bit as much of a competitor for Princess Leia's heart as Han Solo was, and the outcome of the situation was a hot topic among fans. The *Making of Star Wars* documentary which had aired on American television on September 16, 1977, covered this very issue. "She's a chump if she goes for Han Solo," said Hamill. George Lucas was noncommittal on the subject, saying, "I think Luke is more dedicated to her than Han Solo is." Carrie Fisher did not venture an opinion either but she did say, "I'd describe Han Solo as the mercenary rogue with the cream filling. He's a nice guy."[34]

Opening to the center of this *Star Wars Official Poster Monthly* issue, readers encountered one of the most influential articles that the publication would ever produce. "The

Derek Dorking's R2-D2 controlled by John Noakes (photograph by Philip Dorking, courtesy Derek Dorking).

Soldiers of the Empire" was based on the flimsiest of information, yet the origin, life and duty of Stormtroopers described by Anthony Fredrickson was so authentic, it seemed as if it had been part of the *Star Wars* backstory all along. Fredrickson's key innovation was describing Stormtroopers as being iden-

tical clones, produced in growth tanks. Once removed, they were drilled over a period of years until eventually joining the Empire's ranks, totally committed to the emperor. The best Stormtroopers were promoted to Squad Leaders and then to the Imperial Guards (the menacing, gray-suited troopers in pseudo-samurai helmets), of which 40 were assigned to Grand Moff Tarkin and 12 to Darth Vader. Sources such as the *Star Wars Program Book* had described Stormtroopers as drones but, what with the mention of *The Clone Wars* and the fact that the Imperial Troopers' faces were never seen, fans reached the logical conclusion that *they* were the clones in question. "Princess Leia says, 'Aren't you a little short for a Stormtrooper?'" says Fredrickson. "So the implication is that the Stormtroopers are of a uniform height. Take that one step further and you can conclude a uniform body type, so the nature of Stormtroopers is suggested in the original dialogue. Clones. No brainer." The Stormtrooper armor was described by Fredrickson as being

Above and opposite page: **Nabisco Shreddies with *Star Wars* transfers—a must for *Star Wars* fans.**

made of super-lightweight impervium worn over a black two-piece body temperature glove. Indirect laser hits were deflected off of the surface of the armor, although it offered little protection against a direct hit. Although explicit mentions of "clones" would not appear again in print outside of Bunch Associates publications (the term "drones" to describe Stormtroopers coming into vogue instead), "The Soldiers of the Empire" provided the basis for all future descriptions of Stormtroopers and their equipment, including the Lucasfilm-endorsed *Guide to the* Star Wars *Universe* by Raymond L Velasco, which credited the information to Fredrickson. Considering how the *Star Wars* saga would develop, over 20 years later the article is nothing short of astounding. How *Star Wars Episode II: Attack of the Clones* came to resemble Fredrickson's article so closely remains a mystery. Perhaps the author was tuned into Lucas' thinking process … or perhaps if the director had cast his mind back to those days the article may have influenced the film.

*   *   *

(courtesy cerealoffers.com)

Witnessing the depiction of the creation of the Clone Army in Star Wars II: Attack of the Clones—*exactly as I had read about as an eight-year old in 1978—was amazing. To my mind it vindicated the assertion that Stormtroopers were clones as described in the poster magazine (although I'm aware that not all fans share the interpretation). Marvel comics and*

later West End Games, in their wisdom, decided to ignore this fact. Perhaps this was inten-
tional. Maybe Lucas was seeking to protect his concept of a clone army. I don't know. What
I do know is that one of the most important elements of Star Wars *became confused and led*
to many publications contradicting the film saga by featuring human Stormtroopers.

The Palitoy Saga Continues

Vehicles for the *Star Wars* action figures from Palitoy began appearing in May. Unlike
the action figures and die-cast toys, the vehicles were the result of Palitoy manufacturing.
Palitoy tooling manager Roger Morison says, "I met Kenner tooling and development president Jim Chips during my trip to the States and he became my main contact. I acquired
product drawings, tool drawings, technical information and manufacturing specification
documents from the different departments at Kenner." The three vehicles for the line were
the X-Wing Fighter, TIE Fighter and Landspeeder but the challenge was for Palitoy to be
able to produce them. Morison continues,

> The metal molds which are used to create each toy's individual plastic pieces, known as "tooling," were
> to be loaned from Kenner which was negotiated by the sales and marketing team at Palitoy. Due to
> Kenner's own production of the Landspeeder and X-Wing Fighter, however, it meant that the tools
> would not be available for loan. Therefore, I had tooling manufactured for them in the U.K. which
> would then be owned by Palitoy. The purchasing and buying department at Palitoy then obtained
> quotes from three injection-molding companies to produce the toys from the tooling.

The TIE Fighter toy was produced under the guidance of Palitoy manufacturing engineer
John Holmes, who recalls,

> Kenner also sent ready-molded examples of each piece of the toy and details of the production line at
> their factory, so we could work out how the toy would be eventually put together at Palitoy. I briefed
> engineers Dave Waters and Aubrey Bale on what was required. The Design Department process manager
> Alec Langton was involved too. We had to organize an assembly line for the TIE Fighter as well as the
> X-Wing Fighter and Landspeeder, which included all of the compressed air screwdrivers, soldering
> irons, etc., that would be required to make all of the individual pieces into the finished toys. When we
> received the thousands of pieces of the toys (and the precious tooling) back from the sub-contractor,
> we produced a dozen of each of the trio of new toys to be sent to the safety lab for testing.

Although John Holmes put 100 percent effort into creating the *Star Wars* toys, he was
not a huge admirer of the film. "I went to see it in Leicester just to see what it was all about,
to help me understand where the products fitted in, etc. Although I was 23–25 years of age,
I was not a lover of these types of films (and I'm still not), but I found it interesting as it
was one of the first of its type. Consequently, I wasn't really excited about *Star Wars* as a
toy line, but realized that the hype behind the film meant that it was going to take off. This
would mean job security because the company would be moving forward."

The resulting *Star Wars* vehicle toys were turned out by Palitoy without a hitch. A
faithful reproduction of the "real thing," the X-Wing Fighter had an opening cockpit and
a non-removable R2-D2 installed in the rear. There was a function where the wings could
be opened by pressing down on R2-D2's head. It was identical to the Kenner version of the
X-Wing but since Palitoy had commissioned its own tooling molds, it had taken the opportunity of simplifying the toy, leaving out the battery box, sound feature and miniature light
bulb in the nose of the craft. The Palitoy Landspeeder too was slightly less detailed than

its American counterpart, in that it did not have an opening bonnet. Even so, the spring-loaded "anti-gravity" wheels made it a prize for many *Star Wars* fans. The TIE Fighter was an exact copy of the Kenner toy and, since it had been derived from the same tooling molds, it retained the light and sound feature. It also had a function where the wings could be "blown off" via hidden activation buttons and then re-fitted for the next game.

The *Star Wars* vehicle range was sold in packaging which was unique to Palitoy. This was the responsibility of Ray Hastings Studio, which was managed by Dave Barnacle. According to Barnacle,

> My primary contact at Palitoy was packaging manager Ken Moore, from whom I would get my initial brief. There was input from marketing manager Geoff Maisey and head of design Bob Brechin. Almost all of the work I did was "Anglicizing" U.S. *Star Wars* packaging. In those pre-computer days, everything was crafted manually. I would overlay a flattened printed packaging sample from Kenner and paste into position changes to spelling, license copy, catalogue numbers, and replace Kenner with the Palitoy logo. Incidentally, my company's name was derived from the founder Ray Hastings. I became a director-partner and took over the company when Ray decided to emigrate to New Zealand.

Since both the X-Wing Fighter and Landspeeder were different from the Kenner versions, new photographs needed to be incorporated into the packaging. In common with its American counterpart, the Landspeeder was described on the box as a Land Speeder. As the TIE Fighter was identical to the American version, Palitoy simply used the Kenner printing for the box and placed a sticker of its own logo over the Kenner branding. Palitoy had produced and packaged a large amount of *Star Wars* toys at its own expense without significant orders from retailers. At this stage, the potential reaction from the toy trade and from customers was a question mark.

Palitoy gained another "sister" at this time in the form of Chad Valley when it was purchased by General Mills and placed in the General Mills UK Toy Group. Two products derived from the Kenner *Star Wars* line were released by Chad Valley: a Slide Projector Set and *Electronic Battle Command Game*. According to Geoff Maisey,

> My understanding was that Chad Valley was acquired by General Mills on the recommendation of the then–Palitoy MD Bob Simpson, as a way to enter the pre-school market, as Kenner had plans to exploit this area. Usually General Mills' decision to acquire companies was related to product or market criteria, rather than corporate infrastructure. In the case of another GM acquisition Denys Fisher, for example, it was primarily to obtain Spirograph. The *Star Wars* slide projector was similar to items already in the Chad Valley product portfolio so it was natural for the company to carry it. I'm not sure why the Battle Command center was placed with them, though.

An Update from the Stars

Issue #3 of the *Star Wars Fan Club Newsletter*, issued in July, included an interview with Mark Hamill, who said that he had first learned about the casting for *Star Wars* from his actor friend Robert Englund, who had already tested for a role. (Englund would later find fame as Freddie Krueger in *A Nightmare on Elm Street*.) Hamill also revealed that he was due to begin filming the World War II film *The Big Red One*: "I read the script and I thought, 'This is a good movie. This is a great World War II movie. I'd want to see it.' Sam Fuller, the picture's writer-director, is a man I respect. After *Star Wars*, I thought I should wait around for another good movie, so good it would equal *Star Wars*, at least in intent.

I've done a lot of television I'm embarrassed of, but that's because I was learning. I wanted to wait for another great picture, but I realized that there's no Great American Novel waiting for me. I'm an actor and I should act. So I'm going to act in this movie."[35]

Starburst #3 contained an interview with Harrison Ford, who described his reaction to *Star Wars*. "Terrific! I first saw it probably a whole year later after shooting. I thought it was just … incredible. [*Laughs.*] Terrific! Fantastic!" The interview, which was conducted after a preview screening of Ford's latest movie *Force Ten from Navarone*, included the actor's take on Han Solo's relationship with Chewbacca: "I just said to myself, 'Look, you've got this huge dog.' You understand? I made Chewie into a pet relationship. But it's like anything in that movie. People say: How did you act with those special effects? Well, it's no different from than in other picture. You just saw us just now, Robert Shaw and I in a cattle truck, pretending that there were walls all around us … chugging along some track in Yugoslavia. It's dress up and pretend time."

Ford's laid-back attitude extended to the subject of fame. "Fortunately I don't have as unique a physiognomy as Carrie or Mark do, so I'm much less recognized in the streets, about which I'm very happy. That could get heavy. It happens infrequently enough, and people are usually very nice because the film is so broadly accepted, so that's a pleasure. But when they know where we're going to be, and they're sitting outside the hotel, all these autograph people, sometimes that's a drag. But none of it really bothers me." The article also contained an update on *Star Wars II*, which included the same information in issue #2 of the fan club newsletter. In addition, it was stated that shooting was scheduled for Lapland and Africa, "costing $10,000,000."[36] Attentive readers would have noticed that in an entry on the magazine's "Things to Come" page, Hamill had provided the additional snippet of information that *Star Wars 2* would open in America on May 25, 1980. The countdown to the film had begun!

The Poster Monthly *Goes Stateside*

Subscribers to the *Star Wars Official Poster Monthly* receiving issue #5 found that it was the version which had been initially released in America in February. The British printing had ceased and the magazine had become, for all intents and purposes, an American publication (albeit created in Britain). The back page contained American merchandise and a contact address in Hicksville, New York. High street shops in Britain no longer stocked the magazine, so if fans did not have a subscription via the mail, they would need to seek out imports at comic shops or from their regular comics dealer. Wherever fans sourced the magazine from, they found that the articles continued in a similar vein. "The Threepio File" by Dr. M.F. Marten provided an interesting slant on the character: "Human-droid relations may not be the most demanding function in the galaxy, but in a fully robotized civilization it is a vital one. Threepio and his kind represent the acceptable face of robotics. His human appearance, emotionalism and buffoonery all serve to make the droids seem less threatening to their human (and alien) masters. In terms of logic, Threepio's a waste of good circuitry. In terms of human psychology, he's indispensable."[37]

Also in this issue, John May tackled the subject of Chewbacca, of whom nothing was known except that he was 200 years old (which May had uncharacteristically left out of the article). His imagination firing on all cylinders, May did put forward the idea of Chewbacca owing his life to Han Solo, explaining why he was following the smuggler through the galaxy. This concept became entrenched in *Star Wars* literature, with Chewbacca described as having a life debt to Han. Although Chewbacca did not receive a medal at the end of *Star Wars*, May asserted that the Wookiee was indeed presented with one by Princess Leia before he and Han left the rebel base to pursue their adventures. May was keeping an eye on the Marvel comics saga, where Han and Chewbacca had indeed left the rebel base shortly after the destruction of the Death Star. It may be a coincidence but the Marvel *Star Wars* story "The Day After the Death Star" would go on to depict Chewbacca receiving his medal at the rebel base from Princess Leia, who was standing on a table.

Fans seeking out imports of the *Official Poster Monthly* discovered that the American schedule was several issues ahead. A detailed explanation of R2-D2 was the lead article in #6, John May asserting that the droid's actions had been instrumental in the destruction of the Death Star. In "An Alien Universe," Dr. M.F. Marten explored the possibility that the struggle between rebel and imperial was a largely human concern, as the film did not show aliens among the ranks of either side:

> In the space bar, humans and aliens appear to mix on quite equal terms, trading, drinking and chatting together. The life-forms which are excluded are the droids, not the aliens. But it's possible that this free and easy intermingling of species is typical only of frontier planets like Tatooine. On the long-inhabited central worlds it's possible that species prejudice keeps humans and aliens separated. Certainly, humans appear to be the dominant species in the galaxy, wielding the ultimate power, and it's likely that this would be resented by the more intelligent of the alien species.[38]

This was an extremely well-thought-out article and the concept of the higher civilization resting in the "central systems," though not new to sci-fi, was to become an important aspect of the *Star Wars* universe. Jon Trux's article "The Spaceships of *Star Wars*" was based on the *Star Wars Sketchbook*, bringing some of the book's unique information to a wider readership. The article underlined the fact that the X-Wing Fighters were second-hand, "refurbished earlier models. Lovingly maintained, with replacement engines and body panels. Basic fighting ships, battered and stripped of all but the essentials."[39]

Issue #7 of the *Official Star Wars Poster Monthly* introduced a new writer, Dr. Humberto Kaminski, whose article "The Droids of *Star Wars*" was extremely wide of the mark. Taking inspiration from Luke Skywalker saying to C-3PO in the novelization "Now isn't the time to force the issue of droid rights"[40] as a basis, Kaminski speculated that there was a droid resistance movement, organizing strikes and revolutions against their owners. John May maintained a much firmer footing with a profile of George Lucas, which included an update on *Star Wars 2*. May revealed that the film had been "tentatively titled *The Empire Strikes Back*... Lucas is financing entirely with his own money and will act as executive producer or advisor."[41] Also in the works, according to May, was a sequel to *American Graffiti* and a secret space project, a unique collaboration between Lucas and longtime friend Steven Spielberg. A Lucas-Spielberg collaboration was quite a prospect, even if the resulting film *Raiders of the Lost Ark* was not quite in the vein of science fiction. Jon Trux's article "Beams, Blasters and Battle Stations!" explored the real-life developments using lasers. Summing up, Trux wrote; "[W]e're still years away from seeing earthly wars fought with direct-energy weapons, and hopefully we never will. There is a bright side to the story—as well as the military uses of high-powered lasers, NASA is studying the possibility of using them to power spaceships across the solar system—and maybe to the stars!"[42]

Star Wars Weekly *Goes Beyond the Film*

On May 3, *Star Wars Weekly* reached issue #13. A free A3-sized color poster was included, with the promise of another in #14. This edition featured "New Planets, New Perils," the first episode to take the story beyond the adaptation of the film. *Star Wars Weekly* used the title of the first chapter of serializations in individual issues of American *Star Wars* comics to describe the entire story. "New Planets, New Perils" was by Roy Thomas and with art by Howard Chaykin. Tom Palmer came on board as inker part way through (he was also credited as co-artist and embellisher). Developing the continuing story had presented a considerable challenge to Thomas, who said in an interview with *Star Wars Weekly*, "I had lunch with Charlie Lippincott, George Lucas and Mark Hamill and we discussed the problem. We weren't sure where we were going with Luke Skywalker and Princess Leia or any of the others. The only character we felt we could do anything with—as long as we kept it open for him to return to meet Luke Skywalker—was Han Solo and his first mate, Chewbacca. So Howie [Chaykin] and I decided to do 'Han Solo' comics for a couple of issues, as kind of a holding action."[43]

"New Planets, New Perils" began with Han Solo and Chewbacca leaving the Rebel base in order to pay Jabba the Hut. Their reward from the rebels is stolen when they are boarded by the space pirate Crimson Jack, who has a captured Imperial Star Destroyer under his command. Han Solo and Chewbacca, impoverished once more, are desperate enough to work for a village on a remote planet, seeking to drive away a group of brigands. To assist in the action, Han gathers a motley band of gun hands at the local spaceport, including a bipedal porcupine Hedji, a deranged former Jedi called Don-Wan Kihotay, the gun-toting moll Amazia, a green man-rabbit called Jaxxon and Jim, a local youth who calls himself the Starkiller Kid.

The similarity of "New Planets New Perils" to the movie Western *The Magnificent Seven* was apparent but it did not jar too much, as *Star Wars* itself contained many pulp references to previous films. Jaxxon was a bit of a stretch for some fans, however. According to Thomas,

> It was interesting to me that someone wrote in a letter recently to the effect that having a six-foot green rabbit was really too much. That struck me as really amusing. Some purists claim that anything that isn't derived from the released version is out of the spirit of the movie. The thing is, there's definitely a spirit to the finished *Star Wars* movie, but there was also a certain spirit to the various [*Star Wars*] scripts I saw for inspiration. One of the characters in the bar sequence, in fact, reminded me of Porky Pig—which sparked me to create the green rabbit.[44]

Since he made that statement, the *Star Wars* films have gone on to feature creatures with pig heads, squid faces and a race of teddy bears, so in hindsight Jaxxon does not look too out-of-place in the *Star Wars* universe.

Thomas decided to leave the *Star Wars* comic before "New Planets, New Perils" was finished, so science fiction writer Don Glut filled in for the conclusion of the story. Glut, who also attended the USC Film School the same time as George Lucas, had a strong interest in dinosaurs and had made several amateur films featuring the creatures. It is not surprising that his contribution to "New Planets, New Perils" was to introduce a rampaging T-Rex-like creature that stomped everything it encountered to death. Han Solo's slaying the beast with a lightsaber provided *Star Wars Weekly* with one of its most iconic covers:

an image of Han lofting the weapon above his head. "It was a great comic and was a big part of my life," says Ian Whitlock. He continues,

> I was upset that I missed the first issue but I made sure that I never missed another. I would always look forward to receiving the next issue and cut out the photographs and stuck them up on my bedroom walls. I was never sure about the other non–*Star Wars* stories included to bulk it out and I never felt the stories after the film adaptation ended were ever quite up to the same standard. (That green bunny Jaxxon was never going to cut the mustard!) That said, though, some *Star Wars* was better than none, and the stories helped to expand the universe that I had created with my figures. I'm not sure kids today get the same joy out of comics as there's so much else to keep them busy but for us '70s and '80s children, it was a big part of affordable entertainment.

The stories that went beyond the film did not suit everyone. "When the *Star* Wars Weekly comic came out, my mother bought me a copy for the first two months," remembers Richard Harris. "But I lost interest when the storylines had nothing to do with the film and went off track with new 'comic-like' characters. Fortunately, I was also bought the 'young readers' version of the novel. As I flicked through, I always went to the photographs of the film in the center." Darren Slade recalls, "I collected *Star Wars Weekly* from the first issue. All of those crazy characters and outlandish plots, I was constantly defending it against derision from school chums and my brother. I assumed though that the stories had been passed by Lucasfilm, so it seemed to be the authentic continuation of the *Star Wars* story."

Star Wars *Becomes Further Flung*

Star Wars began to widen its orbit yet further on the May 7, reaching the satellite towns of large cities. In the Liverpool area, the Birkenhead Classic, Wallasey Unit Four and Skelmersdale Focus. Also in the North; the Oldham Odeon, the Solihull Cinema and the Isle of Man Picturehouse. As the month progressed, there were further openings at the Chester Odeon and in Cornwall at the St. Austell Film Center, the Penzance Savoy and the St. Ives Royal; also in further extremities of the South of Britain. In Kent, the Margate Dreamland and Ramsgate Classic. In Dorset, the Dorchester Plaza, Weymouth Classic and Bridport Palace.

The next bulk release was on June 4 when more satellite towns to large cities finally received *Star Wars*. In the Manchester area, the Urmston Curzon Mayfair, Whitefield Major, the Hyde Royal, Altrincham Studio 1, the Chorlton-Cum-Hardy Classic, Odeon Sale and Odeon Cheetham Ashton-Under Lyne. The releases in Cornwall became further afield on the 4th: the Falmouth Grand, Newquay Camelot, St. Austell Capitol and the Wadebridge Regal. Some venues in relatively large towns such the Basildon ABC in Greater London and the Chichester Granada had been delayed due to contractual clauses with Odeon. Additional venues in Scotland also followed in June: the Odeon Hamilton, the ABC Paisley, the Lancaster 1 2 3, the ABC Coatbridge and the Aviemore Speyside Theatre. Also the Morecambe Empire Lancashire that is geographically close to Scotland. Louise Turner first saw *Star Wars* at this time.

> I went to see *Star Wars* soon after it opened in Paisley. My pal who lived across the street was going to see it and I tagged along. I remember people had been talking about it. I don't remember any queues. All I remember is thinking that Luke was cute (I was nine at the time) and I remember being

completely traumatized by the two burned-out corpses at the Lars homestead on Tatooine! I soon had a bubble gum card of that cute Luke Skywalker.

The Making of Star Wars

On June 16, 1978, the *Making of Star Wars* documentary was televised for the first time in Britain. People who lived in parts of the country which had not yet been reached by *Star Wars* at the cinema could now learn how the film was made before actually seeing it. "I remember very well the agony of waiting for the show to begin," says Darren Slade. "I found the program fascinating and thanks to a recording I made on our first cassette recorder, I enjoyed it, in sound-only, countless times after that. They showed things like Chewbacca's hair being combed and the models being filmed but they kept some of the illusion, which I suppose was a conscious choice. It's like saying there's no Father Christmas. As I recall, though, my mum wasn't all that happy about staying quiet for an hour while I made my audio recording!"

The Making of Star Wars had been made in America by 20th Century-Fox Television and was presented by Anthony Daniels as C-3PO accompanied by R2-D2 on a specially created *Star Wars*–like set. Additional narration was by William Conrad. The program began with scenes of the event at Mann's Chinese Theatre, where C-3PO, R2-D2 and Darth Vader placed their footprints in cement. Dialogue and sound effects had been added to make it seem as if C-3PO was talking, R2-D2 was beeping and Vader breathing. Many of the secrets of *Star Wars* were revealed, with contributions from the stars of the film, along with Gary Kurtz and George Lucas. The program included clips of some of the scenes which had been cut from *Star Wars,* including Han Solo encountering a very much human Jabba the Hut (played by Declan Mulholland) at Docking Bay 94 and Luke Skywalker meeting up with Biggs Darklighter at Anchorhead and the Rebel Base. The "galaxy far, far away" was seen coming down to earth with an enormous thud however, when it was meant to be creating a perfect fantasy in the mind of the audience. Instead of lasers and explosions rocking the Millennium Falcon, it was a group of burly men shaking the set. Instead of zipping across the wastes of Tatooine via the power of anti-gravity, Luke's Landspeeder was seen supported by a counter-balance arm. In rehearsing the escape from the Death Star, Harrison Ford casually pointed his blaster, saying, "Bang, bang."

Not all of *Star Wars'* secrets were revealed in *The Making of Star Wars*. Neither Anthony Daniels nor Kenny Baker made an appearance, apart from the "Bang, bang" rehearsal, where Daniels, dressed in a bathrobe, hurried up the Millennium Falcon's ramp (something that would have been a Herculean feat in his costume). The puncturing of the *Star Wars* fantasy was commented upon by some but the truth was that there was a hunger, at least from the media's point of view, to explain all of the secrets of the *Star Wars* films. Nobody in the moviemaking world would pass up an opportunity to produce a documentary about their film for airing on prime time television, especially a film that was still showing at the cinema. In these formative years of blockbuster film marketing, the special effects and the effects technicians were becoming just as important as the actors and the storyline. Hollywood would no longer be a magic factory which kept secrets from the audience. A ratings success for ITV, *The Making of Star Wars* attracted 11.75 million viewers, making it the twelfth most popular program shown that week, even beating the popular soap opera *Cross-roads*.

Changing the Guard at the Star Wars Comic

On June 28, issue #21 of *Star Wars Weekly* (June 28) featured the new story "Star Search," which was the debut of Archie Goodwin as the regular writer-editor. Carmine Infantino had taken over as the artist, with Terry Austin acting as inker. Roy Thomas was credited as consulting editor. Writing for *Comics Feature* magazine, Kurt Busiek provided his own point of view regarding the change in personnel: "Roy Thomas is a master of comics writing but his four *Star Wars* issues (beyond the film adaptation) indicate that he did not quite understand the special needs of the series. The universe he began to establish as the background for the star warriors was peopled by such interesting inhabitants as intelligent, man-sized, carnivorous rabbits and Don Quixote parodies … a little too tongue-in-cheek, poking fun at the story conventions that *Star Wars* relies upon."[45] Goodwin shared his memories of the time with *Comics Journal*: "Roy was giving up the book and I knew we had to find somebody. What I thought was, 'Well, I'll write a few issues 'til we can settle on another team.' I got Carmine Infantino to draw it and I got Terry Austin to ink it, and we just sort of kept doing it."[46]

"Star Search" began with Han Solo and Chewbacca being recaptured by Crimson Jack's Star Destroyer and finding to their surprise that Princess Leia has suffered the same fate. Leia had flown a spacecraft alone from the Rebel base, searching for Luke Skywalker, who had disappeared while scouting the planetary system Drexel as a possible location for a new base. Unbeknownst to the princess, Luke had crashed his spaceship on a planet in the Drexel system and ended up floating in an escape pod on a seemingly endless sea with R2-D2 and C-3PO. A group of warriors dubbed the Dragon Lords, who rode swimming reptilian creatures, arrived, intent on capturing Luke's escape pod. They were chased off by another armed group, this one driving water skimmers which used technology similar to the Tatooine Landspeeders to fly just above the waves. The water skimmers won the skirmish and took Luke and the droids back to their base, an enormous floating city.

Han and Leia trick Crimson Jack into transporting them to Drexel. During the journey, Crimson Jack's first mate, a fiery female named Jolli, is confused by the friendship between Han and Leia. In her experience, men and women were always antagonistic to each other. Jolli seemed to begin to develop feelings for Han herself. Once at Drexel, Crimson Jack's cruiser is caught in a powerful sonic jammer (or tractor beam) generated by the floating city and has to use full power to avoid being dragged down to the surface. (This was how Luke had crashed there.) Han, Leia and Chewbacca escape and travel down to Drexel in the Millennium Falcon but once there, they became embroiled in a civil war which would see the Dragon Lords victorious. "Star Search" represented a phenomenal debut by Goodwin as writer. With its non-stop action, humor and character interaction, the story captured the spirit of *Star Wars* perfectly. But Infantino's art was criticized by some, with perhaps the statuesque depiction of Princess Leia being the most glaring example.

* * *

    I was captured by the realistic seeming black-and-white art of "Star Search" and the double-dealing aspects of the story, as well as action-packed elements. The back-up stories "Star-Lord" and "Tales of the Watcher" were fascinating also. The cover of issue #21 was dominated by a highly stylized image of Chewbacca, who looked much fiercer than he had in the film. There was a male figure who I assume was meant to be Han but the colorist had given him yellow hair. There was a beautiful depiction of Princess Leia, seeming very young and fragile. Also on the cover were Crimson Jack and his chief crewmate Jolli, who with a cigarette between her lips and an evil stare was the epitome of a femme fatale. I must have read that issue a thousand times!

Chapter 3

The Long Summer
of *Star Wars*

Naysayers had predicted that *Star Wars* business would be short-lived in Britain. In the July 16 edition of the *Daily Express,* city editor Roy Assersohn Bonn wrote, "A new lease of life in the cinema will boost Rank Organization's profits this year. Box office records have been set by space age films like *Star Wars* and *Close Encounters of the Third Kind.* If the weather stays as poor as it has been recently, Rank is looking for a continuation of the 35–40 percent rise in attendance seen so far this year."[1] Despite the gloomy weather, the summer of 1978 was the golden time for *Star Wars* fans. For some, the film arrived in their area just in time for the school holidays. In July, smaller venues began to be awarded *Star Wars*, inheriting prints when they came available. Cornwall was representative of many areas where smaller venues finally got *Star Wars*: the Redruth Regal, Padstow Capitol, Helston Flora, St. Austell Capitol and Wadebridge Regal. Coastal venues too were still being issued the film: the Westcliff-on-Sea Classic on July 2, the Westgate-on-Sea Carlton (West Sussex) from July 16 and the Whitby (North Yorkshire) Empire on the 23rd. A geographically close venue to Whitby, the Loftus Empire began playing the film on the 27th.

"I went to see *Star Wars* when it opened on the second of July at my local cinema," says Derek Dorking. He continues:

The Westcliff-on-Sea Classic was about two miles away from the Southend Odeon, built in a residential part of town, surrounded by houses. It was equipped for 70mm and was the only cinema in that part of Essex that was; but it was only showing *Star Wars* in 35mm at that time. Later on, the cinema was sporadically sent 70mm prints when they were available. In the foyer, they had put together their own Darth Vader costume which looked awful, out of motorcycle leathers, a red-lined Dracula cape and a helmet made out of a Spider-Man mask and a crash helmet! I thought, "I don't know what I think about this." There was also a very basic model of R2-D2 in the foyer, calved out of a polystyrene tube with a Coca-Cola bottle stuck in it. I cheekily said to the manager Ron Stewart, "I like your robot but I can do better." He said, "You're the kid from *Blue Peter*. I've been asking the press for your details but they wouldn't give it to me." I agreed to take along my R2-D2 to help in the promotions at the cinema. By that time, I had made a Luke Skywalker costume for myself. I had bought a couple of Force Beam lightsabers but converted them with a stroboscopic light effect inside to make them a lot brighter. They were very effective but you had to have them connected via a wire to an 18-volt power pack on your belt!

Well, after two weeks of *Star Wars* being at the cinema, Ron Stewart said to me, "Had you ever fancied being a projectionist? We can tell that you're a pretty bright lad, how would you like to work here?" and he offered me a job right there and then. I had left college by that time with a City and Guilds qualification in art, and I had a strong interest in cameras and electronics, so it seemed like a perfect job. Not long after that, I met [soon-to-be girlfriend] Julie, who used to bring her little brother to the kids shows at the cinema and also helped out.

Towns with more than one cinema often had the benefit of *Star Wars* returning during the summer months as the second or third venues were allocated the film. The Hastings Orion began its showing on June 18, the Focus Cinema at Croydon Town Hall began on July 9, the Manchester Deansgate Studio on July 23, the Nottingham Classic on August 6 and the Streatham ABC on August 13. Many cinemas were still in the middle of record-breaking runs, among them the Redditch Classic (9th August–12th April) and the Odeon Bolton (30th September–2nd April). What could be better than seeing *Star Wars* again in your home town during the summertime? People from areas which had yet to see their first showing of the film might have not been so pleased! The Dominion Tottenham Court Road was *still* showing *Star Wars* in an incredible uninterrupted run since December 28. Meanwhile in America, *Variety* reported that Labor Day September 4 would mark the end of the film's initial domestic release except for the Westgate I in Portland which would retain the film due to a contractual clause. That being said, the second release had already begun on July 21, meaning that audiences could still go out for their *Star Wars* fix. The film had already recouped more money in the U.S. than any other, a staggering $260,421,049 by August 20, 1978.[2]

Summer Holiday Star Wars

In Britain, it was a challenge for children to keep themselves occupied during the annual six-week summer break from school. It might be difficult to imagine today but there was not any form of computer game to play in the home, video recorders were extremely expensive at over £650 and there were only three television channels to choose from. Since *Star Wars* toy vehicles were often out of families' price range, children learned to improvise. Every episode of the BBC1 TV program *Blue Peter* featured a craft section which showed children how to make useful things out of everyday items and the indispensable sticky-backed plastic. *Star Wars* was never featured but constructing items such as an Action Man bunk bed and a wearable *Blake's 7* teleportation bracelet fine-tuned children's crafting skills and gave empty washing-up liquid bottles a thousand possibilities.

R2-D2 was the model of choice for hobbyists to construct from scratch. Even if they could not construct one as complex as Derek Dorking's, many notable examples were made. A less ambitious, non-mechanical scratch-built R2-D2 by John Bradley of Whitburn, West Lothian, was featured in *Look-In*. Few fans were as fortunate as John Millbank from Huntingdon, whose father constructed a realistic, life-sized R2-D2 from the sump of a drain which was featured in *Star Wars Weekly*. Craig Spivey's father was no less resourceful: "In Crowle every year, there'd be a Halloween fancy dress disco in the village hall. My dad always put a lot of effort into his costumes and, at the height of the *Star Wars* hype, elected to go as C-3PO in a customized pair of gold-painted overalls and a shop-bought mask. He also made his own R2-D2 out of an old spin dryer and a space hopper, which he rolled around on a pair of my old roller skates all night. Everyone thought it was hilarious and he won the prize for best costume." The Reverend Malcolm Kitchen built his own replica of R2-D2 in his manse in Nottingham. Bev Smith, a reporter from the local ITV television station, discovered that the robot had been put on show in Nottingham City Center and even managed to interview the machine. The reverend spoke about how his R2-D2 was constructed and how he would be incorporating it into his sermons.

My mother is a real craft ace and she helped me construct a magnificent wedge-shaped Star Wars *spaceship from cardboard and silver foil. The cockpit was half of a clear plastic sphere from a vending machine and the rocket boosters were the caps from bottles of "Matey" bubble bath. Naturally, the ship became Darth Vader's personal flagship and it went to war against the Landspeeder. Unfortunately, the homemade craft proved to be as flimsy as the actual craft used by the Empire in the* Star Wars *movies and fell to pieces by the end of the summer holiday.*

Also keeping boredom at bay was a new range of Denys Fisher *Star Wars* kits, which were first advertised in the press in August. Palitoy had turned down the opportunity to distribute the range, as Geoff Maisey explains. "At that time, Palitoy felt that the *Star Wars* kits were specialist items, not mainstream toys, so they passed and Denys Fisher took on the range." The originator of the kits was American company MPC, which was owned by the Fundimensions division of CBC Products Corporation, which was in turn owned by General Mills. The route via which the kits trickled down to Denys Fisher seems easy enough to trace. However, *Star Wars* kits were also sold in Britain in German-language Kenner packaging with a sticker stating that instructions in English were enclosed and that the origin was Canada. The source was the MPC factory in Concord, Ontario, that produced bilingual French-English kits for the Canadian domestic market and also for Meccano's European operation.

No matter where the kits came from, fans could construct Darth Vader TIE Fighter, Luke Skywalker X-Wing Fighter, C-3PO and the all-important R2-D2. The plastic kit version of the little droid was absolutely fantastic, with a retractable third leg, extending computer interface arm and removable panel exposing his innards. The C-3PO model was molded in a golden brown color, so fans could construct it without painting and still have a reasonable-looking version of the droid. The arms, head and waist were held in place via an elastic band, which allowed a degree of articulation. The handsome X-Wing Fighter kit incorporated a hinge which allowed the wings to unfold as they did on the "real" spacecraft. Included were a removable R2-D2 and a very basic-looking pilot figure (the only letdown with the kit). The Darth Vader TIE Fighter was also a very faithful reproduction of the spacecraft seen on the screen, although it was supplied with undercarriage that was not in the film. "They were very nicely detailed kits, very much to scale," says Laurie Calvert. "They looked right, so I was very pleased with them. I couldn't understand why a TIE Fighter wasn't released so I ended up making one of my own."

There was a bonus in purchasing the *Star Wars* models, in that an array of interesting facts and figures was included in the instructions. R2-D2 was described as being a Class A Starship Maintenance/Repair Technician constructed by the Imperial Cybernetics Corporation. His serial number was R2-D2/Y477090. C-3PO had been constructed by the same company with a class/type: Servant/Domestic Translator. His serial number was C-3PO/Z195A46 and he had Class C programming. The descriptions of both droids read like intergalactic sales brochures. The X-Wing Fighter instructions revealed that the craft were powered by four 3.2 kg/parsic thrust ion rocket engines and were able to carry two 250-kiloton proton torpedoes or one 500-kiloton torpedo. The additional information provided with Darth

Vader's TIE Fighter was the most detailed of all. Standard TIE Fighters were described as being "powered by 2 solar converting ionization engines, with a combined thrust of 9.15 kg/parsic. These expendable and cheap fighters are not given any defensive shielding which keeps them fast, light and maneuverable. When necessary, these abilities provide protection through evasive action." Regarding Vader's craft: "The Sith Lord's own fighter is faster, more maneuverable & deadly, with its twin laser bolt cannons, than its predecessors."[3]

There was an additional kit produced for the range which was not distributed in Britain. Darth Vader was cast in a similar scale to the C-3PO and R2-D2 kits and featured glow-in-the-dark eyes and lightsaber. British fans were still able to find rare items, if they knew where to look. "I knew of a local model shop which imported models from America," remembers Pete Dummer. "I picked up the Darth Vader kit there, which at the time was a real find. None of my friends had one and they were really quite jealous."

Making your own film was perhaps the ultimate for *Star Wars* fans, and 8mm film camera equipment was available fairly cheaply to the home market. Anthony Luke from Newcastle produced *The Elementia*, featuring an alien invasion which was only thwarted by the frequencies of the Tyne Tees Television station. Laurie Calvert also turned his hand to filmmaking that summer. "I was 16 in the summer of '78," says Calvert. "Me and my friends decided to make a Super 8 movie. Two and a half minutes long and it was about a sci-fi baddie accidentally destroying his own base. We called it *Space Wars* because we couldn't think of anything more imaginative! We then made another film called *4 or 5* where C-3PO and R2-D2 crashland and can't figure out where they are. By that time, I had decided to change tack with my choice of career. I had been inspired by *Star Wars* to change from working in the aerodynamics industry to take up a career in special effects. Nearly all of my friends who I made *Star Wars* films with ended up with careers in the film industry."

Another popular summer tradition in Britain in the 1970s (and today) is organizing local carnivals which incorporate a procession of floats, marching bands and costume characters. Back then, however, people tended to spend a great deal of effort on home-made costumes, and health and safety was not an issue in constructing elaborate rolling attractions. Naturally, *Star Wars* became a popular theme. Paul Harrington joined in with the Ringwood carnival as a child, dressing as Ben Kenobi and riding with other children in a replica of Luke Skywalker's Landspeeder. He recalls,

> My dad, my uncle and their neighbors built the Landspeeder. The mums and aunties were responsible for the costumes. The Landspeeder was built on an old trailer featuring the front grille from my dad's Vauxhall Viva—it even had lights under it for the night procession. They entered Ringwood carnival pretty much every year in the late '70s but this was my favorite by a long shot. I think we won first prize and the mayor or somebody asked us if we'd like to enter Bournemouth Carnival too![4]

David F. Chapman recalls, "In our little town, we had an annual carnival, and my dad was a fan of dressing up for it. After we'd seen the movie, we dressed up in *Star Wars* gear. I was dressed as Luke, my hero. My dad dressed as Vader. We couldn't get a proper helmet for him, so we made one out of a balaclava and a plastic bucket cut to shape. Sure, he had a square top to his head, but with the cape on and the grill on his face from an old stereo speaker, he looked great!"[5]

The Westcliff-on-Sea Classic entered carnivals every year, as did cinemas all over Britain. "During our run of *Star Wars*, we constructed a float for the 20th August Rochford Carnival procession," says Derek Dorking. He continues:

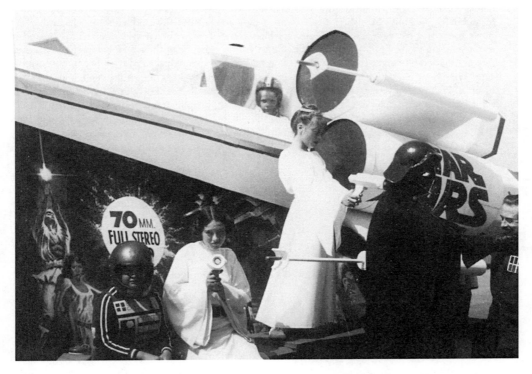

Above and following page: The Westcliff-on-Sea Odeon put a huge amount of effort into their carnival float (courtesy Derek Dorking).

It was organized by the manager Ron Stewart, who was quite a local celebrity due to his enthusiasm for publicity. We built a *Star Wars* display on a 20-foot-long trailer, the kind with two wheels that you might use for car recovery. It was a big X-Wing Fighter mock-up out of hardboard, with broom handles as the guns on the wings. We had got from 20th Century-Fox one of the huge posters that were used for the London Underground and we cut it in half and put it each side of the float to obscure the supports under the model. The canopy lifted up and the model was large and strong enough for someone to sit in. That person was my girlfriend Julie's brother, because he was fairly small. We dressed him in a red football kit, specially decorated pilot's vest and a crash helmet! The overall effect was really good. The cinema still had that dodgy Vader costume though, but Ron Stewart (who dressed as Grand Moff Tarkin on the day of the carnival) was very friendly with a man from Tigon Films, who knew somebody at 20th Century-Fox, and he managed to get hold of a Stormtrooper outfit. I'd made a Tusken Raider outfit and also a Princess Leia gown for Julie. I even persuaded my brother Robin to dress as Obi-Wan Kenobi. He was mobbed by the kids and they all wanted to meet him. Children from our cinema's Kids Club dressed up in various interpretations of *Star Wars* characters and they won first prize. The entire assembly that had been on the trailer was then parked outside the cinema entrance to bring to attention our showing of the film.

After that, I set about improving the Darth Vader costume the cinema had. I made the helmet much more accurate, and constructed quite good replicas of the chest box and belt. What made the difference was when the assistant manager got hold of a glass fiber Don Post Darth Vader mask. Even here, I ended up changing the eye lenses and putting in a proper grill in order to make it more accurate.

Summer Reading

Star Wars Weekly #29 (August 23) featured the story "Star Duel." Although the Drexel civil war was over, Crimson Jack's Star Destroyer was waiting above the planet. Han Solo, Princess Leia and Chewbacca had lessened the odds considerably when they had been aboard the ship by sabotaging all of Crimson Jack's one-man fighter craft, leaving only three of them in spaceworthy condition. Jolli led the trio of fighter craft against the Millennium Falcon, anxious as always to prove she is as good as any man. Han Solo and Luke Skywalker manned the gun ports as they had done in the *Star Wars* movie. The resulting battle left both the Millennium Falcon and Jolli's fighter craft crippled but when she sent a request to Crimson Jack for help, she was callously told that she would have to make it on her own. Han Solo had one ace left up his sleeve: While he and Chewbacca were aboard the pirate star destroyer, they had secretly wiped the memory banks of its navigational computer, which would have left Crimson Jack and his crew marooned in that area of space. Wearing breath masks, Han Solo and Crimson Jack rendezvoused between their craft to exchange vital parts for the Millennium Falcon in return for the navigation discs. As soon as the exchange is made, dozens of Jack's spacesuited men arrived. Jolli joined the fray in her crippled Y-Wing, gunning down her crewmates and smashing her ship into the conning tower of the pirate star destroyer. Crimson Jack was so distracted by seeing his spacecraft damaged beyond feasible repair that he failed to notice as he draws his sidearm that Han had already drawn his. One shot was all it took to rid the space lanes of its greatest scourge.

"Star Duel" was very much in keeping with the spirit of *Star Wars*, although some readers might have been sorry to see the end of two fantastic villains in Crimson Jack and Jolli. The story introduced the concept that a starship's protective force field (referred to in *Star Wars* as a shield) would protect someone against the effects of being in outer space and that they would only need to wear the equivalent of scuba diving equipment. The spacecraft featured in the story were mostly derived from *The Star Wars Sketchbook* including one of the pirate fighters being based on the TIE Boarding Craft that was later used as the TIE Bomber in the *Star Wars* saga.

Issue #8 of *Star Wars Poster Monthly* contained a profile of special effects technicians in "The Special Effects Wizards" by John May. "Until recently the skills of these men went largely unrecognized," wrote May. "No matter how sophisticated the final results were, the technicians and craftsmen who produced them remained firmly in the background. Now, with *Star Wars* and other such effects extravaganzas, the effects men are even getting fan mail."[6] Dr. M.F. Marten speculated in the article "The Ins and Outs of Space Travel" about the future course of true-life space exploration. It was clear however that *Star Wars* fans would not be able to jump into anything even resembling the Millennium Falcon in their own lifetimes. In "Ben Kenobi—Man or Legend," Brian Shepherd painted a vivid picture of the venerable character. Regarding the Force, Shepherd put forward the idea that a Jedi "may well have his own 'signature' in this energy field, a clue dropped casually by Darth Vader to an uncomprehending Tarkin. 'He is here ... a stirring in the Force, of a kind that I have only felt in the presence of my old master.'"[7] The article was a rare example of reference to the Force in the British media (albeit aimed at the U.S.) which contrasted to America, where much discussion was taking place on the subject. Writing for *Science Fantasy Film Classics*, Irving Karchmar seemed to attempt to present the Force as fact by connecting it to alleged theories of Albert Einstein, Zen Masters, Shaolin priests and Kirlian photography. Frank Allnutt's view of the Force was no less literal, as presented in his book *The Force of Star Wars*, which stated that Christianity was in fact the message behind the film. George Lucas gave his take on the Force in the *Making of Star Wars* documentary: "It's sort of boiling down religion to a very basic concept. The fact that there is some deity or some power or some force that sort of controls our destiny, or works for good and also works for evil has always been basic in mankind."[8]

Issue #9 of the *Official Star Wars Poster Monthly* contained "The Brain of the Droid." Dr. M.F. Marten extrapolated upon what was known about R2-D2 and C-3PO to present a detailed examination of robot intelligence, while John May profiled Ralph McQuarrie. "Systems in Collision" by Brian Shepherd focused on the conflict between the Imperial forces and the rebellion. "With Palpatine in his palace, the galaxy is effectively ruled by a bureaucratic elite and the various Imperial Governors—the latter assuming the position of warlords in a semi–feudal society, who hold power by terror in a rapidly disintegrating society." While that statement did not jibe precisely with the concept of the rebels confronting a single, powerful Empire, Shepherd did add weight to the "true" nature of Imperial Stormtroopers: "In *Star Wars* we see in visual terms the workings of tyranny. The Imperial soldiery cloned and institutionalized from youth, bear numbers, not names. Their white body armor adds a further sinister flavor. Stormtroopers are designed for terror."[9] The emperor's name, Palpatine, was derived from the prologue to the *Star Wars* novel, which is another example of obscure information being brought to the fore by the *Official Poster Monthly*.

In September, *Star Wars Fan Club Newsletter* #4 announced the result of the "Name the Newsletter Contest": Preston Pastle of Avon, Ohio, won with his entry "Bantha Tracks." There was an exciting update on the *Star Wars* sequel, revealing that the title had been announced on August 4 as being *The Empire Strikes Back*. While this was the first time that the majority of fans had encountered the title, industry insiders had been aware of it as a "working title" thanks to the January 28, 1978, *Hollywood Reporter* and the February issue of *Screen International*. The article confirmed that George Lucas would not be directing this time; Irvin Kershner would be taking the reins. Stuart Freeborn and John Williams would again be taking up their respective responsibilities from *Star Wars*. Norman Reynolds, *Star Wars'* art director, would be production designer and British special effects impresario Brian Johnson would take over as special effects supervisor. His past work had included *2001: A Space Odyssey* (working with Douglas Trumbull), *The Day the Earth Caught Fire*, *Alien* (which was currently in production) and Gerry Anderson productions including *Space: 1999 and Thunderbirds*. Perhaps the most exciting news of all was that, along with the main character trio announced in the last newsletter (R2-D2, C-3PO, Chewbacca), Darth Vader would be returning. More emphasis would be placed on the characters and their development and the romantic rivalry between Luke Skywalker and Han Solo for Princess Leia would be resolved. Also revealed was that preparations had already begun in the art department and special effects department, with special effects photography due to start in October and principal photography beginning in February 1979. *The Empire Strikes Back* was tentatively scheduled for release in the spring of 1980.

Look at the Size of That Thing!

In September, there was an amazing Palitoy television commercial for *Star Wars* action figures and toys featuring the Death Star, Landspeeder and X-Wing Fighter. The Death Star was a genuine innovation from Palitoy. Bob Brechin designed the major item in the range completely in-house, almost entirely from cheap-to-produce cardboard. The pressure had been on because the toy was due to be displayed at the Birmingham NEC Toy Fair on the 29th January 1978. According to Brechin,

> The Kenner version of the Death Star toy was based on very large plastic moldings. Injection molding requires large production runs to make the process economic. Kenner probably had four times the market in the States as Palitoy in the U.K., so could justify investing in large expensive steel tooling molds for injection molding. We decided to save money on tooling and produce most of our version of the Death Star in printed card with smaller additional plastic accessories. We also decided to make it look more like the Death Star in shape, albeit only one half of the "beast," whereas the Kenner version was really just a segment, like half a piece of a peeled orange. I sat down with designer Brian Turner to work out the basic design of the product. We designed the plain card construction, then invited Dave Barnacle at Ray Hastings Studio to work up the colored illustrations for each *room*.

Dave Barnacle recalls, "The Death Star was a toy that I actually participated in creating. I produced the artwork on the toy itself. After a brief discussion with Palitoy marketing manager Geoff Maisey, I visited the Palitoy Design Department to be shown a mock-up of the playset and discussed with the designers Bob Brechin and Brian Turner how they visualized the artwork for the toy. Based on our discussions, I prepared a color mock-up of the playset."

Brechin picks up the story:

> Palitoy's marketing department needed to get Kenner approval and after this was confirmed, we got Dave to complete the final artworks for all the separate cardboard pieces. The wing cannons from the X-Wing Fighter were used to go in the gun emplacement. We needed some plastic clips to hold the assembled domed part to the base and decided to make the clip in two identical parts which could be injection-molded as a single impression. To aid a child in standing the action figures up, we developed a small circular clear injection-molded base with a pin which fitted into a hole in the figure's feet. Several of the bases were included with each toy. All things considered, I thought it turned out very well.

Brian Turner says,

> When I moved over to design, one of my first jobs was to work closely with Bob Brechin and Dave Barnacle on the Death Star, liaising with them on the artwork and card construction required for each room based on scenes from the film (e.g., the trash compactor). I designed the plastic clips that held

The Palitoy Death Star was the answer to many fan's dreams (courtesy Darren Simpson).

the card of the Death Star together, along with the rest of the plastic injection-molded components. Before working on the design, I went to see the film at the Odeon in Leicester. The experience was great and inspiring and it certainly showcased a terrific range of toys and characters.

In addition to contributing to the toy's design, Barnacle was required to produce the packaging. "The Death Star playset box was one of the few that I was required to design from scratch. I gained approval of a mock-up of the box following the style of the rest of the *Star Wars* range. The photography took place at Neville Chadwick Photography Ltd. in Wigston, Leicestershire. I set up and directed the shoot and the boy used in the shot is my son David Jr."

The finished Death Star was indeed a beast, standing 12 inches high, incorporating many different rooms, a control room and a working Trash Compactor complete with a chute and escape hatch. The action figures and the accompanying vehicles were extremely important in keeping *Star Wars* alive in the minds of children. Not only could they recreate scenes from the film, they could act out their own adventures on a grand scale, with everyday household items becoming props and scenery. The small size of the figures meant that they could travel everywhere with their owners, even if the tiny plastic weapons were often lost in the sand pit, or down the back of the sofa.

Star Wars *Marches Onwards*

Star Wars was still being distributed to outlying areas of Britain in September, as the lengthy runs at cinemas ended and prints became available. The Manchester area provides a snapshot of the process, as its satellite towns were issued *Star Wars*. The Withington Scala and the Heaton Moor New Savoy received the film on September 3 and the Romiley Forum and Middleton Palace Twins on the 10th. The Worsley Unit Four cinema began its run on October 1 and the Marple Regent cinema on the 22nd. *Star Wars* was still showing at the Dominion Theatre, where it was seen by people who could not see it in their local area. "It was around autumn time that my father realized that I had a strong interest in *Star Wars*," says Joe Sales. He continues:

> I had been collecting the comics and some of the toys. I also had the annual. He found that the film was not showing in our home town of Aylesbury (although the town is only 36 miles from London) but according to the listings in the *Daily Telegraph* it was still at the Dominion Theatre and he suggested that he get us both tickets. We made the journey in October. I remember the huge *Star Wars* sign at the Dominion, which had light effects built into it. In the foyer, you could buy the program book and there was a life-sized cut-out standee of Darth Vader brandishing his lightsaber, which looked amazing. I loved the film and how Ben Kenobi was played by an Englishman—Alec Guinness—and I therefore identified with him a little bit. I have learned since through looking through old newspapers that *Star Wars* was not too far away from me in Aylesbury at that time. The Chandos Cinema, a small, cozy venue in the nearby town of Buckingham, got its hands on a print from Sunday, October 29. The advert in the paper included the words in capitals: "WE'VE GOT IT AT LAST!!"

Star Wars was also available for re-release to the major regional venues that had previously shown it, although the only one that chose to do so was the Odeon Newcastle for a two-week run from October 29.

Star Wars' success inevitably led to people questioning why Americans were reaping the rewards from what was a largely British-made film. Cyril Howard, managing director of Pinewood Studios, put his own spin on the situation: "In the short term, anything that creates employment [in the British film industry] is good. Otherwise it is sad, because the money will not flow back to this country but back to the source. Why is British finance so sluggish? God knows. Scared witless like the rest of the country, I suppose. No one wants to invest in anything, do they?"[10] Facing public criticism for not financing profitable films that had been made in Britain (in the case of *Star Wars*, actually filmed at EMI Elstree), Michael Deely, managing director of EMI Films, said, "As for *Star Wars* and *The Omen*, we all wish these pictures had been financed by EMI instead of 20th Century-Fox. Had we been established in America three years ago, we would have been an obviously appropriate company to which the American creators of these projects may have brought their scripts. Unfortunately, at that time, no British company was in Hollywood and the pictures (and the profits) were made by Americans"[11] Peter Beale has his own viewpoint:

> The *Star Wars* production was made in Britain. The money was spent there. The risk and the intellectual asset came from America. All of the finance came from America along with the distribution. So that is normal. Britain did very nicely. A lot of people were employed. Taxes were paid. Studios were rented and that is the normal thing. Britain didn't have the finance and wouldn't have financed it because at the time it was a high risk film. In fact, all of the studios in England at that time were empty. Andrew Mitchell was the managing director of Elstree Studios, and I made the deal with him to rent the entire facility. When we began facing budget problems during the filming, I discussed with Andrew that EMI could defer some of their fees for the rental for a percentage of the profits from *Star Wars* but they wouldn't do it. So in fact they had the opportunity to receive some of the profits but they didn't go for it.

What Does It Take to Be a Space Pilot?

Official Star Wars Poster Monthly #10 contained the article "What It Takes to Be a Space Pilot," where Dr. M.F. Marten declared, "Let's be clear about one thing. The apparently startling transformation of Luke Skywalker from farm hand to X-Wing hero is not the way it happens. It takes hard work, as Luke Skywalker would admit."[12] So much for George Lucas' careful plotting to have Luke being an expert owner-flyer of the Incom T-16 which had identical controls to the Incom T-65 X-Wing, being able to hit a wamp rat with ease and being able to fly through a canyon at high speed. Not to mention the scene in the novel (and on the cutting room floor) of Biggs Darklighter vouching for his friend as being "the best bush pilot in the outer-rim territories."[13] Marten was correct of course but *Star Wars* is fantasy, not science! *The Star Wars Snowball* by John May neatly summed up the success of the film up until that time: "It is well over a year now since *Star Wars* was first launched on an unsuspecting public—and for many people, life has not been the same since. More than 88 million tickets have been sold in the U.S. alone, a gold mine at the box office worth some $219 million. From America, the movie went to Australia, where it exploded all previous box office records, and then arrived in Europe where it earned another $100 million. In Paris alone they calculated that one million chairs had been occupied by spellbound spacehounds." May's article included the public reaction to the characters and the incredible merchandising explosion. "Now it is possible to dress up, wash and dry yourself, sleep, decorate your home, take notes at school, collect stamps, have parties and even blow bubbles—all with *Star Wars*... [T]he snowball just keeps on rolling it seems and is getting bigger all the time."[14]

The story in *Star Wars Weekly* #31, "The Hunter," had Walt Simonson and Bob Wiacek as guest artists. A new character, the bounty hunter Valance, encountered Don-Wan Kihotay bedridden at the Telos 4 Medical Station. Readers would have remembered that Kihotay had been one of Han Solo's hired *guns* from "New Planets, New Perils." The old man's delirious mumblings included Han Solo, Chewbacca and "a boy and his droid." This reminded Valance of an information tape issued by the Empire which stated that they were searching for a boy who kept droids as companions. Valance had an all-encompassing hatred of droids and *the boy's* apparent friendship with a pair of mechanicals only added to his fury. Unbeknownst to Valance, the boy that Kihotay was actually referring to was Jim the Starkiller Kid, another one of Han Solo's hired hands. After attempting to capture Jaxxon, Valance and his men faced off against the man-rabbit, Amazia and Jim. Valance was defeated, and once alone in his ship he peeled at the skin on the left side of his face, revealing that half of his body was in fact mechanical. In his earlier days, Valance had been an Imperial Stormtrooper who had been injured during a skirmish with the Rebels. It was a terrible fate for a robot-hater, that in order to save his life, he had been turned into a cyborg by the well-meaning staff of the Telos 4 Medical Station. Valance was even more determined to find this *boy* being harbored by the Rebels and his wretched droids. Some interesting ideas were introduced in the story such as Luke Skywalker having a bounty placed on his head by the Empire, even though his name was not known. This was also the first Marvel story to introduce the concept that Stormtroopers were ordinary human beings, which was in contradiction to the *Star Wars Official Poster Monthly* (and perhaps the films), in which they were clones.

* ❋ *

"The Hunter" was one of my childhood favorite stories. I considered it to be such a well-crafted story, with some of the best artwork seen up until that time. This was the world of Star Wars *outside of the conflict between Rebel and Imperial and I found it fascinating.*

Valance and his men were realistically drawn, kitted out in their own personalized armor and weapons. I didn't mind the rabbit-like character of Jaxxon, especially as he was depicted in realistic black-and-white artwork rather than the Technicolor splurge of the American version.

Star Wars. Ready, Set, Go!

On October 15, the *Star Wars* Corporation sponsored a sports and equestrian event at Everdon Hall, Daventry, Northamptonshire. Proceeds went to Riding for the Disabled and other charities. Gary Kurtz, David

The gigantic Star Wars presence at the Cross Country Team Event was only advertised in a tiny local newspaper.

Prowse, Carrie Fisher and Peter Mayhew were all happy to speak to the public. Prowse was also on Green Cross Code Man duty (albeit in plain clothes) and was handing out road safety badges. Mayhew appeared dressed in his full Chewbacca costume before changing back to his human form. Lucasfilm set up a long table covered in a *Star Wars* bedcover, each side of which were two identical *Star Wars* pieces of prop scenery from the Death Star. Behind the stall, there was a banner reading *Star Wars: The Empire Strikes Back.* Carrie Fisher and company wore large blue circular badges reading *The Empire Strikes Back.* There was also a group of Stormtroopers at the Daventry event, an R2-D2 prop and a life-sized model of a Jerba, an alien beast of burden from Tatooine seen in the background in *Star Wars'* Mos Eisley scenes. It was more in the style of a donkey though than a horse but that did not put off Fisher, who was photographed, a full glass of wine in hand, sitting astride it. A *Star Wars* team entered the cross country race. Simon Dabbin was one of the fans in attendance. "On Sunday, October 15, I went with my mum and dad to see the *Star Wars* cast at Evendon Hall. I met Dave Prowse and he gave me a Green Cross Code badge. I also met Peter Mayhew and Carrie Fisher. I saw R2-D2 and lots of Stormtroopers. We had a great day and enjoyed meeting the stars who were all very friendly, especially Dave Prowse, who told us that the next *Star Wars* film would not be ready until May 1980. It's a long time to wait but I bet it will be worth it."[15] The local paper's coverage of the event was extremely low-key. It reported that the event raised a record amount for the designated charities but only chose to print a small picture of David Prowse. The *Star Wars* contribution to Daventry had been one-of-a-kind and the *Star Wars* corporation Lucasfilm would not lend its support to another British event again in such fashion.

Summer events were also taking Derek Dorking far and wide. "Nineteen seventy-eight was a fantastic time," says Dorking. "I attended a science fiction convention at the Fulcrum Centre, Slough, where I dressed as Luke and Julie as Leia. Anthony Daniels and Dave Prowse were there doing a signing. The organizer suggested that me and Julie could do a rope-swing up on stage. Well, we were not going to do that! So instead there was a photo shoot of Anthony Daniels driving my R2-D2 model." Sarah Baker-Saunders was in attendance too, and she recalls:

> I was made aware of the event by reading about it in a daily newspaper and that Anthony Daniels was going to one of the guests. With this small news article I managed to persuade my mum to allow me to go! I managed to talk my sister and her boyfriend to take me down from Manchester all the way to Slough by train and experience my first convention. It was a huge adventure going to London, then on to Slough, then finding the Fulcrum Centre. The day was a blur, really. I was dressed from neck to waist with *Star Wars* badges which really embarrassed my sister and boyfriend! I remember the dealer tables, the models on display, particularly the Denys Fisher R2-D2 and C-3PO kits with little lights, and reading that the special effects department at Elstree Studios had painted and made them. I remember Anthony Daniels on stage where he talked about the suit and how bad it was and that the new *Star Wars* film was set on an ice planet. Afterwards there was a huge queue for his autograph and I managed to get one. He asked me where he was amongst all the badges and I pointed him out (as I had checked before meeting him). I still have the autograph, the program from the day and the badges!

Derek Dorking went yet further with *Star Wars* promotions:

> Later in the year, I appeared as Luke Skywalker, with Artoo, at a fete. People were invited to drive around the robot and I drew the raffle (as Luke) after opening the fete. Julie and I also appeared in costume on September 29, 1978, at a black tie charity dinner event at the London Hilton Park Lane. I did a little lightsaber training with Obi Wan and drove Artoo about a bit. We had a free table for dinner

and, once changed into our dinner outfits, we could enjoy the floor show. One up-and-coming little act was a very young impressionist, Gary Wilmot. Some of the guests were Barbara Windsor, Charles Hawtrey, Roy Kinnear and many others. My events usually came from people who had seen the *Blue Peter* show and the BBC passed on the letters for me to deal with. Lots were from little kids asking me to build them a robot R2! It was all a bit daunting as I was only 18. I still have all the letters somewhere.

Returning to Tatooine

The story "Skywalker" began in issue #33 (September 21) of *Star Wars Weekly*. A tale from Luke's past, it began with a large meeting of Tatooine youth at Beggar's Canyon. Racing was the main reason that Luke and Biggs Darklighter were there and the story opened with them pitting their flying skills against each other and other teenage pilots in their T-16 Skyhoppers through the narrow twists and turns of the canyon. The race meeting was interrupted by a large war party of rampaging Tusken Raiders, armed with blasters along with their razor-sharp gaderffii sticks. As the group's only radio communicator was inoperative, Luke decided to make a run for his Skyhopper with Biggs, in order to spread the warning of the attack. Before the pair could reach the craft, Biggs was wounded by a flying gaderffii stick which had evidently been drenched in deadly sand bat venom. Luke took off with the wounded Biggs, but heavy blaster fire forced him to dive into Beggar's Canyon. The only way to pass though the canyon from this point was via the Diablo Cut, an underground route which had never been successfully negotiated in a Skyhopper. With Biggs drifting into unconsciousness, Luke skillfully directed the Skyhopper through the Diablo Cut and crash-landed at his uncle's farm. Biggs would receive medical treatment via the Med pack at the farm and the local militia could be called out by Uncle Owen to deal with the Tusken Raiders. *Skywalker* was derived from issue #17 of the American comic where it was titled "Crucible." It has a reputation as one of the finest *Star Wars* stories that Marvel ever produced and it would be reprinted many times in the British weekly comic. Archie Goodwin was credited as writer-editor with the plot by Chris Claremont. Herb Trimpe and Allen Milgrom were the guest artists. The depiction of Luke hunting wamp rats in his Landspeeder may have been inspired by Dr. M.F. Marten's poster magazine article "Life on Tatooine." Marten's mention of Luke getting his thrills by racing his T-16 Skyhopper through Beggar's Canyon could well have provided inspiration for the racing scene in the comic.

In *Official Star Wars Poster Monthly* #11, Marten presented a detailed discussion of faster-than-light travel in the article "Hyperspace!" John May profiled Kenny Baker, Anthony Daniels, Peter Mayhew and David Prowse in "The Men Behind the Masks." A profile of John Williams was this issue's main article. "The *Star Wars* Symphony" by Zak Jones listed *Midway, Black Sunday, Earthquake, The Towering Inferno, Sugarland Express, Jaws* and *Close Encounters of the Third Kind* as being among the composer's previous film soundtracks. Williams also had an extensive career in recording music for American television including *The Wide Country, The Time Tunnel, Land of the Giants* and *The Cowboys.* According to Jones, "It was Spielberg who introduced Williams to George Lucas, in June 1975. By the end of the year, Williams was contracted to do the score." Williams was quoted as saying, "George and I both felt that the music should be full of high adventure and the soaring spirits of the characters in the film." Jones continued, "Perhaps most satisfying for

John Williams, a man who also conducts a number of major American orchestras, his *Star Wars* music produced an interest in classical music in general."[16]

The Empire Strikes Marvel

The Marvel post–*Star Wars* storyline picked up again in *Star Wars Weekly* #35 (cover date October 4). "The Empire Strikes" began with the Rebel heroes heading back to their base in the Millennium Falcon. In midflight, Luke fell into a strange coma-like state after meditating with the Force. Fearing that Luke was near death, Han brought the Millennium Falcon out of hyperspace in order to seek medical help, but an Imperial Light Cruiser showed up and chased the Millennium Falcon in the direction of the Wheel, a gigantic spacegoing gambling hub, which had a policy of sending people who had run out of credit to the Spice Mines of Kessel. Han decided on a gamble of his own and docked the Millennium Falcon inside one of the Wheel's gigantic hangar bays without landing permission. Here was a refuge from the Imperials and a chance to get medical help for Luke. Finding that the captain of the Light Cruiser, Yul Brynner lookalike Commander Strom, was bold enough to dock with the Wheel and send Stormtroopers after them, the rebel heroes scattered throughout the space station, leaving Luke in the care of R2-D2 and C-3PO, who carried his master in his arms. The rebel heroes were all captured by Wheel Security, and Luke was brought to a medical center aboard the station. R2-D2 and C-3PO's actions to save their master caught the interest of the Wheel's computer, Master Com, who looked like a muscular version of C-3PO. The Wheel's administrator, "Senator" Greyshade, was the embodiment of a '70s lothario complete with a moustache and medallion; he remembered Princess Leia from his days as a politician and rekindled his romantic interest in her. To guarantee that Leia would be unable to leave the Wheel, Greyshade arranged for Han Solo and Chewbacca to enter a gladiatorial contest aboard the station, unaware that their opposite number had done so. Han Solo reached the final death match but found that one of his opponents was none other than Chewbacca.

This cliffhanging situation would not be resolved, for the time being at least, because *Star Wars Weekly* took a break from the story to bring readers the yarn "Silent Drifting," featured in issues #43 and #44. The story was meant to have taken place directly after the rebel heroes had dealt with Crimson Jack in issue #30. Han used an old trick of his to make the Millennium Falcon appear to be lifeless before springing into action to deal with a pair of TIE Fighters. Princess Leia said that her father had told her a tale of Ben Kenobi using a similar technique in the days of the Old Republic. The story then went into flashback to that time, when Ben Kenobi was a passenger aboard a luxurious passenger spacecraft. A C-3PO-style droid 68-RKO stated that he was traveling with the intention of entering the service of Bail Organa and requested that Obi-Wan act as his owner for the duration of the trip. The anti-droid element aboard ship was confirmed by a drunken lout objecting to RKO's presence; Obi-Wan made short work of him with his lightsaber. Augustus Tryll, a corrupt businessman involved in slaving amongst other diabolical practices, offered Obi-Wan a partnership in his business but he refused. While traversing an asteroid field, the passenger ship was threatened by small group of armed spaceships manned by pirates. Utilizing his military experience and his use of the Force, Obi-Wan was able to direct the passenger craft's minuscule armament to fire upon the pirates at the most opportune moment and destroy them. The pirates had evidently been attracted by a signal from aboard the ship and a passenger lynch mob accused Tryll. Obi-Wan stepped in and threw his ignited lightsaber at a fermentation device and destroyed it. Unbeknownst to anyone else, the machine had been emitting microwave signals that the pirates had picked up. The moral of the story seemed to be that even the most disagreeable person should be defended against false accusations and from summary justice.

Enter Mary Jo Duffy

"Silent Drifting" was published in issue #24 of the American *Star Wars* comic directly after the conclusion of the "Wheel" saga begun by *The Empire Strikes*. The writer was Mary Jo Duffy, with Archie Goodwin credited as editor. Duffy began her career with Marvel as assistant editor to Goodwin when the work commenced on the *Star Wars* comic. She remembers,

> I was a fan of some of the cast members before *Star Wars* ever came out and I absolutely lost my mind over the movie. But there were people who already had the writing assignment and I wasn't established as a writer at all. I was quite new but on the other hand you always get into a situation where somebody misses their deadline or in those days it was before FedEx and before the Internet or before even scanners and all different things like that, so if a package was delayed in the mail we might not have an issue ready to go. As a result, it was a practice to have extra stand-alone stories of absolutely every series sitting in a drawer somewhere in case the worst happened. I just clamored—I love these characters. I love this movie. Let me write the fill ins for *Star Wars*.[17]

The reason that Duffy's "Silent Drifting" was used is unknown, but the final result was excellent. It presented a realistic look at the Old Republic time period, although her vision would be replaced in time by the *Star Wars* prequel films.

The Making of the Poster Magazine

The techniques used to make *Star Wars* was proving to be fertile ground for the Bunch Associates writing team. Issues #12, 13 and 14 of the *Official Star Wars Poster Monthly* had a "Making of" theme. Dr. M.F. Marten focused on Rick Baker and the process of bringing the Cantina characters to life, describing how Baker had already built up a portfolio of work before he met with Gary Kurtz and George Lucas. It included David Carradine's makeup in *Death Race 2000* and the gorilla suit for the 1976 *King Kong* remake (he also performed as Kong). "It turned out I was one of the last people [the *Star Wars* people] talked to," said Baker. "They had just seen about every artist in town who did makeup and appliances." Awarded the contract, Baker assembled a team of four animators—Doug Beswick, Laine Liska, Jon Berg and Phil Tippett—in addition to his own assistant, Rob Bottin. "Any shot of a creature drinking, talking or reacting to something when you don't see the main bar or Mark Hamill or Alec Guinness was our stuff," explained Baker. Doug Beswick said, "I think it was the greatest experience of my life just to be connected, even in a small way, with a film of that potential and scope. If they do another one, I hope to get the chance to work on it."[18]

"The Soundmaster" by John May detailed how Ben Burtt had graduated from Allegheny College in Pennsylvania with a physics degree before breaking into the movie business via commercials and TV shows, eventually working on *Killdozer* and *Death Race 2000*. Burtt's interest in sound landed him the *Star Wars* job and by all accounts he was a perfect choice. His determination to make every sound in *Star Wars* unique and other-worldly made him a permanent fixture at Lucasfilm.

The article "John Dykstra—Making Movie Magic" by Larry Hurgan revealed that Dykstra had been working on designs for a new computer-aided camera when he worked with Douglas Trumbull at his company Future General. Dykstra left that company to work on *Star Wars* and eventually perfected what became known as the Dykstraflex camera. Meanwhile, Trumbull completed his own version and put it to work on *Close Encounters*. Trumbull's engineer father had contributed to both cameras. According to Trumbull, the two effects companies worked cooperatively, sharing equipment as well as ideas. John May's "The Machines That Make Lines Move" profiled the computer animation produced by John Wash and Larry Cuba that had been used in the Rebel pilot briefing scene. Readers may have been surprised to learn that filmmaker Dan O'Bannon, who had starred in and provided the effects for the movie *Dark Star*, also contributed to the computer screen and control panel readouts for *Star Wars*. John May's article was very forward-looking, with the writer stating, "As for the future it seems (with computer animation) the only limit is the human imagination. As Larry Cuba puts it: 'The computer as a tool gives us a new way to explore motion, movement and the kind of imagery that we never really had the power to explore.'"[19] It was clear that the interest in how *Star Wars* was made had not diminished and that the *Star Wars Official Poster Monthly* was the ideal source for detailed explanations of many of the processes involved. "I became pretty much an expert on special effects," says John May. "I subsequently studied the history of special effects going back to its earliest days."

Palitoy's Challenge

With Christmas approaching, there was a scramble for *Star Wars* products, both from customers and retailers who were attempting to satisfy the insatiable need. "Once the toy range was widely available, vehicles and figures flew off the shelves," says Carole Deighton. She continued:

We soon found ourselves having to handle some potentially negative media coverage about the product shortages pre–Christmas and of course, all the disappointment that caused! We were inundated with calls from national newspapers, radio and TV and had specially prepared press statements explaining the reasons for the unexpected shortages. In the main, it was still positive publicity but Palitoy and Kenner weren't able to take advantage of the unprecedented demand as the *Star Wars* toy range had completely sold out. I believe there was some talk about the shortages having been deliberately manipulated in the States, but not so much over here. A lot has been said about the brains and planning behind the huge success of *Star Wars* Toys in the U.K. (and other merchandise), but with hindsight, it seems to me that the huge popularity was created, in the main, by the hugely enthusiastic movie going public and the ever-growing fan base and, of course, the media who, apart from genuinely rating the movie and seeing its evident success, lapped up stories about a new toy craze and that it [*Star Wars*] was #1 on the NATR's [National Association of Toy Retailers[Top Selling Toy List in the run-up to Christmas. We just did our best to try to control the unparalleled success and make it work as well as possible for our client. The toys were so well-crafted and photogenic and the figures so highly collectable that it wasn't really surprising the media got behind the phenomenon as much as they did—they were more than happy to feed their readers and TV audiences with 'the *Star Wars* hype' they wanted.

Geoff Maisey explains the reasons for the shortage of *Star Wars* stock. "The intensive p.r. and promotion had unfortunately worked too well and shelves were pretty much empty well before Christmas 1978. We were soundly castigated by the trade for not supporting our brand by letting it run out of stock—no mention of course that we had already taken a massive inventory risk ourselves on their behalf, which even so turned out to be totally inadequate." Peter Beale had every sympathy with the position that Palitoy was in. "If the retailers didn't give them the advance orders, they couldn't expect to have the stuff available when the film was a success. Palitoy went out on a limb and beyond and had a lot of stock. They ran out because of the success. How many millions of items were they expected to make?" *Star Wars Weekly* picked up on the lack of *Star Wars* toys in the shops but its report that there was a 20-year waiting list to stock *Star Wars* toys seems like a *slight* exaggeration.

Laurie Calvert was one of the fans left wanting. "The toy manufacturers hadn't got sufficient stocks into the shops, so there was not much to collect. I had amassed the blue and red Topps cards. I ended up with four or five sets of each. I had bought the soundtrack and the blueprints pack. There were also peripheral things like the stationery and bubble bath. Any film on television with one of the *Star Wars* actors in, I was watching. All of us fans were struggling to collect anything. We were keeping anything from the local newspaper, no matter how trivial."

I can speak of there being a lack of Star Wars *toys in the shops. Earlier in the year, my brother Paul had his heart set on a* Star Wars *vehicle. It was unusual for us to receive toys outside of birthdays and Christmas but our mum agreed to see what was available. When we all went shopping in Romford town center, it seemed as if we would have better luck in the deserts of Tatooine, for there was not a* Star Wars *action or figure or toy for sale anywhere. There was a large market stall at a shopping arcade in town which sold toys and sure enough, there was a sole Palitoy Landspeeder with a whopping big price tag. Mum decided to buy it as a present for both of us and Paul and I were so glad she did. That toy was played with to complete destruction over the next few years, with it being our only* Star Wars *vehicle. I have a few pieces left of it in a cupboard. Like good collectors everywhere, we did keep the box, though, and that is still in good shape!*

Winding Down the Year of Star Wars

November 25 was a noteworthy date: It was the day that *Star Wars* finally ended its titanic 48-week run at the Dominion Theatre, having ranked up £712,738 in the process. The Odeon Kensington was ready to wade in and began a fresh run from December 3, ready for the Christmas holiday season. Fans living in ITV's Anglia region were treated to a repeat of *The Making of Star Wars* but it may have been beyond their bedtimes, being broadcast at 11 p.m. As the end of the year loomed, one of the main points of discussion in *Star Wars Weekly* became the upcoming sequel and what the title would be. Some *Star*

Wars fans of course had already learned of the actual title from science fiction magazines, the *Star Wars Fan Club Newsletter* and/or *Official Poster Magazine* but an announcement had yet to be made in the comic. In November, a reader's letter reported that the sequel would be called *Empire Fights Back*. Whatever the title was going to be, a new *Star Wars* film was a very exciting prospect. Not a single image had been released from the film and even the title logo had yet to appear.

The storyline detailed in *Star Wars Weekly* took a major turn for the worse, if readers genuinely considered the comic to be the actual continuing events of the saga. Issue #45 (December 13) featured the continuation of the story "The Empire Strikes," where Han and Chewbacca were fighting in the same death match. While this was going on, Senator Greyshade had knocked out Commander Strom with a drugged glass of wine and made his way to his personal space yacht just in time to catch Luke and Leia attempting to steal it. Greyshade offered a deal where Princess Leia would go away with him in his yacht, which had been loaded with stolen Wheel profits, and Greyshade would order that the other rebel heroes be set free. None of them were aware that Darth Vader was speeding through hyperspace aboard a Star Destroyer to reach the Wheel, having learned that Princess Leia & Company were there.

Han and Chewbacca finally faced off against each other. There could be only one survivor. At Han's urging, Chewbacca shot him in the chest at point blank range, which seemed to be the end of many fan's favorite character. Luke and Leia had been watching on a view screen and their tears made Han Solo's apparent demise all the more moving. Readers would have to wait until after Christmas to learn if Han Solo had survived.

As a dedicated Han Solo fan, I felt devastated at the turn of events depicted in the story. I thought that Han Solo had actually died and that he would be missing not only from the comics but the film series too!

The December *Starburst* contained an update on George Lucas that would whet the appetite of *Star Wars* fans. According to the article, there would be a total of up to ten sequels, the last of which Lucas would direct himself "about 20 years from now."[20] The article reported that Lucas had set up new companies to deal with his various projects. Medway Productions would make smaller, more intimate films and handle the theatrical reissue of Lucas' hit film *American Graffiti*. Black Falcon Ltd. would be responsible for the merchandising of *Star Wars* and other films by Lucas (Black Falcon was an obscure reference to the 1940s comic strip Blackhawk that Lucas was a fan of). It is curious that the sequel movie was still referred by *Starburst* in December 1978 as *Star Wars II* when the title *The Empire Strikes Back* had long ago been revealed to the media. This might not be too surprising though, as articles were often written far in advance and *Starburst* was released well ahead of the date on the cover. Behind the scenes at *Star Wars Weekly*, the title *The Empire Strikes Back* was known but the news was intentionally held back by Dez Skinn. "I wanted to make a splash with issue 50 [due out in January 1979] announcing and featuring an article about *The Empire Strikes Back* was the cherry on the cake."

The Final Cinema Push

Despite all of the excitement surrounding *Star Wars*, there were areas of Britain which *still* had not received the film, even though it was almost Christmas. Joe Sales was even more thankful that he had seen the film in London, as he was still on the lookout for showings of *Star Wars* at his local cinema. "The film didn't show up at the Odeon Aylesbury until the second week in December 1978 [presumably with the print transferred from the Chandos, Buckingham], and only then as a Screen Three presentation—a screen that occasionally showed horror or soft porn double bills. *The Spy Who Loved Me* was in Screen Two (another deferred release), and *The Cat from Outer Space* in Screen One! I was ever so pleased to see *Star Wars* again. I saw it with both of my parents this time, so it was a real family experience." Aylesbury certainly was not the last area to see *Star Wars*. The Regal Cinema, Cromer, on the North Norfolk coast (judging from local newspaper advertising) opened on Wednesday, December 27. The Gatley Minor and the Hollinwood Minor, both satellite towns to Manchester, finally got the film on December 31. The Bury Classic received the film for the first time on the 31st, although the Bury Odeon had previously run it.

As cinemas that had not seen a first run of *Star Wars* were now fairly far and few between, the film became available for a Christmas release. Venues included the Croydon Town Hall Focus Cinema, Romford Odeon, Bolton Odeon, Leeds Odeon, Liverpool Odeon and Nottingham Odeon from December 17, Brighton Odeon on the 21st, the Cannon Hill Cinema Birmingham on the 24th and the Quinton Classic Birmingham from December 6. The Christmas run in some areas continued until the end of the school holiday in the first week of January. Perhaps the last venue in the whole of Britain to receive *Star Wars* was the Apollo Theatre Birmingham, which ran it for one week, from Monday, January 1, 1979. The initial release of *Star Wars* in Britain over the course of more than a year was quite a contrast to today when it would be shown in almost every available big venue almost instantaneously.

People receiving the *Guinness Book of Records* for Christmas would have been able to read that *Star Wars* was listed as the highest grossing film of all time, with it apparently having earned £24,000,000. The 1979 *Star Wars* calendar, available from Ballantine, was packed full of large format color photographs. A new *Star Wars* annual had not been produced for the traditional seasonal Christmas annuals market, so shops continued to stock the one that had been released earlier in the year. Of course the #1 toy to receive that year was *Star Wars*, if you were fortunate to find any stock for sale.

Readers found that issue #47 (December 27) of *Star Wars Weekly* did not contain the continuation of "The Empire Strikes" or the conclusion of Han Solo versus Chewbacca. Instead it ran the first installment of a new four-part story, "Fugitives in Space." In this slim tale, the rebel heroes ended up on the wrong planet thanks to an R2-D2 malfunction and encountered a vengeful super-computer. This was clearly not part of the ongoing Marvel *Star Wars* continuity. "Fugitives in Space" had been produced by Marvel for its own *Pizzazz* magazine from October 1977 to June 1978, where it was titled "Keepers World." It was written by Roy Thomas with art by Howard Chaykin and Tony Dezuniga. Any fans anxious to learn if Han Solo had survived his confrontation with Chewbacca would have to wait a while longer.

The year 1978 had been quite a spectacular one for *Star Wars*. The film had finally been distributed to every part of the country, even if some areas had to wait until December. The incredible total gross ticket sales had been $19,762,521.[21] *Star Wars* was received in a way that surpassed every expectation, both in ticket sales and merchandise sold. Palitoy's sales had topped £20 million, a record for a single year. The *Star Wars* wave was showing no signs of slowing down, especially with the promise of a sequel which many fans already knew was called *The Empire Strikes Back.* The question was if the momentum could be carried on, up until the release of the sequel and beyond. With the high level of excitement at the end of 1978, it seemed as if *Star Wars* could live forever.

Chapter 4

Dreams of Empire

The year could not have begun in a more exciting fashion for *Star Wars* fans in Britain. On January 17, 1979, *Star Wars Weekly* #50 featured an incredible full-color cover and an article on the upcoming sequel the title of which was revealed as *The Empire Strikes Back*. Readers not only learned the title, they were also informed that Irvin Kershner would take over the mantle of director, that Elstree Studios would again be used and, most importantly, that Darth Vader would return. There was a photograph from the Daventry *Star Wars* event of Carrie Fisher sitting on the Jerba creature, which was described as being a new creation from *The Empire Strikes Back*. Fans were given more of an exclusive than Lucasfilm would have wished for in the *Star Wars Weekly* article, as it was stated, "At one time a *Star Wars* actor told us the secret of Darth Vader, then to be announced in the second movie, was quite simply that, beneath the mask, Darth Vader actually was Luke's father! But though this would have led to an interesting conflict, father vs. son, it seems the idea has now been dropped."[1] Dez Skinn remembers the source of the information clearly. "Dave Prowse had told me this a few months earlier but I didn't believe him! But in case he wasn't pulling my leg, I thought it best to mention such in print, albeit in such a way that we wouldn't look foolish if he had been on a wind-up! But I don't think that Lucasfilm spotted the spoiler."

There was a real-life drama which seemed as if it would lead to fans missing out on their weekly dose of *Star Wars*, as Dez Skinn describes. "A haulers dispute broke out at the height of the various disruptions to industry, nationally crippling deliveries of even the most basic goods, let alone mere comics and magazines, and curtailing deliveries of Marvel's UK titles throughout most of February 1979. Thankfully, breadwinner title *Star Wars Weekly* somehow managed to stay in news agents weekly for a few more issues although it too suffered erratic and random distribution throughout January and February 1979—before undergoing a month's break in publication of its own at the end of February, between #54 [2/14/79] and #55 [3/14/79]."[2] Joe Sales has memories of the time, "I was very concerned that my issues of *Star Wars Weekly* were delayed. I put it down to the bad weather. I was very relieved when the comic returned back to its regular release."

The comic was Marvel UK's biggest seller by far but Dez Skinn had become dissatisfied with the cover art.

> I actually *hated* the cover art. I felt that photo covers were an essential if you were to attract people who had seen the film. That with the increasing text and photo feature content, was a major change I instigated. The photo covers relied on the small amount of images available in those pre-computer days. Boosting the content, with features and competitions, was a luxury as I had no more staff or budget to accomplish such. So sadly they disappeared because, once they succeeded in boosting sales,

we just didn't have time to maintain them. Much to my disappointment, the more "on market" style was short-lived. But it worked, and boosted sales, which was my main role.

The revamped comic boasted of four sci-fi comic strips on the cover; *Star Wars, The Micronauts, The Watcher* and *Warlock*. Skinn wanted to include the comic based on the American television series *Battlestar Galactica* but Lucasfilm blocked the move because that show was seen as a *Star Wars* rival. There were claims and counter claims in the U.S. of the breaching of copyright. Micronauts toys were just as big a rival to *Star Wars* in British shops, however, benefitting distributor Airfix, which was making millions off of the sci-fi wave.

I continued to buy Star Wars Weekly *on a regular basis, with the letters page being my favorite feature. It provided a feeling of being part of a community where there were fans, often a lot older than myself, who were still crazy about* Star Wars. *While I had little time for the hideous-looking* Warlock *strip, I thought that* The Micronauts *was a fantastic addition to the comic.*

John May on a Mission

It was not just Marvel UK who wanted to make the most of the *Star Wars* sequel. Felix Dennis at Bunch Associates was seeking the freshest information from America. Bunch Associates was also due to publish *The Empire Strikes Back Poster Monthly* and *Collector's Edition* book. John May describes how he was chosen to undertake the mission to America:

> Felix Dennis gave me the job at the end of 1978 and sent me to Hollywood to work on the *Collector's Edition* and to collect more information for *Star Wars Monthly*. I left the U.K. on January 17 and stayed until the 25th. I had never been on a plane before so you can imagine to arrive in Hollywood, be picked up by limousine and be whisked to *Star Wars* HQ was all very strange and wonderful. Lucasfilm had begun building a new headquarters opposite Universal Studios but when I went there in January they were operating out of porta cabins. Among the people I interviewed was Russ Manning who was doing the *Star Wars* comic strips which, at the time, were published daily in newspapers in America and Canada.

May wrote an *Empire Strikes Back* update for issue #15 of the *Official Poster Monthly* while on his trip to America. "This report is actually coming to you direct from *Star Wars* H.Q, a nest of trailers near Universal Studios in California and it is clear from just a few days on the lot, that *Empire* excitement is building as the movie begins to get into gear." May revealed that the *Empire Strikes Back* trailer would be included in the *Star Wars* re-release in America on August 15. It would run for just three weeks before it disappeared from the cinema screens for several years. May's trip to *Star Wars* H.Q had certainly paid off as his report contained all of the very latest *Empire Strikes Back* information. In addition to confirming that the main cast would be returning, with Irvin Kershner at the helm and Brian Johnson handling the special effects, May was also able to reveal that, in order to accommodate the production, a giant new sound stage, the biggest in Europe, was under construction. Many of the specialist departments including wardrobe and special effects were currently preparing for the new production. There was also a snippet of information regarding the plot: "Darth Vader discovers the location of a Rebel base, bringing about a major confrontation."[3]

Gary Kurtz on Star Wars II

The December 1977 *Starlog* included the article "Luke Skywalker Is Alive and Well in *The Empire Strikes Back*." Gary Kurtz explained that he and George Lucas had planned to have each *Star Wars* adventure as an episode of a continuing story. Calling the new film *Episode 2* had been ruled out by the fact that three films that the pair wanted to make were set before *Star Wars*. Providing each film with a number was problematic, so Kurtz was ready to abandon the concept and instead provide each chapter with an individual title. "I mean, if we had to give each film its own true number in the series, this movie would be called *Episode Five: The Empire Strikes Back*. The first film would be called *Episode Four*! Can you imagine how confusing that would get? If we released a story like that publicly through a press release, thousands of people would be totally confused. Everyone would want to know what happened to the other three movies."[4] Kurtz revealed that *The Empire Strikes Back* would take place after its predecessor and that the rebels would be fighting from a new base of operations. There would be an emphasis on character development and the relationships between characters, and the romantic triangle between Leia, Han and Luke would be resolved.

Even though fans' thoughts were on *The Empire Strikes Back*, it was still possible to see *Star Wars* at the cinema. The Brighton Odeon showed the film again until the end of the second week of January, with other venues probably following suit as prints were evidently still available.

The Empire Keeps Striking Marvel

Issue #51 of *Star Wars Weekly* (cover date January 24) continued "The Empire Strikes." It transpired that Han Solo had actually survived his confrontation with Chewbacca. He had slid a laser-proof shield under his shirt and faked his death, so that his Wookiee co-pilot could win the contest and collect the winnings on their behalf. Han and his compatriots had yet to make their escape from the Wheel. Issue #52 continued the story. Commander Strom ordered his Stormtroopers to shoot Greyshade and the rebels on sight. Master Com helped R2-D2 and C-3PO blast off from the Wheel in an escape pod before traveling down to the spot where Greyshade's yacht was docked. Greyshade had a change of heart and ran at the advancing Stormtroopers, blazing with his blaster, while Luke and Leia escaped in the space yacht. Greyshade made quick work of the Stormtroopers. When Master Com arrived, Commander Strom held the Senator and his droid at gunpoint. Greyshade dealt his last card, throwing a powerful proton grenade at Strom, blowing him into space dust. Greyshade and Master Com had both been mortally wounded but it seemed that at the end, they had established a friendship. Chewbacca used the antigravity platform that was carrying his considerable winnings from the gladiator contest to ram a squad of Stormtroopers, scattering the coins in all directions. Han and Chewbacca were penniless once more and they were no nearer to being able to pay off Jabba the Hut. Luke and Leia had managed to blast away from the Wheel in the space yacht and pick up the droid's escape pod but ran straight into a Star Destroyer commanded by Darth Vader. Fortunately, Han and Chewbacca were able to attack and damage Vader's ship with the Millennium Falcon, allowing Luke and Leia to escape. Luke and Leia were very pleased to learn that Han was in fact alive and well. Luke, seeing that the Star Destroyer was about to bring all its weaponry to bear against the Millennium Falcon, sent all of his pain and frustration via the Force into Darth Vader's mind; the Dark Lord cried out in pain. By the time he had recovered, both the space yacht and the Millennium Falcon had escaped into hyperspace.

Here ended the most drawn-out, convoluted (or intricately constructed, depending on your point of view) Marvel *Star Wars* story of them all. While the Marvel UK title was "The Empire Strikes," in the American Marvel comic the story was serialized in issue #18 "The Empire Strikes," issue #19 "The Ultimate Gamble," issue #20 "Deathgame," issue #21 "Shadow of a Dark Lord," issue #22 "To the Last Gladiator" and issue #23 "Flight Into Fury." The story was significant in that it marked the return of Darth Vader to the Marvel *Star Wars* storyline. Luke's telekinesis was an aspect of the Force that had not been featured before.

There was to be no rest for the Rebel heroes. *Star Wars Weekly* #53 (cover date February 7), featured "No Mercy Hath Baron Tagge." The story opened with the Rebel's Yavin base under attack by yet another wave of TIE Fighters which seemed to be popping up out of nowhere. The rebels needed to find the source of the attacks, before their valuable fighter squadrons were whittled down to nothing. Meanwhile Luke, Leia and the droids had visited a used spacecraft dealer on the planet Centares in order to trade in Senator Greyshade's space yacht for a more practical and less conspicuous spaceship. Shortly before Luke and Leia took off from Centares, they noticed that a space cruiser belonging to the powerful Tagge dynasty was heading for the Yavin system. General Ulric Tagge, who had been present during officers' meeting aboard the Death Star in *Star Wars* (and who evidently left the station before the rebel attack), was the Tagge family's most influential member. Ulric Tagge's older brother Baron Orman Tagge was at the command of the space cruiser. While his subordinates flew the ship, Tagge practiced with his lightsaber. He was determined to get revenge on Darth Vader, who had blinded him in a previous encounter, leaving him to rely on cyber vision glasses in order to see. On the journey to the Yavin system, Luke and Leia had time to talk. They had not heard anything from Han Solo or Chewbacca since their escape from the Wheel and Leia's concern about Han made Luke concerned that he might be losing out in romancing the Princess. Leia also explained that the Empire was holding back from launching an all-out attack on the Rebel base and had instead installed a blockade around the Fourth Moon of Yavin. Somehow the Rebels had destroyed the Death Star, and the Empire was concerned about suffering another defeat. When Luke and Leia arrived at Yavin, they saw Imperial TIE Fighters flying from Tagge's cruiser into the deadly gas atmosphere of the planet Yavin. General Dodonna concluded that there must be a major spacecraft hiding inside the gaseous atmosphere of Yavin, which generated a whirlwind corridor that allowed TIE Fighters to fly out and attack the Rebel base. Dodonna devised a plan that appeared to be a suicide mission, where a pilot would traverse the whirlwind corridor to its source but there would be no way of returning once the Imperial craft had been destroyed. Luke of course volunteered and was soon on his way to Yavin in a captured TIE fighter. Deep inside the planet's atmosphere, he encountered a massive Turbine Ship generating the whirlwind and immediately began firing on it using powerful proton charges. As soon as Luke's attack began, quick-thinking Baron Tagge made his way to his space cruiser, which was docked with the Turbine Ship. Luke's final shot hit the ship's engines and it exploded in a massive fireball. After the explosion had faded, Luke was left alone in the TIE Fighter but he concentrated using the Force and found his way back to base. Baron Tagge escaped Yavin's gaseous atmosphere in his cruiser but only by following Luke's lead. Tagge vowed to exact his revenge on both Darth Vader and whoever had just blown up his very expensive pet project. If the pilot had a distinctive name, it might help greatly in tracking him down. Luke Skywalker radioing back to base provided Tagge with the information he needed.

The story was very much in keeping with the *Star Wars* style of storytelling in that Tagge's past encounter with Darth Vader was only referred to in the dialogue, introducing the reader to a subplot that was already underway. The fact that Tagge was skilled with a lightsaber brought the tantalizing possibility of a confrontation with both Darth Vader and Luke Skywalker.

The Star Wars Holiday Special

The February *Starlog* featured a fascinating article on the *Star Wars Holiday Special*, which had been televised in the U.S. in December. The two-hour "movie" featured all of the main stars, along with Chewbacca's family and a sequence that recreated the Mos Eisley Cantina. Fans hoping that this new chapter in the *Star Wars* saga would be shown in Britain were disappointed: It was never shown again. This may have been just as well, because the *Star Wars Holiday Special* has not garnered a reputation for being

Above and opposite page: **There was plenty of excitement in early 1979 with the *Starlog* report on *The Star Wars Holiday Special* and the *Sun* newspaper going on location to Finse, Norway.**

high-quality television. *Milwaukee Sentinel* reviewer Greg Moody wrote,

> Well, I have to praise producers Dwight Hemion and Gary Smith for one thing. They certainly know how to disguise the musical-variety format. I was at least an hour into the *Star Wars Holiday Special* before I realized that it was, in fact, a variety show that they were trying to put over on America. Don't be fooled by the spacey surroundings! What we've got here is nothing but a common, everyday variety show, packaged with bright *Star Wars* wrappings, a sure guarantee of healthy ratings. But—is it worth it? Not on your life, bucko… [T]o put it simply, *The Star Wars Holiday Special* is junk. It's a commercial rip-off, not only of the popularity of *Star Wars* and the holiday season, but of your time as well.[5]

"I was blown away when I found out that Boba Fett had appeared in a cartoon segment of the *Holiday Special*," says Jordan Royce. "But without the Internet, there was not any way of seeing it." Sarah Baker-Saunders recalls, "I remember reading about the *Star Wars Holiday Special* in *Starlog*. It was among many exciting things that were only available across the pond."

The Empire Hits the Press

On March 12, the *Sun* featured the major article "*Star Wars* on Ice," in which writer Joe Steeples described how he and photographer Steve Markeson had flown by helicopter and landed at the site where *The Empire Strikes Back* was filming in Norway. They managed to take a few photographs before flying off again. The article contained a lengthy quote from Mark Hamill, derived from a press conference conducted at the Scandinavia Hotel in Oslo on March 8 before location filming began. Hamill joked, "They tell me that all over the glacier there are big fissures just covered by a few feet of snow. A man could fall down one of them and never be seen again. Perhaps I ought to pay my stand-in to walk in front of me, to test out the footholds. I'm quite enjoying the physical challenge, though it's tiresome they don't let us ski, in case one of us breaks a leg." To research the article, Steeples and Markeson engaged in a real-life adventure to reach the location. "The hardest thing about the Hardanger Glacier is getting there," said Steeples. "There is no local bus service, mainly because there are no local roads. And most of the railway line to the isolated halt was blocked in both directions by avalanches [sic]. That is why we turned to the experts: The British Army. Through the British military attaché in Oslo, we got in touch with the Prince of Wales' Own Regiment of Yorkshire and the Army Air Corps, who were in the area preparing for NATO's Operation Hardwinter." The pair managed to hitch a ride with the Air Rescue Corps and land in the midst of the *Empire Strikes Back* location filming camp, but they were not made welcome. "After *Star Wars*, they've become *Star Bores*," quipped Steeples.[6] The article included an aerial photograph of two rebel turrets and another of a windswept crew and equipment. A photograph of Hamill and Carrie Fisher wrapped up in cold weather clothing came from a photo shoot conducted after the Oslo press conference, far from any actual snow.

Also on March 12, the *Daily Express* article "Hop on a Star" featured a photograph of Hamill astride a creature described as a Tauntaun. "That bold space adventurer, Luke Skywalker, rides again," proclaimed the article. "For transport, Luke simply saddles up."[7] The article repeated the information that was already known regarding the filming in Finse, Norway, and that the film would be released in the summer. The photograph had been made available by Lucasfilm to the press as a teaser and was subsequently included in many newspapers and magazines. Lucasfilm was probably aware of the *Sun* article "*Star Wars* on Ice" before it had been printed and in issuing a *teaser* photograph, it sought to deter the press from going to similar lengths to cover the film.

The choice of the photograph had been down to Stanley Bielecki, who after *Star Wars* had been taken on by 20th Century-Fox as a marketing maestro covering publicity and advertising. According to Gary Kurtz,

> Stanley had a great eye. I was continually amazed that we would go through the proof books that he produced of the stills that had been shot on the set. We would go through the pages and he would spot the frames that were the ones to go out, like that one of Luke on the Tauntaun that says nothing about science fiction really. It was a gritty picture that could have been shot on any location in the world if the creature had been real and it was one of those iconic shots that everybody wanted to print because it looked unique and nobody had seen it before.[8]

Competition in the Stars

Despite its incredible success *Star Wars* was not being seen by the media as something that was unique but instead simply representative of a new wave of science fiction and family entertainment films. Writing for the *Guardian*, Bart Mills said, "Films have never been more entertaining than they are today. They have never made more money. They have never been less original escapism. Happy endings."[9] Thompson Prentice, writing for the *Daily Mail*, lumped *Star Wars* together with *Close Encounters of the Third Kind* and *Saturday Night Fever*. "Take your seats, ladies and Gentlemen, the great British cinema revival has begun."[10] David Robinson of the *Times* wrote, "The previously relentless audience decline seems at last to have been arrested, thanks partly to the steady flow of American box office infallibles."[11] Journalists were speaking in terms of there being a new beginning for the cinema. The *Star Wars* formula appeared to be easy to replicate and it seemed that new science fiction projects such as *Star Trek: The Motion Picture*, the Canadian film *The Shape of Things to Come* and television producer Glen A. Larson's *Battlestar Galactica* and *Buck Rogers in the 25th Century* would capture the same spirit as *Star Wars*. Roger Corman was preparing his biggest-ever budget for *Battle Beyond the Stars* and Dino De Laurentiis had secured the rights to handle a film adaptation of *Flash Gordon*. The filmmaking behemoths were heading for the stars too. Walt Disney Pictures had cranked up the production of their own long-in-gestation science fiction epic *Space Probe One* which had been renamed *The Black Hole*. The setting for the next James Bond offering had been changed from the British countryside to outer space, with the title *Moonraker* offering a tidy reference to science fiction that Ian Fleming had certainly not intended.

The Sun ran an article on March 13 which featured some of the upcoming sci-fi films. The piece included a competition to win a set of six Large Size *Star Wars* figures from Denys Fisher Ltd., which had probably been donated by the company as a way of promoting the new range. The paper had fifty sets to give away, which would have been a major investment by Denys Fisher.

The BAFTAs

On March 31, *Screen International* reported on the 1979 awards from the British equivalent of the Oscars, the British Academy of Film and Television Arts Awards (BAFTA). Although *Star Wars* had been released in 1977, it had not been in British cinemas long enough to qualify for the awards in 1978. Subsequently *Star Wars* ended up competing with two other special effects extravaganzas, *Superman* and *Close Encounters of the Third Kind*. John Williams was awarded the Anthony Asquith award for best original film music for *Star Wars*. Sam Shaw, Robert R. Rutledge, Gordon Davidson, Gene Corso, Derek Ball, Don MacDougall, Bob Minkler, Ray West, Mike Minkler, Lester Fresholtz, Richard Portman and Ben Burtt won Best Soundtrack. 20th Century–Fox took out a full-page advertisement in *Screen International* congratulating all of those responsible for winning the two BAFTAs for *Star Wars*.

Marvel Puts Star Wars on Ice

Issue #57 of *Star Wars Weekly* (March 28) began "The Kingdom of Ice." Luke, Leia and the droids embarked on a mission to a rebel base on the icy planet Akuria Two but they were intercepted by a squadron of TIE Fighters and forced to crash-land on its surface. The rebels were then accosted by a bunch of giant furry yeti-like creatures called Snow Demons. They were saved by the arrival of rebel commander Colonel Odan in his giant fortress mounted on skis. Odan and his crew were soon exposed as Imperial agents and it was down to the genuine Colonel Odan to save the day. Luke, Leia and the droids teamed with Odan to defeat the local Imperial forces, the leader of which was fortunate enough to be crushed in the destruction of his base, saving him from having to explain the unlikely events to Darth Vader. "The Kingdom of Ice" was a fast-paced, entertaining story but clearly not part of the ongoing *Star Wars* saga; it was, in fact, another story derived from *Pizzazz* magazine. It was written by Archie Goodwin with art by Walt Simonson and Dave Cockrum. The story was notable for being a precursor to *The Empire Strikes Back*. It is surprising that a story had been approved which was set in a snowbound environment, that contained yeti-like snow creatures and Snow Flyer vehicles. It was well-known that *The Empire Strikes*

Back would include a snowbound environment. At least one science fiction television series, *Battlestar Galactica*, had based an episode on that premise too.

Han Solo at Stars' End

The novel *Han Solo at Stars' End* by New Jersey-born Brian Daley was released in Britain by Sphere. Daley had sought a writer-for-hire project after the release of his first two novels for Del Rey *The Doomfarers of Coramande* and *The Followers of Coramande*. Judy Lynn del Rey suggested he work on a *Star Wars* novel. After his first story treatment was rejected by Lucasfilm as it would contradict the ongoing continuity, Daley set about chronicling the early career of Han Solo and Chewbacca. Daley said, "Everyone else [in *Star Wars*] starts out bad and ends up bad, or starts out good and ends up good. He's [Han Solo] the one who turns around in the middle of his departure and comes back."[12] Set before the events of *Star Wars*, *Han Solo at Stars' End* takes place in a region of the galaxy controlled by the Corporate Sector Authority, on behalf of the Empire. Han Solo delivers a shipment of weapons to a group of aliens who had started a rebellion against the Corporate Sector. This was no act of mercy by Han Solo and Chewbacca but instead just another profitable illegal run. The Millennium Falcon's sensor dish was ripped off during the mission but when Solo sought out a gang of outlaw technicians to replace the dish, he found that the group's leader, his old friend "Doc," had disappeared. Doc's daughter Jessa roped Han into joining a group that was setting out to prove that the Corporate Sector Authority was responsible for covertly arresting dissidents en masse and incarcerating them at a secret location. To assist Han on the mission, she and her colleagues had constructed Blue Max, a powerful briefcase-sized robot capable of retaining and processing massive amounts of information. A companion droid Bollux was modified so as to be able to carry Blue Max in its chest cavity. In the process of telling its story, *Han Solo at Stars' End* took the form of many genres, from spy mission to whodunit to sting operation, building to an action-packed gun-blazing finale.

The character name of the droid Bollux was changed to Zollux for the UK printing, for Bollux is uncomfortably close to *bollocks*, a slang word for testicles in Britain, and would have been the source of sniggers in the playground. Daley expanded upon the character of Han Solo considerably, with all of the information presumably cleared by Lucasfilm. Solo's red piped trousers were described as being from a uniform, hinting that he had served in some kind of military outfit. Han also told a story about a "friend" but was obviously talking about himself: "A friend of mine made a moral decision once, thought that he was doing the moral thing. Hell, he *was*. But he'd been conned. He lost his career, his girl, everything. This friend of mine, he ended up standing there while they ripped the rank insignia off his tunic. The people who didn't want him put up against a wall were laughing at him. A whole planet. He shipped out of there and never went back." During the course of the story, Han also stated, "We're not Jedi Knights or Freedom's Sons,"[13] fueling interest that the latter group had some kind of involvement in the Clone Wars. Daley's book was treasured by fans because—other than the weekly comic—there was not any *Star Wars* story content available.

Keeping the Force Alive

Nineteen seventy-nine had begun well for fans with the exciting issue #50 of the weekly comic, the first images from *The Empire Strikes Back* and the *Han Solo at Stars' End* novel. But *Star Wars* had disappeared from the wider media; newspapers had moved on to the next big thing, *Look-In* was focusing on new fads and girls' magazines had found new hunks to swoon over. Even the Making Of coverage in the specialist scifi press had burned itself out, unless fans went to the trouble of seeking out copies of the *Official Star Wars Poster Monthly*. Little else could be expected, as it was the organic process that followed all fads. When more excitement could be found elsewhere, Lucas' creation became less and less of a priority in the media.

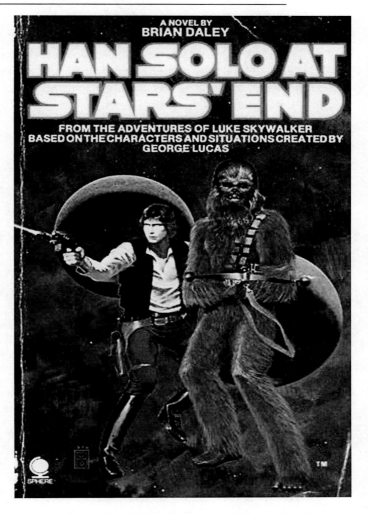

Han Solo at Stars' End **from Sphere was welcomed by fans starved of** *Star Wars.*

But it was still worth looking out for features on the actors in the press. The April *Starlog* included an interview with Mark Hamill, who provided an update on his acting career:

> Since *Star Wars* I've been offered some really amazing deals. I'm not used to playing with Monopoly money yet, so when I hear the offers it's like, "Excuse me, I have to sit down now and splash cold water on my face. Can you hold the line?" Then I come back up and say, "Now, can you repeat that number?" The only trouble is that most of the scripts I have been sent are terrible…. You begin to think: "Well, I'm not working, and I should work." That's what everybody else says, so it becomes hard to turn down offers.[14]

Seeking to adapt to the changing climate Munro/Deighton took a new direction to generate national media coverage. According to Carole Deighton,

> We were responsible for many national newspaper and magazine promotions and competitions. But we made sure we were always "mean" with the amount of prizes on offer so that it didn't affect the currency of the toys. We negotiated some tough deals and found that high-circulation tabloids like *The Sun, Daily Express* and *Daily Mirror* were prepared to offer us spreads way bigger than usual in return for the highly sought-after *Star Wars* product prizes. Formats for these promotions were often created

by us and strictly controlled; great care was taken to ensure the necessary film and licensing copyrights were always protected with correct logos, trademarks and brand names prominently featured.

In the 1970s, celebrities were not put under such scrutiny as they are today and there were no dedicated celebrity-based magazines (or of course websites) in which stories could be published. Mark Hamill could get married and expect his firstborn without a murmur in Britain, while in the modern age, magazines would be queuing up to make a splash of the wedding and paparazzi would report excitedly at the first sign of Mary Lou Hamill's pregnancy. The British stars of *Star Wars* did not make an impact in the media as they did not secure other high-profile roles. Alec Guinness and Peter Cushing continued to be prolific in films and on television but their fame was such that headlines would not begin with "*Star Wars* star…" *Star Wars* was becoming a distant memory, even for fans.

Fans Keep the Force Alive

Without any access to the film, fans were required to use their initiative to keep their interest alive. Darren Slade recalls the time:

> For the millions of children who saw *Star Wars* on its first release, the chances of watching it again any time soon were pretty small. So for a long time after that first fateful viewing, children like me had to recreate the experience in our imagination as best we could. Piecing the film together, doing our best to reconstruct in our memories. The novel helped. So did the comic books but they were in some respects very different from the film, both in style and detail. For me the nearest thing to seeing the movie again was the *Story of Star Wars* record—which stood alongside John Williams' double album of the soundtrack music in practically every music shop. My own copy was played to the point of disintegration. It also bears a long scratch at the point where Chewbacca is introduced—a lasting testament to my ham-fistedness with delicate vinyl and a record player that didn't have a cue lever.

Bob Cole was another proud owner of the *Story of Star Wars* record: "I played that record to death. That's what kept my six-year-old self going in between films. Me and my sister used to open the windows and play it full blast so the entire street could hear it. We didn't care if they wanted to hear it or not!"

Louise Turner had a *Star Wars* diversion of another kind. "I used to play the French horn, and had dreams of joining an orchestra until I finally jumped ship and took up archaeology in my student days. I used to spend hours listening to my *Star Wars* soundtrack and transcribing the horn parts so I could play along—that horn solo that accompanies the scene where a restless Luke Skywalker watches the twin suns go down is sublime."

"A major aspect of being a fan (depending on age, of course) was playing with *Star Wars* figures," recalls Gary Harvey. He continues:

> Craig and I developed a system not unlike the "Dungeons and Dragons" game, where we would take turns at devising an adventure. Craig was a genius at creating environments from bits of wood, polystyrene and other junk. The selection of *Star Wars* figures that we had available was very limited, so characters from other toy franchises were roped in too and provided with new *Star Wars* personas. Our imaginations took us to every corner of the *Star Wars* universe and we explored many issues connected with it. We were collecting too, which would soon take over from "playing with" figures as the driving force behind our fandom.

Sarah Baker-Saunders too was still very much a fan:

> I developed a serious collecting bug for *Star Wars*. I had limited funds and about 25p pocket money a week, so my purchases had to be selective. I also had birthday money and an early purchase was the sound-

track and membership to the fan club. It was £2.95 to join, a lot of money. I was more interested in the filmmaking process than the toys and games and I used to buy magazines and comics that had *Star Wars*-related information. I also started going to film and comic fairs in Manchester, along with some specialist comic shops, and was able to pick up original cinema posters, stills, U.S. magazines like *Fangoria* and *Famous Monsters of Filmland*. Without the Internet, that's what kept me up to date with what was going on. I was hooked! I soon got a part-time job and was able to set a little aside for my little *Star Wars* hobby.

Being able to actually see *Star Wars* was a considerable advantage for any fan. "I had bought *Star Wars* on Super 8 and I had a projector to play it," says Laurie Calvert. "It was only a couple of short sequences but it was special because you actually had a piece of *Star Wars*. It was before video came along. The film could be blown up much larger than any TV set back then and it was in color and in stereo. With all the lights down and the clickety clack of the projector, it was a very special experience." Joe Sales can contest that you did not necessarily need to own a projector to see *Star Wars*:

I went to my friend Mark's birthday party. In those days, you had film shows in the home and his father brought out a projector and put on *Star Wars*. It was a color sound version but it ended at the point where the heroes escaped the Death Star. That was a rare experience and apart from that, the only way I found to relive the film was through the weekly comics. I identified with the comic strongly because it was something to read every week, when you could only see the film once in a blue moon. I was also a member of the *Star Wars* fan club but I wasn't old enough to rearrange addresses when my family and I moved to Colchester, so I ended up missing out on some of the newsletters.

Jordan Royce says:

Buying the *Star Wars* figures was still incredibly important to me at the time and hunting for *Star Wars* news in *Starburst*. Also the *Star Wars* comic, which was like a weekly fix until the next film came along. Carmine Infantino's depictions of Luke, Leia, etc., looked nothing like the way they did in the film, but it was still the characters that we loved. We knew it was Leia—she had the buns hairstyle! I fully believed at the time that the comics were canon. The stories were really good, even including flashbacks to when Ben Kenobi was a Jedi Knight. Han and Chewie having adventures on their own. Looking back, it's clear that the writers had to tread water because they couldn't contradict what was going to happen in the upcoming *Star Wars* films. They couldn't have, for instance, Luke and Leia having a full-blown relationship. Reading the comics as a child, I didn't care about that.

Shaun Dawkins had another way of keeping his fandom alive:

My friend and I were fascinated as to how the film had been made and so we started tracking down actors, technicians and anyone vaguely connected to *Star Wars* for autographs and also for interviews on my tape recorder. We used to sneak off on the train to London and attempt to meet actors such as Denis Lawson who were in plays, etc. It was a genuine passion. In the many decades before the Internet and instant communication, whenever there had been a feature in a newspaper or television about a person connected to *Star Wars*, we used to write to the editor or the TV company and they would often forward your letter. Many of the British actors were completely bowled over by the response they were getting. They were actually part of something pretty momentous. We later began to visit sci-fi conventions in London and up in Manchester and Birmingham. I used to leave Folkestone unofficially, telling my parents that I was doing other things! There were actors from *Star Wars* you could meet on the circuit such as Dave Prowse, Kenny Baker and Peter Mayhew. The American actors didn't do convention appearances. Some of the technical crew would also turn up such as Ben Burtt and Robert Watts and were almost as in-demand as the actors. It was also through meeting people at conventions that you found pen pals, in the days when people used to write letters.

No matter how fans kept themselves going, it seemed that it would be down to their own ingenuity to keep their *Star Wars* alive for some time to come.

To many children and young people, *Star Wars* was much more than a film. Its universe was much larger than what was served up on the screen. Children had an almost perfect environment to explore in their minds that had no connection whatsoever to Earth and every-day existence. The toy line was an ideal way to recreate that universe and for many children the *Official Poster Monthly* and weekly comic helped to expand upon it. Prior to the arrival of *Star Wars* young boys had a great deal of interest in Westerns on television and related dress-up toys were a big part of childhood. Science fiction television shows, including those on the outer edge of the genre such as *The Six Million Dollar Man* and *Batman* were extremely popular but did not present fantasy situations with a great deal of potential. Apart from re-runs of *Star Trek* and *Doctor Who*, nearly all were restricted to planet Earth and did not have the budgets to bring fantastic situations to the small screen. According to Darren Slade,

> Children of the 1970s had plenty of pop culture to enjoy, and it wouldn't all disappear when *Star Wars* came along. But for children who were suddenly *Star Wars*-obsessed, none of it seemed quite as impor-tant anymore.

The greatest sweeping saga that was available to fuel a young boy's imagination in Britain in the 70s was World War II. Fueled by constant reruns of war films on television and by war story comic books, it was set on a massive stage, filled with fascinating vehicles, exotic places and endless tales of derring-do both fictional and very real. The toys for boys were often similarly World War II–inspired. Airfix soldiers were cheap enough to recreate battles on a grand scale with the goodies cast in green and the baddies in blue. Action Man was supplied with every imaginable piece of military equipment right down to his mess kit. The militaristic aspect of *Star Wars* was part of the appeal for many but the events, char-acters, technology and environments entirely eclipsed any kind of real-life war. Even though *Star Wars* is set "In a Galaxy Far, Far, Away," boys' minds were catapulted from the age of their grandfathers to the furthest reaches of the future. Darren Slade recalls

> Boys read WWII comics, they assembled Airfix aircraft and battleship kits. Perhaps more significantly, many of us recreated the war daily in the playground. Then, from the time *Star Wars* was released, we were no longer Germans vs Allies we were Empire vs Rebels.

Girls too found that there was a place for their minds to run free. Previously the fantasy world presented to girls was based around riding ponies, becoming ballerinas and living in a modern house. Their toys were prams, realistic baby dolls, ponies with riders, farms and Lego models of kitchens. In *Star Wars*, there was a female character in Princess Leia that they could claim as their own. The 1970s had offered a string of strong female char-acters: *Wonder Woman, the Bionic Woman* and *Charlie's Angels*. Princess Leia was a woman who, while being undeniably beautiful, lived among, fought with and commanded men without seeking to be glamorous or fashionable in the slightest. She did not possess super-powers, only an acerbic wit and a blaster pistol. According to Sarah Saunders.

> My love of the movies and my family's love of them helped in my love and appreciation of the *Star Wars* films. You can see gender stereotypes in the 1970s and *Star Wars* helped change that. It had such mass appeal and girls too could join in without feeling they had to explain themselves. We had a strong female lead in Leia but it was also a fun adventure film, wookiees, myths, the force and robots. In my life as a fan I've come across many other women and their stories are similar.

Television producers, filmmakers, comic producers, toy companies, computer game manufacturers and those connected to children's media of all descriptions began to mine the vein of science fiction and fantasy gold represented by *Star Wars*. World War II com-mando comic strips and Lego kitchens were not going to cut it any more. *Star Wars* may or may not have saved cinema but it certainly transformed childhood.

Chapter 5

The Merchandise Strikes Back

Buying something connected to *Star Wars* may have not been remotely close to seeing the actual film but every little bit helped and the shops were still chock full of memorabilia in 1979. In the minds of fans, each item was like a small piece of the film, which helped them to recreate it in their minds. Although *Star Wars* had not been showing at cinemas for quite some time, fans' collecting desires had not been dulled. "If it had *Star Wars* on it, I had to have it," says Graham Ogle. "That includes almost everything Palitoy ever released, as well as jigsaws, books, records, watches, soap models, shampoo, stationery, bedding and curtains. The figures were by far my favorite, of course. My bedroom was a *Star Wars* shrine. My favorite item wasn't a toy but the *Star Wars* digital watch by Texas Instruments. My Dad was not keen on buying it as it was quite expensive but I wore him down. It was my first digital watch and I wore it with pride until the strap broke about two years later."

"I was collecting pretty much everything at the time," recalls Laurie Calvert. "I was snipping cuttings from my local paper, even the Odeon cinema listings. When Alec Guinness starred in *Tinker Tailor Soldier Spy*, I cut out its listing out of the newspaper's television listing and stuck it in my album."

"No exaggeration, I probably thought about *Star Wars* for about 75 percent of my waking hours as a six-year old," recalls Bob Fischer, "even though I had only seen the film the one time, the previous year. I voraciously collected the action figures and playsets, and my bedroom was decorated in *Star Wars* wallpaper, curtains and bedspread. I had the books, comics, jigsaws, posters and other assorted ephemera. I even had my picture taken with 'Darth Vader' on the seafront in Scarborough in the summer of 1979. I was wearing my favourite *Star Wars* T-shirt, and in the excitement I completely failed to notice that Darth's costume wasn't an entirely accurate replica! There was a photographer with Darth, who we trusted would send the picture to us in the post, a few weeks later. They were much more innocent times back then." The "Darth Vader" that Bob Fischer remembers had been sighted by a reader of *Star Wars Weekly* in Scarborough the previous year, so his antics took place during two summer seasons at least.

For many, keeping a scrapbook was a vital part of collecting. In creating a scrapbook for its *Star Wars* product line, Letraset had inadvertently introduced an interest to children who may not otherwise have considered keeping *Star Wars* odds and ends. "I kept a scrapbook because as a child everything from *Star Wars* seemed worth saving," says Craig Spivey. "It was where all the cuttings I'd saved from magazines and bits of packaging ended up. I would fastidiously cut things out and glue them in place." Sarah Baker-Saunders was still hoarding too. "I didn't collect many toys, although I did have a few. I was more interested in things like bubble gum cards, Lyons Maid ice lollies with free masks, stationery, and anything unusual. I had a couple of scrapbooks in which I used to collect newspaper and magazine cuttings and some of the *Star Wars*-related items like cinema tickets and leaflets, lolly and sweet wrappers. At the film fairs in Manchester, I picked up movie posters and stills, and any unusual item I could find."

The Large Size *Star Wars* Action Figures that had been offered as prizes by the *Sun* newspaper were also offered to the shops. Designed by Kenner, they were sumptuously made, with authentic clothing and accessories. The likeness to the *Star Wars* actors was fairly good but the bodies featured very little articulation, reducing the play value considerably. Denys Fisher released a partial set of the Large Size figures: Han Solo, Luke Skywalker, Princess Leia Organa, Chewbacca, Darth Vader, Stormtrooper, See-Threepio (C-3PO) and Artoo-Detoo (R2-D2). Palitoy released only Luke Skywalker and Princess Leia, for reasons that Geoff Maisey explains: "We met so much resistance from retailers, who saw the Large Size Figures

The young Bob Fischer meets Darth Vader in Scarborough (courtesy Bob Fischer).

as collector-only items and therefore specialist distribution, that we picked what we thought were the key ones—Luke and Leia. Denys Fisher felt they could sell the rest, as they had specialist customers among their retail listings." Two additional figures, Ben (Obi-Wan) Kenobi and Jawa, were made available in Britain in Meccano packaging. The set proved to be unpopular with retailers, hence their scarcity on the high street. "I was aware of the large *Star Wars* action figures," says Craig Spivey. "They were included in the little catalogues that were packed with the boxed toys, though I never saw any for sale in shops. I was also into my Action Man at the time and when I came across the big *Star Wars* figures in the collections of other children, they seemed sorely lacking in their pose-ability and accessories by comparison. They seemed nice to have but weren't essential."

Nicholas Broome recalls, "I was 15 in '79 and considered myself to be a very serious collector. I couldn't find the large *Star Wars* figures anywhere in my hometown of Romford. I found a Chewbacca but it was only when the Kiddie City toy shop in the center of town received the entire set that I managed to buy them. The shop specialized in buying up unwanted stock and had the entire range of *Star Wars* Large Action Figures on sale at knock-down prices. The Ben Kenobi and Jawa were in stock there until the mid–1980s. If only us fans had known how valuable they would turn out to be!"

The Large Size Action Figures were part of the last gasp of the "12-inch" action figure scale. What had previously been a standard of the toy industry would ebb away over the next few years, as

The Large Size *Star Wars* Action Figures were released by Denys Fisher, convinced that there was a market for them in Britain (courtesy Darren Simpson).

manufacturers changed their emphasis to smaller plastic figures. "When Kenner obtained the license to make *Star Wars* toys, their decision to opt for the 3¾-inch scale was a defining moment for the action figure genre and the history of toys," says Bob Brechin. He went on:

WIN OUT-OF-THIS-WORLD STAR WAR PRIZES!

★ CALLING all children! Here's your chance to stage your own space adventures with superb scale models from blockbuster film Star Wars and its sequel, The Empire Strikes Back.

The Sun is giving away 50 sets of Denys Fisher models

in a fantastic FREE contest. They are new, larger-size figures, ranging from a 7½in high robot R2D2 to a 15in tall all-black villain Darth Vader.

There is hairy good-guy Chewbacca, space hero Luke Skywalker the beautiful Princess Leia and the golden

android C3PO. The whole set of six is worth £36.

To enter, just tell us which Star Wars character is your favourite and why—in not more than 30 words. Send your entry—it must be on a postcard—to STAR WARS CONTEST, The Sun, 30 Bouverie Street, London EC4Y 8DE. Closing date: March 23, 1979.

The Large Size *Star Wars* Action Figures were advertised via a competition in the *Sun* newspaper on March 14, 1979.

Small action figure brands existed but at the time, the established action figure scale ranged from eight inches to 12, with many figures dressed in cloth clothing. Plastics, which most modern toys are made from, is a byproduct of oil, and after the 1973 oil crisis, when OPEC announced an embargo on oil production, the price of oil quadrupled. This had a big effect on the toy industry and it affected many toy companies. The decision of Kenner to go for the much smaller action figure for *Star Wars* was a wise move because there was another oil crisis in 1979 due to the Iranian revolution. It also meant that they could sell many more figures and vehicles than the larger figure brands. The move to smaller action figures also tended to change the way the child played. Smaller figures and vehicles allowed for table-top play whereas large 12-inch scaled vehicles dictated that outside play in the garden was more suitable.

Palitoy's New Wave

The 3¾-inch *Star Wars* action figure toy range was still available in shops; but with only 12 characters available, fans clamored for more. In April, Munro/Deighton launched the *Draw a Droid* competition for Palitoy with a full-page advertisement in *Star Wars Weekly*, *Look-In* and other kids' publications. The six winners (aged four to 14) would be given a tour of Elstree Studios and see the filming of *The Empire Strikes Back*. "I accompanied the winners to Elstree and we met up with Harrison Ford, Carrie Fisher, Mark Hamill and Antony Daniels," says Carole Deighton. "Over time, we got to know Anthony quite well and he was always very helpful. All four stars signed autographs and posed for photos. It's a great pity that subsequently the file copies of them have been lost! However, my nephew does have a copy of the *Empire Strikes Back* film flier autographed by the four stars and I've always advised him to hang on to it!" The competition had been designed to promote the new wave of eight *Star Wars* action figures. The nicknames that the cantina characters had been issued with for filming purposes at Elstree had provided the names of Hammerhead, Snaggletooth and Walrus Man. (Fans may have been fortunate that Kenner did not make figures of Weird Girl, Martian and Local Ugly Man.) Greedo was the only one of the new figures to have been provided a name in the script. Cast in bright colors and each armed with a blaster, the Cantina creatures seemed evocative of far-flung worlds. There were new droid characters, Power Droid, Death Star Droid and R5-D4. The only human figure included in the set was Luke Skywalker X-Wing Pilot, which was a measure of how popular the *Star Wars* aliens and droids had become.

The new *Star Wars* figures were not as big a hit with retailers as with children, as Geoff Maisey explains: "We met with strong trade resistance in 1979 for the second wave of figures, as they only wanted the key characters and did not want the added complication of managing assortments. This we overcame by using assortment packs but weighted towards the most popular characters. This method was continued in the following years."

The poses of the Cantina characters seemed to be more realistic than the figures in the first set, as Kenner designer Steve Hodges recalled. "Once I saw hard copies of my first figure work (the action figures from the first set), the characters looked stiff. My next assignment was the Cantina set. We added bent knees and more detail to make them more natural." Regarding Snaggletooth, who passes by in the blink of an eye in the *Star Wars* film, Hodges says, "The belt buckle design is actually the logo used on my first business card. None of the photos I had showed Snaggletooth's buckle, so I used my old logo temporarily and it got approved all the way up to George Lucas."[1]

Boba Fett had been released in America by Kenner as a mail promotion but Palitoy decided not to release the figure at this time. "The second set of figures came out shortly after I had completed the first 12," says Jason Smith. "But given that it had been so difficult to collect the first set, I stopped collecting *Star Wars* figures and enjoyed the ones that I had, along with the Landspeeder. The thing was that I had a mate who had absolutely everything from *Star Wars,* so I never felt that I missed out on much!" James Simmonds recollects:

> I received a C-3PO action figure and a die-cast X-Wing for my seventh birthday in 1979. The thing was that I hadn't seen the film, so I presumed that the holes in Threepio's feet were there so he could fly! I don't know how or why but I didn't see the film when it was released. Perhaps growing up in a rural village had something to do with it. My friends at school had some of the action figures and I even gave my best friend David a Sand People action figure as a birthday present but I was completely unaware of the film. I vividly remember choosing my second action figure from the die-cast X-Wing backing card, which was R2-D2. Perhaps it was the shiny parts of the two droids that impressed me, I don't know. I've since asked my Mum why she bought me *Star Wars* toys when I hadn't seen the film and she said that they were everywhere in the shops at the time and she thought that I would like them. Thanks, Mum!"

The Mounting Merchandise Snowball

Palitoy was in the enviable position of supplying the two top-selling boys' toys in Britain, *Star Wars* and Action Man. "It was a strange situation," says Bob Brechin. "Palitoy had been given *Star Wars* from Kenner to sell in the UK and yet the company was also selling Action Man, which was on license from one of Kenner's biggest competitors, Hasbro. Although *Star Wars* demanded a big license fee to George Lucas, the toys had all the free publicity from an amazingly successful and very popular film. Action Man had to generate its own publicity."

Palitoy's *Star Wars* range expanded with the release of the Kenner series of miniature *Star Wars* die-cast vehicles that had debuted in America the previous year. They were shipped to Palitoy, fully packaged in much the same style as the action figures but with larger backing cards emblazoned with the Palitoy logo. The set consisted of a TIE Fighter, Darth Vader TIE Fighter, X-Wing Fighter and Landspeeder (again spelled Land Speeder). Kenner seems to have done its homework because the Landspeeder featured C-3PO in the driver's seat, which replicated the scene in *Star Wars* when he and Luke searched for R2-D2 (although in the film, the droid is sitting on the right). "I have great memories of playing with my *Star Wars* action figures" says Richard Harris. "But my favorite toy was the die-cast Landspeeder. (I still have it today minus the windscreen.) I didn't care that the figures sitting inside were smaller than my other figures, and I created the scenes from the film over and over again."

Palitoy also released the second set of die-cast vehicles that were debuting too in America. Larger than the first set, they were blister-packed against a cardboard background, surrounded by a thick cardboard frame that made them seem even more impressive. The Millennium Falcon featured a movable antenna dish and top blaster cannon. The Y-Wing Fighter sported removable engines and a small bomb which could be dropped at the touch of a button and be instantly lost. Perhaps the most impressive of the three was the Imperial Cruiser which came complete with a miniature Blockade Runner that could be captured and fitted inside the docking bay and the door slid shut.

There was a fresh batch of other new toys from Palitoy that was derived from the Kenner line. The Radio Controlled R2-D2 could trundle along at a sedate pace on a pair of oversized feet issuing beeping noises. Two items that children could use in their play were the Blaster Pistol and 3 Position Laser Rifle, which had stock which could be folded and unfolded in the manner of the Sterling machine gun from which the on-screen prop was derived. Both toys would make a satisfying buzzing noise when the trigger was activated. Mark Daniels recalls,

> I was taken to Castle House, a department store here in Newcastle-under-Lyme, just before Christmas. I was told I could choose one item as my Christmas present from my grandparents and it didn't take long before I spotted the 3 Position Laser Rifle in a tub at the end of one of the aisles. The box was huge! I drove my family mad that Christmas morning in 1979 with the dreadful whirring sound it made. I also recall taking it into school the following year on the last day before summer holidays. Another boy had bought a Blaster Pistol—so I was the Empire and he was the Rebels!

Palitoy had also made improvements to its production line, as John Holmes explains. "Initially the assembly included a lot of WIP [work in progress] which meant making up parts of the toys in batches and holding them before they were moved to the assembly line for completion. The Americans wanted us to get rid of WIP and make assembly all on line. We were resistant to that method at first but then realized it was better. When we had the assembly running smoothly, I'd say that we were better than Kenner on performance and minute values, i.e., the time it took to produce each toy."

Another item in the Palitoy range, the Imperial Troop Transporter, was an impressive addition to the Imperial arsenal, with a cockpit which could hold two action figures, compartments on the sides that held six more and space in the rear too. Its main selling point was that it made six authentic *Star Wars* sounds when buttons on the top were pressed. "A notable incident took place at the London toy fair," says Geoff Maisey. "Unfortunately, one of our salesmen had misheard the description of the new Imperial Troop Transporter. The retailer he was selling to walked away, trying to find a character called Stan, as he had been told that the vehicle's mechanism had said, 'There's one. Send for Stan,' when in fact it should have been 'Set for stun!'"

Palitoy also released a product unique to its *Star Wars* line: the Talking R2-D2 toy. It was almost identical to the Large Size Action Figure R2-D2 but this version beeped and actually said lines such as "This message is vital to the rebels" when a button on his chest was pressed. "The Palitoy Talking R2-D2 was not a conversion of the Kenner Large Size Action Figure toy," says Brechin. "I commissioned an external pattern maker to create the prototype from wood, on which the tooling would be based, ready for injection molding by a UK subcontractor. The talking mechanism was a unit from Ozen in Japan which was also used in Palitoy products such as the Kojak car and the Daleks and K9 from *Doctor Who*." Meanwhile, in America, Kenner Parker delivered its first royalty check to 20th Century-Fox on April 4, 1979, totaling $1,067,432.58 and was confident that future amounts would be even greater.

The British Merchandise Continues

British publisher Armada released a series of activity books built around Darth Vader, Chewbacca, Luke Skywalker and R2-D2, They were written by James Razzi and illustrated by Patricia Wynne. Also released were two storybooks aimed at younger children, illustrated with high-quality color paintings. *The Maverick Moon* seemed to take place in an alternative *Star Wars* universe where Luke Skywalker is attending the Space Academy. Princess Leia, R2-D2 and C-3PO are also featured but there is no mention of Han Solo and Chewbacca or an intergalactic civil war against the Empire. Covering more familiar territory, *The Mystery of the Rebellious Robot* showed a decidedly anarchic sense of humor. With artwork from Mark Corcoran, the story

Top: Star Wars 1979 novels displayed in an R2-D2 book stand. *Above left:* A second selection of transfer sets was released by Letraset. *Above right:* A Talking R2-D2 was a unique product from Palitoy.

fitted very much within the existing framework of *Star Wars*, with Chewbacca saving the day and finally receiving a medal from Princess Leia. The Armada range of *Star Wars* books was released by arrangement with Random House in the U.S. and were copyrighted by Black Falcon. Helix re-entered the merchandising fray in August with a fresh advertising campaign in *Star Wars Weekly* for its stationery range from the previous year, timed for the start of the new school term. Also available was a new set of Letraset transfer sets, which told the story of the film in ten parts. The sets were of a much smaller size than the three previous editions but the scenes and transfer characters were much more realistic. Sphere released the *Star Wars* novel with a variation on the original cover that included the words "The Greatest Film of the Century!" A promotional poster was issued to shops with the words "On sale here—in paperback. The best-selling novel of the greatest film of the century. Now over five million copies worldwide!" There was a Special Young Readers' Edition of the novel with a red cover and a version released by the Scholastic Society with a yellow cover. Another major *Star Wars* item released this year was a 24-page book and record set from Disney's Buena Vista Records label. The company had secured the exclusive rights for *Star Wars* "kidisk" spinoffs from Black Falcon Ltd. Fans could listen on the record or tape to an excellent abridged audio adaptation of *Star Wars* accompanied by a narrator and turn the page of the book when they heard R2-D2 beep. None of the voices were of the original cast but with John Williams' soundtrack and Lucasfilm sourced sound effects, the record sounded very authentic.

"For kids in the late '70s without access to the film anywhere but on the big screen, this was a must-have," Mark Newbold recalls "[The record and book] gave a swift summary of the film as well as the movie's sound effects, John Williams music, great stills and in its brief running time, it promised—and always delivered—a great adventure."[2] The record had been produced by 30-year-old Michigan-born Jymn Magon, who had begun working at Disney on children's records in 1978. Magon went on to write for Disney's various animated television shows before going freelance in 1993, writing for many animated children's favorites in films and television.

Robert Beecham and Cliro Perfumeries were still going strong, although the production had not gone entirely smoothly. Beecham recalled:

> We had a factory in Abingdon, Oxfordshire, which produced the *Star Wars* bottled bubble bath, and I couldn't get through to their office on the telephone. I said to Andrew my sales rep, "Could you go up there and see what's going on?" Andrew jumped in his car and about three hours later he phoned me and said, "Robert, the owner's gone." I asked, "Where has he gone?" Andrew said, "He's inside." I replied, "That's great. If he's inside the factory, you can speak to him." Then Andrew dropped the bombshell: "He's inside prison!" My mind began racing immediately. I asked, "What's happened to the factory?" Andrew replied, "All of the production line girls are leaving. Nobody has paid them." So, I thought, what does a young businessman like myself do in this sort of position? I immediately went to see my bank manager and said, "I want £2000 in cash, right now." I drove to the factory and said to all of the production staff, "I'm now going to pay all of your wages," and for three weeks, we ran a bubble bath factory. It wasn't easy but we managed to fulfill all of our contracts. That's business!"

Poster Magazine Progress

Bunch Associates was still making the most of the material sent from America by John May. In "Fan Club Facts," the lead article in the *Star Wars Official Poster Monthly* #16, John

May profiled the continuing work of Craig Miller, in his capacity as Director of Fan Relations. The writer had caught up with Miller during his visit to Lucasfilm. "Since the film opened, Craig admits to being swamped by many thousands of letters," wrote May. "But he is fighting to keep the backlog down to a minimum. All mail addressed to individual stars remains unopened and is delivered to them…. Membership of the club has reached some 35,000 members. Hopes are that by the time the new film *The Empire Strikes Back* is released on May 25th, 1980, the roster will number some 250,000 *Star Wars* fans worldwide." This issue also contained John Chesterman's "Cantina Communications," which included a conversation imagined by the writer between Luke Skywalker and Ben Kenobi regarding alien species, where Ben consulted his *Universal Encyclopedia.* The invented scene was clearly not part of the *Star Wars* story but succeeded in presenting the subject of alien communication in an entertaining way. Dr. M.F. Marten prepared an incredibly tough *Star Wars* quiz for this issue. Among the facts that readers were expected to know was that C-3PO was a Class 3 droid, that the Rebels' base was called Massassi and that the trash compactor monster was called a Dianoga. The quiz was another method of bringing obscure *Star Wars* information to the fore. All of it had been derived from official sources such as the novel and the *Art of Star Wars* book.

John Chesterman wrote another informative article, "Escape Through Hyperspace," for *Star Wars Official Poster Monthly* #17. "It was not clear where Han Solo acquired the equipment, but somehow he had found enough spare parts and using bootleg computer programs he had fitted the Millennium Falcon with hyperspace drive." The article that followed was a highly technical examination of the theories surrounding hyperspace travel. Chesterman made an assertion ("The usual technique was to make small jumps and surface at regular intervals to get your bearings, because the slightest mistake could put you millions of miles off course or right outside the galaxy"[3]) that seemed like good advice for space travelers but did not quite ring true for *Star Wars*, as fans were aware that pilots such as Han Solo kept charts to enable them to plot a precise course with a navicomputer. The writer's description of the physics behind faster-than-light travel seemed totally authentic and made the jump to hyperspace seen in *Star Wars* seem to be something that someone, someday, might accomplish. In the same issue, Dr. M.F. Marten presented a report on the *Voyager 1* mission to Jupiter, which it had reached in January 1979. Fantastic color photographs depicted a gas giant, very much in the mode of the planet Yavin in *Star Wars*. Marten's article presented a vivid picture of an alien world, within our very own solar system, that could well be evocative of a planet in the *Star Wars* universe. There was also an interview with Russ Manning, writer-artist of the *Star Wars Comic Strip,* which John May had conducted during his trip to America. The *Star Wars Comic Strip* was syndicated to newspapers in America and Canada, but it had yet to land on British shores. Manning recounted the first time he saw *Star Wars*: "I think it was the second night it was on in a theater in Orange County when my family and I went to see it. I just couldn't even let go of the seat, it was so incredible. Just the sheer amount of sound that was coming out of the screen and what we were seeing was beyond anything we'd seen in films before."[4]

The *Star Wars* comic strip was created for the *Los Angeles Times* by Black Falcon Ltd. on March 11, 1979. It was syndicated to over 200 American and Canadian newspapers. It had run every day since and had become an important part of *Star Wars* fandom, although it had not appeared in Britain. "Russ Manning ended up on the strip for a couple of reasons," says Craig Miller. He continued:

> One is that he had a relationship with the comic strip syndicate. On the Lucasfilm side, the publishing people came to me and they asked me for suggestions for artists because they knew that I was familiar with comic books. I told them Alex Raymond (the creator of the *Flash Gordon* comic strip) was dead, so we couldn't get him. The next choice was Al Williamson, who was an obvious one. After that, Russ Manning was actually a friend of mine and had enjoyed a very long career. I knew that he was a science fiction fan and he'd done a science fiction book called *Magnus Robot Fighter* which was set in the future. Lucasfilm publishing went to Al Williamson and they were not able to do a deal with him and then they went to Russ Manning; and the comic book syndicate also was very high on him doing it; so it came together.

Enter the Hunter

Issue #61 of *Star Wars Weekly* (cover date April 25) began the story "The Return of the Hunter." Valance was still earning a decent living collecting bounties in the outworld planets, preferring "dead" to "alive." He was determined to collect the large bounty on the rebel boy, and the fact that the youth was a "droid lover" in Valance's eyes made the search even more vital. Having studied rebel activity, Valance had identified the planet Junction as a place where the group obtained supplies, and he waited at the planet's main spaceport. Luke eventually turned up searching for parts to repair R2-D2, not realizing that walking around in his usual Tatooine garb, in the company of a golden protocol droid, was a dead giveaway to his identity. An informant alerted Valance to Luke and C-3PO's presence but the bounty hunter first dealt with the local Imperial Spy, who had also spotted the rebel pair. Valance attacked Luke but his blaster was melted to slag in his hand by Luke's lightsaber. Valance opened fire with a blaster weapon incorporated into his artificial arm, but Luke deflected the blast with his lightsaber, sending it back into Valance's face, exposing his artificial features. Valance soon had Luke at his mercy and intended to blast him with the last shot from his arm weapon. C-3PO stepped in front of Luke to protect him. In true pulp fashion, Valance was so moved by the droid's actions that he had a change of heart and allowed Luke and C-3PO to go free.

"Return of the Hunter" could be seen as one of the weaker stories in the post–*Star Wars* Marvel storyline, as Valance's conversion to the good guys seems to be far too easy. The precedent, set by '50s serials and comics, was that a bad guy would usually change sides if the hero had saved his life, or if he had been converted to his cause. As Michael Marten pointed out in his articles for the *Official Star Wars Poster Monthly*, C-3PO only acts in accordance to his programming, so to be moved by his willingness to sacrifice himself seems a little foolish, especially for a hardened bounty hunter.

Star Wars Weekly #64 (May 16) featured the return of Han Solo and Chewbacca in "What Ever Happened to Jabba the Hut?" After helping Luke, Leia and the droids escape the Wheel in issue #52, Han and Chewie developed engine trouble and landed the Millennium Falcon on the planet Orleon, where they had an old hideout in a cave. Unbeknownst to the pair, Jabba the Hut was aware of the hideout and had installed a monitoring device which alerted him that the Millennium Falcon had landed there. Jabba soon arrived in his well-armed ship, the *Voidraker*, and he and his men laid siege to the cave entrance. This was the same bipedal alien Jabba that had been featured in the Marvel *Star Wars* film adaptation and was the only visualization of the character at this time. A major assault by Jabba's men on the cave disturbed a huge nest of killer stone mites, which proceeded to swarm and devour everything in their path. Han and Chewbacca used the distraction to fly the Millennium Falcon out of the cave but found Jabba's *Voidraker* waiting for them in orbit above the planet. But in their haste to escape the planet, members of Jabba's crew had allowed a large number of stone mites to follow them into the ship. Jabba, the only one not devoured by the nasty insects, pleaded to be allowed to transfer to the Millennium Falcon. Han Solo agreed on the condition that the bounty on his head would be lifted; Jabba was more than happy to agree.

The depiction of Jabba the Hut is one of the most glaring problems in the Marvel *Star Wars* continuity, considering how he would eventually be portrayed in the film saga. Although this was not the intention when it was originally written, another way of looking at the Marvel Jabba is that he is not actually the crime lord but someone whom he has employed to be his physical extension. (Writer John Jackson Miller came up with a similar idea *in Star Wars Insider* #149.) The alternative spelling of the name Hut could be a way of differentiating between the two individuals.

The Making of Star Wars *Up for Grabs*

On May 1, *The Making of Star Wars* became available in Britain in both VHS and Betamax formats. The cassette was packaged in a cardboard sleeve with a photograph from the program featuring R2-D2 and C-3PO on the front. The Film Distributors' Association supplied trade buyers the video at the cost of £15.00. An advertisement by one company in the national press offered *The Making of Star Wars* for sale at a considerable sum, £29.99. "I recall how the video was promoted quite heavily," says Darren Slade. "It was included in the print advertisements for companies that rented video recorders. Part of the deal for buying a video recorder from at least one company was that they were giving the title away free. That was something to dream of at the time."

The manufacturer of the *Making of Star Wars* cassette was Magnetic Video UK, whose American parent company in 1977 had been the first to make pre-recorded films available to the general public by acquiring rights to the back catalogue of 20th Century-Fox films. Initially this had been an untested concept and Magnetic Video America seemed to be taking a considerable risk. Would the general public be interested in *hiring* films? In September 1978, Magnetic Video UK launched the release of its first selection of 27 20th Century-Fox video films to high street shops such as Thorn Electrical Industry's DER chain, with a mighty asking price of between £29.95 and £39.95; *The Making of Star Wars* was not part of the selection.

On May 4, Margaret Thatcher and her Conservative party celebrated winning the general election. *The London Evening News* contained a political advertisement under the banner of "May the 4th be with you, Maggie."

Star Wars Weekly #67 (cover date June 13) featured the story "Dark Encounter" which began with Darth Vader in fine form, torturing a rebel spy. The Dark Lord was searching for a rebel deserter, Tyler Lucian, who coincidentally was also being sought by Valance. Lucian was hiding out at a tower on the banks of an acid lake, bemoaning his bad luck at deserting the rebel base, only to learn that Luke Skywalker had destroyed the Death Star. He did not have long to ponder his fate as first Valance arrived and then Vader. Valance completed his conversion to the "good" cause of Luke by choosing to fight Vader although he knew full well that he had little chance of survival. Even though the Empire was aware of Luke's general appearance and that he was a boy who kept the company of droids, they still had not discovered his name. It was Valance's intention to delay Vader's interrogation of Lucian and discovering the boy's identity. Vader began the confrontation with Valance by attempting to make him see reason and offering him a place within the Empire. Hearing Valance's rebuttal, Vader used the Force to make him drop his blaster

FDA (Film Distributors' Association) advertised that *The Making of Star Wars* was available to the trade only.

but the bounty hunter was able to blast him with the weapon hidden inside his artificial arm. This only enraged Vader further. After a punch from Valance clanged against Vader's mask, a downward slash from the Dark Lord's lightsaber seemed to settle the issue. Valance, not quite finished, clamped his artificial hand around one of Vader's ankles and dove into the lake. Vader was almost pulled into the deadly soup but he severed Valance's arm with his lightsaber in time and watched his enemy dissolve in a puff of smoke. Lucian, realizing that Vader was not going to be the most generous of hosts, decided to jump into the deadly lake himself. Luke's identity was safe for now.

The story is a fitting end to the Valance character and his duel with Darth Vader is considered to be one the highlights of the Marvel comic series. The irony of Valance choosing to fight a man that he could have conceivably found common ground with, being a fellow part-man, part-machine cyborg, was obvious to the reader. If only Valance had known what lay under the Dark Lord's armor. Vader had seemed reluctant to put an end to a potentially useful ally, perhaps for similar reasons. According to Kurt Busiek, Valance's death was not the result of a skillful story arc but a directive from above. "He met his death at the request of the people at Lucasfilm. After Valance's first appearance, word came down that George Lucas had plans for a bounty hunter character [Boba Fett] and Valance had to go. Who knows? If not for Boba Fett, we might have found that Valance was a long-lost Tagge cousin or something!"[5]

The Empire *Gets Closer*

The fifth issue of *Star Wars Fan Club Newsletter* (now titled *Bantha Tracks*) contained a good deal of information regarding *The Empire Strikes Back*, including an interview with

Irvin Kershner, who said, "It's a very profound picture. It's a very deep picture, but on one level it's beautifully simple and on one level it's a delight. It's simple, it's clear, it's easy to read, and below that it's supported by some wonderful ideas and wonderful feelings." The report stated that a full-sized Millennium Falcon had been constructed and that production involving the cast had wrapped in early August, while the filming of special effects was due to continue until early March 1980. *The Empire Strikes Back* was due for release in London on May 17, 1980, and in the U.S. and Canada on May 18. There was further confirmation that the entire main cast was returning and that they would be joined by Billy Dee Williams as a character called Lando Calrissian, "an old friend of Han Solo's who runs the mining colony of Bespin." The screenplay was by Leigh Brackett, "a long-time master of science fiction, as well as a top Hollywood screenwriter, and Lawrence Kasdan, a highly talented newcomer to screenwriting." Also included in this issue was a tribute to John Barry, who had collapsed while directing second unit for *The Empire Strikes Back* at Elstree and died in hospital on June 1, 1979. Since winning an Academy Award for his *Star Wars* set designs, Barry had worked on *Superman* and had been due to direct *Saturn III*. It later transpired that Barry had died from meningitis only two weeks after joining the *Star Wars* sequel production.

This issue of *Bantha Tracks* contained a profile of the intriguing new character Boba Fett, who according to the article wore the uniform of the Imperial Shocktroopers, from the "olden time" that were wiped out by the Jedi Knights during the Clone Wars. "Fett is the best bounty hunter in the galaxy, and cares little for whom he works—as long as they pay."[6] Boba Fett had appeared in the cartoon segment of *The Star Wars Holiday Special*, and a performer wearing the costume made public appearances in America.

Speaking to *Starlog* magazine, David Prowse provided some more details. "I went to dinner with the people from Kenner Toys in L.A. and this guy turned up. This character goes around dressed up as Boba Fett, an intergalactic bounty hunter. They're promoting him prior to filming so that by the time the film comes out, people will want to see what he does. I've heard a rumor that he's going to do away with Han Solo. Or, at least, he's going to be *after* Solo. Boba Fett walks around with a sort of flame thrower in one hand and a rocket pack on his back." Prowse was also able to offer a tantalizing prospect: Vader being unmasked, albeit in a limited way. "[Y]ou'll probably only see either the back of my head or my face hidden by breathing tubes."[7]

Star Wars Official Poster Monthly #18 contributed to the excitement of the impending *Star Wars* sequel. In "The Secret Planets," John Chesterman focused on the Empire's search for the planet harboring the new Rebel base, which was a plot point in the new movie. According to Chesterman, the Empire would be required to search for the Rebels even on planets that seem unattractive to settlers. The article segued neatly into *The Empire Strikes Back*, with Chesterman stating; "With ingenuity and determination it is possible to survive in the most inhospitable environments. The frozen landscape of Hoth, the setting of the second *Star Wars* film, shows that life can survive in the coldest climate."[8] This issue of the poster magazine included the article "The Empire Gets Closer" in which John May described how a life-sized Millennium Falcon model had been made for the film: "This huge construction is no less than 80 feet across and weighs some 90 tons." Included in the article was Lucasfilm's standard black-and-white promotional photograph of Luke Skywalker riding a Tauntaun, which May described thusly: "A giant horned lizard which is capable of living in the frozen wastes of the planet Hoth, and which the Rebels have domesticated and ride like horses. On Hoth, the rebels have gathered for yet another confrontation with Darth Vader, the outcome of which we will all just have to wait for."[9]

There was no mention in the editorial but #18 was the last issue of the *Star Wars Official Poster Monthly*. Behind the scenes at Bunch Associates, preparations were being made for *The Empire Strikes Back*. In the meantime, fans could only await the return of their monthly slice of *Star Wars*.

Marvel's Saga Continues

Even though the poster magazine had finished, *Star Wars Weekly* showed no signs of slowing down. The story "A Princess Alone" began in issue #70 (June 27). Leia had embarked on a dangerous spying mission to the industrial planet Metalorn, which was run by the Tagge dynasty on behalf of the Empire. She had fitted herself out in an appropriate figure-hugging worker uniform. As well as dressing exactly the same, the population consisted of pairs of men and women who looked more or less identical. The fact that Leia fitted the bill both physically and facially would almost guarantee her anonymity. A subplot had Tammi, a small girl living on the planet, determined to plant some seeds on one of the few patches of bare soil that had not been built on, if only the over-zealous Stormtrooper guards would let her. A Stormtrooper spotted Leia's fake ID and a furious chase began through the factory workings and storehouses. Baron Orman Tagge had chosen the very same day to make an inspection of the factory planet and to meet its controller, Governor Corwyth. Leia reached her goal in the cafeteria, a local elder, Professor Arn Horada, who had been one of her childhood tutors. Horada was shocked to see Leia, as he had believed the story told by his Imperial masters, that Alderaan had been destroyed in a meteor storm. Before Leia could speak with the old man at length, Baron Tagge approached the pair, brandishing his lightsaber. Leia tipped the tray of food she was carrying over his head, blinding his cyber-vision and locked his ankle to a table leg with his own pair of energy shackles. Tagge cried out for someone to stop this "enemy of the Empire" but the workers crowding around were confused, having been told that the Emperor had no enemies. Tagge freed himself and chased out of the cafeteria, completely ignoring a woman clutching a small girl, covering her face. This of course was Leia, who had been assisted by Tammi. As Leia stealthily made her way to her waiting transport ship, Tagge and Corwyth argued over who was to blame for letting such a high-profile rebel escape. As Leia was whisked away from Metalorn by her transport ship, content that she had sowed the seeds of a new rebel cell, young Tammi finally managed to plant some seeds of her own in a patch of earth without the Stormtroopers spotting her.

"A Princess Alone" was one of the better *Star Wars Weekly* stories, with Leia displaying all of her resourcefulness and cunning. It was refreshing to see her wearing something other than her white dress (keeping the characters in their familiar outfits was probably a request from on high), but when she peeled back the skin-tight hood of her worker's outfit, she had her space buns hairdo squeezed underneath!

The epic tale "Return to Tatooine" began in *Star Wars Weekly* #73 (July 18). In the prologue, Baron Orman Tagge met with his younger brother General Ulric Tagge, who was in command of the Imperial Space Fleet blockade around the Fourth Moon of Yavin. Ulric ribbed his sibling by referencing his ill-advised schemes such as the wind turbine ship, which had been destroyed in about five minutes by Luke Skywalker. Orman Tagge in turn questioned the value of the blockade that had proven to be practically useless. Ulric countered, "The Empire would soon strike back!" Orman Tagge had greater things on his mind: another grand scheme based around a little-known backwater world called Tatooine.

Unbeknownst to Orman Tagge, Luke was at that very moment revisiting the planet of his birth, in order to recruit some new pilots to the Rebel cause. Traveling with R2-D2 and C-3PO, Luke came across his old home, the ruined Lars Homestead, and found that it was being renovated by his old friends Fixer and Camie, who were finally married. An approaching Imperial Troop Transporter, in the mode of the action figure toy, caused Luke and the droids to flee in their Landspeeder.

Baron Orman Tagge met with another brother, the scientist Silas Tagge, at their base on Tatooine. Orman explained that he'd picked the planet because he had checked the Imperial census record and discovered that Luke had grown up there. This put him several steps ahead of Darth Vader, who didn't even know the name of the pilot who had destroyed the Death Star. Tagge knew nothing about Luke other than that he was a Rebel pilot, nor did he know that Luke was being sought by Darth Vader. Meanwhile, Luke ventured into the Mos Eisley Cantina and to his surprise, he found Han Solo and Chewbacca there. In a typical pulp turn of events, the pair had coincidentally visited Mos Eisley at the same time as Luke, to drop off Jabba the Hut after saving him from the sand mites in their previous adventure. Fixer arrived and told Luke that he'd had no choice but to inform the local Imperial garrison. A large contingent of them arrived, blasting everything in sight. Luke, Han, Chewbacca and the droids squeezed into the Landspeeder and made a hasty exit, heading towards Luke's ship hidden in the desert. But it had been stripped down by Jawas. Han managed to negotiate a ride from the Jawas in their Sandcrawler and soon they came across the reason why Orman and Silas Tagge were on Tatooine: the testing of their Omega Frost weapon which could instantly freeze any object, even in the blistering desert. A furious fight ensued and, despite the odds against them, Han, Luke and Chewbacca, with the assistance of the Jawas, defeat Tagge's Stormtroopers and wreck their transport craft. The Jawas then transported their new rebel friends back to Mos Eisley and to where the Millennium Falcon was parked.

Taking off from Tatooine, the rebel heroes followed Baron Tagge's cruiser to the planet Junction and watched it meet an Imperial Star Destroyer in orbit and begin to transfer cargo. To get a closer look, Luke believed he could don a spacesuit and mingle with the men who were handling the cargo, but he was instantly captured. Han decided against any rash action to recue Luke and instead directed the Millennium Falcon towards the Rebel base to warn them of the Omega Frost weapon.

Baron Tagge performed his duty as a comic book villain, boasting to Luke about his entire plan, so that Luke would have all of the information he would need to stop him. Tagge's scheme was to place the Omega Frost in the asteroid belt that the Rebels used to avoid the Imperial blockade and reach the planet Junction. Luke promptly escaped, and once he had defeated the Baron in a lightsaber duel, he managed to disable the Omega frost before the Millennium Falcon and the Rebel Fleet arrived. The Tagge cruiser then felt the full force of the Rebels and was destroyed.

"Return to Tatooine" was an entertaining story very much in the swashbuckling spirit of *Star Wars,* especially the coincidence of the Rebels being on Tatooine just at the right time to meet each other and also just in time to discover Baron Tagge's plans. The inclusion of the Camie and Fixer characters from *Star Wars'* missing scenes was a satisfying addition. The concept of there being galactic census records doesn't ring true because the administration involved would have been next to impossible. Luke would surely not have been raised on Tatooine bearing his father's surname, if everybody in the galaxy could be looked up on a huge database. Despite Baron Tagge's apparent death in this story, seasoned comic readers may have suspected that the character might return.

The Return of Star Wars

With the six-week summer break from school underway, there could hardly be a better prospect for fans than *Star Wars* reappearing at the cinema. And that is exactly what happened, with the film being added to 20th Century-Fox's catalogue of classic films available for hire to cinemas. Much like video hire shops, but on a larger scale, film studios had a catalogue of films that were available to cinemas to rent on a constant basis, so it was never very long before popular films returned to cinema screens. Classic films were shown when individual cinemas had space in their schedule, or during a holiday season. A large percentage of the income of studios came from rentals to cinemas and for that reason big expensive films were rarely sold to television. The system of renting previously released films to cinemas had begun to erode, however, by the new video sale and hire market. But *Star Wars* was no ordinary cinema re-release, and 200 extra prints were made to cope with the expected demand.

Palitoy sought to make the most of the re-release. "I had the idea to tag local *Star Wars* retailer names to the cinema ads to get guaranteed displays in the stores," says Geoff Maisey. "We would show a *Star Wars* TV commercial in the local cinemas and invite retailers to tag their shop name to the end of the ad: 'Available in XX.' It worked well, but the logistics of tagging and distributing commercials to the right cinemas was horrendous!"

The *Star Wars* re-release began at the Glasgow Odeon on July 14 and Birmingham Odeon Queensway on the 15th. It opened at venues all over the country on the 29th. *Star Wars* opened in central London at the Classic Leicester Square and Odeon Westbourne Grove on August 12, then headed for coastal venues on September 9. The *Empire Strikes Back* trailer was included in the presentation, which would have made it even more of an occasion for fans. "The Westcliff-on-Sea Classic understandably wanted to show *Star Wars* but we could only get it in 35mm," says Derek Dorking. "We couldn't get a 70mm copy for love of money. We did have the very first teaser trailer for *The Empire Strikes Back*, though. We always used to step out of the projection room to see the audience reaction to the trailer reels. When the *Empire Strikes Back* trailer came on, it had the audience's complete attention. This was *Star Wars* but it was something new and different. Once word had gotten around, we'd have people paying for entry, watching the trailer and then leaving. I could hardly believe it."

There was another bonus in that there was a "B" feature released with the film in some areas. *Rock Faces* was compilation of three music videos, including Whitesnake performing

"Day Tripper." The production was by the Townsend brothers, director Ray Townsend, editor David and producer Tony. The trio had enjoyed success with their debut feature *Snakebite*, a trio of videos performed by Whitesnake. Brian Payne at 20th Century-Fox had purchased *Rock Faces* specifically as a "B" feature. "I remember *Rock Faces* very strongly when I saw *Star Wars* again in 1979," says Laurie Calvert. "Although I thought that it was a little odd that this music video compilation was being shown before the film!"

Star Wars' British re-release preceded the American one, which began on August 15, 1979. Video recorders, albeit with a very expensive £600 plus price tag, were beginning to appear more frequently in the shops but *Star Wars* was not still not available to purchase or even hire on video. If fans were unable to catch a local showing in 1979, they could catch a glimpse of the film during *The Making of Star Wars* when it was reshown on ITV on Friday, August 24, at 10:05 p.m.

In August, Palitoy placed quarter-page advertisements in *Star Wars Weekly* and *2000AD*, featuring the nine newest figures in the *Star Wars* range. A cartoon depicted Luke in his X-Wing outfit facing off against the new cantina creatures. On his side were

The Making of Star Wars **was made available in a cardboard sleeve (courtesy Gerald Faget).**

the new droids, including the Death Star Droid. The fantastic artwork was from Brian Bolland, a very well-known artist via his work on *2000AD*. He has since become extremely well known, especially for providing the art for *Batman: The Killing Joke*.

Craig Miller's Campaign Trail

The 37th Worldcon Science Fiction Convention took place at the Metropole Hotel, Brighton from August 23 to 27 and featured a large exhibition of photographs, sketches and models from *The Empire Strikes Back* organized by Craig Miller, who also presented a slide show and a trailer for the film. He was joined in a panel discussion by Gary Kurtz, who also presented a Hugo Award for the best dramatic presentation of a science fiction theme to Christopher Reeve representing *Superman*. Miller says,

> Part of the promotional tour Charlie Lippincott had conducted in 1976 was the World Science Fiction Convention which that year was in Kansas City. He organized a small display room and Mark Hamill was there along with some costumes, artwork and R2-D2 and C-3PO on display. We continued to do promotions at events in the run-up to *The Empire Strikes Back*. The World Science Fiction Convention was in Brighton in '79, which was not that far from where we were filming at Elstree. We arranged a display with the organizers and transported there a full-sized Snowspeeder prop, which we put just outside the main exhibit hall. In a function room we hung up Ralph McQuarrie paintings, we had R2-D2 and costumes including C-3PO and Darth Vader. There were dozens and dozens of photos and some of the miniature mock-ups of the sets that had been used in planning how they would eventually look. We had Dagobah, the carbon-freezing chamber, the rebel base ice hangar and some others. The thing was that when we opened the door to the public, I realized that there was a tiny Yoda on the Dagobah miniature set, who at that time was still top secret. I nonchalantly wandered up to the display as not to attract attention and quickly put Yoda in my pocket! The other thing was that I and the rest of the Lucasfilm team didn't take any photographs of the display and none have emerged in all of these years. We had a sign saying "No photographs." Trust people to have actually taken notice of it! It would be great if someone, somewhere would come forward with some images. During the event, Gary Kurtz and I put on a slide show and showed the trailer to great reaction.

Miller's next stop was Comicon '79, the annual British Comic Art and Fantasy Convention, which took place at the Hotel Metropole, Birmingham, from Friday August 31, to Sunday, September 2. Gerald Crotty has strong memories of Craig Miller's presentation. "He answered a few questions and showed some slides from *Empire*; these were of Star Destroyers and a painting of Luke vs. Vader. It seemed fantastic in an unreal way. I remember trying to imagine a sequel but just couldn't see it, what could top *Star Wars*? Then they showed a 90-second trailer. Wow! The most amazing shot was of the Falcon banking right to avoid the asteroids."

Expanding the Palitoy Range

In September, a full-page advertisement appeared in *Star Wars Weekly* and other children's publications featuring three new playsets for the action figure range from Palitoy; it boasted fantastic artwork again by Brian Bolland. *The Land of the Jawas* consisted of a plastic base and a three-dimensional cardboard version of the Jawa Sandcrawler, which included a lift which could whisk droids or unfortunate humans into its innards. The *Cantina* was made up from a cardboard backdrop and plastic base that incorporated a bar, a table and pair of cardboard doors attached to a plastic frame via strips of silver paper. The *Droid Factory* consisted of either a yellow or blue molded plastic base, with indentations into which an array of droid parts supplied could be installed, including an R2-D2 with a third leg. All three sets were different from the American versions because the injection-molding tooling was not available from Kenner and instead Palitoy had turned to vacuum-forming for the manufacturing process. "There was also the cost of manufacture to take into consideration," says Bob Brechin. "Vacuum-forming tooling is very much cheaper than injection-molding tooling and is useful for short production runs. The molds can be made in epoxy resin, whereas injection molding requires more substantial molds made from steel or beryllium copper that can withstand the heat and pressure involved in the injection-molding process." The Kenner versions of the *Cantina* and *Land of the Jawas* had an injection-molded base which incorporated some child-operated mechanisms which made the action figures move. The *Droid Factory* had a socket for a manually operated crane. "Products that have been injection-molded can be designed to be more intricate and versatile than vacuum forming," says Bob Brechen. He continues:

> In fact, vacuum forming is not a process to consider if too many post-molding operations are required, such as fitting mechanisms. To replace the child-operated features in the *Cantina* and *Land of the Jawas* and yet still give some "action" and child participation, we designed a small stand, with pins that fit the holes in the feet of the figures, on which two characters could fit. The "fighting" stand had two hinges and two handles so that when it was pushed back and forth using the handles, both figures would move and look as if they were confronting each other. We felt that this was a better solution in some respects than the Kenner playsets because it allowed the child to be more creative in play, moving the "action" to anywhere, whereas the Kenner version only allowed the child to have "action" in designated places. We also included several yellow versions of the circular action figure base with the *Cantina* and *Land of the Jawas*. Unfortunately, due to concerns over cost, we were not able to include the escape pod which was supplied with the Kenner *Land of the Jawas*.

At one stage, the *Cantina* came with four free *Star Wars* action figures: Hammerhead, Greedo, Walrus Man and Snaggletooth. They were either supplied in plastic bags or fully packaged with the backing cards folded in half. A large circular sticker was applied to the front of the box. A Palitoy *Star Wars* catalogue, included with the large boxed toys, featured the entire 1979 range.

Gary Kurtz and Craig Miller present the *Empire Strikes Back* preview at the World Science Fiction Convention in Brighton (photograph by John C. Andrews, courtesy Colin Harris).

With few opportunities to obtain action figure playsets outside of birthdays and Christmas, fans often used their creativity to expand their *Star Wars* play world, as Ian Whitlock can testify:

> With some cardboard, pens and Sellotape, you could extend your playset fairly easily. That's one of the main things about *Star Wars* that I loved, that you could really let your imagination run away with you and expand the world so much more than was initially on offer from the toy shops. The only official playsets I owned from *Star Wars* were the *Death Star* and the *Cantina*. It was only as an adult collector that I learned that the *Cantina* came with cardboard doors and sticker hinges along with the fighting stand which were all missing from mine. They were probably swiped from the box before I bought it. Thanks a bunch, whoever that was.

I picked up an American Batman *comic from my local news agent and was surprised to find the center pages contained an advert for* Star Wars *toys depicted via some fantastic artwork. There was a very exotic-looking new toy called an Imperial Troop Transporter which looked like the vehicle the Imperials had recently used in* Star Wars Weekly. *Most of the toys in the shops were well out of the price range of my parents and even if I'd received one of the playsets from Palitoy, I would have been very disappointed that it had no working functions. That* Batman *comic became an indispensable part of my* Star Wars *collection and was the source of many toy fantasies.*

Soon it was not only *Star Wars* figures which crowded the shelves in toy shops, as 3¾-inch action figures began to appear, based on other science fiction films and television programs. The similar scale of all action figures was an advantage of childhood in the 1970s. *Star Wars, Micronauts, Airfix Eagles, Fisher Price Adventure, The Black Hole, Buck Rogers, Battlestar Galactica* and others were all combined by children in a mix-and-match science fiction play world. "My local toy shop set up a window display which featured all kinds of sci-fi figures," recalls Glen Maloney. "They had the Cantina playset with all different science fiction characters rubbing shoulders with each other at the bar, which looked very funny." Peter Davis has similar memories. "Our #1 film was *Star Wars* but this was fueled by anything else space-related; *The Black Hole, Battlestar Galactica,* etc. Whether it was movies, books or the toys. You didn't have the deluge you get now. We weren't kids with parents who spent loads of money on this stuff. My *Star Wars* fix was birthdays, Christmas and very little in between. As brothers, we would get different toys so we could have a variety and share."

In common with many children, I added to my Star Wars *play world with characters from other films and television programs. When Mego ceased trading, many of its product lines flooded the British market at bargain prices; The Black Hole, Star Trek, Micronauts were all sold for pence. Also, I did not let the lack of Palitoy-produced playsets affect my* Star Wars *play world. Like children everywhere, I made use of everything I could get my hands on, which eventually built into a huge pile of junk with which to create scenery and entire environments for my action figures. The source of the characters didn't matter—they all occupied the same* Star Wars *world, at least in my own mind.*

The Empire Creeps Closer

Bantha Tracks #6 revealed more about *The Empire Strikes Back* via an interview with Harrison Ford, who said, "You can pretty much think that everyone who will see the second one, has seen the first one … it had to be more complex. The characterizations had to be more complex. I felt a responsibility to make it better. I mean, you get a chance to do it over again—the only reason is to make it better. If you can't do it better, it's boring."[10] Also in this issue, a further update informed readers that principal photography had wrapped and that the large scale Millennium Falcon prop had been dismantled and placed in storage. Brian Johnson was working alongside his colleagues at Industrial Light and Magic completing the special effects sequences. Harrison Ellenshaw had resumed his matte painting responsibilities (changing his name from Peter Ellenshaw, Jr.). Jon Berg and Phil Tippett, who had created the Millennium Falcon chess sequence, had joined the production again as animators. Richard Edlund was listed as director of photography and Paul Hirsh as editor.

There was another update in the 1980 *Star Wars Annual,* released in the autumn by Marvel/Grandreams Ltd. "Our Marvel offices were on the second floor of a building that had the *Star Wars Annual* producer [Grandreams] on the first floor," remembers Dez Skinn. "U.K. annuals traditionally go on sale about four months before Christmas, despite the following year's date inside. Confusing, but that's publishing for you!" This *Star Wars Annual* bucked the trend of annuals containing the following year's date and was copyrighted 1979 20th Century-Fox and Black Falcon Ltd. It included a reprinting of the "Dragon Lords" story and interviews with Ford, Anthony Daniels, Carrie Fisher, Mark Hamill and Dave Prowse. There was also an exclusive feature on *The Empire Strikes Back*, with a fantastic rendering of the cast and crew filming the logo of Darth Vader in flames and the film's official title font. The article listed the major members of the cast and crew who had been previously announced, along with John Mollo as costume designer and "Ken Russell's favorite camera ace" Peter Suschitzky as cinematographer. The article revealed a fact that some readers may not have not picked up on, that the *Star Wars* sequel would actually be the fifth chapter of the saga. "It's not *Star Wars 2*, because it's not *Star Wars 2!*" proclaimed the writer. "The first film was really, basically *Star Wars 4* and this one is really *Star Wars 5* if you want to be really, sequentially correct."[11] The black-and-white photograph of Luke Skywalker riding a Tauntaun which had previously appeared in the press was included in the article. Two production paintings by Ralph McQuarrie were also included which readers would not have seen before: in one, the Millennium Falcon flies down inside a huge crater in an asteroid, and in the other, C-3PO and R2-D2 are inside a Rebel base control room on Hoth, with the Rebels wrapped in cold weather gear. This was more than an update than any fan might have expected, and to discover it inside a *Star Wars Annual* was all the more surprising.

Shaun Dawkins was seeking all of the information as to the present state of the sequel "It was all systems go to try and find out what was going on with *The Empire Strikes Back*. I started reading *Starburst* magazine and *Starlog* looking for the latest information. We bombarded Elstree Studios with letters and phone calls but despite our efforts we were frustratingly not given access to visit the set."

Darth Vader Strikes

Star Wars Weekly #85 (cover date October 10) began a new story titled "Dark Lord's Gambit." The tale began with Darth Vader torturing a hapless Rebel and learning the identity of the pilot who destroyed the Death Star. Vader concocted a trap for Luke Skywalker in which he would use the troublesome Tagge family members as pawns. Vader revealed to General Ulric Tagge that his brothers Orman and Silas had *not* been killed in the Rebel Fleet attack on their ship and that his men had rescued them from them from the wreckage. Ulric, desperate to inherit the title of baron from his elder brothers, agreed to assist Vader on the promise that their demise would be guaranteed.

The Rebel Base received new visitors in the form of Sister Domina and her followers, whose ship made it through the Imperial Blockade with the assistance of Luke and his X-Wing squadron. Domina was from the planet Monastery; it was run by the Order of the Sacred Circle, who were politically powerful throughout the galaxy but had remained neutral. Domina explained that an envoy on Monastery was making the case for the Empire: Darth Vader! The Rebels decided to send their own representative and Luke was soon on his way. When he encountered Vader on Monastery, he drew and ignited his lightsaber, bristling for a confrontation. Vader was content to observe the traditions of the host planet and walked away. Leia, Han and Chewbacca were shadowing Luke in the Millennium Falcon until they were captured by Darth Vader's Star Destroyer. Vader's second-in-command saw straight through the forged papers that Han Solo presented and ordered an immediate inspection. Well-briefed by Vader, he had recognized Han and Chewbacca and knew that Leia was often their traveling companion and threw them in the Star Destroyer's brig. A search of the Millennium Falcon's smuggling compartments drew a blank, because Leia was hiding in one of them under a false bottom.

On Monastery, Luke and R2-D2 presented themselves before the Council of Elders to make a case against the Empire, unaware that Domina was the sister of the Tagge brothers and had vowed to avenge the apparent deaths of Orman and Silas. Domina revealed that she had been named All-High Priestess and had the final say *over* the council. She condemned Luke and the Rebels as being dangerous, but Luke countered by stating that Darth Vader, who was standing there in the auditorium, had used the Force to cloud the judgment of everyone present. Vader spoke next, suggesting that if Luke was accusing him, they settle the issue with a duel, which was in keeping with Monastery traditions. Luke agreed, unaware that the trap Vader had set was at that moment snapping shut.

In orbit aboard the Star Destroyer, Leia rescued Han and Chewbacca and they flew free in the Millennium Falcon, but Baron Orman Tagge had stowed aboard. As soon as the ship landed on Monastery, Tagge ran off, convinced that his sister must be in danger.

Luke faced off against a towering figure in very familiar black armor, his red lightsaber alight. They dueled at length, but it was Luke who eventually landed the fatal blow. But the figure who fell was not Darth Vader but Orman Tagge. Vader had projected an illusion into the mind of Luke and as the Dark Lord approached, he taunted him about how easy it had all been. Vader challenged Luke to fight him, but Luke understandably thought better of it and made a hasty exit. Han and Leia arrived on foot and led Luke to the Millennium Falcon. Since Orman Tagge had been killed in the duel with Luke, Domina's hatred of the youth intensified. Despite their experience and savvy, the rebel heroes had found themselves outmatched. Vader could have dealt with all of them there and then on Monastery but it would have been contrary to the laws of that world, and he didn't care to upset his allies on Monastery. The Dark Lord had trapped and manipulated Luke & Company so easily, that another chance to deal with these troublemakers would surely present itself, when the Empire could truly *strike back*.

As an epilogue to the story, Jabba the Hut was informed that the wreck of Crimson Jack's Star Destroyer had been found and the ship's log indicated that Han Solo was behind the destruction. As Jabba had invested heavily in Jack's operation, he was enraged enough to reverse the agreement he had made with Solo. A bounty hunter drew on Han Solo on a far-off planet and, after being felled by a well-aimed shot, he spluttered that Jabba the Hut's bounty had reactivated.

In the American comic, the storyline begun by "Dark Lord's Gambit" concluded in April 1980 and was written as the finale to the Marvel *Star Wars* story, which segued directly into *The Empire Strikes Back* (even though one more story, "Silent Drifting," was printed). The daily comic strip was still chronicling the events in between the end of the Marvel storyline and the *Star Wars* sequel but for American fans who only read the Marvel comic, "Dark Lord's Gambit" was the final chapter. All the separate plot points in the Marvel *Star Wars* saga had been brought neatly to a conclusion, except the Rebels finding a new base. "Dark Lord's Gambit" was a story full of the action, intrigue and humor that was the trademark of *Star Wars*. Darth Vader knowing the identity of all of the rebel heroes and of the Millennium Falcon was an important plot point of *The Empire Strikes Back*, and the Marvel comic storyline had explained how that came about. At the end of this particular chapter of the saga, Han Solo was still indebted to Jabba the Hut while Luke had grown in the Force but not enough to make him the equal of Darth Vader. In Britain, "Dark Lord's Gambit" ended on December 5, 1979, well ahead of the American comic schedule, so with *The Empire Strikes Back* roughly six months away, *Star Wars Weekly* would need to continue the ongoing story in some other way.

John May's New Challenge

Bunch Associates was still hungry for fresh material for its publications based on *The Empire Strikes Back* and dispatched John May to America once more. According to May,

I flew with the cartoonist Edward Barker on October 10–11, by which time the *Star Wars* H.Q. had been completed. A kind of hybrid between a Roman villa and a corporate H.Q., a tiled atrium and a staff of about 20. Every day I'd be picked up from where I was staying, just up from Hollywood Boulevard, by limousine and work in a windowless office. They gave me, under high security, a copy of the script, from which I constructed a short-form version of the story of the film, for potential publication in our mag. As it turned out, this was a waste of time because we didn't use it in the end as the film changed so much during the course of production.

I traveled north to San Francisco by train where I met George Lucas for the first time in a milk bar in Modesto, a small town north of San Francisco in which Lucas owned many properties. He was dressed as usual in his check shirt, jeans and Converse-type shoes, was friendly and took me to one of the houses—a little terraced house. We went through the narrow front hall and turned the corner to the front room where I got the shock of my life. There was a giant screen, lots of equipment and several people actually editing *The Empire Strikes Back*. [A] great gee-whiz moment. Later we wandered to a string of cottages set amongst the trees where some of the major players were staying and I met

Irvin Kershner, the director, and conducted an interview with him. A few days later, I went down to San Rafael to Industrial Light and Magic (3160 Kerner Blvd.) which was definitely the highlight of the trip. It was located at the time in an anonymous warehouse on the edge of this small town. I will try to picture the place for you. There was a small reception area, with a big cut-out of the magician logo of Industrial Light and Magic and a schemata drawing of what would become Skywalker Ranch on the wall. I remember meeting Brian Johnson, the British guy who was in charge of the special effects of the film. His desk was covered in books about stunts, dynamiting things, etc. From there I was led into this large space which was the heart of the operation. At one end was the blue screen against which many scenes were shot. In the center was the computer-controlled camera. To the right, in the bay, was the cannibalized VistaVision equipment used for optical printing. I remember being shown the small rectangle of velvet with little fiber optic cables coming out; that was the universe in most of the deep space shots in the film. In another area, the model makers were at work on the AT-AT Walkers. Upstairs was a very tiny computer room with one computer and one bearded guy in charge of it. Further down on the first floor was a giant room entirely filled with plastic model kits, that the spaceship builders would cannibalize for parts for their own creations. Here I met Joe Johnston, in a room where the entire final attack on the Death Star was storyboarded in a series of drawings on the pin board behind him. I had never seen anything like that.

On October 22, there was a special event organized by 20th Century-Fox where British companies interested in producing merchandise were wined and dined and shown a presentation on the upcoming film. Existing licensees such as Bunch Associates were present too. Black Falcon was not engaged with British merchandising at this stage and the company was eventually absorbed into Lucasfilm's main operation in December 1979. This development could only have been beneficial as Black Falcon Ltd. had not contributed a great deal to the *Star Wars* franchise in Britain. The 1980 annual and bedroom ware for *The Empire Strikes Back* from Ratcliffe Bros. are the only exclusively British produced items known (at least by this author) to bear the Black Falcon copyright. With this, Grandreams and Ratcliffe Bros. probably sought out the rights to produce these indispensable items. Looking at the situation in practical terms; the geographical distance, time difference, the astronomical cost of phone calls and the lack of local knowledge meant that any company based in America would be hard-pressed to conduct a merchandise campaign in Britain. In its place, Lucasfilm UK would take over all of the responsibilities for British *Star Wars* merchandising, although 20th Century-Fox would still need to be consulted with any merchandise arrangement.

Charles Lippincott was no longer involved with merchandising as he had parted company with Lucasfilm. Nor would Peter Beale, as he had taken the position of managing director of EMI Films Ltd. Still in the mix, Marc Pevers had been promoted to vice-president of 20th Century-Fox Licensing Corporation, the company's merchandising subsidiary. According to Pevers:

> I had virtually nothing to do with *The Empire Strikes Back*, other than briefing Jerry Van Ness who had been taken on to handle the merchandising at Lucasfilm and introducing him to all of the licensee companies. I had actually met with George Lucas regarding taking the merchandising job at Lucasfilm but it seems that while he loved the *Star Wars* toys, he was unhappy that the deal with Kenner Parker had been made before the film came out and had not been as profitable as it might have been if it had been made after it was a hit. This was despite the fact that the original brief that Charlie and I had been given was to make a toy deal in advance. I got along well with Van Ness and his successor Maggie Young.

Fans who kept their eyes peeled could still see *Star Wars* at the cinema. It was appearing here and there, probably to fill lulls in individual cinemas' schedules. For example, the

Classic Oxford Circus showed it for one week only from October 28, and the Bristol ABC for a single week from November 18.

Star Wars Weekly #94 (cover date December 12) featured "Way of the Wookiee!," a story produced by the regular Marvel team of writer Archie Goodwin and artist Carmine Infantino (with Pablo Marcos) exclusively for *Star Wars Weekly*. It took readers back to a point in time shortly before Han Solo and Chewbacca met Luke and Ben Kenobi in the Mos Eisley cantina. At the behest of Jabba the Hut, Han and Chewbacca were traveling in the Millennium Falcon to the planet Formos, a hub of trader and smuggler activity due to its proximity to "spice-rich" Kessel. The twists and turns of the adventure led to the situation where Han had to dump his cargo of spice. Han was philosophical about Jabba being enraged over the loss of the cargo. "If you and I can't handle a little trouble … who can?" he said in the closing panel. "Way of the Wookiee!" is a fine stand-alone story which presents a realistic series of events, which could be seen as being part of the buildup to the *Star Wars* film. C-3PO's line in *Star Wars* "We'll be sent to the spice mines of Kessel…" was evidently interpreted by Goodwin as an Imperial policy of sweeping up anyone they chose to serve in the mines. Chewbacca's home world of Kashyyyk was featured, albeit in a flashback, which matched the *Star Wars Holiday Special*.

The Christmas Present List

In November, the Ballantine book *Art of Star Wars* was stuffed full of pre-production art and rare photographs. It also contained the *Star Wars* script, labeled as "Revised Fourth

Palitoy's Cantina playset added a great deal to the *Star Wars* play world of children (courtesy Darren Simpson).

Draft January 15th 1976." It was clear that the script had been heavily edited to match the dialogue of the finished film, with elements such as Blue Squadron being changed to Red Squadron. It was telling that despite the changes, the major missing scenes were still included, as if they were still legitimate sections of the *Star Wars* story. Also available was Ballantine's beautiful 1980 *Star Wars* calendar, featuring *Star Wars* poster art from all over the world. It was an item to treasure for any fan. The quality of *Star Wars* products had certainly not diminished since the film had arrived. *The Star Wars Annual, Calendar* and *Art of Star Wars* were at the top of the Christmas gift list of many a fan.

Regarding the Palitoy *Star Wars* range, Geoff Maisey says, "The success of the Palitoy *Star Wars* product line in 1979, selling in huge quantities, especially up to Christmas, without a *Star Wars* film at the cinema surprised everyone in the U.K. toy trade." A new item from Palitoy was Darth Vader's TIE fighter, scaled to action figures that had been advertised in *Star Wars Weekly* #93 (December 5). The toy was essentially the standard TIE fighter fitted with a different style of wings, cast in a dark gray color; but even so, it presented a mighty item for any fan lucky enough to receive it. Also in December, Magnetic Video made additional titles from its catalogue available via high street shops, including *The Making of Star Wars,* all for under £30 per piece. Depending on where fans lived in the country, the Christmas holiday was made extra special. *The Making of Star Wars* was shown on ITV at 11:15 a.m. on December 31 in the Southern and Border regions.

Nineteen seventy-nine had seen the successful continuation of *Star Wars* fandom, which had been supported by the fan club, weekly comic, the novel *Han Solo at Stars' End* and the *Official Poster Monthly.* New merchandise had been produced although not nearly

The Darth Vader TIE Fighter was a top Christmas gift choice.

at the same level as the previous year. Tantalizing dribs and drabs had been released about *The Empire Strikes Back*, which seemed even more exciting with every new revelation.

The air was also thick with news of all kinds of rival science fiction films and television programs. "The countdown has started. Without doubt this is going to be the biggest space or sci-fi movie year in movie history," said the December 15 issue of *Screen International*. The article highlighted *The Black Hole, Star Trek: The Motion Picture, Flash Gordon, The Incredible Shrinking Woman* and *The Empire Strikes Back*; 1980 would also see the release of *Saturn 3, Battle Beyond the Stars, The Final Countdown* and a second *Battlestar Galactica* film. And James Bond in *Moonraker* was still on release. In addition to the huge budgets and massive sums spent to publicize upcoming science fiction films, *Screen International* also focused on the rival merchandise:

> One of America's biggest toy companies (Mego) … is producing six million *Black Hole* dolls…. There are a million copies of the *Black Hole* novel on the way to bookstores, along with 150,000 calendars, 200,000 picture books and 20,000 jigsaw puzzles. Not forgetting 300,000 T-shirts, 30,000 pairs of *Black Hole* pajamas … and if that wasn't enough, a million soundtrack records are coming off the pressing machines. Not to be outdone, Paramount has licensed the production of millions of comic books, coloring books, transfer kits—and even believe it or not, a *Star Trek* cookbook. Plus, a whole range of dolls.[12]

The Empire Strikes Back would need to shine brighter than all of its rivals to compete for the attention of the cinema audiences. Sequels were often shoddily produced reruns of the original film, and people could be forgiven for believing that the *Star Wars* sequel would be little different. Despite being Britain's #3 film in 1979, *Jaws 2* had done little to uphold the reputation of sequel films, with its tired rehash of the events of its predecessor. *The Empire Strikes Back* would face choppier waters than any sequel film deserved to enter.

Star Wars was shown again as a Christmas release at venues including the Dominion Theatre. Newspaper advertisements included the line "The very best Christmas present of all." The Liverpool Odeon ran *Star Wars* from December 23, the only one of the big 13

Star Wars made a welcome return to the Dominion Theatre (courtesy Derek Dorking).

provincial venues to do so. Showings were relatively scarce, probably because of the crush of new films opening in December. Fans would have considered themselves to be very fortunate indeed if they had picked up on the advertising for a showing of *Star Wars*, because in those pre–Internet days, such events were truly a local affair. There could hardly have been a better Christmas present for a fan. Anyone who was fortunate enough to see *The Empire Strikes Back* trailer at the cinema in December would have witnessed a rare glimpse of the film to come that most fans could only dream of.

Chapter 6

The Empire
Gathers Its Forces

On January 1, 1980, there was a change in the production of *Star Wars* toys in Britain, not that *Star Wars* fans would notice any difference. While still being owned by General Mills, Denys Fisher and Chad Valley began trading as "The Palitoy Company." There was also very nearly another major change at Palitoy, as Geoff Maisey explains:

> The Palitoy board decided to switch sales of the upcoming *Empire Strikes Back* products to Chad Valley, which was under the control of Palitoy, to try to bring stronger and more successful lines to its portfolio of products. This was met with very strong resistance from the Palitoy marketing group and the case was made that Chad Valley was predominantly a pre-school brand and the company had no experience of selling a complex and varied product line like *Star Wars*. The decision was not an easy one, as we still had Action Man in the Palitoy line, a key competitor of *Star Wars*. However, we won the day and *The Empire Strikes Back* line stayed at Palitoy!

Chad Valley got as far as producing a 1980 trade catalogue that featured *Star Wars* but all of the packaging remained Palitoy-branded. The ITV Anglia region broadcast *The Making of Star Wars* on January 5 at 4:30 p.m.

The Christmas release of *Star Wars* at the Dominion Theatre Tottenham Court Road had proven successful enough for it to be booked at the cinema for an open-ended run, which was probably an exclusive presentation in Britain at that time. The Dominion's continuing run of *Star Wars* was a litmus test of the film's popularity. This was a top-flight venue in a prime London location and could show any film, including new releases, but it was showing *Star Wars*.

Issue #100 of *Star Wars Weekly* (cover date January 23) sported a fantastic wraparound photograph of an X-Wing dogfighting with Darth Vader's TIE Fighter. Inside was a listing of all of the past comic stories and the writers and artists who had produced them. More importantly, there was news about *The Empire Strikes Back*, including an updated official logo for the film. Via a breathtaking double spread advertisement, it was revealed that the film would have its world premiere on May 16, 1980. The milestone of the 100th issue provided another opportunity to launch a revamp, with photographic covers and "Star Profiles" of the *Star Wars* actors, which included the latest information on their film roles, along with photographs of them out of their *Star Wars* guises.

The story "The Long Hunt" began in #100, with "Guest Artists" Mike Vosburg and Steve Leialoha, along with "Guest Writer" Chris Claremont serving up a more mature story than the usual Marvel fare. Luke, Leia, Han, Chewbacca and the droids stopped off on the planet Tirahnn for supplies in the Millennium Falcon. At a bustling bazaar, Luke and Leia were spotted by a local informant. Perhaps the farm boy clothing and the white dress and space buns hairstyle was a poor choice of attire for two people wanted by the Empire! An extremely interesting character, an alluring black woman called Katya M'Buele, with whom Han Solo had "old business," was murdered almost as soon as she arrived. Despite an apparent attempt at a more mature tone, "The Long Hunt" does not seem to fit in with the post-*Star Wars* storyline and can be seen as an individual, separate story. The story's winged warriors had stepped directly out of *Flash Gordon.* Many fans consider the story a contradiction to the events in *The Empire Strikes Back,* as Luke's Father *and* Darth Vader are mentioned, but it can also be seen as one of many red herrings Luke encountered on the path to learning the truth about his father. "The Long Hunt" was originally printed in color in the American *1979 Star Wars Annual.*

Star Wars Weekly #104 (February 20) featured the beginning of another story exclusive to Britain. "The Weapons Master" began with Luke and C-3PO being wowed by Leia's skills with a blaster during an escape from Stormtroopers, and they asked her how she became so skilled. The story went into flashback to a time when she was beginning her first term as an Imperial Senator. Her constantly challenging the emperor's increasingly restrictive policies provoked General Emir of the Imperial forces into hiring the Assassin's Guild to get rid of her. Leia's father had anticipated the potential danger to his daughter and had hired one of his colleagues from the Clone Wars, Giles Durane, to act as protector and a trainer. Leia took a break from her senatorial duties and traveled aboard Durane's spaceship, where he schooled her in marksmanship and the use of starship gun turrets. After Leia's training, Durane was hired by the Assassin's Guild himself and perished in a shoot-out with Leia.

The Muppets

The February 21 episode of *The Muppet Show* had a *Star Wars* theme. Mark Hamill appeared in his new costume from *The Empire Strikes Back*, along with R2-D2, C-3PO and Chewbacca, who was strangely naked without his bandolier strap. Although it appeared to be an American program, *The Muppet Show* was filmed in Britain, which partially explained the absence of Carrie Fisher and Harrison Ford. Fortunately, Miss Piggy and Kermit the Frog filled their roles with some gusto, especially Miss Piggy, who sported a full Princess Leia hairdo. Hamill took to the Muppets' stage with huge enthusiasm in what proved to be a fantastic show. "*The Muppet Show* was one of the best spinoffs," said Anthony Daniels. He went on:

> For the first time, I felt like I was on a set where people understood how it was for an actor to wear a difficult costume, because most Muppeteers are in awkward positions to animate the characters. I also felt for the first time I was part of a team that really got that. To be working with Kermit, Miss Piggy and the others was such a remarkable treat, I loved the show. They also asked me to be in *Sesame Street* in New York. I wanted to stay there for the rest of my life, as the team consists of the most lovely people who love what they are doing and do it superbly well. These two things are really great memories.[1]

The ever-resourceful Craig Miller had been responsible for organizing Daniels' trip to *Sesame Street*. "It was sort of amusing that me and my crew, we all wanted photographs taken with Big Bird and the *Sesame Street* guys wanted photos taken with R2-D2 and C-

3PO because, of course, we saw the robots all the time and it was no big deal for us. But Big Bird, wow, that was really something. The *Sesame Street* people saw their characters every day, so it was R2-D2 and C-3PO that were special."

Picture Previews

There was an exciting glimpse of *The Empire Strikes Back* in a March 17 *Daily Mirror* article by Tom Merrin titled "*Star Wars* on Ice!" *Star Wars* fans may have been savvy enough not to believe plot revelations so far in advance of the film's release. "All of the characters from the original film are back plus a monster lineup of new faces to help hinder Luke and Co. as they are hounded through space by the wicked Darth Vader," wrote Merrin. "Two bounty hunters Boba Fett and Grido make their bow by helping the villainous Darth Vader. There are also automations, war Droids and medical Droids."[2] The article included several new photographs from the film. One was of Chewbacca with his hands around the neck of a kneeling Lando Calrissian. C-3PO appeared to be in pieces and strapped to Chewbacca's back. The *Daily Express* also printed a preview of *The Empire Strikes Back* on March 17. Under the headline "C-1½ PO" was the same photograph of Chewbacca strangling Lando Calrissian. There was also a new photo of C-3PO in one piece next to R2-D2. The article confirmed what many fans knew, that the live action photography had been finished and that the special effects were being filmed. "The film, to be premiered in May, will give audiences another chance to escape their earthly confines as Luke Skywalker, Han Solo and Princess Leia stride the cosmos…. Let the Force be with you."[3] *The Daily Star*'s *Empire Strikes Back* preview, printed on April 21, was front page news, with a photograph Darth of Vader on the top right hand corner under the headline **Darth Vader is back**. The article "Back in Force" by Alan Frank featured a photo of the Rebel heroes posing in an ice cavern and another of Rebel soldiers standing next to a large dish-like weapon. Gary Kurtz was quoted as saying, "The emphasis again is on action and adventure. But having established the main characters, we intend to develop their emotional aspects, their relationships with one another." For the *Daily Star*, Alan Frank wrote, "With creator George Lucas overseeing the special effects, *The Empire Strikes Back* has all the ingredients for a smash hit. And if it does make money there will be nothing to stop the producers from carrying on with the original idea of NINE films in the *Star Wars* epic."[4] A teaser poster, distributed to cinemas by 20th Century-Fox for promotional purposes, depicted Darth Vader against a star field background.

Palitoy was gearing up for the toy release for *The Empire Strikes Back* but the design department had much less to do. "Palitoy's product line for *The Empire Strikes Back* was identical to Kenner's," says Bob Brechin. "So the Palitoy design department did not have an influence on the line. One of the jobs we did do was to 'dress' the stands at the British Toy Fair which opened on the last weekend in January each year. Many of the *Star Wars* dioramas, etc., that were used at toy fairs and for in-store promotions were produced by Nick Farmer. He was formerly a brand manager at Palitoy and worked on the marketing of Action Man. He left the company to take over a family business which he turned into a display and promotions company." Carole Deighton also remembers Farmer. "Nick was a very talented individual and he created these incredible and rather beautiful dioramas of scenes featuring *Star Wars* toys which were much in demand from retailers for shop windows and in-store displays. They were highly detailed and featured realistic-looking terrain, stunning backdrops and action scenes as well as the figures and vehicles which were all painted by hand."

On March 31, there was a photo shoot in London's Oxford Street featuring Darth Vader and two Stormtroopers. The trio posed in locations as diverse as a bus stop and some road works. Perhaps Darth Vader's reputation had preceded him, as the road works contractors had cleared off before the photographer began the shoot. Although it appeared totally authentic, the Darth Vader costume was not an original prop but one of a small number of replicas authorized by Lucasfilm and manufactured by Farmer's company N.J. Farmer Associates. From his studio in Leicester, Farmer had contacted David Middleton, the construction store man for *The Empire Strikes Back,* who was able to lend one of the original Darth Vader costumes to base the copies on. Instead of fragile vac-formed plastic, the new costumes were constructed from Fiberglas and other hard-wearing materials. Farmer had the skills and the equipment on hand to produce complex display items and promotional aids such as the Vader costume. It would have taken an expert to tell the difference between the N.J. Farmer versions and the costumes produced for *Star Wars* films. There would presumably be no more of the Darth Vaders of previous years that were produced by individual cinemas and department stores, as appearances could be organized using officially sanctioned costumes which were almost perfect replicas.

Empire Promotions Gear Up

Italian-born Ascanio Branca had taken over as the head of 20th Century-Fox Distribution from Percy Livingstone. Branca was a man who was small in stature but who doubled up in tenacity. He had become concerned about the reduction in cinema attendance since the massive surge in 1978 and 1979 for films such as *Star Wars, Close Encounters of the Third Kind* and *Superman* and pointed out the state of cinemas as being part of the problem: "No country in Europe is so badly served as Britain as to the condition of its theaters. Many of the multi-auditoria put up are lousy. There are continual complaints about sound and comfort. It is pitiful… [British exhibitors] have no faith in the business."[5] There was much concern within the British film industry regarding the growing competition from video, which was borne out in a stream of doom-laden articles and commentaries in the press.

Lucasfilm UK was working flat-out on the *Empire Strikes Back* merchandise campaign. It had moved in 1980 from temporary offices at 20th Century-Fox's Soho Square address to its own headquarters at 3A Queens Gate Mews, London SW7. "Caroline Nelson was the director of Lucasfilm U.K., assisted by Sally Dale," says Andrew Maconie. "I was sales manager. We reported to Maggie Young, the head of worldwide merchandising for Lucasfilm Inc. We had several Darth Vader suits stored at the office for promotions, some of which involved Dave Prowse. The move to our own headquarters made a huge difference. Our previous office at Soho Square was on the top floor where 20th Century-Fox used to keep old reels of film, so it was far from ideal." The Lucasfilm UK team worked in conjunction with the 20th Century-Fox UK marketing director Colin Hankins and his team to promote

The Empire Strikes Back. At the same time, Munro/Deighton was still handling p.r. for Palitoy. Maconie recalls how the various strategies that had been employed for *Star Wars* were put into place once more: "I and the Lucasfilm team handled all of the licensing contracts and approvals. Key trade shows such as the Spring Toy Fair at the Birmingham NEC were attended by Lucasfilm personnel and prospective licensees were approached at these events. The primary vehicle for promoting licensing programs was to invite prospective licensees to private showings of *The Empire Strikes Back* at London theaters."

Carole Deighton adds: "The reaction was remarkable from the selected audiences invited to preview the movie screenings of *The Empire Strikes Back*. I think we [the agency] felt that many of our media guests preferred this film to the original *Star Wars*; most people agreed it was visually superior and, of course, by then, everyone was familiar with the main characters. If anything, this film featured both characters and 'toy' space and land craft models even more strongly, introducing not only the fabulous AT-AT but a great new character, Yoda!"

To increase public awareness of the film, a display at the Ideal Home Exhibition at London's Olympia exhibition center featured some of the spacecraft prop models from *Star Wars*, along with R2-D2 and C-3PO in glass cases. In April, the models formed part of a larger prop display at the Selfridges department store, which also included a gallery of pre-production artwork. "I was lucky enough to be taken by Mum to see the *Empire Strikes Back* exhibition at Selfridges," recalls Ian Boyce. "She made me dress up in my smartest clothes which seemed a bit odd, but it was well worth it. There were Ralph McQuarrie paintings on show, lots of the original props used in the film and even mannequins dressed in the costumes from *The Empire Strikes Back*. Absolutely fantastic." A quad (horizontal) version of Roger Kastel's one-sheet (vertical) American poster for *The Empire Strikes Back* was issued for publicity purposes. The London Underground's hoardings were used extensively. The art was not the same as the American version however, with much more simplistic depictions of the characters. In order to change the vertical American poster to the horizontal British format, the entire poster was repainted by a yet-unknown British artist. The *Empire Strikes Back* presskit listed the key production staff members who had returned to work on the film. It followed the standard style of movie presskits, being made up from plain white sheets with printed text and a selection of black-and-white photographs. It did contain a significant fact regarding the *Star Wars* film series: that it would be extended to nine parts.

Readers of *Star Wars Weekly* #107 were treated to yet another exclusive story. "World of Fire" began with two rebel pilots discovering that a group of their colleagues on a survey mission on the planet Alashan had all been wiped out. These two pilots were themselves killed by the same unseen force but not before they had sent a report to the Rebel base. Luke, Leia, the droids and a new female character, Mici Shabandar, had stolen a new Imperial spacecraft, the Staraker, with the intention of flying it back to the Rebel Base, but General Dadonna redirected them to Alashan. Luke and Leia struck up a truce with a ragtag squad of Imperial Commandos in order to deal with the alien menace. "World of Fire" was very much in keeping with *Star Wars*' pulp style, which drew freely from archetypes established in films and literature. The Mici Shabandar character had a great deal of potential but after a promising gun-blazing start, she spent the rest of the story incapacitated. For the first time in the comics, Leia's ordinarily impervious space buns hairdo unraveled on two occasions.

"World of Fire" introduced some interesting concepts. The Imperial Commandos were dressed in irregular uniforms and seemed to be a group of mavericks in the style of James Coburn's platoon in the film *Cross of Iron*. Luke and Leia engaged in another kiss for luck, which seemed completely above board at this time. "I found this story to be very interesting," says Joe Sales. "I was reminded of the film *Hell in the Pacific* where an American pilot and a Japanese navy captain have to work together. *Alien* too seems to have been an inspiration for the story." *World of Fire* ended in #115 (May 7), with *The Empire Strikes Back* imminent.

A Meeting of Minds

In February, with the release of *The Empire Strikes Back* looming, Michael Hutson, the London-based head of RSO Records, took the initiative to organize a meeting at the Hotel George V in Paris to plan the movie's European launch. Emile Buyse, the president of 20th Century-Fox International, flew in from California; he was joined by Jean Louis Rubin, Fox's head of marketing and distribution, and John Simenon, Fox continental manager. Ascanio Branca was joined by his 20th Century-Fox counterparts Hellmuth Gattinger from Germany, Gaetano Scafidi from Italy and Robert Balk from France. Lucasfilm's head of sales Ashley Boone and senior vice-president Sid Ganis were in attendance, along with Michael Baumohl from Black Falcon Ltd. (which evidently was still a separate entity within LFL). Lucasfilm put on a presentation which explained that *Star Wars* was the largest grossing film of all time, with worldwide rentals amounting to $247,923,000. Summer re-releases of the film throughout continental Europe would increase awareness ahead of the release of the sequel.

"We took advantage of the RSO meeting to organize an integrated launch strategy for *Empire*," Emile Buyse told *Variety*. "RSO is planning a global release of the album of the music by John Williams for April, one of the few times that a record has been brought out in advance of the motion picture. Their marketing will constitute an important part of the overall plan for exploiting the motion picture, music and merchandising package."[6]

Sphere released *Han Solo's Revenge* by Brian Daley, which had Han Solo and Chewbacca going head to head with space slavers. Assisted by the droids Blue Max and Zollux, they teamed up with Fiolla, a woman working for the Corporate Sector Authority, who was intent on stopping the slavers. An alien called Spray, working as a repossession agent, initially wanted to impound the Millennium Falcon but he too came along on the adventure. The slavers were tracked to the planet Ammuud, where Han encountered the professional gunman Gallandro, who was working for one of the planet's warring clans. Han, Chewbacca, Spray and Fiolla faced off against the slaver's spaceship in the Millennium Falcon but for once the Corellian freighter was bested and all seemed lost. Both craft were then captured by a tractor beam from a warship of the Corporate Sector Authority; Gallandro was directing their operation. Spray revealed himself to be an important Corporate Sector Authority agent. When Han made his play to escape, he successfully used the creature as a hostage. Gallandro had been itching for a quick draw but he lost the opportunity when Han handed him a booby-trapped briefcase that temporarily paralyzed his gun arm.

The excitement surrounding the release of *The Empire Strikes Back* was given a further boost within the fan community by issue #7 of *Bantha Tracks*. Interviewee Anthony Daniels said, "This time was better because people knew that they were on to a winner with *The Empire Strikes Back*. You only had to look at the script to see that it was very, very good. Most times watching a scene in the studio is very dull, especially for the thirtieth take. But there were some scenes where people were actually crowding around to watch. There was certainly a sense of excitement about this project."[7] In this, the final update on the *Empire Strikes Back* production, it was stated that plans for the film's release had changed since the last issue, with the American premiere due to take place on May 17 and the European premiere on the 21st. This issue also introduced readers to the new character Lando Calrissian, played by Billy Dee Williams, and it profiled the actor's career to that date.

The Ad Campaign Strikes Back

Seeking to mirror the success of the *Star Wars Soundtrack* album, RSO embarked on an advertising blitz and issued posters and standees to shops with the slogan "May the Sound Be with You." *The Empire Strikes Back Soundtrack* was available in Britain on a single album disk and cassette, but if fans searched hard enough in record shops they might locate the American version which sported two disks and a beautiful booklet, set between a gatefold cover. As was the case with *Star Wars*, the *Empire Strikes Back* soundtrack album from RSO was not the only one available, although there was no repeat of the *Star Wars* "rip-off" album blitz. In fact, all but one of the other major albums available had been issued by RSO. The *Empire Strikes Back* story record, titled *The Adventures of Luke Skywalker*, was also gatefold but contained only one album disk. It opened to reveal a gallery of photographs depicting the events of

Above and following page: RSO intended to make an impact for the *Empire Strikes Back* soundtrack with shop standees and magazine advertisements.

the film in sequence. The cover featured a beautiful original painting (by Jeff Wack) of Luke Skywalker battling Darth Vader on Bespin Cloud City. Wack was an established artist working extensively in the music, film and adverting industries. An alternative choice of the soundtrack was provided by Russian-born disco pioneer Boris Midney with his disco-esque version, with Wack again providing cover art. The artist displayed his best work on the sleeve for the *Empire Jazz* album, which contained jazz interpretations of the main soundtrack themes produced and arranged by Ron Carter. Wack's sleeve painting depicted Darth Vader sitting at a table in a bar watching a jazz band made up of Chewbacca on the piano, C-3PO on double bass, a Stormtrooper on saxophone and R2-D2 on the drums! A major album release for *The Empire Strikes Back* outside of the RSO stable was the version of the soundtrack by Charles Gerhardt and the National Philharmonic Orchestra, released by Chalfont Records Inc. Gerhardt again presented a different take on the soundtrack, with "Han Solo and the Princess" and "The Asteroid Field" being the full-length movements prepared by John Williams.

May the sound be with you.

STAR WARS THE EMPIRE STRIKES BACK

Soundtracks composed by John Williams and performed by the London Symphony Orchestra. Available on RSO records and tapes

'Star Wars' and 'The Empire Strikes Back' are registered trademarks of Lucasfilm Ltd.

Palitoy launched a Boba Fett action figure offer in April via a full-page advertisement in *Star Wars Weekly* #110 and in other children's publications. Fans could obtain an exciting new figure from the *Empire Strikes Back* range in exchange for three names cut from figure card backs and 20 pence postage and packing. The advertisement contributed a great deal to the mystery surrounding the new character. According to the heading on the advert, "Boba Fett fights for the highest bidder. But he's yours for free." The figure looked amazing, standing 22 centimeters tall in the monochrome photograph. Boba Fett's equipment was listed: a "carrel view and finder," grappling hook, rocket pack, storage pack, rocket pack controls and a laser rifle. Knee darts and tools were strapped to his legs. All of them were "non-functioning" on the figure, as the ad pointed out.

A fantastic television commercial which premiered on April 7 advertised the offer. A dramatic scene was set before the camera, where the Princess Leia action figure had been captured on a dining room table by Darth Vader and legions of Stormtroopers. Leia was held beneath a large electric lamp which was the only source of light in the commercial, casting all of the other figures in partial shadow. "Who is this mysterious figure?" said the narrator. "Boba Fett! Will he save Princess Leia or side with Darth Vader? See comics and toy shops for details of the Boba Fett special offer now. He is waiting!" "Who was this Boba Fett?" fans were asking. Would he live up to his awesome appearance when *The Empire Strikes Back* arrived? "The offer to send off for Boba Fett was amazing," says Jordan Royce. "All the children I knew did that and they were all waiting for the figure to arrive. They all pretty much came on the same day and we were all bringing them to school."

Also in April, advertisements for *Empire*'s opening at the Odeon Leicester Square (the main Odeon venue in Leicester Square) began to appear in London newspapers. They incorporated the Darth Vader teaser poster and a ticket application form. At the bottom of the advert was the message "Talk to C3PO on 01-409 2961!" and a photograph of the droid. If one dialed that number, they heard a recording of Anthony Daniels performing as C-3PO. In the U.S., a whole series of phone recordings was organized by Craig Miller featuring the main cast members talking in character.

To build public awareness of *The Empire Strikes Back*, small advertisements began appearing in the British press featuring the Darth Vader in flames logo and the words "Empire Day is May 20." This was a reference to the celebration of British Empire (called "Empire Day") that traditionally took place on May 24, even though by 1980 it had become a relatively obscure event and had been known as Commonwealth Day since 1958. The enigmatic adverts could not have failed to draw attention, even if their meaning was far from clear.

Palitoy made a splash with magazine advertisements and this flyer for its mail-away Boba Fett offer.

Gerald Crotty was determined to be one of the first to see *The Empire Strikes Back*. "I heard that there'd be a Royal premiere on May 20. Now I imagined that those sorts of things were invitation only but I decided to write off to see if I could get a ticket, what had I got to lose? To my surprise, I received an application form for tickets. The prices ranged from £5 to £40, not as steep as I'd expected, so I went for a £5 ticket and got one. From then, my excitement grew each day." Sarah Baker-Saunders was also anxious to get a ticket:

> The double center page in issue #100 of *Star Wars Weekly* advertising the premiere prompted me to call the Odeon in Leicester Square and ask about tickets for its release and how to obtain them. The assistant said I could send through the post a postal order and book tickets to be picked up on the film's release date. So that is what I did, I sent a stamped addressed envelope and letter, along with a

£5 postal order, for the day after the Royal premiere. I eventually received by return post, a receipt and instructions to go to the box office and pick up my tickets on the day. I was excited more than words.

Despite all of the secrecy surrounding the latest chapter in the *Star Wars* saga, the film's story could be read in full in Donald F. Glut's *Empire Strikes Back* novelization, which was made available in Britain by Sphere in April. (Fans may have recalled his contribution to the story *New Planets New Perils* in Star Wars Weekly as Don Glut). The book had a cover featuring the American poster art by Roger Kastel and included eight pages of color photographs, including one of the top-secret Yoda. The Kastel poster referenced the poster of *Gone with the Wind* in its depiction of Princess Leia in the arms of Han Solo but it unfortunately gave away the key plot point of who the princess would end up with. Sphere promoted the book heavily, issuing leaflets and posters to shops. A hardback version of the novel was printed by Severn House, minus photographs. The Marvel comic strip adaptation was available in a novel-sized format, distributed in Britain by Arrow Books. In common with the novelization, the comic disclosed all of the major plot points of the film. Fans would also notice that Yoda was pictured much differently to the one that would eventually appear on movie screens, with him having been based on early design sketches. Anyone wanting to know what was going to happen in *The Empire Strikes Back* need look no further than their local branch of W.H. Smith.

"I was annoyed that the comic adaptation and the novel came out weeks before the movie," says Gerald Crotty. "It was hard not to look at them. I wanted to see *Empire* fresh and get all the surprises in the cinema." Jordan Royce says, "Everyone that I knew who had an interest had the comic adaptation as soon as it came out. It was the biggest excitement since *Star Wars* had been released. I don't know why it was released so early and it isn't something you would see today."

Crotty remembers that another glimpse of the film was available. "About a month before the film opened, there were two posters on the wall of W.H. Smith. One showed a Star Destroyer chasing the Millennium Falcon. The detail on the Star Destroyer was so incredible, I just stared at it for ages. The other poster was of a shot of three AT-ATs in profile which I just adored."

There were other ways to get a sneak preview of *The Empire Strikes Back,* as Peter Davis remembers:

> Our neighbor had been on holiday in America and returned with Topps trading cards from *The Empire Strikes Back.* I can still visualize that hot day in next door's shed, with this kid's enormous stack of cards as he flicked through them with a group of friends speculating on how the film was going to pan out. We were looking with drooling wonder at the images of the next *Star Wars* movie. All I wanted to do was to get these cards and stare at them more, to insure that I would imprint those images onto my eyelids. These cards were like gold dust. God knows how but my brother managed somehow to persuade him somehow to swap a few doubles for something. The card "The Fate of Han Solo" had us apoplectic with frenzied frothing. What the hell had happened to Han Solo?! Was he a statue? Or whatever it was. I can remember we stared at this card for days, weeks, wanting to know what the hell was happening.

The Press Previews

On April 23, the *Sun* newspaper began an *Empire Strikes Back* serialization, which provided a digest of the storyline supported by photographs. (Some of them, including an image of the top-secret Yoda, were culled from the *Empire Strikes Back* novelization.) Although the film's release was imminent, an actual review was extremely difficult to find. All of the magazine features leading up to its release were based solely on the press material that had been provided and what journalists had managed to glean from exterior sources. Specialist movie and science fiction magazines packed their pages full of *Empire Strikes Back* material, so much so that only a fan with a considerable budget could have hoped to collect every single publication. The June *Film Review* contained a four-page preview: "*Star Wars* fans have been waiting with ever-growing impatience for two years watching imitations fly across their cinema screens, each lacking that certain something which turned *Star Wars* into a cult and little piece of history. At last the wait is over." In common with much of the media, a feature in *Film Review* had a patriotic flavor. "One of the most gratifying aspects of *Star Wars* was that it was made by technicians in British studios. The same goes for *The Empire Strikes Back* for, although the saga's creator George Lucas, new film's director Irvin Kershner, and producer Gary Kurtz are all Americans, they chose Britain once again as the best place to film the most important scenes and the amazing special effects."[8]

Darth Vader was featured on the cover of the June *Photoplay*. The excellent feature by Mike Nunn included quotes from Lucas, Kurtz and Carrie Fisher. The article revealed that *Star Wars* had been retitled *Star Wars: Episode IV—A New Hope*. The official title of the sequel was *Star Wars: Episode V—The Empire Strikes Back*.

Also in May, *Sunday Times Magazine* interviewed Kurtz for the article "A New Empire of Illusion." It revealed that the producer has had an interest in science fiction all his life and described how had made 8mm films as a child in his birthplace, Los Angeles. Fans eager to know more about Lando Calrissian would have received the June issue of *Starlog*, released in early May, very warmly. Billy Dee Williams painted a vivid picture of the character: "I love the name; the name alone is fantastic—he's a brownskin, he's charming, adventurous, bumbling. And he's the best kind of hero you can create. He's very handsome, very cavalier."[9] Lando Calrissian was described in the article as being the governor of Bespin—one of the new locations featured in *Empire*.

The same *Starlog* also featured a detailed interview with special effects supervisor Brian Johnson, who had been charged with coordinating the effects crews working at Elstree, Norway and California. (He was eventually listed simply as "Special Visual Effects" in the credits.) "You know, every movie that comes along is advertised as 'the greatest thing since sliced bread' or whatever," said Johnson. "But *Empire* is a different movie

The press coverage began to crank up but it was not at the level it had been for *Star Wars*.

from *Star Wars*. The pace of *Empire* is pretty brisk—there isn't time to dwell on any particular shot. I think that the quality of the English and American teams working on *Empire* is unsurpassed and that it will be immediately apparent on screen."[10]

George Lucas Does *Time*

The May 19 edition of *Time* magazine was difficult to miss with Darth Vader dominating the cover. Inside was a six-page feature by Gerald Clarke featuring a wealth of photographs including Yoda and a frozen Han Solo. Clarke's article began with a digest of the film's story up until the point where Luke encounters Vader at Bespin, stopping short of the film's major revelation. The article went well beyond an examination of the film as it included George Lucas sitting for perhaps his most personal interview to date. According to Clarke, Lucas is a "devout believer in the Force" and one might have been inclined to believe him upon hearing Lucas say:

> When you are born, you have an energy field around you. You could call it an aura. An archaic description would be a halo. It's an idea that has gone all the way through history. When you die, your energy field joins all the other energy fields in the universe, and while you're still living that larger energy field is sympathetic to your energy field. The Force has two sides. It is not a malevolent or a benevolent thing. It has a bad side to it, involving hate and fear, and it has a good side, involving love, charity, fairness and hope. If you use it well, you can see into the future and the past. You can sort of read minds and you can levitate and use that whole netherworld of psychic energy.

Clarke brought the article back down to Earth by saying "So far Lucas can do none of these marvelous things."[11] Well, as far as he knew. Up until that point, Lucas had been the cinematic equivalent of a wizard.

Perhaps the greatest source of information for fans was the 41st issue of *Mediascene* magazine, available from the growing number of comic shops such as the Sheffield Space Center and London's Forbidden Planet. The fantastic wraparound painted cover boasted "Almost 40 pages of exclusive photos, art and interviews" and the contents certainly did not disappoint. There was even a special message from Lucas, who was concerned about what the fan reaction to *Empire*. Lucas said,

> In the first one, the mood is joyous and triumphant, exciting and funny, all at the same time. The second one is exciting and funny too, but it's also sad; it's more of a tragedy than a triumph. That's why I'm concerned at how it will be received. The third one won't have this difficulty because that's the film with the great climax. At this point *The Empire Strikes Back* is practically finished. It's probably as presold to the public as any film has ever been, but that doesn't mean that everyone will love it. As I say, it's different from *Star Wars*, and I think it stands just as much of a chance as being a hit as not being one. I guess I'm the biggest pessimist around here. After all, I said the very same thing about the first one.[12]

With these words from the great man in mind, fans were prepared for anything that *The Empire Strikes Back* could throw at them. Lucas expressed similar sentiments in an interview in *Bantha Tracks #8*, which was issued on the eve of *Empire*'s release. He also provided a wonderful window on the future of the saga. "After the third film, we'll go back and make the first trilogy, which deals with the young Ben Kenobi and Darth Vader."

If that was not enough for fans, the third chapter in the *Star Wars* saga was announced in the same issue as *Revenge of the Jedi*, which would begin production in January 1981, with a scheduled release in the spring of 1983. The report also stated, "*Revenge of the Jedi* will complete the middle trilogy of the nine-part *Star Wars* epic. Following its completion, the first trilogy will be filmed, and then finally, the last trilogy. Should production on the nine films continue at the same rate, we can expect the ninth film released in the spring of 2001."[13]

Television Coverage

The April 14 edition of *Film 1980* included a feature on *The Empire Strikes Back*. On May 9, BBC2 ran the documentary *The Risk Business*, in which presenter Michael Rod visited the *Empire* set. The program featured comments from Harrison Ford, Anthony Daniels, Mark Hamill, producer Kurtz and director Kershner. On May 18 at 7:15, BBC2 aired the program *Star Wars, Music by John Williams*, which featured contributions from Lucas, Kurtz, Kershner, Steven Spielberg and Ben Burtt. John Williams talked through his inspiration, technique and the process for composing and conducting film soundtracks, between clips from *The Empire Strikes Back* and other films he had scored. The program contained a fascinating segment where Han Solo and Princess Leia expressed their feelings for each other in the carbon freezing chamber, with and without music.

The television coverage did not end there. On May 19 *The Empire Strikes Back* was featured on *Clapperboard,* where familiar presenter Chris Kelly interviewed Anthony Daniels, David Prowse and Brian Johnson, who explained the processes used to create the visual effects seen in the film. Some long clips of the film were shown including Han Solo being frozen and Luke Skywalker confronting Darth Vader. Revealing spoilers to the plot were perhaps less important to 20th Century-Fox than showing dramatic scenes that might draw the audience to cinemas. An episode of *Jim'll Fix It* granted the wish of a young boy to visit the *Empire* set. During the production of the film, on the Dagobah set, the boy and Mark Hamill (in his Luke Skywalker costume) had a picnic. Back in the BBC studio, a "Jim'll Fix It Badge" was hung around the boy's neck by Chewbacca, again without his bandolier strap. This act had a tinge of irony about it, because the "badge" was almost identical to the medal that the Wookiee did *not* receive at the end of *Star Wars*.

On *Blue Peter*, Hamill and Carrie Fisher were interviewed by Sarah Green and were fed "rebel stew" that had been based on a recipe sent in by a young viewer. The two actors also guested on the Radio One children's program *Playground* where they sang "The Rebel Flight Song." On May 25, the BBC1 religious program *Heart of the Matter* featured a Jungian psychologist and a science fiction writer, discussing the appeal of *Star Wars*. A guest on the early morning BBC1 program *Multi Colored Swap Shop*, Anthony Daniels was interviewed by Noel Edmunds. All of the media hype and coverage whipped up a frenzy among fans. Jordan Royce says,

> It was incredible. It seemed like it was something that everyone was talking about, in the weeks leading up to the release of *The Empire Strikes Back*. The expectation was enormous. Almost like the release of an album of massive importance. It was seen as being an event rather than just another film coming out. I had been following the progress of the film in *Starburst* but I hadn't seen any footage. The first clip that was shown on television was of Princess Leia being captured and Luke following. Then Luke makes his way to where Vader is, who says, "The Force is with you, young Skywalker but you're not a Jedi yet." They had chosen such a strong, iconic scene to release first, it was absolutely potent. The next day at school, people were talking about nothing else.

Now the Screenings Begin

On the 3rd and 4th May there were special cast and crew screenings of *The Empire Strikes Back* at the Odeon Leicester Square at 10:15 a.m. each day. Harrison Ford, Carrie

From left, Harrison Ford, David Prowse, Carrie Fisher, Peter Mayhew (rear), Kenny Baker (front) and Mark Hamill pose outside the Dorchester Hotel on May 19, 1980 (Mirrorpix).

Fisher and Mark Hamill joined Anthony Daniels, David Prowse, and Peter Mayhew on the 5th May at the Selfridges department store (that was still hosting the props display) for a signing that drew huge crowds. The next day the stars attended a press preview screening of *The Empire Strikes Back* at the Odeon Leicester Square at 8:15 p.m. After the film there was a lavish luncheon and conference for critics and provincial journalists hosted by 20th Century-Fox, who were evidently doing everything in their power to impress. The next significant event was *The Empire Strikes Back* premiering on May 17 at the Kennedy Center in Washington, D.C., in a benefit performance for the Special Olympics. The audience contained over 600 local children, many of them Special Olympians. The stars in attendance included Hamill, Ford, Fisher, Prowse, Billy Dee Williams, Kenny Baker, Peter Mayhew and Frank Oz. Lawrence Kasdan, Irvin Kershner and Gary Kurtz were there but George Lucas was not. Ford, Fisher, Williams and Hamill then took a flight from Washington to London on the 18th (the latter two with their wives and children) on the same Concorde and were photographed presenting the aircraft's captain with a model of the Millennium Falcon.

On Monday 19th there was a final preview showing at the Dominion Theatre at 10 a.m., which was a last chance to invite reviewers and interested merchandising companies. At the Odeon Leicester Square, a huge photographic blow-up of the British Empire Strikes Back poster by Tom Jung with light effects was still being put together by workers. On the Thames Embankment side of the nearby Savoy Hotel Mark Hamill, Carrie Fisher, Harrison Ford, Dave Prowse, Peter Mayhew and Kenny Baker posed for photographs with some Stormtroopers who had arrived from 20th Century-Fox's Soho Square headquarters on the back of Jeeps driven by Imperial Officers. The Empire's finest then fanned out to invade Leicester Square and the surrounding area of London, handing out film logo stickers to bemused shopkeepers and members of the public. These antics, including the ever game-for-a-laugh Carrie Fisher kissing and being carried by a Stormtrooper, would be perfect fodder for the press that would combine the photographs with their coverage of the premiere the following day.

Issue #116 of *Star Wars Weekly* (cover date May 14) began the story "Trapped in a Galaxy Gone Mad!" by Archie Goodwin. The art was by Michael Golden, who would become very well-known via his work on the Micronauts comic for Marvel. Luke and Leia were brought aboard a spacecraft that was initially a house of horrors. It may have been the final story in the *Star Wars* cycle (as was the case in the USA where the story was called "Riders in the Void" in issue 38) but it seemed to be a flash back story since they were back in their original movie costumes instead of the more functional space faring gear they had worn in recent UK stories (Luke's being based on his outfit from the *Star Wars* medal ceremony). Luke and Leia initially had to fight for their lives but ended up with a greater knowledge of the galaxy at large, via a sobering story from the ship's pilot. Issue #117 had "The conclusion to the Star Wars Epic!" on the cover and at the end of the story was printed "Next: The Empire Strikes Back!"

It had been an astronomically long wait for fans but *The Empire Strikes Back* was finally due to arrive in Britain. The entire efforts of 20th Century-Fox UK, Lucasfilm UK, Munro/Deighton and Palitoy Marketing had been put behind the film's launch. Could lightning strike twice? Could *The Empire Strikes Back* catch the imagination of the public as *Star Wars* had done?

Chapter 7

The Empire Strikes Back

The long-awaited European Royal Charity Premiere of *The Empire Strikes Back* took place on May 20, 1980, at the Odeon Leicester Square. The cast members who were present included Carrie Fisher, Mark Hamill, Harrison Ford, Kenny Baker, Peter Mayhew, Billy Dee Williams, Anthony Daniels and Alec Guinness. Irvin Kershner and Gary Kurtz were there but George Lucas did not attend. Also at the event: Steven Spielberg, Art Garfunkel, Paul Simon, Martin and Janet Sheen, and the Carradine brothers Robert, Keith and David. Representing Lucasfilm was Sid Ganis, Michael Baumohl, John Moohr and Caroline Nelson. Princess Margaret was the representative from the Royal Family.

Gerald Crotty was not going to miss this event for the world. "On Tuesday, May 20, I went down to London. I wasn't bothered that much about seeing the stars, I just wanted to see the movie. I kept hanging about in the lobby but ushers kept moving me and others into the auditorium." Laurie Calvert also bought tickets for the premiere. "My mate let me down at the last minute so I went with my mum. When I took my seat, I looked back and all the stars were there, taking their own seats. That was a really weird thought, that I was about to watch the film with the people who were in the film. Television presenter David Jacobs was the compère for the evening and he was interviewing the stars as they came in for an outside broadcast, which was projected on to the cinema screen in black and white. It was like an additional treat for the audience." Gerald Crotty says, "As the stars arrived, they were interviewed by a lady with a microphone. She asked the most stupid questions. At one point she was talking to two young girls, Kurtz's daughters I think, and they looked at her as if she was an idiot. Well, the audience was roaring with laughter at this and they must have heard us in the lobby. After that, there was an orchestra, some trumpeters and the national anthem. Then it began."

The May 20 *Evening News* dedicated its entire front cover to the premiere with the headline **It's Empire Day Today**. "After two years of intensive planning and production, *The Empire Strikes Back*, the eagerly awaited follow-up to the cinema's all-time box office champion *Star Wars*, is unveiled in London. ...The new film exceeds the spectacular special effects of the first while at the same time delving deeper into the human interest."[1] The *Sun* newspaper printed a major piece on the 20th with the headline **Empire Day**. The film was described as having "a lively sense of humor, a love affair and some of the finest special effects ever." There was little doubt which element of the film had made the greatest impression: "[T]he real star of *The Empire Strikes Back* is going to be a new character—Yoda. He is worked by Frank Oz, the Muppet Show Master who is the voice and personality of Fozzie Bear and Miss Piggy. Yoda is a being, somewhere between a gargoyle and a tea cozy, who has spent 800 years training the Jedi Knights to fight evil." There was a photograph of Yoda, the embargo on his image having being lifted. Bringing the article to a close was a fact that most fans would have guessed for themselves, although they might not have appreciated the spoiler: "Even at the end of *The Empire*—Darth Vader lives."[2] Also on May 20, at 4:45 p.m. on ITV, the children's television program *Magpie* showed some clips from the film. At 5:40 p.m. on BBC1, an episode of *Ask Aspel* featured a recorded interview with Mark Hamill. Part of the program's format was to ask the guest questions sent in by the audience.

The Empire Strikes Back opened to the public on May 21 at the Odeon Leicester Square to huge queues, which was not surprising as it was the only British venue showing the film. Performances were preceded by *Black Angel*, a B feature made on behalf of Lucasfilm by Roger Christian and a small crew at the Scottish castle Eilean Donan (which was later used in the film *Highlander*). It was set shortly after the Crusades, with its earthy depiction of the period presenting a great contrast to the glittering armor and perfect smiles of standard Hollywood medieval movies. The excellent cinematography transformed the natural sunlight shining through the tree cover into a magical hue. Much of the same look could be detected in the film *Excalibur* and the *Robin of Sherwood* television series.

"I traveled into London to see *The Empire Strikes Back* at the Odeon Leicester Square the day it opened," says Shaun Dawkins. "It lived up to my expectations, especially the revelation of Darth Vader being Luke Skywalker's father. Despite my gathering all this information, I hadn't got wind of that. It came completely from left field—wow." Sarah Baker-Saunders made the journey on the same day; she recalls:

The Odeon Leicester Square had a huge illuminated poster sign for *The Empire Strikes Back*. The cinema was very busy with lots of queuing customers, similar to how it had been over two years earlier when going to see *Star Wars*. I had collected my ticket earlier from the box office, so I bypassed the queue and was in!

The advertisement for *The Empire Strikes Back*'s opening at the Odeon Leicester Square (Mirrorpix).

As I climbed the stairs to the circle, the walls of the cinema were filled with images of the new movie and special posters advertising the Royal premiere the night before! When the lights went down and a hush descended upon the audience, on the screen came a movie called *Black Angel*. Confusion and panic started to set in. Had I gone into the wrong cinema? Had the Odeon got it wrong and were showing the wrong movie? After 25 minutes, the movie finished and I was ready for the main feature. Finally the familiar 20th Century-Fox fanfare and the John Williams score bought tingles down my back and a smile to my face. After such a long wait, all the effort getting to London and finally the *Star Wars* sequel was there in front of me. The movie went by so quickly but as I left the cinema I was smiling from ear to ear. I was left thinking, "Darth Vader is Luke's father? No, that can't be true!"

The Odeon Leicester Square on the day of the *Empire Strikes Back* opening (courtesy Sarah Saunders).

On May 22, David Prowse made a special appearance at the Forbidden Planet shop in London. Laurie Calvert remembers that the event on the 22nd was much more than had been advertised. "Dave Prowse was there but Mark Hamill and Brian Johnson made an appearance also. They had a life-sized radio controlled R2-D2, the Millennium Falcon prop and one of the X-Wings." Derek Dorking was there too. "I visited 20th Century-Fox and met Colin Hankins. I then walked to the Forbidden Planet and saw David Prowse and Mark Hamill. There were badges and flyers available with 'Empire Day' and the logo on them." Anthony Daniels had been booked to appear at the Forbidden Planet the next day but he reportedly cancelled.

The May 24 edition of *Look-In* featured one of its trademark cover paintings of *The Empire Strikes Back* cast and contained a color centerfold article and a color poster of the rebel heroes posing with their weapons drawn. *Star Wars Weekly* #118 (cover date May 28) was rebranded as *The Empire Strikes Back Weekly*, in which the comic adaptation of the film by Archie Goodwin and artist Al Williamson began. Readers had never before seen the *Star Wars* characters, places and technology so accurately depicted in a comic. The monochrome print reflected the dark tone of the film perfectly and displayed Williamson's artwork off to the full. "The artwork was absolutely incredible," says Jordan Royce. "Because unlike all of the other artists that had worked on the *Star Wars* comic, Al Williamson had drawn the characters to perfection." A set of rub-down transfers printed by Letraset on behalf of Kraft Foods was given away free with the first issue, with one of the pages containing a scene to rub them down on. An advertisement for Kraft Dairylea cheese spread was printed on the back cover of *The Empire Strikes Back Weekly*; stickers were included in each tub, which included a scene printed on the bottom to rub them down on. Fans could even send off for a "Bumper Transfer Pack" in exchange for lids from the

Mark Hamill and David Prowse sign for fans at the Forbidden Planet shop, London (courtesy Derek Dorking).

tubs, consisting of a sheet of transfers and a background scene featuring three environments from *The Empire Strikes Back*.

Reviewing the Empire

In contrast to the press articles which had covered the buildup to release of *The Empire Strikes Back* with breathless enthusiasm, a great many of the reviews were less than enthusiastic. Nicholas Wapshott reviewed it for *The Times* on May 23 under the heading "The recipe is not quite as before":

> This sequel misses the magic of the original. There is very little humor. The Laurel and Hardy of C3PO and R2D2, the mismatched robots, are kept apart for most of the story…. The new characters, a glum plastic puppet and a black space pirate, do not grip the imagination. Put simply, Lucas has done better. Without his intelligence and the novelty of meeting the *Star Wars* menagerie for the first time, the film fails to involve and seldom charms.[3]

"The Empire Strikes Back and Misses" was the heading of William Hall's review for the *Evening News*:

> [T]here is so much bang-bang-you're not dead (how on earth can those ace laser pilots be such rotten shots?) and so little character definition, that one feels that director Irvin Kershner has to keep up the frenetic pace to paper over the cracks in the plot…. I shall be surprised if George Lucas can keep up the pace, or the interest [of a nine-part series]. Luke Skywalker is no space-age James Bond. Already the characters are showing the same signs of wear and tear as Solo's battered old space craft.[4]

In a withering three-page destruction of the film, Andrew Rissik of *Films Illustrated* wrote, "Rather than invent a new plot, they've kept the old one running by dividing it into strands, throwing in little things to complicate matters, and refusing to resolve it all. This is the time-honored, continued-in-our-next manner of the television serial. It's useful as a way of doing things because it's essentially plotless and it can be kept up forever."[5] Writing for *Time*, Gerald Clarke presented a more measured view: "Sequels of giant hits, like children who follow Daddy's favorite, always have an unfair burden. They are not examined on their own merits but in relationship to the picture everyone loved. In many ways Lucas and Kershner have overcome that handicap. *The Empire Strikes Back* is a more polished and in some way, a richer film. But to imitate Yoda's way of speaking and to answer the obvious question, as much fun it is not."[6]

Fortunately, there were positive reviews too. "Crash, bang, wallop, what a picture!" was the heading for Cecil Wilson's *Daily Mail* review: "This inevitable sequel should allay fears that George Lucas and his team of technical wizards reached the limit of bizarre space fantasy with *Star Wars*. It was just an appetizer."[7] (It was stated that Margaret Hinxman was "away," which may have been extremely fortuitous, considering the tone of her review for *Star Wars*.) Ian Christie's *Daily Express* review was titled "It's a monster of a hit!" and he wrote, "Would producer Gary Kurtz, director Irvin Kershner, their scriptwriters and special effects men be able to come up with something which would retain the appeal of the original and yet interject some novelty into the inter-galactic proceedings? I asked myself. The answer I'm pleased to say, is yes.... There is enough excitement, spectacle and humor to make the epic enthralling."[8]

The tabloid newspapers in general swung in behind the film with bold headlines and more than enough pictures to keep scissors-wielding fans happy. In his *Daily Mirror* review, under the heading "Weird and wonderful. Striking back with a winner," Arthur Thirkell said that *Empire* "retains the high technical standard of the original and has the added appeal of a charming new Muppet-like creature called Yoda to rival those old favorites, the almost human robots See Threepio and Artoo Detoo.... *The Empire Strikes Back* will keep children from eight to eighty entertained for a couple of hours."[9] In *The Sunday Mirror*'s review under the heading "The Empire hits back even harder," Madeline Harmsworth called *Empire* "even more imaginative than its predecessor."[10]

"Blockbusting!" was the front page headline of the May 31 issue of *Screen International*, which reported that in seven days, this second story in the *Star Wars* series netted an astonishing £94,241 at the Odeon Leicester Square. The first eight days' play netted, in total, £103,397. And not only was a new house record set, but also a new one-day gross and admissions record. On Saturday, May 24, the film took £22,154 gross, with 8624 admissions. The article reported that *Empire* would open in UK keys on June 15, with coastal situations following in early July. The June 2 *Variety* reported that the Odeon Leicester Square had netted £213,562 from only 32 performances. *Screen International* devoted much of its May 24 edition to *Empire*. Such coverage was reserved for big British films or those that had been made in Britain, such as *Alien* and *Superman*. Interviewee Brian Johnson said,

> There have been a lot of articles in the press and on television recently about how wonderful British special effects are and how we are the best in the world. I would like to say that unless we do something about paralleling the developments in America, we are going to be left way behind... [L]ook at *Empire*. If anyone says that it is due to English special effects in its entirety, they are out of their skulls. Just

like the first *Star Wars*—the reason it won the Oscar was not because of the British special effects content, but because the motion control equipment produced those very exciting model shots. That's what fired everyone's imagination. And it's the same with *Empire*... [W]e could partially replicate it [in Britain] but it would have to be a compromise. And it wouldn't be such a good result.[11]

Reading the Empire

The Empire Strikes Back Official Poster Monthly from Bunch Associates was launched in time for the film premiere. This time around, the publication would be identical in America and Britain, except for the price printed on the cover. Bunch had been sent a memo stating that under no circumstances should images of Yoda be released in either country ahead of May 20. This was an innovation of Stanley Bielecki, as Gary Kurtz recalled. "It was Stanley who suggested that the shots we had of Yoda not be used in the first run of press stuff and should be released later."[12] *The Empire Strikes Back Official Poster Monthly* was produced at Bunch Associate's London offices; the writing team remained anonymous except for regular Dr. M.F. Marten and newcomer Richard Voorhuys. The first issue began with an editorial:

> Welcome to the first issue of a brand new series of poster magazines aimed at providing you with the essential information and the finest pictures on the new screen adventure, *The Empire Strikes Back*. Our editorial team has followed every stage of the picture's production and in future issues we will provide insights into the fascinating special effects work that makes *Empire* the best space spectacular.[13]

Articles for the first issue included a profile of Bespin Cloud City, which revealed that the planet Bespin was made entirely from gas and that the floating city was kept aloft via a reactor at the base of the huge column on which it rested. The city's great wealth was derived from its source of Tibana gas. Fans who had not picked up the names from the comic or the novel would have learned that Lando's aide on Bespin was named Lobot and the small pig-like beings which inhabited the city's junk room were called Ugnaughts. It was precisely these kinds of facts, which were not included in the film, that made the poster magazine worth seeking out.

A publication which was a must for many fans was *The Empire Strikes Back Collectors Edition* by John May, which was sold in high street shops and also at cinemas as a program book. It contained interviews with the key behind-the-scenes personnel and also a digest of the film's plot, which included a missing scene: During the Imperial assault on the Rebel Base, General Rieekan is killed in the command center explosion. Whether this event had been culled from a script that May had access to, or was a leap of the writer's considerable imagination, it did explain why the general suddenly disappeared from the film. May had been provided with full assistance from Lucasfilm and 20th Century-Fox on the British side of production, along with the American. A special visit to Elstree Studios had been arranged for May during the filming of the Dagobah scenes. "I was picked up by limousine, something like a big old black Bentley, and traveled north of London in the company of Carol Titleman, the head of *Star Wars* publishing," May remembers. "She was most concerned about my footwear and insisted that we stop at a shoe shop in Elstree High Street and purchase a pair of brand new Wellingtons—suitable for the bog planet. Elstree Studios was a magic place where dreams are manufactured." May included an account of his visit to Dagobah in the *Collectors Edition*:

It's a struggle to get impressions in order when faced with the most monstrous film set you've ever seen. School plays were never like this. The sound stage recedes into the background as far as you can see, and everywhere you look there's movement. On my left stands a giant artificial forest of gnarled, steel framed trees which reach up to the roof and are hung with lianas and Spanish moss. The trees back on to a lake of muddy, oily water with a full-scale X-Wing Fighter lying half submerged in it. On the far right is a glass-painted backdrop, as long as a football field. It is covered in vague grey shapes, giving the impression of immeasurable reaches of forest disappearing into the distance. At the far end of the lake, in a leaf-strewn muddy clearing, is a battered and forlorn R2 unit, the only static object in sight. We climb six steps up and wander into the forest … the illusion quickly shatters. Behind one tree a crew member sits reading *Variety* in a garishly striped deckchair. Behind another, steaming blocks of dry ice wait to be fed into the machine. Fat, rubber-coated electrical cables snake in all directions.[14]

May says of his work on the title, "*The Empire Strikes Back Collectors Edition* was the most amazing job. I was very fortunate to have visited Lucasfilm and Industrial Light and Magic. It was the highest level of filmmaking at that time. It was one of the highlights of my working life."

Palitoy Strikes Back

The Palitoy range from *The Empire Strikes Back* was soon available. Palitoy had made merchandising kits available to toy stores, including shelf talkers, signs and a window sticker, proclaiming that the new range was in stock. The new additions to the action figure selection were Han Solo (Hoth Outfit), Luke Skywalker (Bespin Fatigues), Leia Organa (Bespin Gown), Lando Calrissian, Rebel Soldier (Hoth Battle Gear), Imperial Stormtrooper (Hoth Battle Gear), FX-7 (Medical Droid), IG-88 (Bounty Hunter), Bespin Security Guard and Bossk (Bounty Hunter). Boba Fett was not made available in the shops at this time. The packaging followed the same style as the *Star Wars* range, but with the *Empire Strikes Back* logo. On the reverse, there was a photograph of hand-painted prototypes of the new figures, which varied

John May poses on the Dagobah set at EMI Elstree Studios (courtesy John May).

slightly from the ones in the shops. Also pictured on the back was the Imperial Troop Transporter and Droid Factory. The 20 *Star Wars* figures were pictured too but they were only being sold in the *Star Wars*-style packaging at this time. "I remember it being as a total bun fight to get your hands on figures from *The Empire Strikes Back*," says Tim Drummond. "The day they hit my local toyshop, the Kiddy City in Lewisham, it was mayhem with adults wading in and grabbing armfuls and the shelves being totally cleared of all new figures!"[15]

New vehicles for the action figure range were also available; the Rebel Armoured Snowspeeder (the title of which was changed by Palitoy to reflect the English spelling of Armor) and the Twin Pod Cloud Car. The Snowspeeder would prove to be the most iconic of the pair, with blaster cannons that lit up noisily at the press of a button, spring-loaded undercarriage, space for two figures back to back and a removable grappling hook ready to trip Imperial Walkers. If only the string attached to the hook had been a great deal longer, it would have been the perfect toy. The Twin Pod Cloud Car had all of the sleek lines of its on-screen counterpart but was bereft of working features, apart from a pair of opening cockpits and manually operated landing gear. The Palitoy Twin Pod Cloud Car was even less of a bargain, compared with the Kenner version, due to it being manufactured in a too-bright orange color, and with landing gear that was often too loose to keep the craft off of the ground. Even so, the compact nature of both vehicles in *The Empire Strikes Back* allowed their toy counterparts to be perfectly scaled with *Star Wars* action figures. There was also a Tauntaun which figures could "ride," via a spring-loaded trap door in the beast's back.

Also from Palitoy: a Boba Fett Large Size Action Figure. The toy had been provided with much better articulation than its *Star Wars* predecessors and was armed with a blaster and a non-functioning rocket to which a length of string was attached. Peering through the back of the figure's head would provide a fish-eye view. Boba Fett was packaged in Kenner branded boxes in Britain with Palitoy not developing its own design, although some were adorned with a Palitoy sticker. Palitoy had also chosen not to issue Boba Fett's counterpart figure IG-88, which had been released in America by Kenner. "Palitoy felt that the IG-88 large action figure was not suited for mainstream distribution," says Geoff Maisey. "It was too expensive for our market."

A standout item from the new range was the Millennium Falcon Spaceship scaled to action figures, which had been released in America in 1979. What more desirable item could there be? There was no shortage of features: an opening cockpit, a removable roof panel, chess table, gun turret chair, training remote ball and a chamber in the floor in which the rebel heroes could hide. The front landing gear foot doubled as a handle, which was perfect for children to use as they made the Millennium Falcon swoop and dive, narrowly missing obstacles both real and imaginary. Another new item was the Force Lightsaber, which was a much better attempt by Kenner at producing a child-friendly-sized version of the Jedi weapon than the Light Saber (from 1978). The new toy featured a sturdy hilt that was large enough for a double-handed grip, attached to a solid plastic blade cast in red or yellow. There was not a light-up feature but instead a function where the weapon would make sounds reminiscent of a lightsaber via the air passing through it. Fans had a choice of Jedi weaponry as the *Force Beam* toy was still available from Loydale Ltd. If the company was breaking copyright, Lucasfilm and 20th Century–Fox were extremely slow to act.

Palitoy included a double-side poster with all of its big boxed *Star Wars* items picturing the entire *Star Wars* range, which included the majority of the items from 1978 and 1979. The X-Wing Fighter had been issued in a new box with a Dagobah-based picture and the *Empire Strikes Back* logo. The Blaster Pistol too had been rebranded for the new film. The majority of the range continued to be sold in their original *Star Wars* packaging: the Death Star, Landspeeder, Cantina, Land of the Jawas, Droid Factory, Imperial Troop Transporter, TIE Fighter (Kenner box with a Palitoy sticker), Radio Controlled R2-D2, Talking R2-D2, Three Position Laser Rifle and the die-cast range.

Items from Palitoy's sister companies were also included in the poster, which was part and parcel of the new Palitoy Company group: the *Electronic Battle Command Game* from Chad Valley and the *Adventures of R2-D2* game from Parker Bros. The Large Size Action Figures range from Denys Fisher was featured but not Ben (Obi-Wan) Kenobi and Jawa from Meccano. The Denys Fisher Darth Vader TIE Fighter and X-Wing Fighter kits were included on the poster. A fantastic new 1:87 scale Millennium Falcon model kit was announced too but collectors have yet to find one in Denys Fisher packaging.

The June 21–28 edition of *2000AD* featured a *Star Wars* cover, with artwork depicting the Large Size Action Figures and *Electronic Battle Command Game*. Inside there was a competition negotiated by Munro/Deighton to win one of 15 *Electronic Battle Command Game*s or one of 20 Large Size Action Figures. Palitoy also organized live promotions with the costumes it had available. The Darth Vader suits by Nick Farmer and movie-costumed Stormtroopers began making the rounds. So did Boba Fett who, as part of his tour, visited Gammon Toys in Lowestoft on August 22, Tortoise Toys in Rochford, Essex, and Martins Toys in Kingswood, Bristol. "I was so pleased that Boba Fett visited Martins," says Ian Whitlock. "I got his autograph and stuck it in my scrapbook next to Darth Vader's. So I proudly had the two big baddies' autographs." Sarah Baker-Saunders encountered Boba Fett in her area:

I used to go into Manchester most Saturdays, sometimes to shop, other times to go to film and comic fairs. Whilst going through the Arndale Centre one day, I noticed a new toy store with a large poster in the window: "Boba Fett will be appearing at this store on 26th July." As well as that, they would be displaying a new range of Palitoy *Star Wars* figures.

One of the promotions for *The Empire Strikes Back* was a competition in 2000AD (Star Wars Magazines Encyclopaedia).

This store was huge with two stories, and Boba was visiting the following week! So armed with my camera and taking my younger brother along, I went to Manchester on the day. I took some photos, including me with Boba when he finally turned up. There was a huge crowd, and staff were giving out Boba Fett figures in little Baggies and I was lucky enough to grab one! I was a great day. Afterwards I asked the store assistants if I could have the large cardboard sign from the window and lucky they said yes! I had some strange looks on the bus going home!

Fans may have let their imaginations run away with them as to who it was under Boba Fett's mask but it was not Jeremy Bulloch who was dressed for the part on tour. As was the case with David Prowse, it did not matter who filled the Boba Fett costume for promotions. It would not have made financial sense to hire Jeremy Bulloch for promotional work and in any case, he was extremely busy with his acting career. Darth Vader was putting on another kind of performance at the time, at the

Watch out. Boba Fett is out and about on tour (courtesy Sarah Saunders).

rock band Queen's live shows. During the song "We Will Rock You," Freddie Mercury would appear on stage on the shoulders of the Dark Lord, to huge reaction from the audience. Photographer Tom Callins captured an iconic image of Freddie sitting on Vader's shoulders wearing a Flash Gordon T-shirt at Houston's Summit Center on August 10, 1980. "I'm sure it was a roadie they hired [to play Vader], or maybe a bodyguard. I guess you had to be a pretty bulky guy to carry Freddie around. It was pandemonium. Everyone thought it was so funny, so Freddie. It was so over-the-top. Everybody got a chuckle out of it."[16] The fun reportedly came to an end when the band was served a cease-and-desist order by lawyers representing Lucasfilm.[17]

C-3PO for a Day

An important *Star Wars* promotion landed in Southend-on-Sea ahead of a special premiere event of the film on July 24 at the local Odeon. According to Derek Dorking,

Every summer, the Southend-on-Sea Odeon used to share movie promotions with Keddies department store. The store always put on a big display based on the biggest film release and in 1980, it was due to be *The Empire Strikes Back*. I just happened to pass the main display window and saw to my amazement the original Princess Leia gown on a mannequin and the C-3PO costume sort of propped up. I met with the manager of Keddies, who recognized me. He explained that the display was being organized in conjunction with Palitoy and he invited me to bring along the R2-D2 model again. A few days later, I met with some representatives from Palitoy at the store and I said to them, "I hope you realize that the C-3PO costume is an original" and they said, "We have no idea. We just got it from France." They said that they had the costumes for two weeks, after which they would be sent to Germany. I said, "I'm sure that I can figure out how the suit works." I added that I had even met Anthony Daniels. "I'm about his size, I bet I could wear it." They agreed and I even figured out how to make the lights behind the eyes work. On the day at Keddies, there were a couple of people dressed in Hoth Rebel soldier costumes from the film, someone in a movie Hoth Stormtrooper outfit and Julie in the original movie Princess Leia outfit. The C-3PO suit weighed a ton and as I attempted to walk, I found that the reason that C-3PO walks the way he does is that the person inside has to pull their body weight up to lift the leg joints, so you have no choice but to shuffle. Also, like Anthony Daniels has said, it was rough as old boots inside.

The kids went absolutely berserk. They loved seeing C-3PO and I was literally mobbed. I had a go at a high-pitched, posh voice but I sounded very muffled. At the end of the event, I had gotten so hot inside the suit that the top half had expanded the fastenings and I found that I was locked inside! The guys from Palitoy put their heads together and after a bit of brute force I was freed. I didn't get paid— I'd done it for the love of it—but I was given a Palitoy Radio Controlled R2-D2 by Keddies. When I got home, I found that I had sores all over my body, so I have every respect for Anthony Daniels wearing the outfit for hours on end, especially out in the desert—and it was a much rougher version back in '76. Despite the toll it took on me physically, it was a fantastic experience that I'll never forget.

20th Century–Fox was also organizing promotional stunts for *The Empire Strikes Back*, although they did not always appear in the national press. On June 21, Londoners were treated to the odd spectacle of Darth Vader and a Stormtrooper standing in the back of an open-top Rolls-Royce which was being driven leisurely through the streets. Vader waved royally until the car arrived at Fatso's Pasta Joint in Central London, where the Imperial duo presented a cup to the winner of the *Evening News* Space Invaders Championships and other prizes to the runners-up. A scantily clad model was photographed in the street with Vader and the Stormtrooper—perhaps a degree of glamor was deemed necessary to catch the eye of newspaper editors. Not all had gone according to plan, however, as the Stormtrooper was

Above and opposite page (top): **Derek Dorking's shining hour: appearing as C-3PO (photograph by Philip Dorking, courtesy Derek Dorking).**

Darth Vader and a Stormtrooper travel in style through the streets of Central London (Mirrorpix).

dressed incorrectly, wearing his back plate on his chest. Standards in the Empire had obviously slipped since they had menaced the rebellion in *The Empire Strikes Back*.

In *The Empire Strikes Back Official Poster Monthly #2*, the focus was on Darth Vader and the Imperial forces. The story was repeated of Darth Vader being terribly injured by Ben Kenobi, resulting in him wearing his black armor as a life support system. Other facts were revealed such as Vader's personal Star Destroyer being called *The Executor.* Imperial Walkers were described in this issue using the acronym AT-AT (All Terrain Armored Transport) Walkers, with it being explained that the machines were 50 feet tall and traveled at 10 to 20 miles per hour. These were the kind of facts that fans craved and that were indispensable in forming a detailed *Star Wars* universe.

Much of this information was derived from *The Empire Strikes Back Sketchbook* by Joe Johnston, *Empire*'s art director, and his assistant Nilo Rodis-Jamero. Packed full of design sketches and fascinating information, this book explained a great deal about the *Star Wars* Universe. For fans who were interested in such things, Imperial Probe Droids were also known as Probots; the Rebels had designed and built the Snowspeeders; and the Rebel Transport ships were hollowed-out space liners. Most importantly, the two-legged Imperial walking machine seen fleetingly in the Hoth battle was introduced in the book as an Imperial Scout Walker; it was revealed that it was piloted by one man and used by the Imperials for reconnaissance. The vehicle had been fully realized in both design and as a detailed model but its use in the film had been reduced to almost nothing. The Scout Walker would however become an important ingredient of the growing *Star Wars* universe.

The July edition of *Fantastic Films*, which was now available from shops in Britain, dedicated a great deal of space to *The Empire Strikes Back*. Screenwriter Laurence Kasdan, interviewed for this issue, explained how he had begun writing screenplays at the University of Michigan; "Three years ago I started selling them." Kasdan explained how his second script, *Continental Divide*, had been bought by Universal and Steven Spielberg which in turn led to him writing the *Raiders of the Lost Ark* screenplay. "When I finished it, George had just received the first draft of *Empire* from Leigh Brackett…. [H]e had some problems with it as they always do with first drafts. He called her up to talk to her about it and she was in the hospital and she never came out. When I finished *Raiders*, George said that they were really up against the wall [and] he asked me if I would come in and write it and that's how I got onto *Empire*."[18]

The September *Starlog* included yet more *Empire* coverage. Sporting a fantastic Boba Fett cover, it brought the news that the second *Star Wars* sequel, *Revenge of the Jedi*, was due to begin filming on January 13, 1982; that Englishman Richard Marquand would be in the director's chair; and that *Raiders of the Lost Ark* producer Howard Kazanjian would produce. This information *ahead* of *The Empire Strikes Back* in general release was enough to make any fan's head spin.

Merchandising the Empire

Arranging a merchandise campaign for *The Empire Strikes Back*, which was essentially a sequel movie, was never going to be easy. The core products had been secured, however; the toy line, soundtrack, novelization, comic, Collector's Edition book and poster magazine. The *Empire Strikes Back* annual from Marvel/Grandreams, which contained the comic adaptation of the film, was released in conjunction with the film as a souvenir piece, well ahead of the traditional autumn schedule. Companies that had produced *Star Wars* merchandise had returned to the fold. Bedroom ware from Ratcliffe Bros. was available in the form of pillowcases, duvet covers and curtains. Vymura produced wallpaper which was of the same high standard, depicting various scenes from the film. Lyons Maid produced themed ice cream lollies with free stickers. Trebor released a chew bar and Mountain Films distributed part one of the Super 8 film glossily packaged in a plastic box. Chappell & Co. released sheet music of Han Solo and the Princess ("Love Theme"). A read-along book and record/tape was released by Buena Vista Records, with Jymn Magon again behind the production. Also available was a *Storybook* from Armada, a *Pop-Up Book* distributed by Franklin-Watts and a *Punch Out and Make It Book* from Random House. Factors of Delaware USA was also listed but there was not a British distributor for the company's range of badges and T-shirts. Anyone wishing to stock the items would have to inquire at Factor's American headquarters. Topps of Ireland was listed but its only product was a set of Initial Stickers, which were part of the third, yellow bordered trading card set in America.

The *Empire Strikes Back* presskit was also able to boast of new blood: The Craft Dairylea cheese products. A range of children's plastic cups, mugs and plates by Decca Plastics Ltd. (imported from America by Dolphin Impex Ltd.) featured photographs of the main cast. The presskit also listed items which unfortunately did not come to fruition. Waddingtons House of Games was listed as producing a jigsaw but it did not emerge. Coffee mugs from Staffordshire Potteries Ltd. of Stoke-on-Trent do not seem to have made it to the shops either.

The relatively small amount of tie-in merchandise for *The Empire Strikes Back* compared to that of *Star Wars* (although still impressive in its own right) could be explained by other science fiction films seeming to be more attractive propositions. For instance, for *The Black Hole* there was a trading card set, a four-part Letraset transfer set, jigsaws, a soap model and a coloring book but not for *The Empire Strikes Back*. *Flash Gordon* and *Star Trek: The Motion Picture* had secured breakfast cereal promotions. It was a natural progression for companies to back the very latest films

Above and following two pages: Initial Stickers from Topps, Lyons Maid lolly wrappers and the Dairylea Bumper Transfer Pack—just some of the items released for *The Empire Strikes Back* (courtesy Darren Simpson).

PRINCESS LEIA ORGANA™
Once a senator and princess on Alderaan, Princess Leia is now a dedicated leader of the Rebel effort. Beautiful but outspoken and courageous, Leia is undaunted in her struggle to overthrow Imperial tyranny.

BOBA FETT™
Boba Fett is the best bounty hunter in the galaxy, and cares little for whom he works—as long as they pay him well. He wears a modified uniform of the Mandalore supercommandos who were wiped out by the Jedi knights in the Clone Wars.

DARTH VADER™
Darth Vader is the seven-foot Imperial lord of the Sith. As a young Jedi knight he was seduced by the dark side of the force. His face is obscured by a grotesque breath mask.

Lyons Maid
STAR WARS™
FREE STICKER INSIDE
TOFFEE FLAVOUR AND MINT ICE LOLLY WITH CHOCOLATE FLAVOURED COATING AND SUGAR BALLS

YODA™
Yoda is the wise, old Jedi Master who has trained Jedi knights for over 800 years. Dressed in rags and little more than two feet tall, he lives on a swamp planet in the Dagobah System.

LANDO CALRISSIAN™
The suave and dashing administrator of Cloud City, Lando Calrissian is a former associate of Han Solo. Han calls Lando a gambler, con artist, and all-around scoundrel, but nonetheless seeks his assistance in evading Darth Vader.

and television programs, so it is understandable that *The Empire Strikes Back* was overlooked, even by those who had done well with *Star Wars* products. "I think the feeling at Helix was that in general, follow-up films tended to be weak," says David Giddings. "I also seem to recall that we had to job out some *Star Wars* stock at year end in 1979, which might have affected our thinking." Robert Beecham makes another valid point: "By that time, it was being seen that Kenner, and Palitoy in Britain had monopolized the business. We're

talking about hundreds of millions of dollars worldwide. It was an extraordinary phenomenon and at some stage the public were going to limited in what they were going to buy."
A lack of distinctive new characters in *The Empire Strikes Back* may also have been a factor
in companies turning away from producing tie-in merchandise. The *Star Wars* campaign
after all had on the whole been based around the strange new robots and creatures rather
than the human stars. Darth Vader was then brand new but his image had reached satu-
ration point. Writing for the May 1980 *Starburst*, Tony Crawley focused on this very issue:
"[S]ince 1977, *Star Wars* has become more than a movie. It is a multi-million-dollar business
corporation. And so, merchandising requires new characters. The toy manufacturers cannot
keep churning out R2 and 3PO toys from here to doomsday. And so, enter a cuddly, friendly,
eight-foot-high beastie called a Tauntaun…. It's no vast rival of Chewie, you ride this beast
like a camel."[19] Crawley also highlighted Lando Calrissian and the mysterious Yoda as new
characters but, in common with the rest of the British media, he did not mention Boba
Fett. Palitoy had used Boba Fett and the theme of Bounty Hunters to great effect but other
companies had not picked up on the importance of the character. Palitoy representatives
visited Elstree during filming, so it is not surprising that the company had an edge over
other manufacturers. In hindsight, it seems amazing that Boba Fett had not been introduced
to Britain in a blaze of publicity as a new villain. Most surprising of all is that Boba Fett
had not even been included in the British film poster or the cover of the novelization. It
could be imagined that if a "Boba Fett and the Bounty Hunters" theme had been part of
Empire's promotional and merchandising strategy, the story may have been different. In
America, Boba Fett had been included in a cartoon segment of the *Star Wars Holiday
Special,* was released very early as an action figure and had even made live appearances at

public events; but still, his potential as a new character for *The Empire Strikes Back* had not been fully exploited.

That said, the promotion of a blockbuster movie in 1980 was still in its infancy and the concept of a highly successful series of sequels telling a continuing story was very much unknown territory. In June 1980, *The Empire Strikes Back* campaign had only just begun.

Empire of Britain

On Sunday, June 15, *The Empire Strikes Back* opened in 40 British cities and large towns. Employees at cinemas showing the film wore T-shirts featuring the *Empire Strikes Back* logo during the release and gave away circular stickers depicting characters from the film. There was not a program book for the film, so cinemas stocked *The Empire Strikes Back Collectors Edition* in its place. This initial release was much wider than that of *Star Wars* but smaller venues still had to wait. Cinemas receiving *Empire Strikes Back* included the Birmingham Gaumont, Edinburgh Odeon, Nottingham Odeon, Glasgow Odeon, Exeter Odeon, Bradford Odeon, Aberdeen Odeon, Bristol Odeon, Leeds Odeon, Cardiff Odeon, Sheffield Gaumont, Hanley Odeon (Stoke-on-Trent), Southampton Odeon, Norwich Odeon, Jersey Odeon, Liverpool Odeon, Manchester Odeon and the Newcastle Odeon.

In researching the release pattern of The Empire Strikes Back *via physically reading through old newspapers in archives (there was not an electronic database for modern local newspapers at the time), I found the 40 venues opening the film on June 15 to be very elusive. Large venues that had snapped up* Star Wars *did not play its sequel immediately. The smaller venues filling in the gaps (if indeed 40 venues did open the film) were difficult to locate, considering the number of cinemas in Britain.*

There was huge demand for tickets as the June 29 edition of *Screen International* reported. "*The Empire Strikes Back* opened to outstanding business. At the Gaumont Birmingham, Odeon 2 Cardiff and the Odeon 1 set new records while at other screens, new year's highs were notched up."[20] According to a 20th Century-Fox memo sent to licensees, 63 coastal venues had originally been earmarked to receive *Empire* on June 26 and cinemas were more or less on schedule; the Portsmouth Odeon, Weymouth Classic, Bude Picturehouse and Southsea Salon opened on the 29th. The Westgate-on-Sea Carlton bucked the trend by showing *Empire* early, on June 2. Also, the Great Yarmouth Regent on June 19. Cinemas including the Plymouth Drake Film Center, Torquay Odeon, Hastings Classic, Clacton Mecca Cinema, Thanet Dreamland Twins, Herne Bay Classic, Deal Classic, Ramsgate Classic, St. Ives Royal, Margate Dreamland and the Redruth Regal opened *Empire* the first week in July. Meanwhile, the featured cinemas in *Screen International* were taking roughly £1000 less in takings per week, every week. The profits were still higher than would be the case with most films but it was clear that *The Empire Strikes Back* did not have the staying power of its predecessor.

The Empire Strikes Back Poster Monthly #3 featured a profile of Yoda, drawing upon the film and novel to paint a vivid picture of the character. Yoda's habit of chewing on a Gimer

Stick, a small twig with three small branches at the far end, was an idea presented in the novel and comic but did not pan out in the finished film. Yet the article presented as many questions as answers: How old is Yoda? What species is he? Why does he live in such isolation? Such matters were left to the imagination of the reader. Also in this issue, "The Lessons of Luke" drew upon the novel to flesh out Yoda's masterly advice. Training methods that had featured in the novel and comic, such as Yoda throwing a metal bar in the air for Luke to cut with his lightsaber, and using a pair of "seeker balls," was also featured, providing a further insight to how the film had been intended to progress. "The Indignities of Artoo" was a playful examination of the events on Dagobah from the little droid's perspective. One of the incidents that R2-D2 was involved in was a major scene featured in the novel, where Luke is zapped unconscious by Yoda's seeker balls (presumably having more kick than the one aboard the Millennium Falcon) and the droid gave his master a mild electric shock to revive him. What with the terrible weather, being swallowed whole by an underwater beast and being levitated during practice sessions with the Force, R2-D2 was glad to leave Dagobah far behind!

The Stars Have Their Say

The August issue of *Film Review*, published in July, included excellent interviews with Carrie Fisher and Mark Hamill by Dave Badger, under the title "Leia and Luke Look In on London." Despite the success of *Star Wars*, both actors still suffered the ignominy of being referred to by their character names in the British press. "The princess is too good to be real," said Fisher. "I've decided that in the next film that she's gonna take to the bottle. After all, she's been tortured, fired at, almost blown up, been in a spaceship hurtling through an asteroid field, almost eaten by monsters, orphaned and left stranded on her first date. In the first two films, the princess never really smiles either, so she is also finally going to grin." Hamill told Badger, "I don't think that it would be a bad thing if all I am ever remembered for is being Luke. …A lot of actors spend their whole lives doing marvelous work but don't get a break and are not remembered for a single thing."[21]

The July 24 issue of *Rolling Stone* had a cover photo of Harrison Ford, Mark Hamill, Carrie Fisher and Billy Dee Williams in their civvies. The center pages contained a humorous photograph of Fisher in the arms of Ford, who is pushing away Hamill. Ford put forward his own view of the cliffhanger ending of *The Empire Strikes Back*:

> I have heard frequently that there is a certain kind of disappointment with the ending. I've heard people say, "There's no end to this film" or "I can't wait to find out what happens" but they *will*, and that's exactly the effect intended by the ending. People who are expecting a repetition of the emotional experience of the first film are not going to find exactly that. The audience that saw the first film is more sophisticated now, three years later, in the same way that the techniques are more sophisticated.[22]

The Empire Strikes Back Poster Monthly #4 contained a detailed article focusing on the film's special effects: "During the shooting of *Empire* the ILM crew worked six-day weeks with long hours. Nightshifts often took over where the day shift left off. The optical department, for instance, was in operation 24 hours a day. While a group of older hands are in charge of operations, most of the artists, technicians, model-makers, engineers, cinematographers and others who work at ILM are incredibly young. The average age is under 30."[23] The same issue contained an article by Dr. Michael F. Marten titled "Asteroids!"

Marten provided a detailed report on the genuine asteroids known to science, including a prediction that real-life astronauts may begin mining asteroids within the next 10 or 15 years. The article "AT-AT Attack" revealed that the rebel Snowspeeders' tow cables had been originally designed for towing heavy loads across the ice wastes of Hoth. Without this information, people may have considered the tow cables to be a little too fortuitous a gadget to be at the pilot's fingertips. Also included was a description of an event during the Hoth battle cut from the film but described in the novelization, where the Rebel pilot Hobbie, wounded and unlikely to survive, bravely made a last ditch kamikaze attack on the lead AT-AT Walker, wiping out General Veers in the process.

The Empire Continues Its March

Some large venues that might have been expected to open *Empire Strikes Back* as soon as it was available did not do so until the week beginning August 3: the Scarborough Odeon, Blackpool Odeon, Bournemouth Gaumont, Eastbourne Curzon and ABC Dover. Individual cinemas juggled their schedules to accommodate all of the summer films on offer. Although *The Black Hole* had been released in December, the delay in releasing it nationally led to it crashing directly into *The Empire Strikes Back* in some areas. *The Final Countdown* and *Mission Galactica* were competing for space in the schedules too. The 10th saw the release of *Empire* at the Folkestone Curzon and the Falmouth Grand. "I became interested more in the making of the film during the build-up to its release," says Darren Slade. "When I eventually went to see it at the Bournemouth Gaumont, I found the film to be surprising, bright and fantastic. I had a terrific time; the spectacle was satisfying enough. I don't recall being unsatisfied with the ending at all." James Simmonds recalls:

> I saw *The Empire Strikes Back* with my brother and dad at the Bournemouth Gaumont. We were on holiday in Bournemouth and it was pouring with rain so my dad only took us to see the film for something to do. The queue stretched right down the street and the place was packed when the film began. Funnily enough, I have no memory of seeing the film but it must have had an impact on me because I hunted high and low for a Luke Bespin figure and it took until the end of our holiday for me to find one. I also bought a Princess Leia Bespin at the same time, although my dad wondered why I wanted the girl toy. And the rest is history, as far as my collecting *Star Wars* goes. As my collecting reached crazy levels in the years that followed, Mum used to joke that taking me to see the film was the worst thing that my Dad ever did!

Derek Dorking says,

> I first saw *The Empire Strikes Back* with Julie at the Southend Odeon at the premiere on July 24 and we thought it was fantastic. I couldn't wait to begin showing it at the Westcliff-on-Sea Classic. There was a bar for two weeks but we would be showing it in 70mm, which would be a draw because the Southend Odeon couldn't. We had already been sent the *Gone with the Wind*-style poster but within the same week Fox had changed it to the new more action-packed artwork with Vader standing astride the other characters. The first poster had to go in the bin.

On August 14, *The Empire Strikes Back Weekly* #129 included a full-page advert proclaiming the news that *Empire* was finally now in release in "key cities" throughout the country. One hundred fifty cinemas opened the film on August 17; those in Greater London including the Bromley Odeon, Ealing Odeon, Barnet Odeon, East Ham Odeon, Elephant and Castle Odeon, Barking Odeon, Chelsea Odeon, Finchley Gaumont, Ilford Gants Hill

Odeon, Kensington Odeon, Kingston Granada, Lewisham Odeon, Peckham Film Center, Purley Astoria, Stockwell Classic, Streatham Odeon, Tooting Classic, Westbourne Grove Odeon, Basildon Odeon, Well Hall Odeon and Wood Green Odeon. Nationally: the Ayr Odeon, Bognor Regis Picture House, Cambridge Victoria, Chester Odeon, Colchester Odeon, Croydon Odeon, Dundee Odeon, Falkirk ABC, Greenock Gaumont, Guildford Odeon, Luton Odeon, St. Albans Odeon, Haslemere Rex, the Hull Mecca, Sale Odeon, Twickenham Odeon, Oxted Plaza, Romford Odeon, Sevenoaks Focus 123, Staines ABC, Stockwell Classic, Taunton Odeon, York Odeon, Watford Odeon, Westcliff-on-Sea Classic, Whitby Empire and Woolwich Odeon. The film began its run at the Dominion Theatre Tottenham Court Road on August 21 and at the Odeon Marble Arch, in 70mm Dolby Stereo, on the same day. August 24 saw additional provincial releases including the Redditch Classic, Havant Empire, and Evesham Regal, and Chichester Granada on the 27th.

"The 70mm print we got to show at the Westcliff-on-Sea Classic was absolutely fantastic," says Derek Dorking. "I had learned that the cinema had originally been an Essoldo chain cinema, which explains why it was equipped with stereo sound and 70mm. With *The Empire Strikes Back*, if cinemas could play 70mm, they got it. I was tied to the projector so to speak, so I got 'Empired out.' We were on a two-projector system so you couldn't leave it running. I saw it hundreds of times so I know every frame!"

Louise Turner says,

When I saw *The Empire Strikes Back*, I remember thinking it was wonderful and I think that it was the music that really blew me away. I *loved* the music—in retrospect, I realize now that it was the Imperial March that I really fell in love with. But I still thought Luke Skywalker was kind of cute, and I liked the Tauntauns. My dad—not a science fiction fan by any stretch of the imagination—was so baffled by the Tauntauns that he did a series of carton drawings featuring 'torn-tauns' (their horns grow so long that they pierce their necks and kill them) and 'tan-tauns,' which can be found lying in huge numbers on sun-loungers along the coast of warm countries!"

The wait was finally over for the majority of fans as *The Empire Strikes Back* went into wider release.

Graham Ogle shares his memories:

I saw *The Empire Strikes Back* on its opening weekend at the Odeon Stoke-on-Trent. Before seeing the film, I knew almost nothing about it, save for a synopsis that one of the national newspapers ran. This was also the first time I had seen photos from the film, Luke on his Tauntaun and Vader, Boba Fett and Lando Calrissian on Cloud City. Boba Fett looked cool. The morning I was due to see it, there was a clip on *Tiswas* that whet my appetite even more. My brother was adamant that we would not be able to get in, but we did. The cinema was full that day, mostly kids of course. For the next two hours, I was spellbound. I absolutely loved Hoth, the Walker battle had me transfixed, and we were only half an hour into the movie!

Ian Whitlock also saw *Empire* at this time. "A child at my school told me the Vader reveal before I saw the film in Bristol, so that pretty much ruined my chance of finding that out while the film played. I do remember feeling quite shocked at the time and I didn't quite believe it and I also never hung out with that kid again!" Bob Cole says that when he saw *Empire* in Worcester, "I was excited beyond anything, being only seven. The trouble was that as I took my seat with my mother and sister, the screen's curtains hadn't opened as the film began. It took until the sequence where Han finds Luke in the snow for the curtains to kick into action. I shouted out, 'That's one small step for man' but nobody laughed! I rekindled my love for Princess Leia with that film. None of the rival space princesses on television came anywhere near." Declan McCafferty recalls,

The first *Star Wars* film I saw was *The Empire Strikes Back* upon its release, possibly during its first day in Glasgow. I was six years old and had a brother eight years my senior who had been hyping me up for it. Any stills I'd seen from *Star Wars* just looked the greatest thing imaginable. The Odeon in Renfield Street was queued right around the block that day. My legs were actually trembling when I saw the Odeon sign and, as we neared the front of the queue, that quad poster. Due to my brother's books and comics, I knew who they all were in advance, even Boba Fett. My brother really liked the film and he took me to see it again before the end of summer. By this time, he'd outgrown the comics, but I inherited his order at the local news agent. One thing that, with hindsight, was a shame. I had known, probably from said brother, that Vader was Luke's father. I had assumed this was always known in *Star Wars*, so at the climax of *The Empire Strikes Back*, I thought that must be Luke just finding out what we knew all along!

I had waited expectantly for The Empire Strikes Back. *I still didn't watch a great deal of television, so the only clip of the film I had seen was Luke Skywalker watching Princess Leia being dragged away and then confronting Darth Vader. I avoided reading anything that would have given the plot away but the novel and the soundtrack were pretty much everywhere you looked and the cover art gave away who Leia would fall for. I was very pleased that it would be Han Solo and that was the only plot point that I expected to see. My father drove Paul and me again to the Odeon Gants Hill, Ilford. The reason that Gary was not with us has been lost in time, except for a vague recollection that as 11-year-olds, we were much more tied to the whims of our families when it came to watching films.*

As I took my seat, it was partway through Black Angel, *which I thought was utterly bizarre. I could not make any sense out of it. During the opening scenes of* The Empire Strikes Back, *I sensed that the tone was a great deal bleaker than its predecessor. As it unfolded, I found the film to be very dark and not just in tone. Modern reproductions on video, DVD and Blu-ray show the film with everything bright and clearly visible, which was not the way it was shown at the cinema. Many of the scenes were obscured in gloom, adding considerably to the feeling of menace. When the camera pulled away from the spacecraft in the final scene, I was left feeling that the film hadn't finished. I felt like shouting to the projectionist to show the final reel! As an 11-year-old, I considered myself to be quite a mature cinemagoer. I had been expecting a film with a familiar structure, like* Star Wars, *a Harryhausen production or* The Black Hole. *If I had had the choice, I would have seen it again because there was so much to take in.*

The Local Letdown

For *The Empire Strikes Back*, there were do-it-yourself promotional activities and costume hijinks organized by cinemas of the kind that had featured in the run-up to the release of *Star Wars*, but it was not as widespread. 20th Century-Fox arranged for a small number of costumed performers to make appearances at key venues dressed in movie accurate costumes of Darth Vader and Stormtroopers. The Bradford Odeon and the Plymouth Drake Film Center had Darth Vader in attendance. Susan Burton recalled seeing Vader at Plymouth: "I walked two miles in the pouring rain without an umbrella to see him and I was not disappointed. He's my favorite character and he can't be such a bad guy because he helped me with my shopping bag which weighed a ton!"[24] The St. Albans Odeon too had the benefit of a Darth Vader to accompany a visiting Stormtrooper but it was a costume left over from the Rank Organisation 1978 campaign. *The St. Albans Post-Echo* featured a

The *Empire* tour lands at Keddies department store, Southend-on-Sea, on the July 29, 1980 (*Southend Echo*).

full page of advertisements for local businesses surrounding the advert for *The Empire Strikes Back* opening locally. Darth Vader and Stormtrooper posed for photographs taken inside the local Wimpy restaurant, Derann Home Entertainment Center and Carpet Supermarket. Unfortunately, the Stormtrooper was not dressed properly and had the back plate on his chest! Darth Vader and Stormtroopers also appeared at schools such as the Ashley Road Primary School in Aberdeen and department stores such as Keddies in Southend-on-Sea.

According to Derek Dorking,

> For the Westcliff Classic, I had constructed a complete Darth Vader suit from scratch, apart from the Don Post helmet. I had noticed from the back cover of *The Star Wars Storybook* that Vader's cloak has a blue lining and did my best to replicate that. The suit was by no means as accurate as the screen one but I thought it worked out very well. I timed the blinking lights on the chest box to the exact timing seen in the film. We had the breathing sound on a loop on a cassette derived from a 70mm soundtrack of *The Empire Strikes Back.* These days it's easy to get Vader's breathing but for that era it was quite a revolution. I also made Princess Leia's Hoth outfit that Julie wore.

Some cinemas used extra-large advertising blocks in local newspapers to advertise *The Empire Strikes Back* utilizing the film poster and the quote "Crash, bang, wallop, what a picture!" from Cecil Wilson's *Daily Mail* review. A highlight of the publicity campaign was that local newspapers featured photographs of R2-D2 and C-3PO on a reconstructed piece of the Death Star set that had featured in the Selfridges display. In each instance, C-3PO was pictured holding an example of the local newspaper as if he was reading it. This was an extremely innovative and eye-catching publicity method, which had required a great deal of forward planning by 20th Century-Fox, to set up the scene with the robots and contact local newspapers to inquire if they would like to participate. "We didn't do that promotion at our cinema," says Dorking. "But I remember some of the nationals like the *Sun* or *Mirror* with a picture of Threepio reading the paper." Local newspapers ran competitions and printed serializations of *Empire*'s story, but this time around the features were few and far between.

In researching this book, I came across a huge number of local newspapers featuring Star Wars *serializations. In contrast,* The Birmingham Evening News *was the only example I came across which serialized* The Empire Strikes Back. *Even here, only the early edition of the newspaper featured the serialization.*

It seemed that in 1977 and 1978, *Star Wars* had been a phenomenon that everyone just had to grab a slice of, while on the whole *The Empire Strikes Back* was treated no differently from any other summer film. The lack of interest in the local press seems surprising. Although there were a whole slew of science fiction films riding the *Star Wars* wave, *Empire* represented the actual *source* of that wave and journalists seemed to have lost sight of that in the excitement over seemingly more fantastic upcoming films. The film review section of newspapers often contained a photograph of *Mission Galactica* or *The Final Countdown.* 20th Century-Fox made a concerted effort to engage with the local press, especially with the Leicester Square launch dinner, touring Vader and Stormtroopers and the C-3PO reading newspapers photo opportunity. Munro/Deighton and Palitoy marketing had been at full pelt too, with the Boba Fett tour being a highlight of their campaign. Derek Dorking recalls,

> There seemed to be less interest in *The Empire Strikes Back* from the local press in general, as I didn't see any coverage of the massive *Star Wars* event at Keddies and my stint as C-3PO or the costumes I made for my cinema. I think maybe then people who did film reviews thought that *The Empire Strikes Back* would promote itself and mentioned other films instead. *Star Wars* had kickstarted the whole phenomenon and there was a science fiction film every month coming out. *The Empire Strikes Back* was darker in tone and the images from the film looked very dark too. The reviews I remember seeing and reading were along the lines of that it was more adult and that the kids might not find it such a party as *Star Wars*.

Shaun Dawkins remembers the release of *The Empire Strikes Back* in his local area: "When the film hit Folkestone, there just wasn't the same level of press interest. Maybe it was because *Empire* was the middle of a story arc. It takes a fan to see that it stands on its own merits."

It was not only at the cinema that *Empire* faced fierce competition. It also came from television science fiction, of a kind that did not exist in 1977 and '78. Universal Studio's *Buck Rogers in the 25th Century* had not been a huge threat to the *Star Wars* franchise upon its UK theatrical release on July 26th 1979 but producer Glen. A Larson had since turned the successful concept into a television series. Premiering on ITV on Saturday, August 30, at 6:15 p.m., the program offered a string of breezy, lightweight adventures packed with heroes, over-the-top villains, robots, scantily clad space women and special effects which were at least on a par with *Star Wars*. It was with a joke and a smile, and with the universe being saved once again by Buck Rogers that each episode ended. Larson's previous sci-fi TV creation *Battlestar Galactica* arrived slightly later in Britain, first airing on Thursday, September 4, on ITV. While more heavyweight and thoughtful than *Buck Rogers*, it provided outer space action, compelling characters and high-quality space dogfight effects direct from the motion control camera of John Dykstra. It may have been to counter the competition from *Buck Rogers* and *Battlestar* that newspaper ads for *Empire* began to include the words "The one you will not see on the TV screen."

The Reaction

The Empire Strikes Back is a film with many subtleties, which were enjoyed upon its release by those who were mature enough to understand and appreciate them. "I loved the movie from start to finish," says Sarah Baker-Saunders. "All of my favorite characters were back and there were so many visual delights: Hoth, the ice battle, Yoda, the Force and Luke's training, the chase through the asteroids and Cloud City, and the duel between Luke and Darth. There was a great deal of character development. All of this excitement and adventure. There were even more questions by the end and another three years to wait for answers." According to Shaun Dawkins, "It was such a cliffhanger that you were definitely going to see the sequel but I was happy to go along with that. They did a great job with the production and they hadn't fallen into the trap of making it simply a special effects extravaganza. It focused on the characters and there was more of Luke exploring the Force. It was all building up to something pretty impressive."

Laurie Calvert was impressed too:

I was kind of expecting a rerun of *Star Wars* because up until that time, that was the style of sequels. *The Empire Strikes Back* was not like that at all. It ended on kind of a down note. I walked out of the cinema thinking two things. The first was that my hero had had his hand cut off. I was struggling to come to terms with that. The other was that I couldn't believe that Darth Vader was Luke's father. I didn't find the film disappointing, though. It was a complete positive although I had these shocking feelings that weird things had happened. Overall the quality had been maintained but the film had been taken in a different direction. I thought that was a very bold move and I was so proud of the saga.

Gerald Crotty noticed a negative tone in much of the media in the wake of *The Empire Strikes Back*:

The reviews varied but many of them complained about similar things. In *Starburst* #23, John Brosnan said, "It begins with an exciting bang then fragments into all directions, splitting up the characters along the way and ends on a very bleak note…. I guess what I wanted to see after all was a remake of *Star Wars* done differently." I found it amazing that he should have said this, since everyone would have slammed Lucas for sure if he'd just remade *Star Wars*. I know what most of the reviewers were trying to say, it was just that they were too busy trying to sound clever to admit it. Basically they were disappointed. Because *The Empire Strikes Back* wasn't as much fun as *Star Wars*. *The Empire Strikes Back* was not an easy ride, it wasn't meant to be. That's not to say you didn't get your money's worth, as Harrison Ford said: "I figure that there was at least 11 dollars worth of entertainment in *Empire*. So if you paid four bucks and didn't get an ending, you're still seven dollars ahead of the game."

Darren Slade says, "I was really impressed. I wasn't bothered about the film not having an ending. There was so much action, that it was satisfying on that level alone. Like most people I imagine, I was left with the puzzle over whether Darth Vader was Luke's father. I discovered that the *Empire Strikes Back* novelization had a line where it reads something like 'They looked at each other, father and son,' so in my mind it clinched it that Vader was telling the truth."

The Empire Strikes Back was not a film which was aimed specifically at children, and many pre-teens had mixed feelings. According to Tim Drummond,

When I saw the film as a ten year old, I remember being bored by Dagobah, confused by the cave scene, being very disappointed that Luke and Han didn't get to hang out as buddies like in the first film and not being able to understand why Lando was easily forgiven when he was clearly a traitor. I was beside myself that the film didn't end properly with everything neatly resolved. It was absolutely awesome, however, and kept me coming back for any opportunity to see it again. In total I saw the film six times over the summer, and when not watching it, I relived the film with a diet of ice lollies, Dairylea, the sticker album and most memorably recreating it all with every one of the toy figures.[25]

Craig Spivey shares similar sentiments:

I was nine when I saw *The Empire Strikes Back* at the Doncaster Gaumont. I didn't believe for one second that Darth Vader was Luke's father. In fact, I'd never really considered that behind that mask, the "electronic" voice and the scary breathing that there was even a human under there. It was Han Solo's fate that had the most impact on me. He was far and away my favorite character and they "turned him to stone." I remember being quite upset by that and I didn't trust Lando one bit either. The nuances of his coercion and redemption sailed way over my head.

Joe Sales recalls,

I had a lot of ideas of how the story would go myself. The comics also had covered a lot of sequel-style material and had provided lots of ideas themselves. One of the stories in the comic, "The Empire Strikes," was set on a giant space station which was very reminiscent of Bespin Cloud City and the very title of the story is a very interesting coincidence. I had always identified with Luke Skywalker and thought that Princess Leia was his ideal partner. It just didn't make sense. Han was brasher than her, and not even of the same age, unlike Luke. I also missed the presence of Alec Guinness and instead the Jedi master is a strange little creature whom I didn't identify with at all. I was quietly disappointed by the film, as it was not quite the story I had wanted to see.

Jordan Royce says,

I was disappointed. My grandparents went to see it with me and they were disappointed too. We left the cinema and they said, "That wasn't as good as the other one, was it?" When I next went to school, everyone I spoke to was disappointed. The consensus was that we had wanted something more swashbuckling, with the same characters that we loved. Like the first one but with a different story. I thought it was amazing in many areas, though, and was rich in new characters. I actually liked Yoda and ended up defending him against people who were saying that he was a "daft puppet." I remember the negativity and how it seemed that the film was not a hit at that time in people's eyes on the street level.

To me, The Empire Strikes Back *seemed to be more like a series of events, albeit exciting ones, rather than an actual story. I too did not understand all of the Dagobah scenes. I did not have any feelings over the Vader father revelation because all of my thoughts were on Han Solo. I cared so little for Luke Skywalker that anything could have happened to him. He could have been cut in half! In contrast, the capture and freezing of my hero Han Solo was akin to a punch in the gut. The settings and technology of* The Empire Strikes Back *were fascinating but the actual story did not hold any elements that I was interested in at that time. I kept going as a* Star Wars *fan though, with the comics representing a more authentic* Star Wars *experience. The toys and other memorabilia were as desirable as ever.*

If pre-teens on the whole did not appreciate the subtleties of *The Empire Strikes Back*, there were certainly enough highlights. including the Hoth battle, the asteroid sequence, the final escape and duel. The film was also chock full of amazing new vehicles. Children trusted that *Empire*'s more shocking aspects would be cleared up in *Revenge of the Jedi*, such as Han Solo being frozen and the question of whether Darth Vader was actually Luke's father. *Empire* had expanded the *Star Wars* universe beyond the wildest dreams of fans. The AT-AT Walkers and Snowspeeders became instant fan favorites and the Millennium Falcon's cool was cemented in people's minds. The Tauntauns and Yoda were so realistic that they appeared to be actual living creatures. The Tauntauns even had icy breath.

The new environments were the greatest addition to the *Star Wars* Universe: Hoth, Dagobah and Bespin. Fans had a genuine feeling of being transported through space and thanks to the professionalism of the effects crews, each location was so authentic, it seemed as if they could be visited and explored, if there was some way of getting there. George Lucas had perhaps been inspired by the television repeats of his cherished Saturday morning serials, in leaving the ending of the film hanging in deep space, but instead of seven days, fans had three years to wait for the continuation of the story. Such a prospect was agonizing to fans, and to young children the delay seemed inconceivable.

Palitoy reissued the ten figures from *The Empire Strikes Back* in packaging that was virtually identical to the release in May, except that the photographs of Leia Organa (Bespin

Gown) and Luke Skywalker (Bespin Fatigues) had been changed on the front of the backing card. The hair of Luke Skywalker (Bespin Fatigues) was changed from yellow to brown. The original set of 20 *Star Wars* figures were also included in this wave, making their debut in packaging from *The Empire Strikes Back*, as did Boba Fett (although Greedo and Snaggletooth have yet to be found by collectors).

Jordan Royce was still collecting: "Even though the film was not quite right in my eyes, it was still *Star Wars*. Then the next step was to get the toys. All of a sudden, the assignment for me and my friends was to get a Yoda or an FX-7 and the rest of the set. It was still like a fix for me at the time."

Once Upon a Galaxy

In August, *Once Upon a Galaxy: A Journal of the Making of The Empire Strikes Back* by Alan Arnold was released by Sphere. It contained new interviews with all of the main cast and many of the crew members. Arnold had traveled with the production to Norway and to Elstree Studios. The book included interviews with personnel who had been previously overlooked in the Making of coverage such as costume designer John Mollo. Mollo's deep interest in historical military costume led to him joining the production of period films, including *The Charge of the Light Brigade*, as a historical advisor. Mollo scored a triumph in garnering an Academy Award in his debut in the role of costume designer. He had gone on to be costume designer for *Alien*, with him finding the genre somewhat liberating, as he was able to explain. "In a period film, you're limited by the conventions of the period. In a space fantasy, you're not; you can draw from any and every period. But one essential we had to convey was a convincing functionalism."[26]

Alan Arnold also caught up with production designer Norman Reynolds, who despite his *Star Wars* Oscar win had not been featured greatly in the press and *Star Wars* publications. Reynolds explained the key rationale behind the design of *The Empire Strikes Back*: "Everything must relate to Earth, to what we know about our own planet. This prevents us from getting too carried away into realms of science fiction. We're making adventure stories for which the terms of reference are in the here and now. We're not trying to convey a world of scientific wonder. We're merely illustrating George's imaginative tales."[27] *Star Wars* and *Empire* editor Paul Hirsch had remained a remote figure too but in *Once Upon a Galaxy* he was able to explain that his connection to Lucas and *Star Wars* had come via Lucas' friend Brian De Palma. Hirsch was only 23 when he cut his first feature film, De Palma's *Hi Mom!* This instigated a regular collaboration between the two men, with Hirsch editing De Palma's *Blood Sisters, Phantom of the Paradise, Obsession* and the highly successful *Carrie*. Hirsch explained what an editor brought to a motion picture: "Editing is popularly considered to be the director's job, and the editor is considered to be simply the director's tool. But that's far from the truth. The director wants an editor who will take the film he has shot and put it together.... [I]f it's a funny scene, he wants the pieces put together so that it's as funny as possible. If it's a scary one, he wants his editor to make it as scary as possible. That's an interpretative thing, so different editors will interpret the film in different ways."[28]

Bantha Tracks #9 covered the Washington premiere of *The Empire Strikes Back*: "As it is everywhere, the film was fantastically received. In fact, so great was the excitement that nearly half the dialogue was drowned out with squeals of joy and welcoming applause for each character. But missed dialogue or not, the *Empire* screening and party were events that these children will long remember."[29] Richard Voorhuys elaborated on the Tauntaun theme for *The Empire Strikes Back Poster Monthly* #5, describing the advances made by ILM in the stop-motion process. This issue also contained a profile of Han Solo which included information that was barely mentioned in the film: that Solo had had a close shave with a bounty hunter on the planet Ord Mantell. There was also an obscure fact from the novel: Jabba the Hut's reward was double if Solo was captured alive. Both of these elements were subsequently used by Archie Goodwin for the comic strip story "The Bounty Hunter of Ord Mantell." In this, the final issue of the magazine, Dr. M.F. Marten speculated about the potential of real-life laser weapons in a well-researched article, stating, "The range of laser weaponry visualized by George Lucas in the *Star Wars* saga is not as far from reality as many may think. It is all too possible that a simple laser handgun will replace the bullet-firing revolver in the lifetime of this magazine's readers."[30]

Additional provincial cinemas began to be issued *The Empire Strikes Back* in September and October, among them the Crewe Focus, the Bolton Odeon, Oldham Odeon, Stockport Classic, Wilmslow Rex, Bury Odeon, Gatley Luxury Cinema, Petersfield Savoy, CBA Dereham Entertainment Center and the Stockport Luxury Twins. The major cinemas in *Screen International*'s chart however had begun to finally close *The Empire Strikes Back*. New films were of course arriving every week that had the potential to be more attractive offerings. At the Birmingham Odeon for instance, the newly released *The Fiendish Plot of Dr. Fu Manchu* made £3264 in the week ending September 14 where *The Empire Strikes Back* accrued £2601. The *Star Wars* sequel had enjoyed an extended run which had eclipsed every other film so far that year but now it was time to step aside for newer releases. A hugely popular new film which replaced *Empire* in many cinemas was *Airplane!*

The last of the big regional venues to stop showing *The Empire Strikes Back* was the Manchester Odeon, which closed the film on Saturday, September 20, after a 15-week run, making over £87,000. In London, the Dominion Theatre Tottenham Court Road was still going strong.

New Merchandise

The Empire Strikes Back Weekly #134 (cover date September 18) included a comic strip-style advertisement for the toys of the film from Palitoy. Some additional merchandise had arrived from other manufacturers since the film had been released: children's slippers from British Shoe Corporation, pajamas produced by Apparel and a shampoo set from Consumer Products. A set of Topps candy heads consisting of Boba Fett, Darth Vader, Stormtrooper, Chewbacca and C-3PO were imported from America by House of Clarkes Ltd., Dagenham, Essex. Each of the character's likenesses was hollow and contained sweets; the American price was covered up on the display box by a sticker giving it in pence. An item to get fans' pulses racing was a set of stickers and an accompanying sticker book from F.K.S. Publishers. Although the stickers were on the small side and the printing was not of top quality, the set included unusual photographs and once completed it made for an excellent method of reliving the entire film. One of the best ranges of merchandise ever produced for the *Star Wars* saga was a set of metal boxes from the British company Metal Box Ltd. The trouble was that the range was manufactured for the U.S. market and did not appear in Britain in any great numbers.

The lack of *Empire* products in the shops gave mail order companies the opportunity to fill the gap, placing adverts in the weekly comic, including Bradley Quartz *Star Wars* watches from Zeon Ltd. and Factors T-shirts supplied by Maybe Baby Fashions. In issue #135, there was an advert for the "newly re-organized" *Star Wars* Fan Club. For £3.45, fans could join a dedicated British branch of the club and receive four issues of the quarterly *Bantha Tracks* newsletter and a membership kit. "Lucasfilm thought it was a great thing," says Craig Miller. "It wasn't like we were going to get rich from it. The club barely broke even. It really just was a way to keep the really dedicated fans interested between movies."

On October 10, a new *Star Wars* television commercial began airing. It featured Princess Leia in the same predicament as the previous commercial, being held captive by Darth Vader and his troops on a table-top underneath an electric lamp. "Our heroes are threatened by an Imperial Troop Transporter," intoned the narrator. "Will the mighty force of the Millennium Falcon be enough to smash Darth Vader?" The Imperial Troop transporter and Millennium Falcon were featured, the latter shown with its rear section interior exposed. The advert ended with a dramatic shot of Darth Vader menacing Leia with his lightsaber. "The new Palitoy *Star Wars* models are in toy shops now. They're waiting!" said the narrator. The Palitoy line of products and the range of periphery merchandise elevated *The Empire Strikes Back* far higher than any average "sequel."

Marvel's Empire Expands

Marvel readers expecting a continuation of the story beyond *The Empire Strikes Back* would have been disappointed that issue #136 of the weekly comic (cover date October 1) contained the first episode of "The Third Law," which seemed like a throwback to the *Star Wars* comics, with artwork by Carmine Infantino. The story was written by Larry Hama. There was no mention of the events in *The Empire Strikes Back* and Princess Leia was back in her white gown, pitting her wits against Darth Vader. The story could have conceivably have taken place after "Dark Lord's Gambit," as Vader was still attempting to ensnare his rebel quarry in an entirely *legal* manner. Leia had chosen to visit the planet Aargau, a major banking center in the galaxy. Vader arrived on the planet and appeared to take action against her using an array of alien assassins but he was in fact operating a covert operation of his own which required the princess stay alive. Leia was under the impression that she had outsmarted Vader, but it was he who walked away gloating, leaving the princess in a tight spot with the planetary authorities. "The Third Law" concluded in issue #139 (October 22), which included an announcement that the comic would be published monthly from the next issue. In the American comic, "The Third Law" was printed in issue #48, the fourth comic after the adaptation of *The Empire Strikes Back*. The British schedule perhaps worked out better, as the story could have easily been interpreted as being a flashback to events in the saga's past.

"Death Probe," a stand-alone tale featured in the November monthly #140, had an Imperial Probe Droid invading and taking over a Rebel Blockade Runner craft. The intention of the droid's Imperial masters was to fly the ship into the midst of the Rebel Fleet set to explode. Luke and R2-D2 boarded the ship, tackled the Probe Droid and sent the ship on a collision course with the Star Destroyer that was controlling it. Written by Archie Goodwin and drawn by Carmine Infantino, "Death Probe" was printed in issue #45 of the American comic and was the first story set after *The Empire Strikes Back.*

Along with The Third Law, *this story did not seem to me to be a very convincing continuation of* The Empire Strikes Back. *While it included Luke reminiscing about the events of the film and it featured a Probe Droid, there was no mention of rescuing Han Solo or an explanation of how Luke obtained another lightsaber.*

There was a new face at Marvel UK: Tim Hampson:

I was brought into Marvel to oversee the production of all its comic titles at the time the *Star Wars* comic went monthly. Immediately prior to that, I was the production editor of a weekly newspaper. However, I had had a great deal of experience working with top-class artists and photographers to produce quality images. I was responsible for the production of all the Marvel titles—weeklies, monthlies and specials—and my name was often put into the titles, sometimes as production manager, editorial manager or even editor. The day-to-day work on the title would be done by others!

The decision to move to a monthly *Star Wars* title was already made when I got to Marvel. I had a lot of contact with Lucasfilm. The comic was the visible face of *Star Wars* and the merchandising companies were always keen to know what our publishing and editorial plans were.

Dez Skinn had left Marvel by that time. "My job was done," says Skinn. He continues:

Basically, Stan Lee and Jim Galton had hired me to try to turn the company around. I'd managed to make the company profitable with various editorial changes to their existing reprint titles and then bolstered their output with originated material (*Doctor Who Weekly* and my own *Starburst*, which Stan had offered to buy to secure my joining the company, so I would not need to desert my own audience to help theirs). This took only 18 months of my working life so, with that challenge met, it was time for me to move on to other projects—which in retrospect was the right move as it resulted in the cult film *V for Vendetta* ultimately spinning out of my 1982 launched anthology *Warrior* and the creation of a comics trade paper in *Comics International*, which I actually stuck with for 16 years before selling that on. I'd had a pretty free hand when I was at Marvel. But my duties after I left were split between Brian Babani (the new number one, as a consultant publisher—Brian ran his own company Grandreams), Paul Neary as editor-in-chief, Alan McKenzie as senior editor and Tim Hampson. Brian had been handling the areas I'd told Jim Galton I'd be too busy for, although I didn't report to him. When I left, he became supremo!

The December issue of *The Empire Strikes Back Monthly* featured "The Dreams of Cody Sunn-Childe!" It began with Lando Calrissian and Chewbacca searching for Han Solo in the Millennium Falcon, which was intended to link in with the final scene in *The Empire Strikes Back.* The pair ended up in another dimension where they encountered a city floating like an island in space. It was run by someone who once fought for the rebellion: Cody Sunn-Childe, who had incredible powers over matter. Cody had used his power to create the city as an oasis of peace where individuals could spend their time in contemplation but Lando argued that such power should be used to fight the Empire. Soon a squadron of Imperial Star Destroyers turned up and Lando and Chewbacca took off in the Falcon to tackle them by bizarrely ramming their hulls. Cody used his power to create terrible creatures which ensnared the Imperial ships, but then he had a change of heart and withdrew them. The Imperial fleet commander ordered all ships to open fire and the city was destroyed, killing Cody and all of his followers. They had decided to stick to their pacifist beliefs and not to fight, even though it would lead to their end. Lando and Chewbacca, moved to tears, found a way out of that area of space but the Imperials could not, and they remained marooned forever.

"The Dreams of Cody Sunn-Childe!," written by J.M. DeMatteis, was printed in issue #46 of the American comic, which was the second set after *The Empire Strikes Back*. Although Tom Palmer's inking had provided Carmine Infantino's art with more of an authentic look, the story could be seen as more of a New Age parable than a slice of *Star Wars*. The script had been approved by Lucasfilm but perhaps understandably the feedback had not been entirely positive. DeMatteis remembers,

> It seemed that, to them, the very idea that a character in the *Star Wars* universe would voice an opinion that in any way contradicted the Skywalker worldview was offensive. The word came down that Sunn-Childe, in rejecting violence, made their characters look bad. In other words, their universe wasn't big enough to contain *one single person* with a point of view that suggested that non-violence was a reasonable alternative to war. (So much for my follow-up story about Princess Leia traveling through time to meet Martin Luther King and Gandhi.)

Editor Louise Jones took steps to change the story: New dialogue was written for the last page of the story, much to the chagrin of DeMatteis. In response, he demanded that his name on the story be changed to Wally Lombego. "To her credit, Louise totally understood my position and no one at Marvel ever gave me any grief about it. (In fact, not long afterwards, I signed an exclusive writing contract with the company, so clearly no harm was done.) Of course I never wrote another *Star Wars* story, but the good news was—I didn't want to."[31] DeMatteis did not know that "The Dreams of Cody Sunn-Childe!" had been printed in its original, unedited form in *The Empire Strikes Back Monthly*, credited to his real name. British fans had the opportunity to decide if "The Dreams of Cody Sunn-Childe!" fitted within the *Star Wars* Universe based on the untainted original material.

The 1981 *Empire Strikes Back Annual* from Marvel/Grandreams (or *The Empire Strikes Back Annual No. 2* as it was officially titled) was timed with the traditional autumn release pattern, where annuals were printed with the following year's date. It featured a color reprinting of the American version of "The Dreams of Cody Sunn-Childe!" credited to Wally Lombego and the story "Crimson Forever" by Archie Goodwin, with art by Al Williamson; the latter had been produced for Marvel's bumper-sized issue #50 of the American comic. This would be the only British printing of "Crimson Forever" at this time as it did not grace the pages of the monthly comic (although it would be included in forthcoming years). The story followed on directly from *The Empire Strikes Back*: Lando and Chewbacca were flying through space in the Millennium Falcon, being menaced by TIE Fighters. Leia came to their rescue in a Blockade Runner craft and brought the grave news that an unknown ailment had left Luke in a comatose state and had turned his eyes red. Luke and a group of other rebels had fallen ill after boarding an Imperial Star Destroyer. A large red gemstone aboard the ship seemed to be the cause of the infection. Leia had sought out Chewbacca because she remembered Han (whose frozen form was being transported to Jabba the Hutt at that very time) had once told her of an adventure he had had with the Wookiee that involved a pair of giant red gemstones. The story went into flashback as Chewbacca described how he and Han had been press-ganged into joining a raid on a temple in the Red Nebular to steal a pair of red gemstones which may have been connected to Luke's predicament. The flashback tale starring Han Solo and Chewbacca was one of Goodwin's finest and it was a clever method of featuring Solo in the comic. If the Marvel comic stories printed in the wake of *The Empire Strikes Back* had been in a similar vein to "Crimson Forever," with Goodwin continuing the story and Williamson providing the artwork, it would have suited the comic perfectly. But "Crimson Forever" remained the only post–*Empire* story from the pair printed by Marvel at that time.

In November, Ballantine released *The Art of The Empire Strikes Back*, which in common with its predecessor was full of beautiful pre-production paintings and sketches (but it did not contain the script of the film). There were a great number of additional facts filling in the background of the film that were of interest to fans. Bespin Cloud City was in the business of exporting the rare anti-gravitational Tibana Gas and was once the headquarters of great leaders, with the skyline of monumental buildings being a leftover of that age. The verandas along the city's sides were designed to be landing ports and the purpose of the giant structure that Luke and Vader fought on at the conclusion of their duel was to create changes in airflow which control the city's movements and to route gasses to be processed. The book also explained that Darth Vader's *Executor* was the Empire's top-of-the-line vehicle with twice the firepower of any other craft in the fleet. The Stormtroopers' cold weather gear incorporated a heating system under the hood and, perhaps most interesting of all, the medical droid 2-1B had a human brain inside its metal casing.

In contrast to this official information from Lucasfilm, the December issue of *Fantastic Films* contained an article by Bill Hays, speculating on the possible plot elements of *Revenge of the Jedi*. Hays' research was thorough and while some of his imaginings were fanciful, such as Boba (or "Roberta") Fett being female, he did make some insightful comments. The Jedi mind trick was familiar to fans, but Hays pointed out that it could lead to an uncomfortable situation if a Jedi was to fall in love. "Luke agonizes that he could make her (Leia) love him by planting the suggestion in her mind, and she would never know. Thus, Luke discovers his own dark side." While this did not end up as a development in the third *Star Wars* film, the prequel movies would cover such tricky terrain, with Anakin appearing to *make* Padme love him via the Force. The fate of Han Solo was correctly guessed by Hays: "[H]e'll still be inside the carbonite, propped up in Jabba's spacecraft like a Picasso sculpture." Another of Hays' statements was in accordance with an earlier version of the *Revenge of the Jedi* script, where the confrontation between Luke and Vader, along with the final fleet battle, took place at the Imperial capital world. "[T]he final battle will take place above the emperor's home planet, where Leia used to work as a Senator, at the bright center of the Galaxy." Hays' version of the film's finale correctly guessed that the Rebels would require new allies to make up for the puny number of ships glimpsed in *The Empire Strikes Back*. The Rebels would rely on craft loyal to Jabba the Hutt. "[T]he Rebels don't have enough ships to defeat the Imperial Fleet. Han arrives at the crucial moment leading the pirates. Afterward, Jabba points out that his ships won the battle, not the rebels, and demands his share of the spoils. Han suggests a compromise. He will marry Leia and establish a duel monarchy, one from the pirates and one from the rebellion, until the Republic is restored throughout the galaxy."[32] This was the kind of action-packed finale to the *Star Wars* trilogy that many fans expected and hoped for. The possible outcome of *Revenge of the Jedi* was a top discussion point among fans as the year came to a close.

Evaluating the Empire

Anyone expecting that *The Empire Strikes Back* would do as well as its predecessor in Britain would have to have been an optimist, to say the least. The launch of *Star Wars*, where an enormous head of steam was allowed to build up over the course of six months or more, had been one-of-a-kind. By the time the film finally turned up in people's local area, a state of hysteria had developed. Another major difference between 1980 and 1978 was the sheer volume of films that were competing directly with *The Empire Strikes Back*, many of them in the science fiction mold. When *Star Wars* had been finally snatched from the hands of cinema managers in '78, to be released elsewhere in the country, it was often old films that had been shown in its place such as *Jaws* and *2001: A Space Odyssey*. There were few new films available in 1978 that would appeal to the *Star Wars* audience. By the time 1980 came around, film companies had begun to produce all kinds of family- and teen-friendly films, from comedies to action films. While *Star Wars* ran for months on end, outside of the large venues *Empire* suffered from short runs at cinemas including some only allocating it a single week. It was telling in the *Screen International* chart of the most profitable films screened at independent cinema chains, that *Empire* was mostly outside the top three and was not the #1 film in any of them. At the AIC cinema chain for instance, *Empire* was at #4 behind *Monty Python's Life of Brian*, *Escape from Alcatraz* and *Airplane!* This was undoubtedly down to short runs at the independents and some venues not showing the film.

Empire was the undoubted British box office champion of 1980 but it had fared only slightly better than other science fiction efforts chasing *Star Wars'* phenomenal $19,762,521 British box office return. The eventual total United Kingdom gross in December was $9,012,117,[33] which may have been entirely predictable. Yardsticks had been provided by *Star Trek: The Motion Picture* earning $7,400,405[34] and *Alien* making $7,886,000.[35] *Superman* did slightly better than *Empire*, earning $10,721,285[36] but only after a publicity campaign of gargantuan proportions. That was not to say that Lucas & Company were crying into their respective coffees. *Empire* had been the highest grossing film in Britain in 1980 and by December 31, 1980, it had made $181,353,855[37] in America alone. Profits continued to roll in, with the film still in release both in the U.S. domestic market and in other parts of the world. The run at the Dominion Theatre Tottenham Court Road was continuing.

It was obvious as the dust settled from the science fiction stampede of 1980 that despite all of the hype and marketing, not one production company had produced anything even resembling *Star Wars*. Out of all of *Empire*'s rivals, only *Star Trek: The Motion Picture* appeared in *Screen International's* top 20 for the year, at #3, and *The Black Hole* at #8. If the film at the #1 spot, *The Empire Strikes Back*, had proved nothing else, it showed that George Lucas' formula was far from easy to replicate and that the *Star Wars* saga was far ahead of any competition, and would undoubtedly remain so for the foreseeable future.

However, if *Revenge of the Jedi* was to catch the imagination of the filmgoing population in Britain, and accrue *Star Wars*-like profits, the film would need to be of a different tone than *Empire*. In 1980, the country had not entirely emerged from the woes that had dominated the 1970s and there was every chance that the situation would not have changed by 1983. A *Star Wars* film relied on repeat viewings and if it did not provide people with an uplifting experience, they would be unlikely to see it again. Children would not accept another film that was confusing and, in some ways, shocking. A darker, more thoughtful middle chapter was survivable for the *Star Wars* franchise in Britain. But *Revenge of the Jedi* would need to deliver the buzz that people craved. As the slick American science fiction programs that had arrived during the cinema run of *Empire Strikes Back* had proven, audiences could get their fix for free on television and when a film did not deliver that kind of kick, the word soon spread. *Revenge of the Jedi* would potentially be required to compete with other science fiction films *and* television and would chase exactly the same kind of demographic.

Christmas in the Stars

There was a treat for *Star Wars* fans on December 13 when *The Two Ronnies* television show featured the extended musical comedy sketch "Space Wars." No expense seems to have been spared on the lavish number that had Ronnie Barker and Ronnie Corbett dressed as C-3PO and R2-D2 (or RB-PO and RC-Tar-C as they were described), although the satire-laced songs were truly cringeworthy (at least in this author's opinion). Darth Vader, Princess Leia and Luke Skywalker pirouetted around with dancers in spangled outfits. Despite the elaborate setup, the comedy was based entirely around the words of the songs, when there was ample opportunity for sight gags in the midst of the elaborate set. The Daleks (with paint tin bodies) came on at the end and blasted Corbett to pieces.

Watching The Two Ronnies, *I was pleased to unexpectedly see this enormous song-and-dance routine based on* Star Wars *but the message from the comedians was that* Star Wars *was basically rubbish. A joke for adults to share rather than children. I felt that a funnier end to the sketch would have been the Death Star appearing at the back of the set and blasting both comedians to bits mid-song!*

The Empire Strikes Back Notebook was released by Ballantine, which presented the script for the film along with a large number of pre-production sketches and storyboards. The script was based entirely on the completed film, however, indicating that any cut scenes had been removed from the overall *Star Wars* saga. *The Empire Strikes Back 1981 Calendar*, available from Ballantine Books in time for Christmas, was produced to the highest standard, which was in keeping with other *Star Wars* printed material. With its color photographs highlighting some of the film's most exciting and poignant scenes, it made a terrific souvenir, especially as it was probable that fans would not be able to see the film again for quite some time. Palitoy remained the main standard bearer for *Star Wars* merchandise and kept shops well-stocked. At the close of 1980, fans could still make the journey to Dominion Theatre Tottenham Court Road where *The Empire Strikes Back* would be showing until the end of the year and perhaps for some time to come. There was clearly interest in the film still, and as local cinemas had ceased their performances, audiences gravitated to the capital. Short local runs of *The Empire Strikes Back* were to the benefit of the Dominion Theatre, and those who craved repeat viewings knew where to go.

Chapter 8

A Long Road Ahead

The year 1981 began well for *Star Wars* fans, for on January 1, the *Clapperboard Pick of the Year* on ITV featured *The Empire Strikes Back*, including an interview with Brian Johnson, who explained the various effects techniques used in the film. *SPFX The Empire Strikes Back*, a documentary from 20th Century-Fox television, was shown on ITV on January 2. Presented by Mark Hamill, the one-hour program covered aspects of the behind-the-scenes filmmaking processes that had brought the film to the screen. Special effects created by amateur film-makers were also featured, focusing even on a notorious comedy spoof of *Star Wars* titled *Hardware Wars*, where kitchen appliances battled it out in hilarious outer space dogfight sequences. This short film had been shown at American cinemas with great success.

Tom Hutchinson, a *Now!* magazine film critic, was less than impressed however with *SPFX The Empire Strikes Back*. Writing to *Screen International*, he said,

> Magic matters. Still more do I believe this after watching the appallingly self-destructive [*SPFX The Empire Strikes Back*] on ITV on Friday, January 2nd. In detailing all of the special effects and the way they were achieved, romance and illusion were skimmed from the idea. Who were they trying to convince? Certainly not my young daughter, Janetta, who said: "I don't want to watch any more. I'm already put off the film!" As a BAFTA lecture, fine [but] people remember how things are done. And yet, deep down, they don't really want to know the ignition for the flame of illusion. Whatever I bring to criticism I hope to bring something of enthusiasm also—and (still!) an innocence. Houdini can rest easy with his shackles, I DO NOT WANT TO KNOW. Magic should still matter."[1]

Hutchinson put his point forward eloquently but the Making of aspect had become a permanent feature of promoting the *Star Wars* franchise. Even though the documentary would not be of benefit in publicizing the initial release of *The Empire Strikes Back* in Britain (unlike America where it was shown during the release on September 22, 1980), the program remained valuable to British publicity as it would not be long before the film would be put on re-release at cinemas.

Shaun Dawkins was not satisfied merely with Making of documentaries. His passion for contacting people involved in the *Star Wars* saga continued unabated. "As characters were introduced such as Boba Fett, there were new actors to track down. We even met John Williams when he appeared in concert at the Barbican. When he emerged after the show, we excitedly approached him for an autograph and we were pleased to find that he was a really nice guy."

Marvel's Shaky Saga

Fans may have thought that they had been catapulted forward in time, as the January issue of *The Empire Strikes Back Monthly* was dated December 1981. In the story "Droid

World," R2-D2 and C-3PO were sent on a mission to the artificial satellite Klingson's Moon that had become known as Droid World due to its population being made up entirely of robots. The Rebels had captured a gigantic war robot developed by the Imperial forces but when R2-D2 attempted to scan its innards in order to produce a schematic, the machine melted into a molten mass, leaving only the gun turret head intact. A plan was hatched where C-3PO and R2-D2 would visit the artificial moon to ask its leader, the cyborg Klingson, to repair the war droid. As soon as they arrived, an Imperial faction of droids aboard the station used the intact turret head to complete a similar robot that they had under repair and use it in a coup. After huge mechanical carnage, the Empire faction was defeated. R2-D2 managed to obtain a schematic of the war droid but Klingson piloted his metal moon into deep space in order to distance himself from any further conflict. This story by the Archie Goodwin and Carmine Infantino pairing did not seem to sit very well in the post *Empire* period, but there was worse to come.

In "The Last Gift from Alderaan," featured in February and March issues, Princess Leia crash-landed on Sheva IV, a planet where rippling bare chests, swords and square jaws were mandatory. The Empire arrived right on cue and captured the princess, the Stormtroopers looking as out of place as they would have done if they stepped into the original *Flash Gordon* serial. In the midst of a rescue attempt by the gallant sword-wielding warriors of Sheva IV, Luke, Lando Calrissian and Chewbacca popped up out of nowhere and helped to seal the victory. After leaving the planet aboard the Millennium Falcon, the rebel heroes encountered a Star Destroyer which gave chase. Luke managed to use the Force to lure the hapless Imperials into a black hole. The story, printed in issue #53 of the American comic, was written by Chris Claremont with art by Carmine Infantino and Walt Simonson. The reason the story jarred so much with the established *Star Wars* universe was that it mainly derived from unused art that Infantino had prepared for the Marvel comic series *John Carter, Warlord of Mars*.

Jordan Royce was keeping up with the Marvel *Star Wars* adventures, although he was well aware of the constraints that the writers were working within. "A large problem the comic writers had in the lead-up to the new film was that Han Solo couldn't be in it. They had lost one of the main characters. There had to be a search for Han going on but they couldn't find him, and you knew when you were reading the comics that he wouldn't be found because it was something that would be revealed in the film. For the same reasons, Luke couldn't have been depicted becoming a fully fledged Jedi Knight in the comic."

As a young fan reading the comic, I did not appreciate the difficulties that Marvel faced in filling in the gap up until the new Star Wars *film. I felt that the stories fell well short of what I expected from the* Star Wars *saga. I became an occasional purchaser of the comic and I settled instead on reading copies in the shops. There was no Han Solo, so for me there seemed little point in buying it. Stand-alone stories did not work as well in the post–*Empire Strikes Back *period because the film had ended on a cliffhanger and the dramatic momentum needed to be maintained. To have the rebel heroes go off and have adventures, leaving Han Solo to his fate, did not ring true for me at all.*

* * *

Lucasfilm UK Winds Down but Star Wars Rolls On

The January 24 edition of *Screen International* brought the news that Lucasfilm UK, operating out of 3A Queens Gate Mews, London SW7, was to be wound up on March 27, with redundancies including that of director Caroline Nelson. Andrew Maconie was unaffected by the change because he was contracted as a freelance by Lucasfilm to handle European *Star Wars* licensing, working at Queens Gate Mews.

The Empire Strikes Back's 21-week run at the Dominion Theatre ended on January 10. The film was picked up by the Odeon Marble Arch on February 8 and ran there until March 28. The Dominion Theatre took over again from April 19. Other major cinemas were not showing the film at this time, so it is likely that the Dominion had an exclusive presentation in Britain. *Empire* finished showing at the Dominion Theatre on May 2, which finally brought the film's extended London run to a close.

On March 31, the 53rd Academy Awards show was broadcast; *Empire* was in the running for awards for Best Set Direction (Norman Reynolds, Leslie Dilley, Harry Lange, Alan Tomkins and Michael Ford) but did not win. An Oscar was won for Best Sound (Bill Varney, Steve Maslow, Gregg Landaker and Peter Sutton); also a Special Achievement Award for Visual Effects (Brian Johnson, Richard Edlund, Dennis Muren and Bruce Nicholson). The Academy of Science Fiction, Fantasy and Horror films awarded *The Empire Strikes Back* Best Actor (Mark Hamill), Best Director (Irvin Kershner), Best Science Fiction Film and Best Special Effects (Brain Johnson and Richard Edlund). For *Empire*'s score, John Williams received an Anthony Asquith Award for Film Music at the BAFTAs, a Golden Globe and a Grammy for Best Album of Original Score Written for a Motion Picture or Television Special, and a separate award for Best Instrumental Composition.

Dengar was the poster boy for Palitoy's Bounty Hunter promotion.

The March issue of *The Empire Strikes Back Monthly* featured a bonus in the form of a full-page Palitoy advertisement for the Dengar action figure which was available via the post in exchange for

Bill Barry from the Advertising Agency (right) and Les Cooke at the Palitoy trade stand at the Earls Court Exhibition Centre in January 1981 (courtesy Brian Turner).

three names cut from *Star Wars* action figure backing cards. The character was photographed, looming large on the page as Boba Fett had done the previous year. Dengar was part of a new range of Palitoy action figures from *Empire*: Lobot, Yoda, Han Solo (Bespin Outfit), Ugnaught, 2-1B, AT-AT Driver, Imperial Commander, Rebel Commander, Bespin Security Guard and Leia (Hoth Outfit). Dengar was held back at this time, due to the mail-away offer. The Imperial Officer backing card featured a photograph of General Veers as played by Julian Glover. John Ratzenberger also missed out on the prestige of being made into a *Star Wars* figure, as while the toy seemed to be modeled on his face, his character name in *The Empire Strikes Back*, Major Derlin, was not used and the backing card photograph was of a different Rebel General. Kenner probably avoided referring to specific characters with these two figures because there was better play value in generic command characters. Darth Vader could be made to strangle any number of Imperial (and Rebel) officers instead of just one. The picture on the reverse of the backing cards was the same as the figures already on sale, which depicted 30 in the set, so the new figures were not included.[2]

Star Wars *on the Radio*

Bantha Tracks #11, dated February, brought the news that principal photography of *Revenge of the Jedi* would begin at Elstree Studios and on locations in Europe in the autumn. George Lucas would write the first draft screenplay and serve as executive producer. Howard Kazanjian would produce and Gary Kurtz would serve as a story consultant. This edition of *Bantha Tracks* also contained other exciting news: "*Star Wars* is coming to radio!" The article proclaimed. "In March, National Public Radio will broadcast 13 episodes of *Star Wars,* part IV, now titled *A New Hope,* starring Mark Hamill and Anthony Daniels." The article described how the story had been greatly expanded and would include a great deal of new material such as Princess Leia on Alderaan, Luke's friends on Tatooine, the first time R2-D2 and C-3PO met and Han Solo and Chewbacca's encounters with Tatooine's underworld. The series executive producers were Richard Toscan of KUSC-FM and Carol Titleman of Lucasfilm Ltd. and the story was by Brian Daley."[3] The March 8 edition of the *Times* reported that the BBC had bought the series and had been awarded the right to broadcast it three times.

British fans did not have long to wait for the *Star Wars Radio Series* as it was broadcast on Easter Monday, April 20 on Radio One. This was a major event which had been featured in many articles in the national press. Photographs used in the coverage had been derived from a photo shoot on April 7 with Anthony Daniels and a life-sized cut-out of his C-3PO alter ego which had been produced by Factors Inc. for their promotions in America. The BBC had reportedly purchased the series for £13,360. Although the initial run would be broadcast in mono, at a 12:00 p.m. weekday time slot which was inconvenient for school-children, it was stated in the press that there would shortly be a repeat broadcast. Hamill explained why he had revisited his role for the show: "In some ways I have become Luke Skywalker. I feel propriety toward his character and that's why I wanted to do my—his— voice on radio."[4]

It was not mentioned in any media at the time but the *Star Wars Radio Series* was essentially a co-production with the BBC, as its budget had depended on the BBC purchasing it for broadcast in Britain. The BBC had suggested Bill Morrison in the first instance as writer and he had flown to Los Angeles in April 1979. His adaptations for BBC radio of Dostoevsky had apparently landed him the job. "You may also say they picked me simply because I was the best in the business,"[5] said Morrison before the writing position was awarded to Brian Daley. A more successful BBC choice was producer John Madden, who was instrumental in bringing the series to life. "Our emphasis, as in the film, is on action and adventure, bit since the public will already be familiar with the basic theme and char-acters, we decided to develop their relationship a little more deeply."[6] Madden later found fame as the director of films such as *Mrs. Brown, Captain Corelli's Mandolin* and the Oscar-winning *Shakespeare in Love.*

"I was very excited by the radio series," recalls Shaun Dawkins. "Especially as it expanded on the story presented in the film. I thought that the production quality was excellent. And to me it really underscored that there was a lot more that could be mined from the *Star Wars* universe." Laurie Calvert has strong recollections too. "I recorded every episode on cassette tape, which was easy to do in those days with a standard cassette radio. I loved the way the story was expanded with the scenes where Luke raced through Beggar's

Canyon with his friends and a lot more besides." Jordan Royce says, "I thought that the radio adaptation was incredible. Me and my friends recorded the episodes and would sit and listen to them in each other's living rooms."

I didn't have a radio that I could take to school and my home was not exactly around the corner. I did rush home though and managed to catch part of some of the episodes. It was not until my teens that I managed to contact a fellow fan who supplied me with a copy on tape. I thought the radio series was fantastic. It expanded upon Star Wars *greatly, with the first two episodes covering the events which led up to the film.*

Palitoy Keeps the Force Alive

Palitoy began releasing the *Star Wars* and *Empire Strikes Back* figure range in a new style of packaging, including Dengar, who made his debut in shops. The reverse of the new backing card featured individual photographs of all the figures and also a selection of the vehicles available. There were actually two styles of this backing card, with one depicting vehicles with a Hoth theme and another featuring spacecraft. The Turret and Probot playset mounted a rebel defensive armament and Probe Droid on the same white plastic base. The Imperial Attack Base was intended as a base for the Imperial troopers on Hoth but it was more use as a Rebel defensive snow trench, which is what many children used it for. Another impressive item was the Darth Vader's Star Destroyer Action Playset, which incorporated a main gun, bridge control room and Vader's meditation chamber. Pocket money-priced Mini Rig vehicles had been added to the range, but did not appear in the *Star Wars* films; The MTV-7 (Multi-Terrain Vehicle), a one-man vehicle on spring-loaded roller wheels, the MLC-3 (Mobile Laser Cannon), a one-man tank, and PDT-8 (Personnel Deployment Transport) which could accommodate two figures.

In a new television commercial, the rebels faced off against the Imperials in a scene depicting Hoth. The Rebels had a MLC-3, a PDT-8, a Tauntaun and a Snowspeeder at their disposal while the Imperials massed around the Imperial Attack Base. "Will Han Solo on his Tauntaun and Luke Skywalker in his Snowspeeder dare attack the Imperial base? Only you can decide, with *Star Wars* toys," said the narrator.

There were other items from Palitoy too: A new set of die-cast models were issued by Palitoy in Kenner packaging, consisting of the Twin Pod Cloud Car, Snowspeeder, Slave 1 but not the TIE Bomber that had been released in the U.S., although it appeared in Palitoy's 1981 trade catalogue. Palitoy also issued a Yoda hand puppet that allowed the user to raise and lower the Jedi Master's head. Also plain white figurines of Yoda, and Luke riding a Tauntaun, each supplied with paints and three "Glow" paint-by-numbers sets. Palitoy again issued a poster with the large boxed items, picturing the entire range, which included all of the die-cast models that were still being issued in their original *Star Wars* packaging. Also being sold in *Star Wars* packaging was the TIE Fighter toy and the Darth Vader TIE Fighter and Imperial Troop Transporter that had the addition of Bounty Hunter offer symbols.

Airfix suffered a downturn in its fortunes and was bought by General Mills and put in Palitoy's charge. The April 23 edition of the *Times* reported, "Airfix crashed owing £15m to its banking creditors after the banks rejected a financial reconstruction scheme. Meccano (UK) and Dinky (which Airfix owned) produced cheaper ranges in the last months of the group's life which were understood to have been well received, but its cash flow problems proved too much after Christmas."[7] The model kit production was transferred to the General Mills-owned Paris Meccano factory, much to the consternation of the British press. Airfix's factory in Haldane Place, London SW18 was stripped of everything vital to model kit production and sold. Unfortunately any legacy material pertaining to the company's other products and business activities were thrown into a skip. Airfix's profitable toy business would no longer be a rival to Palitoy, including its top selling Weebles and Micronauts. "General Mills acquired Airfix on the basis that its products could be distributed across all of the GM European subsidiaries," says Geoff Maisey. "GM was strategically committed to build up the volume of Airfix's European sales. Since Palitoy was behind the wheel of Airfix, we felt that the line needed freshening, so developed the 'character merchandising' element, of which *Star Wars* was a natural part." Munro/Deighton immediately launched an Airfix p.r. campaign. "We began to handle Airfix as soon as Palitoy took it over," says Carole Deighton.

> The initial p.r. strategy was to target existing and would-be hobbyists and then begin to create (in those less pc days!) a "Dad and Son" niche and of course, get Airfix kits featured in the Father's Day and Christmas gift round-ups in the media. It has to be said, the mainstream consumer press was pretty lukewarm initially about the Airfix brand but we spent time identifying journalists who were potential fans, dads or hobbyists themselves and put them on a privileged mailing list to receive specially presented press samples of all the best new kits before they were available in stores. We also planned to promote the *Star Wars* line of kits via high-profile competitions in specialist youth magazines and the *Star Wars* comic.

The 1981 Palitoy *Star Wars* poster included new model kits but it is not clear what manufacturer's name—Airfix, Palitoy or Denys Fisher—was on the packaging in this year. The Imperial Star Destroyer was sizable and highly detailed but the actual scale was open to question, because the "actual" size the craft had not been properly defined in any *Star Wars* media. Built in roughly 1:32 scale, the Snowspeeder kit was very faithful to the prop seen in *The Empire Strikes Back*. The only letdown was the pair of pilot figures, which looked stunted and poorly detailed. The Millennium Falcon kit was also included on the poster.

Other new objects of desire for *Star Wars* fans included a lampshade for *The Empire Strikes Back* from Scanlite, a subdivision of Scandecor. It included a folded poster of Darth Vader and two Stormtroopers. Bunch Associates published *The World of Star Wars—A Compendium of Fact and Fantasy from Star Wars and The Empire Strikes Back,* which presented a selection of pages from past issues of the *Star Wars* and *Empire Strikes Back Official Poster Monthly* magazines. The content (which included Anthony Fredrickson's exposé on Stormtroopers being clones) must have been seen as being legitimate because the publication was edited by Lucasfilm staffer Kristine Johnson. The cover design was by her LFL colleagues Rio Phior and Melanie Paykos. "I picked up the compendium of the *Star Wars* poster magazines at my local book shop," says Darren Slade. "It was great to read articles from the poster magazine issues that I had missed somehow. I only ever found 1–4 in the shops."

Also on sale was *The Empire Strikes Back Panorama Book* from Random House. It presented a trio of fold-out, three-dimensional scenes that could be populated by the punch-out characters supplied. The design was extremely innovative and even incorporated a large hole in the front cover that served as a "window" for the scene behind it and also allowed C-3PO and R2-D2 to *look out* at the reader. The book had its origin in America but was released in Britain with a sticker with the words "Random House" and the price of £1.95.

Andrew Maconie recalls:

We did a deal with Thermos at the Spring Toy Fair, which was kind of a breakthrough for building the licensing program. Licensees were finally realizing that *Star Wars* was not just a toy brand, that Palitoy had developed an impressive range of action figures and playsets for *Star Wars* and that this enthusiasm could be transferred to other products. The Icarus Company came on board for placemats and plastic accessories. I do recall though that companies were a little reticent to buy a license for a movie, having

Above and below: **The small number of new items released in 1981 included a lampshade from Scanlite and a Panorama Book from Random House.**

been used to TV programs. There was one particular screening that we did of *The Empire Strikes Back* for potential licensees where a number of people came on board including duvets and bedcovers from Hayjax Manufacturing and H.C. Ford for stationery. The fact that we were doing merchandising so far in advance was certainly groundbreaking at the time.

Planning the merchandise two years ahead of the release of a film was unheard of at the time but considering the importance of the third chapter of the *Star Wars* saga such a strategy was vital.

Han Solo and the Lost Legacy, the final book in Brian Daley's Han Solo trilogy, was released by Sphere. This time, Han and Chewbacca were engaged in locating the famed lost treasure of Xim the Despot. One of Han's old acquaintances Alexsandr Badure and a woman called Hasti Troujow claimed to have found the logbook disk of Xim's treasure ship *The Queen of Ranroon*. An insectoid professor called Skynx had translated the ancient language in the log and joined in with the search. The planet Dellalt had fallen on hard times since the days of Xim but even though treasure hunters had searched there for generations without success, it remained the focus of Han's mission. The owners of a mining operation on the planet were interested in the treasure too and when they stole the Millennium Falcon, the adventure was from then on was mainly ground-based. Gallandro was added to the mix and a shoot-out with Han Solo seemed to be inevitable. The pair teamed up to raid the treasure vaults of Xim that were protected by ancient devices that would incinerate any being carrying a weapon. Inside the vault, Han was wounded in a quick-draw against Gallandro but the man stepped into range of one of the weapon detectors and was incinerated. As his companions joined him in the vault, Han realized that the treasure was so ancient that it was made up of materials that were no longer valuable. Han seemed to have had the opportunity to get the girl—a first for this trilogy—but he and Chewbacca simply left, consoling each other over their disappointment. The story included some interesting information including Han's red piping on his trousers being referred to as a Correllian Blood Stripe. Also Chewbacca having a "life debt" to Han which seems to have been inspred by John May's article in Poster Monthly #5.

New Blood at Marvel

The Empire Strikes Back Monthly #145, printed in May, featured Mike W. Barr's "The Last Jedi," the first story drawn by Walt Simonson and Tom Palmer (although both had been occasional contributors to the comic). The pair had been recruited by Marvel in the U.S. as regular artists and between them, they captured the look of the *Star Wars* universe far better than other artists working regularly on the comic, with much more accurate depictions of the characters, vehicles and environments. In "The Last Jedi," another standalone story, Luke, Leia and the Droids assisted a pro–Rebel prince to claim the throne of the planet Velmor, which had fallen under the influence of the Empire. The prince's guardian was Jedidia, an alien biped who had suffered head injuries in the past and, as a result, had the delusional belief that he was a Jedi Knight and had armed himself with a lightsaber. Over the course of the story, the prince was reinstated but poor Jedidia was killed in the final confrontation with the Imperials. Luke was so moved by his passing that he gave Jedidia a grand send-off, firing his body into deep space in a transparent capsule.

The July issue of the monthly comic again featured art from Simonson and Palmer and a new writer: David Michelinie, well-known for *The Avengers* and *Iron Man*, had been sought out by Marvel editor Louise Jones. "I hadn't even thought of *Star Wars* because Archie Goodwin had been writing it for three years and it seemed that he would write it forever," said Michelinie. As he undertook the challenge, Michelinie was aware of the restrictions of writing in George Lucas' universe. "There are a lot of special problems with *Star Wars* not only from what's been but what's to come. As far as what's been, we can't really change anything from the end of *Empire*. We can't have Han Solo located and then have him frozen for the next movie." Michelinie was especially sorry not to have Han available for stories; "He could quite possibly be my favorite character if I could write for him."[8] Instead of writing individual stand-alone stories, Michelinie provided the post–*Empire Strikes Back* storyline with some much-needed direction. The stories "Resurrection of Evil" and "To Take the Tarkin" told the story of the Rebels, having regrouped after their escape from the planet Hoth, learning of a new Imperial super-weapon. The *Tarkin* was basically a duplicate of the *Super-Laser* from the Death Star, with a huge spacecraft fuselage wrapped around it. To deal with this new menace the Rebel heroes were ordered to abandon their separate missions; Luke and Leia were investigating planets which might serve as the location for a new Rebel base while Lando Calrissian and Chewbacca were aboard the Millennium Falcon, searching for Boba Fett and Han Solo. Luke, Leia, Chewbacca and the Droids launched a covert operation to destroy the new weapon. Lando was still being viewed as untrustworthy and was due to be left behind, but he hid in one of the Millennium Falcon's smuggling compartments. An interesting subplot had dissatisfied Imperial officers plot to assassinate Darth Vader. The officer's ringleader attempted to bump off Vader by remotely activating a door which led to the vacuum of space, but this only succeeding in enraging the Sith Lord with predictable results. Meanwhile Luke, Leia & Company made short work of the Tarkin but, escaping in the Millennium Falcon piloted by Lando, they found themselves pursued by Darth Vader in his personal TIE Fighter. To bring the chase to a conclusion, Luke dumped the Millennium Falcon's water supply, which froze into blocks and critically damaged Darth Vader's craft. Vader was fortunate that he had chosen to pursue the rebels personally because the Tarkin exploded spectacularly, leaving him in much the same position as when the Death Star was destroyed.

Fans have different ideas over which stories are considered to be part of the overall Marvel Star Wars *saga. Personally speaking, the only Marvel stories printed in the post–*Empire Strikes Back *period that are part of the story are "Crimson Forever" and those written by David Michelinie and Mary Jo Duffy. I can recall my relief at the Michelinie stories beginning, because I felt that the authentic view of the* Star Wars *universe had returned.*

Star Wars *Reading Matter*

In May, *Bantha Tracks* #12's interview with Steven Spielberg covered *Raiders of the Lost Ark*, which Lucasfilm was seeking to introduce to *Star Wars* fans. More important for fans in this issue was an update on *Revenge of the Jedi*. The article reported that George Lucas had completed a rough draft of the screenplay and that production designer Norman Reynolds was currently scouting locations all over the world. On Saturday, July 4, the *Star Wars Radio Series* began a repeat run in Britain, which was timed with the school summer holiday and broadcast in stereo. Readers of *The Empire Strikes Back Monthly* were tipped off about the repeat by a letter printed in the June issue's Cosmic Feedback.

Among the interviewees in the July *Starlog* was George Lucas, who provided some tantalizing clues to the future of the *Star Wars* saga. "Well, the next trilogy—the first one—since it's about Ben Kenobi as a young man, is the same character, just a different actor.... The first trilogy will not be as much of an action adventure kind of thing. Maybe we'll make it have some humor, but right now it's much more humorless than this one. This one is where all the excitement is, which is why I started with it. The other ones are a little more Machiavellian—it's all plotting—more of a mystery."[9] Mature fans may have questioned whether Lucas genuinely had an overall story arc in mind consisting of nine films when he had made *Star Wars* and some may perhaps have doubted if it had been intended for Darth Vader to be Luke's father. Lucas however was the filmmaking version of a magician, who employed tricks and illusions both on and off the screen. Lucas was intent on making the *Star Wars* experience as fulfilling as possible and to say things like "That was the way it was planned from the beginning" was a lot more satisfying than "I'm making up the film saga as I go along." That would not have been showmanship.

The Empire Invades Again

The Empire Strikes Back was made available for re-release at cinemas in late July, which was in line with the July 31 reissue in the U.S. (the initial $181,379,640 domestic run had only just finished on July 23). Only a smattering of British cinemas took up the offer. Out of the main regional venues, only the Nottingham Odeon chose to show it from August 6, and then only for seven days. In London, *Empire* had been shown to death and its run at the Dominion Theatre had ended comparatively recently, so it can be imagined that the film was not an attractive prospect to the big venues. The ABC Edgware Road opened *Empire* on July 26 for one week and Odeon 2 Westbourne Grove on August 9, also for seven days. A second main regional venue, the Southampton Gaumont, waded in on August 23 with a week-long showing. There seemed to be little appetite among venues for *Empire* at this time, which may in part have been due to the huge number of previously released films on offer. The re-release of films at the cinema was then still a vital aspect of the business. Cinema managers could choose to show any other classic film they wished that was available to their chain. It was in keeping with the standard cinema re-release treadmill that there was not any national advertising for *Empire*, with cinemas relying on local advertisements. "We ran *The Empire Strikes Back* re-release in 70mm again at the Westcliff-on-Sea Classic for two weeks," says Derek Dorking. "We still had reasonable attendances but there was no fanfare from 20th Century-Fox, or costumed appearances. It was all pretty quiet as it was a reissue. The print we got initially was from Ireland but it was scratched to pieces, so we sent it back and then we got one that had been showing in London."

In August, *Bantha Tracks* #13 contained the first of three pre-production reports on the progress of filming *Revenge of the Jedi*. The article shed light on how Richard Marquand was chosen as director. "Our director has to have a good sense of humor, a vivid imagination, and enough talent to handle a picture like *Revenge of the Jedi*," said Howard Kazanjian. "We did not need a man who was going to direct a picture about Vader and all the heroes and heroines, but couldn't really believe in them. In *Jedi* as with every chapter of the *Star Wars* saga, our director will be required to film a tremendous amount of special effects. Some directors just can't handle that."[10]

Andrew Maconie was finding himself increasingly busy with *Star Wars* licensing so he was thankful to receive a new staff member. "I came to work at Queens Gate Mews in September 1981," Jackie Ferguson recalls. She continues:

> Jackie Moore is my maiden name and I met my husband through working with Andrew. I believe that Andrew had asked Lucasfilm if he could take on somebody and it was them who paid my salary. I had just returned to the U.K. from working in the Middle East. I fell into the job as a friend of mine found it all too high-powered and she did not have enough time to play tennis, as she told me over lunch. So she gave me the office address in Queens Gate Mews and there I found Andrew battling with a DHL courier. I handled this and said I would stay for three days. I subsequently worked with Andrew for 11 years and learnt everything I know about licensing during that time!

Maconie's licensing brief stretched far beyond the shores of Britain:

> The licensing program expanded across Europe to coincide with the launch of the new *Star Wars* film and local agents were appointed in each country to help build the merchandise portfolio. Initially there was resistance to the concept of being a licensee for a movie but having demonstrated that there were a number of licensees operating successfully in the United Kingdom, the local agents were provided with Lucasfilm presentation material and they were able to build the program in their individual markets. All contracts and approvals were routed through the London office.

Bounty Hunters Wanted

In September, issue #149 of the monthly comic featured a full-page advert announcing Palitoy's *Bounty Hunter Capture Log* promotion. Booklets distributed to toy outlets catalogued the entire range of items that fans could send off for in return for three names cut out from *Star Wars* figure backing cards. "We previously had a great deal of success with an Action Man loyalty program," says Geoff Maisey. "It was called the star scheme where children could collect star symbols printed in every Action Man pack to redeem against free figures or accessories. The larger the item, the more stars were on the packaging. It seemed a natural adaptation to launch a similar offer with *Star Wars*."

Fans also had the opportunity of obtaining an action figure Survival Kit which consisted of some fantastic items with which to enhance their play: two Hoth backpacks that figures could wear, a training harness that allowed Yoda to be strapped to Luke's back, an AT-AT grappling hook belt, three asteroid gas masks and five assorted laser weapons. The major item from the selection available for six names was the Darth Vader Carry Case which was molded in the shape of the Dark Lord and split open to hold 32 figures. This item was especially desirable as it was not available from shops in Britain.

✳ ✳ ✳

As a fan who opened his Star Wars *figures by opening the bubble very carefully with a pair of scissors, I was not about to cut the names out of the precious backing cards. Since many of my fellow schoolchildren hadn't heard about the Bounty Hunter offer, they were willing to let me have their discarded backing cards! Perhaps I wouldn't have adopted this strategy if my hero had been the goodhearted Luke Skywalker, instead of the roguish Han Solo.*

Marvel UK Turns to the Dark Side

The Empire Strikes Back Monthly #149 featured "Death Masque," the first in a long-running series of stories by writers Steve Moore and Alan Moore (who were unrelated) that had been commissioned for the British comic. Alan Moore subsequently became a very well-known comic book writer, with high-profile movie adaptations of his work including *The League of Extraordinary Gentlemen* and *Watchmen*. The rationale behind the new stories was to bulk up the amount of *Star Wars* material available to the comic. Tim Hampson explains,

> The problem of using only repro stories from issues already printed in the States is that sometimes the material can run out, or trying to take a U.S. format story—say 28 pages—and then break it

The Bounty Hunter offer advertised in the weekly comic.

down into sections which made sense for the British format, which might have only five pages of comic strip just wouldn't work. The editorial team on the *Star Wars* comic were articulate advocates for the use of new work, especially from people as talented as Steve and Alan. The publisher wasn't always happy as it was a cost they'd rather not have.

The subsequent stories by Alan Moore and Steve Moore were all stand-alone tales featuring very dark subject matter, all of them independent of the main *Star Wars* storyline. If it had not been for the presence of the *Star Wars* characters, the stories could have been set in any far-flung galaxy.

In "Death Masque" (written by Steve Moore, art from John Stokes, inking by Howard Chaykin), Luke is menaced by a monkey with a skull for a head, which caused him to suffer hallucinations of a landscape made entirely of skulls and of his friends being killed one by one. The Force allowed Luke to be able to break the monkey's spell—and the fact that the creature was sitting directly in line with Luke's deactivated lightsaber helped immensely. One press of a button ended the monkey's evil plan. In October, the cover of #150 advertised "An untold story starring Han Solo!" and also "The shocking story of Leia Organa and Han Solo caught in the Hell Hoop!" but inside was a reprint of "The Hunter" from issues 31 and 32. Issue #151, published in November, included the story "The Pandora Effect" (which was no doubt the delayed "Hell Hoop" story). This was another dark tale by Alan Moore, drawn by Adolfo Buylla, where Han, Leia and Chewbacca were captured by five immortal miscreants who had nothing better to do than to murder people who fell into their trap. Fortunately, Chewbacca was mistaken for a dumb animal by the immortals and was left chained up. The Wookiee escaped with ease and set free a highly dangerous energy-like creature called Wutzek that had also been caged. The creature was even more ruthless than the five immortals and reduced them to smoking skeletons. Han & Company were relieved that the Wuztek allowed them to leave unscathed but they were left wondering what danger the galaxy faced now that the energy creature was free to roam. Fortunately, this was a sector of space controlled by the Empire, the heroes chirped.

In November there was a further update in *Bantha Tracks* #14 in the form of an interview with *Revenge of the Jedi* art director Joe Johnston, who reported that the film was at the stage where the storyboards were being assembled. Regarding the script: "It is still in treatment form. George has a rough idea of how he wants the sequences to work but he's very much open to ideas." Johnston admitted that he could not reveal too much but he did say, "It will resolve a lot of questions raised by the first two films. It is packed with new hardware, new characters, new environments as always. There is a battle in *Jedi* that *A New Hope* and *Empire* were just warm-ups for."[11]

The next chapter of the *Star Wars* saga was a hot topic in the Cosmic Correspondence section of the monthly comic but readers were also discussing the continuation of the saga beyond *Revenge of the Jedi*. There was little doubt that fans were expecting the *Star Wars* films to stretch far into the future, which was not surprising considering the proclamations from LFL.

On December 27, the Goodies *Snow White 2* Christmas Special was broadcast on ITV; the finale was an epic lightsaber duel, where Graham Garden dressed as Buttons battled Tim Brooke-Taylor dressed as a fairy godmother. The skit was as hilarious as it sounds and Bill Oddie also performed a *Star Wars* version of sword swallowing. The Goodies team were experts in staging sight gags and they managed to make the lightsabers appear functional and dangerous, hacking a pantomime horse in two and reducing people's attire to underwear. Kenny Baker, Jack Purvis and a whole host of their fellow dwarf actors also appeared.

In December, issue #152 of *The Empire Strikes Back Monthly* took a break from the Steve Moore and Alan Moore material and instead treated readers to the story "Plif" that had been produced for issue #55 of the American comic. Written by David Michelinie and with art from Walt Simonson and Tom Palmer, the story began with Princess Leia landing with a Rebel scouting party in a forested region of the planet Arbra, seeking a location for their new base. The first night camping outdoors was interrupted by a clutch of rabbit-like creatures which drained all of the rebels' blaster weapons of power. These telepathic creatures, called Hoojibs, explained to the rebels that they used energy as food and that an alien creature had invaded their cave where naturally occurring energy rods could be found. Leia, Chewbacca and their Rebel comrades agreed to assist the Hoojibs evict their unwelcome guest. In return, the Hoojibs offered to share their enormous cave with the Rebels. The story was not as bad as it may have appeared to the casual reader as it included plenty of the action and character interaction familiar to the *Star Wars* films.

Available towards the end of the year was a British exclusive 1982 *Star Wars* calendar from Thomas Forman and Sons which featured images from both films. There was no Marvel/Grandreams annual, however, with Grandreams probably having the policy of releasing titles surrounding current cinema and television productions.

Nineteen eighty-one had been a fairly uneventful year for *Star Wars,* although the Palitoy range, comic and fan club newsletter had kept fans entertained. The Palitoy range was still selling in huge quantities. The highlight of the year for many had been the *Star Wars* radio series which was almost as good as receiving a new film. It brought the story of *Star Wars* a large degree of freshness at a time when the film was unavailable (except for good old Super 8). The response in the press for the radio production had been encouraging, showing that there was still interest within the media for *Star Wars* if there was something to report about. Apart from those who had managed to catch a local re-release of *Star Wars,* memories of seeing it at the cinema in 1977 and '78 were becoming increasingly distant. *Revenge of the Jedi* seemed more exciting with every new revelation but it was agonizingly still well over a year away from appearing at the cinema. Even though the various production arms of Lucasfilm were working to bring the film to fruition, for fans the coming year had the promise of being a long one indeed.

The Star Wars *Fans Keep Going*

With such a long time to wait for a new *Star Wars* film, and with very little to purchase outside of the Palitoy toy line and not a great deal of reading material apart from the weekly comic, fans found ways to keep themselves occupied. Darren Slade says "It was my love for science fiction in general that kept me going. I saw *Superman II, Raiders of the Lost Ark* and *Clash of the Titans* and if I'd had sufficient pocket money, I would have seen the likes of *Excalibur* and *Time Bandits....* On TV, we had *Buck Rogers in the 25th Century.* I also heard *The Hitchhiker's Guide to the Galaxy* on the radio for the first time, thanks to a repeat. So the world seemed to be full of *Star Wars'* influence—we just didn't have access to the original film!" Laurie Calvert too was turning to other science fiction. "I knew that there was a long time to wait. There was *Raiders of the Lost Ark, Star Trek* movies and *Blade Runner* and other 'pulp sci-fi' whilst I was waiting for the more meaningful stuff." Sarah Saunders was keeping up her collecting. "The hype of *Empire* had died down and we had a long wait until the next film arrived. There wasn't anything really that was new in the shops for *Star Wars* but there were small ads in magazines with dealers offering catalogues of collectibles and I bought a few things that way. The collectors fairs in Manchester continued to be a good source of memorabilia. I used to take trips down to London, usually once a year to search out shops that sold posters and other *Star Wars* items."

* ✳ *

I continued to be a Star Wars *fan; collecting the Palitoy range, model kits and other items as far my pocket money and birthday present budget would stretch. Christmas 1981 was an exciting time, as there was the possibility of* Star Wars *related gifts but my feeling was that with so little to support it, George Lucas' saga had become very distant universe indeed.*

Chapter 9

More Than a Hint
of Revenge in the Air

The year 1982 got off to a good start for fans as *Starburst* #43, available in January, was full of *Star Wars* content. On the cover was a color photograph of Luke and C-3PO piloting the Landspeeder and on the reverse was a photo of C-3PO from *The Empire Strikes Back*. An update on *Revenge of the Jedi* stated that filming had begun on Monday, January 11, at Elstree-EMI Studios. *Starburst* had also attempted to clarify the position over the film's title. *Return of the Jedi* was apparently being touted by sections of the American press as the new title, but reportedly Lucasfilm's London office had allegedly heard nothing about it when *Starburst* had inquired. Another article in this issue reported that Lucasfilm had apparently been displeased with the recent sale of *Star Wars* to America's CBS-TV network with Sid Ganis quoted as saying, "If it were up to Lucasfilm we wouldn't sell *Star Wars* to TV. There is considerable theatrical life in the film. And that's why Lucasfilm will not sell the TV rights of *The Empire Strikes Back* or *Revenge of the Jedi*."[1]

"I remember reading this statement," says Darren Slade. "I thought 'Quite right, George' that the *Star Wars* films should only be shown at the cinema; but at the same time I was still desperate to be able to see them on TV or video!" Stuart Tendler, writing for the *Times*, had highlighted the fact that *Star Wars* was in fact readily available as an illegal video cassette. "In Hollywood they talk about *Star Wars* in the reverential terms reserved for the world's most profitable film. Say the word 'video' and the awed tones are likely to change to anger. *Star Wars* has been issued on 70mm and 35mm but never as a video cassette. Yet copies are available all over the world. The film is reported to have earned its makers hundreds of millions of pounds but no one knows what the cassettes have made nor how much more the original film might have made (upon its cinema re-releases) if the pirates had not struck."[2] In a time of rapidly changing technology, to simply use rentals to cinemas as the source of income from the *Star Wars* saga was beginning to appear old-fashioned. *Starburst* #43 also included a new interview with Harrison Ford, discussing his past films and his new film *Blade Runner*. The actor confirmed what many fans already suspected, that the upcoming *Star Wars* film would be his last. "After *Jedi*, the next sequence of *Star Wars* films goes back in time," said Ford. "So, Solo's not in them."[3] To complete this "Special Issue" of Starburst, there was a ten-page retrospective on *Star Wars* which included an A3 sized color poster. Not at all bad for 70 pence!

The January *Empire Strikes Back Monthly*, issue #153, contained another British exclusive story, "Dark Knight's Devilry" by Steve Moore, with art by Alan Davis. On the desert world of Jerne, Leia, Luke and R2-D2 had been captured by the Empire and were being held aboard an Imperial Troop Transporter when local guerrillas attacked and freed them.

Luke and Leia explained that they had learned that a nearby temple contained an ancient device that was able to wind back time. They hoped to be able to change history so that the Empire would not come to power and Alderaan would not be destroyed. The guerrillas agreed to assist but only because they wanted the device for themselves. It turned out that the temple was a fake and that Darth Vader had organized a false trail. The Dark Lord booby-trapped the temple entrance and when it exploded spectacularly he hoped to have killed Luke and Leia. Fortunately for them, they emerged with R2-D2 from the rubble unscathed and Luke threw a grenade at Vader that exploded at his feet. As the Rebel heroes escaped in an Imperial ship, a black glove emerged from the debris. "Dark Lord's Devilry" clearly had nothing to do with the *Star Wars* storyline. Vader was depicted as having none of his extrasensory powers and had instead resorted to the comic book villain tactic of setting an elaborate trap instead of sending in his men for the kill. So much the better for Luke and Leia!

Bantha Tracks #15, sent out in February, featured an interview with Ralph McQuarrie where he spoke about his early discussions with George Lucas. "The scope of *Star Wars* was so vast and so visual that no script could convey it all. George felt he could use a few of my paintings to convince the people at Fox his movie idea would be interesting. They listened to George's presentation and were convinced enough to give him some more money to finish the script and do some more paintings." The artist's work was used as the inspiration of much of *Star Wars'* imagery. Some scenes such as the Millennium Falcon entering the Death Star docking bay had been copied almost exactly from McQuarrie's paintings. "I didn't think they were going to keep so much of what I did," said the artist.[4] In this *Bantha Tracks*, there was also a copy of the Lucasfilm press release regarding the upcoming *Star Wars* film:

> Principal photography began January 11th on *Revenge of the Jedi*, the third film of the *Star Wars* saga, at the EMI Elstree Studios on the outskirts of London. Once more the *Star Wars* team takes all nine sound stages at EMI Elstree which was the shooting base for both previous productions. Principal cast and key technical crew is a mixture of old friends and new faces. Luke Skywalker, Han Solo, Princess Leia, Lando Calrissian, C-3PO, R2-D2, Chewbacca, Yoda and the dreaded Darth Vader are all back in action as the Rebel Alliance again attempts to outwit and out-strike the dark forces of the Empire. *Revenge of the Jedi* is a Chapter III production, produced by Howard Kazanjian, and directed by Richard Marquand. George Lucas is Executive Producer with Robert Watts and Jim Bloom serving as co-producers. The film stars Mark Hamill, Harrison Ford, Carrie Fisher, Billy Dee Williams and Anthony Daniels, with Dave Prowse, Kenny Baker, Peter Mayhew and Frank Oz in supporting roles. *Revenge of the Jedi* will be released by 20th Century-Fox with a May 27, 1983, opening scheduled for the United States and Canada.[5]

Star Wars was still in the public eye in Britain, albeit in the realm of television parody. On January 30, the ITV quiz show *3–2–1* had a science fiction theme. The program was based around comedy sketches and musical numbers and at one point an authentic-looking Darth Vader strode onto the set. The helmet was taken off to reveal Prime Minister Margaret Thatcher of all people, as played by well-known impressionist Faith Brown, to great reaction from the studio audience.

I was not hugely interested in 3–2–1 but I decided to watch this episode in case there were any Star Wars *references or if any related personalities would be on the show. The Darth*

Vader joke worked well because there was so much speculation over what he actually looked like, whether it was human, alien, robot or something even more outlandish. To have Margaret Thatcher under the helmet worked perfectly because at that time she had an extremely formidable reputation. Depending on people's political affiliation, Thatcher was often considered more of a hate figure than Darth Vader!

Comic Revamp

The Empire Strikes Back Monthly #154, published in February, sported a revamp. "As the magazine was sold on a newsstand," says Tim Hampson, "I was very keen that all the titles should have the best possible covers, which were appropriate to the U.K. I thought that the content needed beefing up too." The opening page was headed by the title "Lift-Off!" and included a friendly editorial and a list of contents. The feeling was of a publication tailored specifically for *Star Wars* fans and was all the better for it. Crucially, in addition to the original stories produced in Britain, every issue of the comic would henceforth contain an installment from David Micheline's ongoing storyline continuing on from *The Empire Strikes Back*. On the cover there would either be a color photograph or original artwork from UK artists. The artist who was to make the greatest impact was Liverpool-born John Higgins. He reminisces:

> I hadn't really noticed all of the hype leading to the release of *Star Wars* in 1977. I had just got my first full-time employment in London at a Medical Art Department in the Royal Marsden Hospital and was just beginning to break into SF and comic fan circles in London. Gary Leach, who I had just met, and who is now a very successful comic book artist, rang me up the day after he'd seen *Star Wars* and gave me a rundown with sound effects over the phone. He is a great storyteller. We went to see the film the following Saturday and I thought it was utter magic. For the first time in my life as a fan of SF, someone finally showed me the science fiction movie I had craved.

While working on some early black-and-white comic strip work for *2000 AD*, Higgins was employed to produce cover art for Marvel UK. "Most comics were black and white at that time. Marvel was one of the few companies that I went to looking for color work. I was probably one of the first comic book artists to do fully painted SF imagery since the great days of the *TV21* magazine and Eagle comic. I think they were intending to make *Empire Strikes Back Monthly* look more like a mature comic magazine. It was a great outlet for my painted SF cover work." Tim Hampson recalls, "John made a very important contribution to many Marvel titles including *Star Wars*. At the time, Marvel U.K. was commissioning very little new work. Being able to commission artists of John's skill was a small investment in new talent, which I think with hindsight has been proved absolutely right."

Issues #154 and #155 contained "Coffin in the Clouds" by David Michelinie. Lando Calrissian decided to travel to Cloud City in the Millennium Falcon, as he was concerned about its fate since the events of *The Empire Strikes Back*. The city was seemingly deserted except for Lobot, who was malfunctioning and intent on doing Lando harm. An Imperial shuttle arrived bearing an Imperial bomb disposal squad led by Captain Treece, whose mission was to disable explosive devices left by militant Ugnaughts. In the mode of the bombs in the film *Dark Star*, the first device the Imperials encountered was able to talk and appeared to be very willing to assist in the process of making itself safe. Judging that there was only a handful of Imperials present in Cloud City, Lando decided to go on the offensive, even though he was still attempting to avoid the murderous Lobot. The disposal squad dealt with a bomb that proved to be less helpful than it appeared, and it exploded. With Cloud City on the brink of complete destruction, Lando surmised that Lobot might be able to *talk* to the bombs. After agreeing to a truce in order to catch and repair Lobot, Captain Treece kicked Lando off of Cloud City. Lando seemingly plummeting to his death was a fine cliffhanger to end the issue on.

The Alan Moore story in issue #154 of the monthly comic was "Tilotny Throws a Shape," with art by John Stokes. Leia was wandering around a desolate moonscape, chased by the Empire, when she noticed a Stormtrooper helmet lying on the ground that appeared to have been there for thousands of years. Leia and the Stormtroopers were unfortunate enough to run into Tilotny, a being which had powers over matter, life and death and time itself. The Stormtropers were cruelly transported back to a point in time thousands of years in the past. Leia alone was spared but was still marooned on the dust bowl planet. Alan Moore followed this story by another penciled by John Stokes that was perhaps his most

Above and opposite page: The *Empire Strikes Back* monthly comic underwent a transformation.

effective: "Dark Lord's Conscience" in #155 began with a chess-like game, Firepath, where Darth Vader was pitting his wits against an octopus-like resident of the planet Cheelit. The giant game pieces moved around the room-sized board automatically and were incinerated by the opposite player in a huge fireball once taken. Vader had been drawn to the planet because he had learned that a local group, the Guild of Vindicators, intended to assassinate him and letting them *try* was a source of amusement to the Dark Lord. While the game was underway, a black-robed individual called Clat the Shamer cut a swath through Vader's protective cordon of Stormtroopers by reaching into their minds and convincing them all in turn that they were so crime-ridden, that they should all shoot themselves. Clat the Shamer finally confronted Vader in the games auditorium and attempted to use his mind powers to shame the Dark Lord into committing suicide. Vader's response was to press the button to take the piece that Clat the Shamer was standing next to. The last panel depicted the doomed Shamer's surprised expression as the fireball began to form beneath him. "Dark Lord's Conscience" was reprinted by Dark Horse Comics as part of its *Classic Star Wars: Devilworlds* series in 1996 but with an extra page that depicted Clat the Shamer being incinerated by the gaming piece. This was supposedly a missing page from the story but its inclusion spells out exactly what happened. The original ending causes the reader to think for a few seconds and the realization of what happened to Vader's opponent is a lot more satisfying than seeing it.

Palitoy Promotions

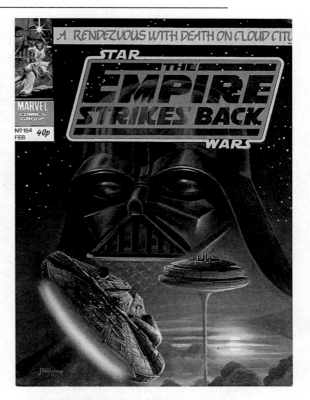

Issue #155 of the monthly comic included a major new competition run by Munro/Deighton on behalf of Palitoy. Readers had the challenge of naming and drawing a new *Star Wars* bounty hunter. The first prize for a pair of winners would be an AT-AT Walker toy and a visit to Elstree Studios to watch the filming of *Revenge of the Jedi*. One hundred runners-up would receive mini-rig vehicles. A new piece of artwork for the competition had the rebel heroes, Han Solo included, being chased down a film set corridor by a lightsaber-wielding Darth Vader! April 12 brought a new *Star Wars* television commercial. In its brief 20 seconds it contained a digest of the two previous commercials depicting Princess Leia's plight (captured under a large electric lamp). Darth Vader's TIE Fighter, the Imperial Troop Transporter and Millennium Falcon were featured. The familiar narration stated: "Who

can challenge the might of the Imperial Forces? Who dares to defy Darth Vader? Who can command the Millennium Falcon? Who can bring victory to the Rebels? You can, with *Star Wars* toys!" Ever mindful of how to keep *Star Wars* in the public eye, Geoff Maisey sought to make the most of a significant milestone. "We tried to set up a shoot at Heathrow for Darth Vader to meet the plane bringing in the next big shipment to Palitoy, including the five millionth *Star Wars* figure to arrive in Britain, but we were refused permission on security grounds. Carole Deighton was extremely adept at getting the most out of a situation, especially overcoming any obstacles, and she somehow managed to get us in the cargo apron area along with Darth Vader!"

Deighton recalls the event: "One of our 'actors' was in the Darth Vader costume. We had massive, whole pallets of *Star Wars* products in the background with Darth Vader holding a carton of figures. The photos were taken as close as we could get to one of the huge, secure, main commercial loading bays at Heathrow. Those shots appeared in both national newspapers and the trade and marketing press."

On Friday, April 16, BBC Radio began the third and final broadcast of the *Star Wars Radio Series*. There was a slim chance that fans would be able to listen to it, as each episode was broadcast on Radio 2 at two a.m.! Considering how much the BBC had spent on the series, the scheduling seems bizarre. "I was aware of this repeat," says Darren Slade. "As I recall, it followed *Trucker's Hour*! I didn't attempt to stay up for that ridiculously late broadcast. I was quite a night owl but staying awake that long after the TV closedown was a tall order." Fans had a slightly better chance of watching a repeat of *The Making of Star Wars*, depending in what ITV region they lived in and if they could stay up late. The Yorkshire region showed it at 11:05 p.m. on Monday, April 19, and the TVS region showed it at 10:25 p.m. on Wednesday, July 28.

Issue #16 of *Bantha Tracks* contained a further update on *Revenge of the Jedi*. Three production paintings by Ralph McQuarrie were included. One was of a giant craft exploding above an expanse of sand dunes, with Han Solo, Chewbacca and two other figures riding a smaller floating craft beside it. The caption read, "In *Revenge of the Jedi*, Luke Skywalker, Han Solo, Princess Leia, Lando Calrissian and Chewbacca fight for their lives on the desert wastelands of Tatooine. The massive 80-foot-high, 212-foot-long sand vessel and its satellite skiffs were constructed in a remote desert location." On the same page, there was a painting which depicted Han, Chewbacca and several other figures fighting hand to hand with a group of aliens aboard a smaller floating craft, while faces framed by the windows of the larger craft looked on. The last painting depicted C-3PO and R2-D2 encountering a strange looking alien in a darkened hallway. The caption read; "A massive metal door filters out the blinding Tatooine sunlight, closing off their only escape route, as C-3PO and R2-D2 are intercepted in the entrance hall to Jabba the Hutt's desert palace by his sinister major domo Bib Fortuna."[6]

Interviewed for this issue, Carrie Fisher said; "I like the script for *Jedi*. It's going to be a spectacle. It will transport you. Leia's character undergoes quite a change in *Jedi*. They found a way for her to be very nice while staying strong and committed. Leia is quite feminine, her character is as defined as 'the boys' are, and she even dresses 'like a woman.'"[7] Attentive readers might have noticed that Fisher had referred to the film as *Return of the Jedi*. There was also an update in this issue for the American members, stating that there would be a summer release of *Star Wars* on August 13 with *The Empire Strikes Back* appearing at Christmas. Cinema re-releases was something that British fans could perhaps expect to happen but an announcement that *Star Wars* was to be made available to hire in the U.S. on video on May 17 was a news item to generate genuine envy.

Marvelous Times

Issues #156 and #157 of *The Empire Strikes Back Monthly* concluded the Bespin Cloud City saga. Lando was saved from certain death by Lobot, who grabbed an emergency jet pack and dived after him. The pair landed on the surface and made an accord with the Ugnaughts, whose grievances were based on the corrupt practices of Captain Treece. Luke and female Rebel pilot Shira Brie arrived at Bespin Cloud City in X-Wings. Lando and Lobot returned to Cloud City with a clutch of Ugnaughts who bizarrely were more intent on making a film documentary than dealing with the Imperials. Cloud City was rocked by explosions, causing the Imperial contingent to make a hasty exit, fearing that it was about to fall. Lando and Shira were intent on escaping too and the Ugnaughts planned to capture the spectacular fall of Cloud City on film. Luke revealed that he had used the Force to set off only the bomb primers and that the city was in fact safe. The citizens of Bespin returned and Lando concocted a way to send the details of Captain Treece's corruption to Darth Vader.

"Hello Bespin, Goodbye!" presented an interesting depiction of the planet Bespin, with its surface shown as being inhabitable. Tibana gas was sourced in liquid form from swamps and was useful for its anti-gravitational properties. The gas being described as being anti gravitational in The Art of the Empire Strikes Back *is another example of a tied together expanded universe.*

Issue #156 contained the British exclusive story "Rust Never Sleeps" by Alan Moore with art by Alan Davis. R2-D2 and C-3PO were on a mission to the planet Ronyards, an enormous dumping ground for inert and obsolete droids. The plan was to encourage the robotic inhabitants to resist the Empire using the scrap materials for its military. An enormous bipedal droid called Fivelines turned up, and via pseudo-religious ramblings it stated that the planet was the living body of a god. Hot on the heels of C-3PO and R2-D2 was an Imperial Star Destroyer, which landed among the mountains of scrapped droids. Its Stormtroopers were not impressed with the Fivelines robot and blasted it. The god that Fivelines spoke of may have been something of a reality because a whirlwind of scrap consumed all of the Stormtroopers and the Star Destroyer, leaving no trace.

"Flight of the Falcon," the British exclusive story in issue #157, was drawn by John Stokes and written by *2000AD* and Marvel comics stalwart Steve Parkhouse, who presented a unique vision of the origin of the Millennium Falcon. The story began with Grand Moff Tarkin announcing the ship as a new spacecraft design for the Imperial Navy. Freebooting spacecraft had been outperforming Imperial ships so the Millennium Falcon had been designed to deal with them. A test pilot whose face was permanently covered by a mask had been contracted to fly the new ship but when he arrived, he and his men simply stole it. The man behind the mask was none other than Han Solo, and he seemed to have

Lando Calrissian at his side. The factory that produced the Millennium Falcon was then bombed by the Rebels, thus preserving the ship's status as a one-off.

Issue #158 of the monthly comic did not contain a British-produced story and instead printed "Sundown" by David Micheline in its entirety. Leia's plan to hide the Rebel fleet from the Imperial's prying eyes by hiding it within a sun seemed so risky that even C-3PO questioned it. Five massive shield generator spaceships had been acquired by the Rebels to project a pyramid-shaped field around the fleet to protect it from the extreme heat. No sooner had the fleet descended into the sun, one of the shield generator ships malfunctioned. It was fortunate that C-3PO and R2-D2 were aboard because they were not affected by the toxic fumes that incapacitated the crew. The droids were able to endure the extreme temperatures outside the ship and remedy the situation by attaching a long cable from one of the large Rebel cruisers to the shield ship to keep it powered up until it could be fixed. This came as a huge relief to Leia as she had believed that the fleet had been lost. Meanwhile Luke and Lando had set off on a mission to the space station *Bizarre* that was a hotspot for the criminal underworld.

Star Wars' *Triumphant Return*

May 20 was the day when one of the most important events for *Star Wars* fans happened: The world's first showing of a double bill of *Star Wars* and *The Empire Strikes Back* commenced at the Odeon Theatre Leicester Square and the Odeon Marble Arch, both in 70mm Dolby Stereo. Fans had been alerted to this double bill in issue #158 of the monthly comic via a double-page advertisement which was enough to take the reader's breath away. A special double bill poster combined the *Star Wars* poster by Tom Chantrell and the *Empire Strikes Back* poster by Tom Jung. The attraction of seeing both films in one performance proved to be phenomenally popular, as *Screen International* was able to report: "[O]nly one billing has drawn the crowds [this week]. *The Empire Strikes Back* and *Star Wars*, which played to excellent business as solo features, have come together for the first time as a double bill. The two set a new high at the Odeon Marble Arch with £10,066 over £9,973 and taking a net of £19,375 at the Leicester Square Theatre."[8] The *Star Wars* double bill went nationwide on Sunday, May 30, to 409 cinemas, including all of the major regional venues featured in *Screen International*: the Gaumont cinemas in Birmingham and Sheffield and the Odeon cinemas in Manchester, Glasgow, Liverpool, Nottingham, Southampton, Cardiff, Newcastle, Bristol, Bradford and Leeds. The exceptions were the Edinburgh and Glasgow Odeons. Double bills were hardly anything new at the cinema but blockbuster films took the concept to an entirely different level. The *Jaws* and *Superman* film duos had been released to huge success as had *Monty Python's Life of Brian* paired with *Airplane!* New releases such as *Gregory's Girl* and *Chariots of Fire* were also being paired on their initial run in an attempt to revive flagging audience numbers. In this climate, a double bill of *Star Wars* and *The Empire Strikes Back* must have presented an unbelievable opportunity and this was borne out by the number of cinemas booking it, which was a light year away from the handful of venues which had shown the re-release of *The Empire Strikes Back* the previous year. 20th Century-Fox sent out a trailer for the double bill to cinemas, followed by a publicity pamphlet packed with ideas how to make the most of the event, including

The Double Bill was a sensation across the country.

specially prepared in-house promotional aids and T-shirts for staff to wear. The message of the pamphlet was that the double feature had huge potential and that venues should make the most of the opportunity.

Palitoy was not going to let such an opportunity pass: Geoff Maisey reveals, "We used the tactic we had employed for the 1979 re-release of *Star Wars*: tagging information of local stores to the end of *Star Wars* toy advertisements. Due to the difficulties we encountered in administering the scheme the last time, we limited it to selected major retailers only!" *Look-In* #23 began a six-part "Collect-A-Page" feature, timed with the release of the *Star Wars* double bill. Each edition featured a photograph of a member of the *Star Wars* cast and a list of facts such as previous jobs, pets and favorite food. Adverts were placed in the national press and in the June issue of the monthly comic. The June 5 issue of *Screen International* excitedly reported that the double bill had been estimated to have taken £502,000 gross nationally in the first three days.

The showing of both films in one sitting was an amazing experience, especially for fans who had only seen *Star Wars* the one time only, several years past. Many had not seen the film at all, so a national cinema re-release was more than overdue. Instead being of a distant memory, supported by comics and other media, *Star Wars* was brought dramatically into the here and now. Contributing to the excitement was the fact that there was a teaser trailer for *Revenge of the Jedi* too. "We showed the double bill at Westcliff and it did really well," says Derek Dorking. "There was a lot of interest from our regular customers, as they'd bring their families in and the grandchildren would come along, because for the younger ones it was their first chance to see *Star Wars*. This started the snowball of the franchise again. For me personally, I wondered if I would still enjoy *Star Wars* again as much, being in my early twenties, but I still viewed it with a childlike fascination. As I was essentially paid to watch films, I could have the mindset of a big kid." Darren Slade says, "The double bill was the first time I had seen *Star Wars* since 1978. I found it surprising and different from the mosaic of different elements in my mind. In those days, you could watch one performance and wait for the next one to begin, so me and my friends watched *Star Wars* and *The Empire Strikes Back*, sat in our seats and watched it again. In between the films, there was a trailer for *Revenge of the Jedi* that I have not seen since, which was made up from stills, the title and nothing much else."

According to Susan Burton, there was nothing better than "a good dose of *Star Wars*, washed down with a liberal helping of *The Empire Strikes Back*. I went to see them at the cinema just after finishing my O levels and came out of the cinema totally rejuvenated."[9]

James Simmonds finally had the chance to see *Star Wars*:

> That was a fantastic experience after waiting so long. I went to see the double bill at the Russell Street cinema in Kettering. My dad had recorded about half of *SPFX The Empire Strikes Back*, so it was great to see the bits I had seen on the small screen on the big screen. I am reminded of that showing whenever I see the asteroid field scene in *The Empire Strikes Back*, because it was at that point that the projector broke down and we had to wait for the film to restart! I remember thinking that Luke was played by a different actor in the second film due to how much his appearance differed from 1977 to 1980. I even asked my dad if this was the case and he didn't know! *The Empire Strikes Back* remained my favorite even after seeing *Star Wars* for the first time at the double bill. I think it was probably because *Star Wars* seemed like the new one to me, even though it was released first. I suppose it's like preferring a group's debut album to their latest release.

Shaun Dawkins was not going to miss the double bill. "I saw it a few times in London at the Odeon Leicester Square. I had seen *Star Wars* on re-release a few times after my binge in 1978 but it was the first time for a while I had seen it on a big screen as a 70mm presentation. It was pretty cool. It was interesting seeing them one after another as you could see how the characters were evolving. It was also great meeting up with people—the whole day talking *Star Wars*." Declan McCafferty recalls,

> I didn't see *Star Wars* until the double bill. It seems hideous now to think that I spent two years being this avid fan having only seen the sequel. I had the novel, storybook, parts of the Marvel adaptation and some of the radio version taped so I knew everything that happened in it. I spent that first showing annoyingly whispering every plot point to my sisters: "This is the bit where Artoo gets caught by Jawas," "This is the bit Luke gets attacked by Sand People." I even remember saying, "This is the bit where Luke sells his Landspeeder." Every single thing in it seemed utterly important. Funnily enough, neither sister has had the inkling to watch a *Star Wars* film since!

According to Jordan Royce, "I didn't hear about the double bill. Information about film showings came via the local newspaper in those days. Living in Stockport, our nearest showing was Manchester and I would have had to have passed by the cinema there to notice it. At my age, a journey to Manchester with the family was fairly uncommon. The access to information that young people have these days is incredible and it just wasn't like that then."

The June 12 *Screen International* reported extremely impressive figures for the double bill: "In an otherwise disastrous week for provincial box office there was one ray of hope. The double bill did excellently at the 11 screens recorded in *Screen International*—and its figures would have been even higher had it been possible to squeeze more than 14 screenings during the week. Due to the length of the double bill, this was the most cinemas could manage." The showing set new records at screens including the Bristol Odeon Broadmead 1, Liverpool Odeon 1 and Newcastle Odeon Pilgrim Street 1. This issue contained 20th Century-Fox's double-page advertisement proclaiming it "The greatest double action feature of all time. £1,057,879 in the first 8 days of release."[10] There was no doubting that the *Star Wars* franchise in Britain was as strong as ever, with the double bill undoubtedly exceeding all expectations.

Diehard fans attending showings would have not failed to notice that the print of *Star Wars* had changed to incorporate the new title *Star Wars: Episode IV—A New Hope*. Despite this, *Star Wars* remained the popular title of the film among fans and in the media (and in this book).

The Star Wars *double bill that I attended with Gary and Paul in Romford was a complete revelation. It was the first time that I viewed* Star Wars *and been able to truly appreciate it. Watching* Star Wars *as a 12-year-old was completely different than it had been as a seven-year-old. That was the day that I knew that I would be a* Star Wars *fan forever.*

Action Figure Reinforcements

Palitoy released another set of *Star Wars* action figures consisting of Luke Skywalker (Hoth Battle Gear), AT-AT Commander, (Twin-Pod) Cloud Car Pilot, Bespin Security Guard, 4-Lom, Zuckuss, Imperial TIE Fighter Pilot, Artoo Detoo (R2-D2) (with Sensorscope) and C-3PO (with Removable Limbs). The original R2-D2 and C-3PO were not included in this wave as they had been replaced by the new versions. The front of the new-style packaging featured an advertisement to "Become a *Star Wars* Bounty Hunter," continuing the theme launched the previous year.

The picture of the action figure range on reverse of the backing cards was indispensable at this time for fans as it was their main reference. But strangely, only 45 figures out of the 48 available were included. Imperial TIE Fighter Pilot, 4-Lom and Zuckuss were missing although it is believed that they too were released in this style of packaging. (Zuckuss has yet to be found by collectors.) A large number of figures appeared in Britain with Kenner backing cards but they were not necessarily illegal imports from America. "Palitoy was constantly trying to keep in stock across 45 or so figures," says Geoff Maisey. "We would resort to taking any U.S. stock we could get to plug gaps. These were usually over-stickered with legals and the Palitoy logo to comply with CE regulations." The Imperial TIE Fighter Pilot and Zuckuss did not feature on the reverse of the American backing cards either. There was an offer on the Kenner cards for a product only available via mail order, the Action Figure Display Arena. It consisted of four L-shaped interlocking plastic bases and four double-sided cardboard *Star Wars* background scenes designed to display action figures. Palitoy covered the offer with a sticker of its own, with details of how British customers could send off for the item by sending four names from action figure backing cards plus £2.50.

Kenner *Star Wars* action figure backing cards soon appeared with an offer to send off for 4-Lom in the post, to which Palitoy added a sticker with the British offer for the character. It was not until Kenner figures appeared in Britain later in the year with an offer for Admiral Ackbar (a new character from *Revenge of the Jedi*), that all 48 in the set were depicted on the reverse of the card. Palitoy again used a sticker to provide purchasers with the British details. Some of the *Empire Strikes Back* vehicles and playsets were available in Britain in Kenner packaging too. These toys contained the Kenner 1982 *Star Wars* catalogue which introduced British collectors to toys that were not available in their high street shops. There was an action figure-scaled Scout Walker, a Rebel Transport vehicle that doubled as a carry case for action figures and, most eye-catching of all, the Micro Collection, a new range of miniature metal, ready-painted figurines with accompanying playsets and vehicles. The Kenner catalogue was the source of collecting fantasies among many *Star Wars* fans and it filled the pockets of toy dealers who would import those toys into Britain in subsequent years.

I remember clearly, reading through the Kenner catalogue as a young collector and ogling products such as the Micro Collection and the Large Size IG-88. My brother Paul and Gary were also collecting at the time. We were all savvy enough to know that Kenner was the American brand and that we were unlikely to see such exotic items in the shops in our home town.

Palitoy *Star Wars* action figure packaging changed again later in the year, with the removal of the Bounty Hunters advert on the front of the backing card and also the Palitoy logo. The photograph of the figures available on the reverse still still depicted 45 out of the 48 in the set. Geoff Maisey explains that there had been a major change at the Coalville factory. "In order to overcome in-house stock imbalances, we began to package the *Star Wars* figure line in the U.K., sourcing the bulk figures from Hong Kong and producing everything else in the U.K., including pack-out (attaching action figures individual to blister cards and packing as assortments into shipping cartons). We sourced the corrugated shipping cartons, all of which began with the supplier code CP, followed by a code number." John Holmes takes up the story:

> When the decision was made to buy the figures bulk from Hong Kong and do the blister packing in the factory, Dave Mugglestone and I went up to Black and Decker in County Durham to look at their machines and how they operated. Palitoy bought six or eight German Illig machines for the job which were intended to seal the blister (or bubble) to the card. The figures were ordered unpackaged from Hong Kong, bulk-packed individually in little plastic bags. To package them at Coalville, the blister was placed in a nest, the figure, and any accessory, placed into the blister. The card was placed over the blister, then a hot plate would come down to seal the card to the blister. Initially we had some problems getting the card to seal to the blister, as after sealing, the card would have a certain amount of distortion where the sealing took place. The figures were mainly blister-packed on the twilight shift (5–9 or 5–10 when busy). I used to supervise sometimes, one or two nights a week on the twilight shift for some overtime. Not the greatest job but someone had to do it!

As part of the new range, Palitoy released a "Battle Damaged" version of its front line X-Wing toy, which was in line with Kenner refurbishing its own X-Wing as a "Battle Damaged" design. While Kenner re-cast the toy in light gray plastic, provided it with a smoked canopy and included a sheet of *Battle Damage* stickers, Palitoy simply reissued the same white-colored toy that it had done previously and included the new sticker sheet. The new

Palitoy's Battle Damaged X-Wing: the same as the previous one but with new stickers!

box design from Kenner was airbrushed for the Palitoy release, so that the activation button and the red light in the nose were obscured. Some fans were less than impressed with the *Battle Damage* stickers, especially when they found that if they attempted to remove them, the stickers that lay underneath would be torn off too. The *Battle Damage* process was permanent!

Palitoy also issued new Mini Rig vehicles: INT-4 Interceptor (a small fighter craft that was meant to fold inside the AT-AT) and CAP-2 Captivator (a four-limbed contraption that could trap an action figure in spring-loaded jaws). The Tauntaun was re-released in new packaging and with an opening belly feature that allowed action figures to be fitted inside. Slave One Boba Fett's Spaceship included a model of Han Solo frozen in carbonite, which was just one of many fantastic features. There was also a Wampa toy which was scaled to action figures. The Dagobah Action Playset included Yoda's house, a bog and various levers and control switches that allowed Luke and Vader to fight and for various items to be "levitated."

The standout action figure accessory vehicle of the year must have been the mightily impressive AT-AT All Terrain Armoured Transport, the Palitoy name for which again reflected English spelling. The toy had presented a mammoth challenge for Palitoy to produce. "Along with the tooling molds, we got build specifications from Kenner which included a bill of materials and instructions with drawings and diagrams on how to put it together," says John Holmes. He continued:

There were no precise details as to how the production line was to be set up, so we had to work that out ourselves. I knew that the Kenner production of the AT-AT was a bit like a car factory with overhead conveyor with hooks to put the legs on; that fed down to the assembly belt. When Palitoy received all of the pieces for the AT-AT toys from the molding company, deciding how to assemble it was a bit like piece of self-assembly furniture. Often you would end up with a spare screw or a bit of card which should have fitted behind the pilot's seat and have to take it to pieces again. We did have a bit of trouble with the AT-AT, but it was probably my favorite *Star Wars* toy to work on. It was a challenge and it stretched your mind. A lot of work went into that toy—I'm sure more than children at the time would have appreciated!

A television commercial depicted the Rebel Snowspeeder toy attacking the AT-AT, flying through its legs and toppling it over. The commercial included a clip of the snow battle from the film which proved problematic at first. Geoff Maisey recalls the time:

> For the *Empire Strikes Back* campaign, Palitoy became one of the first companies in the U.K. to introduce live action footage into TV commercials. This was resisted by the Advertising Standards Agency at first, but it was eventually accepted under strict guidelines relating to the number of seconds per ad. We also had to demonstrate through child actors what was actually possible with the toys. For example, after a movie sequence showing a vehicle moving or flying, we had to show the same sequence with the toy being manipulated by a child moving it or holding it aloft. The rules were gradually relaxed by the ASA over time.

The narrator of the commercial stated that the toy was called an *Att-Att* instead of *Aetie-Aetie*, which has fueled controversy over the pronunciation ever since. Palitoy again issued a poster in the large boxed items, which included images of the Millennium Falcon Spaceship, Darth Vader's Star Destroyer Action Playset, Rebel Armoured Snowspeeder and the die-cast range from *The Empire Strikes Back*. Also the Darth Vader TIE Fighter and Imperial Troop Transporter, which were still being sold in their original *Star Wars* branded packaging with Bounty Hunter offer symbols. Any fan who had collected these symbols would have wasted their time, as Palitoy did not launch a campaign where they could have been redeemed for a corresponding prize.

Airfix released new kits for the *Star Wars* range derived from MPC, albeit under the control of Palitoy. *Encounter with Yoda on Dagobah* was a 1/14 scale diorama which included models of Luke, R2-D2, Yoda and the Jedi master's abode. The well-crafted scene was given additional authenticity by an array of accessories such as snakes and supply boxes. *Battle on Hoth* was a fantastic diorama which included everything required to recreate the iconic scene in miniature. AT-AT Walkers, a Scout Walker, Snowspeeders, rebel turrets and a generous supply of tiny Rebel and Imperial troopers could be set out on a pre-formed plastic diorama base, which incorporated rebel trenches and the power generator. This set bridged the divide between model kits and toys, much as the Airfix range of miniature scale soldiers did. Model makers could create a satisfying diorama while children could purchase the set and use the array of vehicles and figurines to set up their own displays and play with the individual pieces. The scale of the individual items did not match, but that was not a huge concern because the set was produced more in the spirit of play than of serious model making. The standout item from the new range for more experienced model makers was an individually boxed AT-AT Walker. It was supplied with two Snowspeeders and a pair of Rebel defense turrets in a larger size to that of the *Battle on Hoth* diorama.

Revenge of the Merchandise

Parker Bros. released the first *Star Wars* computer game, *The Battle of Hoth*, for the Atari 2600. It was a side-scrolling game, with extremely good graphics for the time. Up to two players could tackle AT-AT Walkers with Snowspeeders and if they hit them 48 times without being hit too many times themselves, the machines would be destroyed. Occasionally the Snowspeeder would glow with the Force and be invulnerable. Since Lucasfilm had already licensed *Star Wars* to existing games manufacturers, it prevented its new in-house company Lucasfilm Games from developing one of its own. The developer of *The Battle of Hoth* for Atari was another of the young guns working on the *Star Wars* franchise. Rex Bradford started working for Parker Bros. directly after leaving the University of Massachusetts, where he had taught himself programming. "I got hired to work on electronic games," recalls Bradford, "but happened to be in the right place at the right time when they made the move to make Atari games. I got the nod to be the programmer for their first game, *The Empire Strikes Back,* and that launched me into video and games as a career." Although this was the first Parker Bros. video game, they only employed two people to work on it. "Sam Kellerman got picked to be the game's designer, and me its programmer, something of a far cry from the 100-plus game development staff these days. There was no spec *per se*; Sam came up with most of the basic play mechanics, though I participated in those and also eagerly took on the stuff that's hard to spec—the technical elements that are over most people's heads."[11]

For lovers of the *Star Wars* soundtrack, Music for Pleasure released a new album, *John Williams Symphonic Suites,* from the London Symphony Orchestra and the National Philharmonic Orchestra conducted by Frank Barber. Although the driving force behind the album was enthusiasm for *E.T. the Extra-Terrestrial*, it contained several fresh *Star Wars* recordings by the National Philharmonic Orchestra. Purchasers expecting a faithful reproduction of the film music may have been disappointed, as nearly all of the tracks included some very out-of-place laser sound effects. Music for Pleasure specialized in repackaging previously released recordings from owner company EMI aimed at the budget market and retailers other than record shops such as W.H. Smith. MFP had notably scored the prestigious Christmas #1 position on the singles chart in Britain in 1980 with "There's No One Quite Like Grandma" by St. Winifred's School Choir, which has been widely derided since. Constantly seeking to capitalize on crazes and the most popular recording artists, Music for Pleasure had judged that there was a large enough market for Williams' science fiction film music to add it to their compilation catalogue.

The new *Star Wars* merchandise arranged the previous year by Andrew Maconie and his office began to arrive in the shops. "There was a coordinated range of merchandise in 1982," Maconie recalls. "This was achieved by holding licensee meetings prior to the launch on a market-by-market basis. Although companies had the option of using branding from *The Empire Strikes Back*, all of the merchandise released in 1982 bore the *Star Wars* logo." From Thermos Ltd. there was a lunch box cast in red plastic with artwork depicting Darth Vader on Hoth. Inside was a flask decorated with Vader and Stormtroopers. British manufacturer Icarus released its striking range of house wear with fantastic original artwork from *Star Wars* and *Empire*. Branded with the original *Star Wars* logo, the range included placemats in two different sizes, framed pictures and wipe boards. The artwork was by British artist Andrew Skilleter, who is best known for providing the cover art for the Target Doctor Who novels, videos and issues of the *Radio Times* magazine. "My involvement with Icarus was a complete fluke," says Skilleter. He continues:

> It came about via a local design agency that I did occasional work for. The guys who were setting up the Icarus company were using the same agency and they got to hear of my *Doctor Who* artwork. They needed an artist for their placemats and so after several meetings the commissions evolved. They were specific as to the characters they required but the compositions and color were left to me. As part of

the process, I had to visit to the offices of Andrew Maconie, the agent in London who was handling the *Star Wars* merchandising and licensing and I selected photographs for reference. I later attended a private screening of *The Empire Strikes Back* in mid–1981 that was shown for the benefit of licensees. All quite something looking back.

Although Skilleter approached his work with the utmost professionalism, he was not a *Star Wars* devotee. "I was aware of the phenomenon but I was very consumed by whatever else was going on in my life and career. *Doctor Who* had by then become a big part of my life professionally. But I was impressed by how solid a creation *Star Wars* was and I was immediately caught up with its rich scenarios, characters and hardware and the exciting possibilities it offered illustratively." Skilleter says that he was reaching a level of success that he had long strived for:

> I always wanted to be an illustrator from an early age. I drew a lot and created my own strips and magazines. There was never a question of which career I wanted to pursue. I went to art college for four years doing a mainly design course but heavily influenced by other illustrators outside of college that inspired me. So I regard myself as self-taught as far as my technique went. I received my first commission while in college and then doggedly stuck to my ambition to be a pro and so my career gradually evolved.

Scanlite released 12 posters, all branded with the *Star Wars* logo although featuring a number of *Empire Strikes Back* images. Han Solo and Chewbacca were not included which may have been to do with doubts over the new film. The posters were distributed via news agent shops and were sold rolled in cellophane, with a small photograph at the end of the roll showing what the poster depicted. Frankel and Roth International produced school

Above, opposite and following page: **The *Star Wars* merchandise campaign in 1982 included placemats from Icarus and stationery items from H.C. Ford.**

bags, branded with the *Star Wars* logo but with photographs from *Empire*. H.C. Ford began producing a new range of wonderfully presented stationery, based almost entirely on *Star Wars*. There were a few references to *Empire*, with Yoda and Han Solo in Hoth gear pencil-top figurines and a stationery gift set depicting Luke and Vader on Bespin Cloud City. It seemed as if the clock had been turned back to 1978 as H.C. Ford *Star Wars* stationery seemed to be everywhere in the shops. Perfumed erasers, pencil tops, domed pencil sharpeners and stationery sets all gleamed in fantastic display boxes decorated with scenes based on the original *Star Wars* poster art. There were also square pencils, tag pencils and four-in-one pencils. "I eagerly bought as much of the new merchandise as I could," says James Simmonds. "The H.C. Ford stationery especially, with the scented erasers being my favorite items along with the tag top pencils. I didn't consider at the time that it was weird that *Star Wars* logo

items were appearing in 1982 but years later I thought that it was a little odd. I missed the Helix *Star Wars* stationery range when it came out in the '70s so it was the H.C. Ford range that was part of my childhood." Sarah Baker-Saunders was finding new items too. "I was a fan of the movie posters, so I collected the Scanlite posters when they came out. I couldn't resist some of the H.C. Ford stationery too."

The 1982 *Star Wars* merchandising drive covered key areas that children connected with: posters to collect and hang up, placemats to use at the dinner table, a lunch box and stationery to use at school and bags to carry it in. Counting Marvel, Bunch Associates, RSO, Palitoy/Airfix, Buena Vista International and Atari, there were manufacturers covering at least 12 vital merchandise aspects.

The return of Star Wars *merchandise in 1982 is one of my fondest memories. The posters from Scanlite were especially exciting, although there were none of Han Solo or Chewbacca. I thought that the H.C. Ford stationery was great and I bought as much of it as I could afford. Display boxes could be obtained from shops when they were finished with, and to me they*

were better than the actual products they contained. It would have been fairly expensive to pick up all of the Icarus range, so I bought just one of the small sized placemats featuring a fantastic painting of Chewbacca, Han, Lando and the Millennium Falcon with my holiday spending money that year. I didn't notice that the bags were available but at 12 years old my schoolmates, who didn't understand my devotion to Star Wars, *would not have been impressed if I had arrived carrying one!*

Considering the amount of time new products took to design and produce, deals needed to struck for 1983 too. According to Jackie Ferguson,

Bridge Farm Dairies were very much a farming enterprise. They were actually two farmers who came into our office for some reason. They only supplied small, independent shops at the time. We thought it was a really good idea to do *Star Wars* yogurt, with the flavor colors corresponding to the individual characters; black currant for Darth Vader for instance. The farmers thought this was completely off-the-wall but we eventually signed a license with them. Another deal I recall very well was with Worlds Apart kites. The owner walked into the office and he was only around 18 years old. He had this kite company and he said that he would like a *Star Wars* license. I must admit that I was a little cautious (compared to some people in licensing who are more brutal and will sign people regardless) because when you do sign, your money is really on the line. I think he guaranteed us £10,000 which was an awful lot. I said to him that I was going to go through the agreement with him clause by clause.

In July, issue #159 of *The Empire Strikes Monthly* was re-titled *Star Wars Monthly* which was in line with the 1982 *Star Wars* rebranding. This was a bumper issue of the comic which included a free poster by John Higgins, probably designed to smooth the transition to the new title. There was also a full-page color advertisement from Palitoy, offering a set of four Action Displays (the Action Figure Display Arena previously advertised on action figure backing cards), which could be claimed in return for four names cut out from *Star Wars* action figure backing cards. The back cover of the comic featured a major new competition devised and organized by Munro/Deighton on behalf of Palitoy and Airfix that was also printed in other comics and magazines. Prizes including the AT-AT Walker toy and the Star Destroyer model kit were won by fans who could correctly identify the four *Star Wars* vehicles pictured in the advert.

"Bazarre," a story printed in its entirety in #159, took Luke, Lando and Chewbacca to the space station Bazarre to negotiate the purchase of four Imperial TIE Fighters from Orion Ferret, an underworld businessman. He had no intention of delivering the them and instead intended to bump off the rebels in such a way that no one would notice. Luke and Lando traveled to an adjacent world to collect the TIEs leaving Chewbacca behind with instructions to pull Ferret's head off if anything went wrong. The enormous garbage pile where the craft had been hidden was guarded by a massive insectoid creature, but Luke and Lando prevailed and towed the four TIE fighters back to the Rebel base with the Millennium Falcon's tractor beam.

Issue #159 also contained the last of the British-exclusive *Star Wars* stories. Written by Alan Moore and drawn by John Stokes, "Blind Fury" was the very peculiar tale of Luke visiting an ancient fortress where the souls of long-dead Jedi were being held inside crystals. Luke discovered the eons-old corpse of the High Shaman of the Order of the Terrible Glare, who before his death had fed his personality into a computer to enable him to communicate with any unfortunate Jedi who fell into his trap. Luke told the Shaman that he must have lost track of time, because the conflict between the Jedi and the Terrible Glare had not happened months but thousands of years ago. The Shaman was so shocked at the revelation that the fortress self-destructed, with Luke escaping just in time. The words "The End" were printed at the bottom of the page, stating that this was the final chapter in the Moore and Moore saga.

The Video Laser Blast

A magnificent event occurred on July 1, which for fans seemed to come out of nowhere. *Star Wars* was made available to hire in Britain on video cassette by 20th Century–Fox Video (it was *not* available to buy). The film was released on VHS and Betamax formats, both of which were only compatible with the corresponding video-playing equipment. 20th Century–Fox had sought to produce the video cassette for some time. It was only the complex final negotiations over *Revenge of the Jedi* that had finally provided the approval from Lucasfilm, which had previously insisted that renting the film to cinemas was far more lucrative.

20th Century-Fox Video erected a *Star Wars*-themed stand at the Earls Court Consumer Electronics Exhibition manned by Jim Howell, Steve Hampson and Darth Vader in an N.J. Farmer brand costume. The release was also publicized by making copies available to newspapers and magazines as competition prizes. The magazine *Popular Video* featured the *Star Wars* poster on the cover and the caption "*Star Wars* exclusive: You can win it and keep it! Video's most wanted film is released for rental only but we've got copies to give away!" In an attempt to beat the video pirates (the name given to those who dealt in illegally copied video films), 20th Century-Fox Video marked the cassettes and covers with "uncopiable Polaproof" labels issued by Polaroid to prove that every copy was genuine. Derek Dorking played a part in the video release:

> I took part in a promotion at a video shop in Southend-on-Sea where the Westcliffe-on-Sea Classic assistant manager Jon Ashman dressed in a Darth Vader costume that we had made from scratch, except for the Don Post helmet. He was assisted by the projectionist Paul Clarke dressed as Han Solo, which was a good job because there was a huge crowd there. I also appeared with Julie at the main video shop in Romford, where we did our usual Luke Skywalker and Princess Leia and we handed out the official leaflets for the release. We then stood outside the shop and people would take photographs.

It was for the little children mainly, because the older ones obviously knew that we weren't the real characters. I found out later that the owner was the son-in law of the original owner of the Westcliff-on-Sea cinema, so it's kind of weird how these things seem to encircle you! A *Star Wars* fan called Laurie Calvert turned up; at the time, he was working as a special effects man. He had his movie camera with him and took some footage. We exchanged letters and he sent me a photograph of himself at his special effects studio.

Laurie recalls the occasion. "I remember meeting Derek very well. He was with his girlfriend doing promotions in Romford town center. They were giving out leaflets and I was filming on Super 8 film. We walked all around Romford and I filmed them interacting with the crowd and they were attracting a lot of interest. Pictures of them were printed in the *Romford Recorder* the following week."

Jon Ashman menaces the crowds at a Southend-on-Sea video shop, accompanied by Paul Clarke (*Southend Echo*).

Star Wars was finally released on video for hire only.

According to Jordan Royce, "The video release was a game changer in so many ways. My family had recently bought a video recorder, so I was lucky to be able to play films at home. It was the first time me and my friends had seen *Star Wars* since 1978 and we ended up watching it so many times, we could recite every line in the film. Any film you hired then, you felt like you had to watch it three or four times in order to get your money's worth which I can't imagine doing today." Gary Harvey also remembers the video release:

> My family wasn't exactly what you would call well off but my dad had managed to buy a video recorder; a top loader with huge buttons which was modern at the time. I made sure that I reserved a copy of the *Star Wars* video the very first day the local video shop received it. There was a large folder on the counter with the covers of all of the videos available, with only room for a small selection actually on display on the shelves. When the shop owner handed over the cassette, I ran home as fast as I could, breathlessly burst indoors and shoved it in the machine. The thing was that it wouldn't play no matter what I tried. The treacherous video recorder had chosen that very moment to break down! In complete desperation, I went across to the house across the road where a friend of my mum lived. Understandably, playing *Star Wars* on their video wasn't exactly a hard sell to the family!"

The *Making of Star Wars* documentary was released to the video hire market alongside *Star Wars*, with a cover featuring C-3PO and R2-D2 against a purple background. The *Eagle* comic ran a competition to tie in with the *Star Wars* release, with copies of *The Making of Star Wars* as prizes. These cassettes were the 1978 version from Magnetic Video, packaged in the old-fashioned cardboard sleeves. 20th Century-Fox no doubt inherited these older cassettes when it bought out Magnetic Video in 1979. The previously risky business proposition of hiring videos and also making them available for sale had proved to be such a success that 20th Century-Fox could not help but want a slice of the market, forming 20th Century-Fox Video earlier in 1982. This new concept in home entertainment meant that fans could finally enjoy *Star Wars* in their own homes, with children whose parents had video players suddenly becoming very popular. Owning video recorders was beyond the pockets of many, so families often rented the equipment from companies such as Radio Rentals. The company also operated a film hire service, with *Star Wars* being one of the titles on offer. Independent video hire shops, springing up all over the country, supplied a wide range of film titles on cassette. Despite 20th Century-Fox's stipulation that *Star Wars* could not be offered for sale on video, it was relatively simple to make copies, even using home equipment. *Star Wars* was also made available on laserdisc by Laservision. The cumbersome 12-inch disk was recorded in CLV (Constant Linear Velocity), which required the viewer to flip the disk over after 60 minutes of play. The quality of laserdisc was far superior to that of video, if you had a small fortune to spend on the equipment.

The double bill was still on release at the cinema, with extended runs at many venues. In London, the Odeon Marble Arch and Odeon Leicester Square handed over to the Classic 2 Oxford Street and Cinecenta 1 at the end of July. On August 21, the Nottingham Odeon registered its year's highest profits for a single week probably because the double bill was due to end that Saturday. The Liverpool Odeon ended on August 21 too, both cinemas having notched up impressive 15-week runs. On August 9, the Southampton Gaumont took over the double bill from the Odeon for a further two weeks. Back in London, the tiny 116-seat Scene 3, Swiss Centre, Wardour Street, opened the double bill on August 5 with its run due to last for quite some time, and the ABC Edgware Road showed the double bill for one week, from September 5.

A Story to Marvel At

In the August issue of *The Empire Strikes Back Monthly,* "Shira's Story" brought the character Shira Brie to the fore. Previously introduced as one of Luke's most trusted pilots and a close companion, Shira asked that she be allowed to travel to the planet of her birth. Luke insisted on tagging along, so he and Shira journeyed to the planet in the company of two of their pilot colleagues. Once there, Shira visited an ancient stone circle alone but she was interrupted by a large group of attacking nomads which quickly had Luke and his companions pinned down. Shira took action by using a tunnel to reach her X-Wing, take off and strafe the nomads until they fled. The September *Star Wars Monthly* featured the culmination of all the Rebels' preparations in previous issues, an attack on an Imperial space armada escorting a craft carrying the Teezl, a giant energy creature that the Imperials intended to use to transmit their communications instantly across the galaxy. Luke and Shira joined other Rebel pilots flying the four purchased TIE fighters to penetrate the Imperial armada. Luke found a TIE Fighter was blocking his path and, using the Force to determine if it was friend or foe, destroyed the ship before blowing up the craft carrying the Teezl. Upon returning to the Rebel base, Luke found everyone to be ashen-faced because it was revealed that he had actually shot down the TIE Fighter piloted by Shira Brie. A closeup image of poor Shira's face frozen in death aboard her ship was one of the comic's biggest-ever shocks and set up an extremely tantalizing situation for the next issue. Jordan Royce says, "When Luke Skywalker had shot down Shira Brie and was ostracized by his comrades, there was a scene where he was sitting in his room, staring at the medal that he had been awarded for destroying the Death Star. I thought it was great to have subtleties such as that."

Major Star Wars *News*

The September 1 *Variety* brought the news that on August 25, Sid Ganis and Industrial Light and Magic general manager Tom Smith had put on a presentation at the Advertising Age Annual Creative Workshop held at the New York Hilton. They explained that the buildup to *Revenge of the Jedi* in America would include a major re-release of *Star Wars* on Labor Day September 4 in 1200 theaters, all of which would be issued the *Revenge* trailer. The re-release would be followed by the video release of *Star Wars* to the hire market and also on pay-per-view television. *The Empire Strikes Back* would be released at Christmas along with a longer trailer for the new *Star Wars* chapter. The most important revelations concerned the future of the *Star Wars* saga: "Following *Jedi*, the next picture to be filmed in the nine-part *Adventures of Luke Skywalker* will be episode #3, a prequel to the original *Star Wars*, with #2 and #1 backtracking sequentially to the beginning of the story. After the history of the rebellion against the Empire, the final sequels #7 through #9 will be filmed in chronological order."[12]

The presentation in front of the assembled press was the strongest statement to date regarding how the *Star Wars* saga had a definite future beyond *Revenge of the Jedi* and that Lucasfilm had made a commitment to bring the remaining chapters to the screen. Smith also showed film clips and slides displaying how Industrial Light and Magic had been employed to produce effects for the non–Lucas projects *Dragon Slayer* and *Star Trek II: The Wrath of Khan*. As time went on, it would transpire that the second half of the presentation was far more significant to the future of Lucasfilm than the first.

Armchair Star Wars

The video release had been exciting enough but in September, ITV began running advertisements for every *Star Wars* fan's dream: a showing of the film on television. The release of *Star Wars* to TV had been another result of the Lucasfilm-Fox negotiations over *Revenge of the Jedi*. ITV had bought the rights from 20th Century-Fox for a reported £1,500,000. Fans had been tipped off in advance by a letter in the September issue of the monthly comic. The *Eagle* comic broke the news to its readers in its news section. *Star Wars* on TV was a massive media event, with a great number of stories printed in the national press during the run-up to the showing on Sunday, October 24, at 7:15 p.m. At this time, big-budget films were rarely shown on television so *Star Wars* seemed to have literally arrived from outer space. Newspapers searched around for every possible related angle. A story by reporter John Hiscock headed by the title "*Star Wars* stars axed!" revealed that *Revenge of the Jedi* would be the last *Star Wars* film to feature the main cast. Another story reported on the profits made by Alec Guinness and the other cast members under the heading "Making a Bomb Out of *Star Wars.*" The story "Star Warrior's Holiday for Love" reported that Harrison Ford had apparently pledged to take time off from his career to spend time with his screenwriter girlfriend Melissa Matheson. "Spook War on Darth" alleged that David Prowse was menaced by a phantom haunting his gym. *Look-In* #45 featured a *Star Wars* cover and a two-page feature. Munro/Deighton were not going to let the opportunity pass them by. Among the promotions they negotiated was a *Daily Mirror* competition for readers to win the complete set of 45 *Star Wars* figures.

Not all of the coverage was positive. Writing for the *Daily Mail's* television review section, Margaret Hinxman was as negative as ever, moaning about the "wiz-bang electronic gadgetry and the sensation of zooming through the cosmos [that] has the same numbing effect on the mind as endlessly playing those press-button *Star Wars* video games." She complained that *Star Wars* had "virtually killed the adult film as a money-making proposition,"[13] although she would have struggled to list any profitable *adult* films that that had immediately preceded *Star Wars.* Hinxman cited the British film *Chariots of Fire* as an example of the type of film that she would like to see more of, but would an uplifting family film based on athletics have even been made in Britain without *Star Wars'* success?

The October 23–29 *TV Times* magazine was crammed with *Star Wars* material. The cover sported artwork culled from a poster by Boris Vallejo, featuring an iconic image of Darth Vader erroneously wielding two lightsabers. There was a two-page feature with illustrations by Martin Asbury that depicted, in comic strip form, the events described in the opening crawl of *Star Wars*: X-Wing Fighters flying away from a giant explosion, the lead ship exclaiming that they had won their first victory against the Empire, while a Rebel spy transmitted a message to Princess Leia's ship and Darth Vader ordered her ship captured. When the evening of the 24th arrived, fans who had access to a video recorder taped the showing. The ad break preceding the film included the Palitoy commercial for the AT-AT. According to Graham Ogle, "We had not long had our first video recorder, so of course I was recording it. I was editing the adverts out with the pause button, but our video was primitive and didn't have a remote control. I had to get up and squat in front of the telly during the ads." Lorraine Malby recalls, "I didn't get to see *Star Wars* on its initial release at the cinema and for some reason it didn't occur to me that it would eventually be shown on television. I believed that *The Making of Star Wars* was going to be my only chance of seeing the film and so I eagerly watched and videoed it. I tried not to let it spoil my enjoyment too much but seeing *Making of* first meant that there were few surprises. The big battle at the end? Poof, I'd seen it all before."

"I had a brand new Betamax tape waiting to tape *Star Wars*," remembers Ian Whitlock. "And I ended up watching it endlessly. My next door neighbor's boys, who were younger than me, had never seen *Star Wars*. They had missed the television showing and were very happy to hear I had a copy of it. I remember disappearing into their house many times after. It's always a good feeling to spread the *Star Wars* joy and I got to play with their *He-Man* figures."

"It was good for me because it was the first time that my dad saw it," says Laurie

Calvert. "He was amazed, although I get the feeling that he really didn't want to admit it. It was the old science fiction films that were special for him but he knew that *Star Wars* was something quite extraordinary as well. My mum watched it as well, so it was a real family thing." Richard Harris was also ready to record the film. "This was the first time in four and a half years I had the chance to see *Star Wars*. Through collecting the cards, reading the novel and playing with the action figures I was hooked on everything *Star Wars* and my parents knew it! My father had set the video as we eagerly gathered in the lounge.

Above and following page: Star Wars on television was a national phenomenon (above only: courtesy **The Star Wars Magazine Archive**).

I was ever so excited about watching 'my' film whenever I wished and throughout the next couple of months I watched the recording countless times with my younger brother, re-enacting all the lines word for word." Some fans without a video recorder made an audio recording of the film.

I was one of the fans who made do with an audio recording of Star Wars *but even that was simply amazing. I'd recently been given a Walkman-style cassette player and I listed to* Star Wars *everywhere I went. That way, I learned the script of the film by heart. I was fascinated by the comic strip by Martin Asbury in the* TV Times. *The "Rebel victory" mentioned in the opening crawl of* Star Wars *had been a bit of an enigma and it was great to see a depiction of it.*

"It was a massive deal for me and everyone I knew," says Peter Davis. He continues:

> Nobody had a video recorder and it was quite late on a Sunday evening. My brother and I had a long sleep after lunch so we could stay up late and watch it. My dad, who was not normally bothered by such nonsense, became intrigued by our frenzied anticipation. We had seen *Empire*, but this would be the first time we would have seen *Star Wars* where our memories would be fresh and the story given context to what we witnessed in the sequel. That anticipation we experienced, the country experienced, can never be repeated today. It was a national event.

"My introduction to *Star Wars* was the British television premiere," recalls Grant Criddle. "Even as a three-year-old, I understood that it was a special occasion as my parents sat me down to watch the film with

them. I sat behind my mum and peeked over her shoulder. This was a strategy of mine at the time, in case things got scary, such as the 'bang' at the end of the credits of *Doctor Who*. I remember having the confidence to leave mum's sanctuary at the moment C-3PO has his oil bath and sitting next to her feet. My parents later told me that I barely said a word and just stared at the screen." *Star Wars* was the highest rated program on British television that month, notching up 16.1 million viewers, beating the regular ratings champion *Coronation Street* (15.56 million).

An Autumn of Star Wars

The October *Star Wars Monthly* included a competition to win the 1983 *Star Wars* annual from Marvel and Grandreams Ltd. which sported Paul Neary cover art depicting a montage of rebel heroes. Confusingly, the opening page contained a copyright of 1981 but that simply referred to the Marvel artwork and not the annual's release date, which was not included. The annual was filled with color reprints of the stories "The Third Law," "Death Probe" and "Droid World." There was no other content such as interviews and features, which was similar to the style of other annuals available at the time.

The October and November issues of *Star Wars Monthly* contained the stories "Pariah" and "The Mind Spider" by David Michelinie where Luke Skywalker sought to find out why the Force had told him that the opposing TIE Fighter piloted by Shira Brie was an enemy craft. Luke and Chewbacca travelled back to Shira's home planet of Shalyvane and found that Shira's story of her birth and upbringing on the planet had been a lie. Luke discovered that the stone circle Shira had visited contained communication equipment with a direct link to none other than Darth Vader! The next stop for Luke was an Imperial data storage center built inside what appeared to be the husk of an enormous spider, where he found that Shira had been a top Imperial secret agent. Luke blowing the complex sky high was of little concern to Vader, as he had already secured a valuable prize: Shira had survived and was immersed in a healing tank of bacta.

On October 22, ITV's Central News featured a report on *Star Wars* toys, filmed at Palitoy's Coalville production line. It was stated that Palitoy had manufactured and sold over £150 million worth of *Star Wars* toys. The new Admiral Ackbar action figure was featured in the report, seated behind the controls of an AT-AT, which was the key toy product that year. Jackie Ferguson recalls the demand for the AT-AT:

> We were permanently in touch with Palitoy and met with them at least once per month, because you can't have a merchandising program if you don't coordinate things. There were not enough AT-AT Walkers for Christmas, so we air-freighted them in. They were huge and in big boxes, so you're not going to get many in a container. So that in itself shows the demand for *Star Wars* merchandise. The AT-AT was the hero product that year and was priced very highly.

Geoff Maisey recalls, "I remember having regular meetings with Jackie and Andrew and we did indeed air-freight stock of AT-ATs in as the demand was so high. It had to go through the appropriate safety checks and have CE labels applied to the outer packaging."

Another glimpse of the upcoming *Revenge of the Jedi* was provided by *Voyager* magazine's winter issue, which included three fantastic paintings from Ralph McQuarrie that had appeared in black-and-white in *Bantha Tracks* but this time they were in color. The December *Starlog* included an interview with Mark Hamill, who provided a few hints about *Revenge of the Jedi* which he had just finished filming. "It's ironic that the last one would be the best one. But not really. The roles reflect the growth of Luke. I mean, it's not the most satisfying thing in the world to play that sort of 'Golly—you don't believe in the Force, do you?' character." Regarding the film's title, Hamill appeared to be as much in the dark as anyone else as to who would be taking revenge: "[T]he thing is, which Jedi is it? Is it

Vader, Obi Wan, Yoda or me or the other? It's so confusing, too. George has so many ways he can go."[14] A lengthy report from *Star Wars* fan Joe Copeland, who had been chosen as Mark Hamill's stand-in, was a very nice taster of the film to come. Joe was a resident of Yuma, Arizona, where the Sail Barge set had been erected. Without giving any vital details away, Joe described the filming process of the action scene set on the sail barges which had previously been depicted in Ralph McQuarrie paintings released to the media.

The December issue of *Star Wars Monthly* took a break from the David Michelinie storyline to present "Serphidian Eyes," which was simply a filler story that had nothing to do with the overall continuity. Medieval stone castles, plate armor and jousting places this particular story a long way outside the overall *Star Wars* continuity.

The Close of an Amazing Year

The Christmas holiday season was the perfect time for cinemas to book the *Star Wars* double bill and that's exactly what many did. The Liverpool Odeon opened on December 12 along with the Manchester Odeon and Glasgow Odeon, with no doubt many others following suit. In London, the ABC Fulham Road opened the double bill on December 22, while the Scene 3 was still going after an incredible 17 weeks. Taking into consideration the cinema double bill, video release and television broadcast, brand new merchandise and a huge amount of press coverage contributing to the work done by 20th Century-Fox, Palitoy, Munro/Deighton, the fan club, the comic and Andrew Maconie's office, 1982 had been a dizzying year for fans, which contrasted strongly with the dull year that had preceded *The Empire Strikes Back*. The double bill came in at an impressive #12 in the *Screen International* top 20 earners for 1982, beating popular films such as *Poltergeist, An American Werewolf in London* and most surprisingly *Star Trek II: The Wrath of Khan* (*Star Trek* not being able to beat *Star Wars* even on re-release). *The Making of Star Wars* and the radio series had been repeated, although the nighttime scheduling had not been ideal. The slower release of new merchandise by Palitoy compared to the U.S. had resulted in some of the best items from the range launching in 1982 such as the AT-AT Walker. The release of *Star Wars* on video and television had been the result of hard negotiating between 20th Century-Fox and Lucasfilm (with the latter apparently hard-pressed to let it go) but few could have complained about the effect these events had on Britain. *Star Wars* had been catapulted into the forefront of media coverage once more and had generated headlines that were a dream for any publicist. The level of interest in *Star Wars* had been underlined in a dramatic way, with the saga appearing to be up-to-date and viable. Merchandise-producing companies could not have failed to take note, especially with the large number of firms already launching successful new *Star Wars* lines during the course of the year.

Lucasfilm and 20th Century-Fox may have been pleased by the fact that there was not an army of rival science fiction films seeking to challenge or cash in on *Revenge of the Jedi*. Other large films such as *Octopussy, Superman 3, Spacehunter: Adventures in the Forbidden Zone* and *WarGames* were going to be released around the same time, but on the whole, the sixth chapter of the *Star Wars* saga would have an unchallenged sci-fi run. Legions of fans could hardly wait.

Chapter 10

The Force Returns

Nineteen eighty-three was certainly a year of promise for *Star Wars* fans. A new *Star Wars* commercial, which began airing on January 1, started with a narrator stating dramatically, "Darth Vader has found the hiding place of the Millennium Falcon." Darth Vader's TIE Fighter was shown moving past the camera and the Millennium Falcon guarded by Rebel Hoth rebel soldiers. A human hand assisted R2-D2 to board before the ship took off. Fantastic photography placed the camera inside the Millennium Falcon and the figures appeared to be life-sized. Luke rotated in the gunner's chair and Darth Vader was shot down. "Is this the end of Darth Vader?" asked the narrator. "Only you can decide with *Star Wars* toys."

The editorial for the January *Star Wars Monthly* was: "Happy New Year! And what a year it's going to be. In case you had forgotten, 1983 is the amazing year that will finally bring us the long-awaited *Revenge of the Jedi*. Yes, this wonderful film is slowly but surely getting nearer and nearer to its release date. Until then however, we hope we can keep you amused with our Marvelous monthly. So now that you have finished the Christmas pudding, sit down and relax with your captivating copy of *Star Wars Monthly*"[1] This issue brought the post–*Empire* storyline back on course with David Micheline's "Golrath Never Forgets." Luke was exonerated for killing Shira Brie at a hearing at the Rebel base when he presented evidence that she had been an Imperial agent. With Shira gone, Luke and Leia seemed to be growing closer but the Rebels subsequently found that one of its personnel had in his possession a crystal from their previous base on the planet Golrath which had somehow recorded the events that happened around it. (Golrath had been introduced in the story "Crimson Forever" in the 1983 annual). Fearing that the Empire, who had since garrisoned the planet, would discover that shining a light through similar crystals found in and around their old base would reveal some of their secrets, the Rebels launched an attack on Golrath and destroyed the base. Coincidentally, the freshly demoted Imperial officer who had been in charge of the Imperial armada had been put in charge of the base on Golrath. Even though the facility and the promising lead to the rebels had been reduced to rubble, he still boarded a shuttle that was due to take him to report to Darth Vader. A further demotion seemed unlikely at that stage!

At this time, I considered that both the storytelling and the art featured in the monthly comic had reached an extremely high level. This was clearly the actual continuing story of Star Wars, *leading up to* Revenge of the Jedi. *I got a sense however that the search for Han Solo had been sidelined considerably. Even if the main cast of Rebels had been ordered by*

their superiors to concentrate on tackling the Empire, they would at the very least have kept tabs on the Rebel agents who were out in the field attempting to establish what had happened to Han.

The Sunday Express Saga Begins

An unexpected bonus for fans arrived on Sunday January 2: *The Sunday Express Supplement Magazine* began printing the *Star Wars* comic strip, written by Archie Goodwin and with art by Al Williamson. The inclusion of the strip was part of Lucasfilm's promotional drive for *Revenge of the Jedi*, with the first story of 1983 featuring Admiral Ackbar who was due to appear in the film. Incredibly well-drawn and with accurate renditions of the characters, spacecraft and other hardware, the strip soon became a favorite with fans. Internationally, Goodwin and Williamson's first strip had been printed on February 9, 1981. They had taken over the writing and art duties of the comic strip, after their adaptation of *The Empire Strikes Back* had proved so popular, and the existing writer-artist of the strip Russ Manning became unwell. Goodwin had already created much of the *Star Wars* expanded universe, given his previous stewardship of the Marvel comic. He had also co-plotted the comic strip with Manning towards the end of his run under the pseudonym "Russ Helm." In addition to producing the art for *The Empire Strikes Back* comic adaptation for Marvel and also the "Crimson Forever" story, Williamson had submitted two weeks of strips based on the opening scenes of *Star Wars* for consideration by the *Los Angeles Times* when the strip was first being planned. But Williamson's commitment to another strip, *Secret Agent X-9*, meant that he ended up turning down the assignment. Now that he had flung himself into the *Star Wars* universe, he sought to make his artwork as realistic as possible. Eagle-eyed readers could sometimes spot that depictions of the spacecraft were often based on the *Star Wars* die-cast toys that Williamson could hold in one hand and draw them from any angle. Williamson also referred to a wealth of photographs from the films and used life models (including members of his family) to pose for his initial sketches. Even after going to these lengths, Williamson still strived for greater perfection with the strips. "I wish I could do them a little better," the artist said with typical modesty. "In fact, quite a lot better but they haven't complained yet."[2] Fans cut the *Star Wars* comic strip out of the *Sunday Express Supplement* every week, often sticking them in scrapbooks.

David Robertson became a fan of Williamson's work via the *Sunday Express* strip. "I became aware of him when he did the Marvel Comics adaptation of *The Empire Strikes Back*. Back then I could instinctively tell that his artwork was superior to other stuff being published. Its classical style clicked with me and, coupled with the excitement about a new *Star Wars* film, it was irresistible. I cut a bunch of them out of a huge pile of *Sunday Express* magazines that were sat in the back of my biology classroom in the late '80s. They really are beautiful"[3] While the comic strip was ordinarily published in black-and-white (or at the most with some fairly basic coloring), the British version had been transformed into a painterly delight. Each colorful panel could have been framed and hung in a gallery.

Goodwin wrote the comic strip as an extended prequel to *The Empire Strikes Back*, beginning with the Rebels attempting to find a new planet to build a base, while defending their existing Yavin IV base from Imperial attacks. The Empire was so concerned about

Top: My own self-made compilation of the *Star Wars* comic strip from the *Sunday Express*. Time has taken its toll. *Above:* The first instalment of the *Sunday Express* strip.

suffering another damaging defeat that a full-scale attack was not launched against the Rebels and a blockade put up in an attempt to keep the rebels hemmed in, as had been depicted by the Marvel storyline. Somehow a weapon as awesome as the Death Star had been destroyed by the Rebels by unknown means and the fact that Luke, a powerful user of the Force, was defending the base was known to the Empire. Since the Marvel *Star Wars* comic left the story in such a position, the comic strip forms the bridge between the end of the Marvel post–*Star Wars* story "Dark Lord's Gambit" and *The Empire Strikes Back*, forming an unbroken storyline from *Star Wars* to the third film chapter and beyond.

Although working in a time period set in the past made plotting easier than constructing a current story leading up to a new *Star Wars* film, Goodwin still found himself working within someone else's universe. He said,

My interest is generally a little more toward plotting than character, anyway. So it doesn't bother me not having control over the characters. Actually, I find it kind of a relief in a way, because it sometimes seems to me that on a regular [comic] book you become so involved in the characters' lives that maybe you become a little boring. Lucas has created a lot of nice archetypes and they're all basically fun to write. Han is a little funnier and off-the-wall. Luke is a little bit more of a problem to write, just because you don't know where he's going to wind up; it gets a little trickier.[4]

The comic strip story was written in such a way that the Sunday installments provided a roundup of the week's events. Monday to Saturday, the strips only filled in the small details. In that way, readers on Sundays could follow the story without realizing that they had missed anything. It was in the spirit of *Star Wars* to begin in the middle of the action and that was exactly the case with the *Sunday Express* comic strip. American and Canadian fans had been able to read a considerable build-up to the story including Luke's initial encounter with the planet Hoth, so readers in Britain had to catch up quick. The *Sunday Express Supplement* comic strip saga began with Han, Leia, Chewbacca and C-3PO picking up Luke and R2-D2 from Hoth in the Millennium Falcon. Luke felt that the planet would make an ideal base. The Mon Calamari were valuable potential allies for the Rebel Alliance but the delegation led by Admiral Ackbar had been ambushed by the Empire before a meeting with the rebels could take place. The rebel heroes set out to rescue Ackbar and his crewmates from the remote planet they had crash-landed upon, but had to deal with the local Imperial garrison and a clutch of giant serpents for good measure.

I was extremely pleased, to say the least, to begin collecting the Sunday Express *comic strip, especially as Han Solo was featured strongly. I constructed my own comic book out of the individual installments. As my dad bought the paper every Sunday, I never ever missed a single edition. Looking back, I wonder if he began buying the* Sunday Express *because he knew that I'd like the* Star Wars *strip (he spotted it, not me). My devotion to the saga had become pretty extreme by then. If that is the case, I hope that he realized how much it meant to me and I should say a belated, "Thanks, Dad."*

Revenge *Updates*

The cover of the February issue of *Fantastic Films* was eye-catching: A banner above the magazine title promised "*Revenge of the Jedi*—New Facts and Photos." A terrific cover painting depicted Yoda alongside Jen from *The Dark Crystal* and E.T. from *E.T. the Extra-Terrestrial*. Inside there was a detailed report on a *Revenge of the Jedi* presentation that had taken place at the Chicago 40th Annual World Science Fiction Convention, by Lucasfilm vice-president Sid Ganis and executive producer Howard Kazanjian. While few British fans would have made the journey to the convention, the article provided a vivid picture of the events. Ganis and Kazanjian brought with them a 10½-minute film showing the behind-the-scenes process of creating various new alien characters, including a pig guard and a musical troupe. There was also footage of the shooting of the Tatooine battle scene that fans had previously been introduced to in various articles and Ralph McQuarrie artwork. A question-and-answer session with Ganis and Kazanjian confirmed that all of the main cast members would be returning, Yoda would be included again on Dagobah and Jabba the Hutt would be seen. Ben Kenobi would return in his ghostly form and be featured more extensively this time. John Williams was on board to write the score. The film was due for release in America and the United Kingdom on May 25. The article included a fantastic double-page photograph of Han, Chewbacca and others being captured by Imperial troops in a jungle environment. What was described as a chicken walker (Scout Walker) loomed above them menacingly. *Bantha Tracks* #17 featured a photograph of Admiral Ackbar, who was becoming the poster boy for *Revenge of the Jedi*. The caption read, "In *Star Wars*, Princess Leia leads only a small part of the Rebel Alliance. The Commander of the entire Rebel Fleet is Admiral Ackbar—a member of the Mon Calamari race of master chess players from the water planet Dac. We'll see Admiral Ackbar and the amphibious Mon Calamari in the next chapter of the *Star Wars* saga: *Revenge of the Jedi*." Sound designer Ben Burtt, interviewed in this issue, said, "None of my rough cut is approved yet because neither George [Lucas] or Richard Marquand has heard it. They're waiting for a rough cut [of the entire film] to see the film for the first time. I've seen the rough version—I'm probably the only one outside of the editors who has seen the whole movie—*it's great!*"[5]

A fantastic source of information on the upcoming film came in the form of a special *Revenge of the Jedi* supplement to the *Yuma Daily Sun*, Yuma, Arizona, being the American city where the Sail Barge scenes had been filmed. It was originally released in May 1982; the publishers subsequently placed an advertisement in *Starlog* allowing fans all over America to obtain a copy. Since the minimum order was five issues, there were plenty of spares which could be sent to penpals in Britain. The 20-page magazine was a fantastic item, including a wealth of photographs and interviews with the cast and crew. Lucas shed light on the nitty-gritty world of financing films which fans, giddy with excitement over *Star Wars,* may not have immediately considered. "If this film is as big a hit as the last film, then one might conceivably be willing to take the risk [to make another] if one could figure out a way of making it for the same costs that this one was made for. But you know that you can't in this world. You're talking about three years from now, and you're talking about everything costing 20 to 30 percent more than it costs right now… [E]ven though they're giant, huge hits they cost such tremendous amounts to make."[6] This was a rare admission from Lucas that, even after all of the announcements from Lucasfilm, the *Star Wars* film saga may not actually extend beyond the upcoming chapter.

I did not have any American pen friends in 1982 and I did not manage to obtain a copy of the Revenge of the Jedi Yuma Daily Sun *until I won one at an auction at a* Star Wars *convention in Australia. It had been donated by Lucasfilm Fan Club staff writer Lisa Cowen, a guest of honor. This example seemed to be very well-traveled and when I saw an owner's name written inside, I understood how true that was. In my late teens, I had learned via some friends that a* Star Wars *fan named Bob Bains lived apparently only a mile or two from me. As hard as I tried, I could never find Bob. Well, to my surprise the name written inside the* Yuma Daily Sun *was Bob's! He had evidently obtained this copy from an American pen friend, had then sent it to Lisa Cowen in America, who had brought it with her to the Australian convention and donated it to the auction. I won it and brought it back to Britain, only a mile or so from where it came from! So, my message is: "Bob, where are you?"*

Bantha Tracks #18 profiled Stuart Freeborn. Despite his considerable contribution to the *Star Wars* films (creating makeups including Chewbacca, Yoda, Tauntauns, Sand People and many of the Cantina creatures), he had remained fairly anonymous in previous Making of coverage. The veil of secrecy was such that *Revenge of the Jedi* was hardly mentioned in the article except for Freeborn constructing a new Yoda. He also stated: "We've mostly finished shooting creatures in the sets in England but now we're going over to the States to shoot them on location. We'll have to make a batch of new costumes for filming over in the States, because we'll be fitting completely different actors."[7]

There was a definitive statement in this issue regarding the title of the film:

> Both *Revenge of the Jedi* and *Blue Harvest* were working titles for the third film in the *Star Wars* Saga trilogy, "The Adventures of Luke Skywalker." *Revenge of the Jedi was* used during filming at EMI Elstree Studios in England, while *Blue Harvest* was used by our crews during filming in Yuma, Arizona and Crescent City, California, U.S.A. *Return of the Jedi* has always been the title of the film and appears on the first draft of George Lucas' script. For now, and evermore, we'll call it by its proper name…. *Return of the Jedi*!![8]

There was also a page of exclusive photographs from the new film including portrait shots of the main cast members and of a new alien character named Nien Nunb. The April *Star Wars Monthly* provided confirmation of the *Return of the Jedi* title via a statement in the "Cosmic Correspondence" section.

A *Return of the Jedi* teaser poster by Drew Struzan consisted of a large depiction of Darth Vader and a smaller image of the Dark Lord dueling with Luke Skywalker. A number of posters had been printed with the title *Revenge of the Jedi* and they have subsequently become very valuable. Derek Dorking says,

> I remember how there was this great expectation before *Return of the Jedi*. People had seen that cliffhanger with Han Solo frozen in carbonite and wanted to see what was going to happen. The reaction to the first trailer was stupendous. People were saying "This looks fantastic" and couldn't wait to see it. A lot of the publicity was self-generated because people were so excited. The advertising saying that the story will complete. The fact that it was initially called *Revenge of the Jedi* stirred up a lot of interest in the film. When the title changed, all of the cinemas were told to destroy the *Revenge* trailers. The posters that we had been sent had to be ripped up too, although I couldn't help but keep one for myself.

The April *Starlog* sported a fantastic new photograph on the cover of the main cast at the controls of a spacecraft. The heading was "First look: The Next *Star Wars* Saga." This was the first extensive news on the film that had been released, so this issue was a must for many fans. Anthony Daniels was able to provide a few tidbits about *Return of the Jedi*, without giving anything away. "I must say when I read the script, I put it down, rang the producer and told him I loved it."[9] *Return of the Jedi* producer Howard Kazanjian explained why security on the film had to be so tight. "George, Steven and other successful filmmakers have seen themselves ripped off by other people. They don't want to see their characters show up on television three months before the movie opens. There were only *three* full scripts in existence. All of our actors, even Dave Prowse, only received *their* sections of the script."[10] The article included some tantalizing photographs including Darth Vader at an Imperial parade with some sinister red-cloaked guards, Han Solo in the midst of a forest battle scene and a pig-faced alien described as Jabba the Hutt's bodyguard. In a *Mediascene Preview* interview, Richard Marquand was able to be a little bolder in his revelations about the film:

There are many new characters. We meet the emperor, which is a tremendous throw. He's played by a brilliant English actor named Ian McDiarmid, who has worked principally for the National Theatre. He gives a shattering performance that will scare the pants off you. It's a difficult part to play, because he's got to top some very bad people. We meet Jabba the Hutt. You couldn't guess how amazing he is. He comes high on my list of surprises, I could not believe that this character could work with me as an actor. I'd give him eye movements, arm movement, motivations, turn your head, slow up, do this, do that, wonderful!

Jabba the Hutt was one of the most eagerly anticipated of the new characters. He had been mentioned in the two previous films but not seen, and a veil of secrecy still surrounded him during the buildup to *Return of the Jedi*. "There's a wonderful character who's sort of a layabout hanger-on, a drinking buddy of Jabba named Bib Fortuna," Marquand continued. "He's taller than Darth Vader with kind of a ghastly slug-like pinkish color, as though he's never seen the sun. Then there's Admiral Ackbar, who is a Calamari man. The admiral involves the whole Calamari race in the Rebel fight at the climax. He brings his battalions of space ships into the conflicts, and masterminds the final attack. He's a glorious character."[11]

Shaun Dawkins, not simply content to read reports in the media, had his own ideas on how to gather extra information on the new film:

There were various rumors going around about the title. Is it *Revenge*? Is it *Return*? It was a year of anticipation. I managed to get hold of a couple of the actors from the film. I met with Caroline Blakiston who played Mon Mothma and she told me that the sets were very impressive. I managed to find Ian McDiarmid in a play, who refused to let me interview him until I bought a ticket! He didn't give away too much but told me that there was a lot of interaction between Luke Skywalker and Darth Vader, so I had an idea that it was going to be something special. By this time, I had gotten very active with *Star Wars*. I had pen friends all over the place and I had some of my star interviews printed by fan produced magazines in America and Germany. A Thames Television program called *Freetime* contacted me—they got me up there with my collection and to talk about *Star Wars*. I even sent some of my typed interviews and photographs of the stars to *Bantha Tracks*. The Americans had a fascination with the British stars but at that time very few had ventured on to the American convention circuit, so people over there had very little access to them."

The Search for Han Solo

The April issue of *Star Wars Monthly* featured David Michelinie's "The Search Begins," where the main cast of characters had finally been given leave by their superiors to make a concerted search for Han Solo. Although the rebels were aware that Boba Fett had Han in his possession, frozen in carbonite, they believed that the bounty hunter had yet to rendezvous with Jabba the Hutt. Leia and C-3PO took charge of a two-seat Y-Wing, Chewbacca and Lando boarded the Millennium Falcon and Luke and R2-D2 flew in an X-Wing, with all of them heading off in different directions. On the trail of the bounty hunter Dengar, Leia and C-3PO traveled to the planet Mandalore, where she encountered a human slavery operation which had the support of the local Imperial garrison. An armed group which at first seemed to be led by Boba Fett was attempting to tackle the slavers. But the individual dressed in the iconic costume was Fenn Shysa. Shysa and his colleague Tobbi Dala had been part of a unit of identically clad Mandalorian Supercommandos who had fought with Boba Fett as their leader, on the side of the Emperor in the Clone Wars. Out of 212 Supercommandos, only Fett, Shysa and Dalla had survived the wars. Fett went on to become a bounty hunter, while his two remaining comrades had returned to Mandalore to tackle the slavers. The swaggering Shysa operated a "Robin Hood and his Merry Men" operation from the woods. Leia and C-3PO were captured by the local Imperials and transported to the Imperial's base, constructed inside the gargantuan skeleton of a long-dead beast. One of the Stormtroopers on guard was in fact Fenn Shysa in disguise. He freed Leia, C-3PO and Tobbi Dala and led them on a rampage which did not leave a great deal left of the base. Dala was killed, leaving Shysa and Boba Fett as the two remaining Mandalorian Super-commandos. "The Search Begins" was an exciting turn of events as it seemed that, on the eve of *Return of the Jedi*, the comic was depicting the events that were leading directly up to it. The story contained the most detailed description of the Clone Wars printed up until that time. The facts surrounding Boba Fett's past seemed 100 percent official, matched what had been previously printed in *Bantha Tracks* and was gladly added to the knowledge base of fans. Also in the story was an early depiction of a Scout Walker vehicle that would be featured in *Return of the Jedi*.

The Marvel *Star Wars Summer Special* cover featured a color photograph of Luke with Yoda on his back. Inside there was a reprint of the Alan Moore-Steve Moore stories which, depending on a fan's point of view was either a bargain or a huge disappointment.

Palitoy's Campaign Begins

In April, Munro/Deighton launched another major competition for *Star Wars* Toys via double-page promotions in selected children's publications and also distributed attractive leaflets to toy stores nationwide. The May edition of *Star Wars Monthly* contained a double-page advert featuring the competition, which looked stunning in full color. The in-store leaflet contained an exciting comic strip which featured Luke battling a squad of Stormtroopers and encountering a clutch of AT-AT Walkers. The strip ended on a cliffhanger, with an unseen assailant challenging Luke. The winner of the competition would be the fan who drew the most imaginative continuation of the scenario, based solely on a gnarled yellow hand depicted in the final panel of the strip. It was telling that new characters such as Nien Nunb, Admiral Ackbar and the red robed Imperial Guard were featured prominently in the color painting. "Craig and I picked up a pair of Palitoy competition leaflets in our local toy shop," says Gary Harvey. "We were so caught up in the excitement surrounding *Return of the Jedi* that we thought that the comic strip contained events that would actually take place in the film! We didn't take part in the competition but we came up with lots of ideas regarding whose hand that was, because we were convinced that it would be a new character in the film."

In readiness for the new film, Palitoy began issuing *Star Wars* and *Empire* figures in *Return of the Jedi* packaging. No new characters from the film were featured on the photograph on the reverse of the backing card and TIE Fighter Pilot, Zuckuss and 4-Lom were still excluded. The backing card advertised an offer for a mail-away Nien Numb figure from *Return of the Jedi*. The offer was also featured on Kenner-carded figures released by Palitoy, with the text covered with a sticker that described the British details of the offer. The Battle Damaged X-Wing toy was changed for the *Return of the Jedi* range, so that it actually resembled its American counterpart. For the first time, the X-Wing was derived from the Kenner tooling molds, was cast in a light gray color, had a smoked canopy and featured an activation button for the light and sound feature. But examination of the toy revealed that there was not a red light in the nose, nor were there any electronics inside, and the box for the battery

Above and following two pages: **A major competition in 1983 was advertised via this colorful leaflet.**

HOW TO ENTER

Would you like to be one of the first to see the Third Chapter in the Star Wars® Saga–the new film 'Return of the Jedi'?™ You would? Then take a look at the unfinished story above.

Using that as a starting point we want you to complete this exciting Star Wars® adventure. That means letting your *imagination* run wild.

And as it's your story you can introduce any new characters you like. They can be Rebels, bounty hunters–or perhaps, someone–or something from the Dark Side of the Force™ You might even invent some droids or space vehicles (or discover a deadly space monster).

It's up to you. Once you've thought of your story draw and colour it in, on a *single* sheet of paper, and send it to us – with the official entry form you'll find overleaf.

But don't forget, the judges are looking for the most *imaginative* and *exciting* story.

was a dud. This was a strange hybrid which sported the much-improved styling of the Kenner version but lacked the internal workings. Palitoy was supplied with the new X-Wing by the Meccano factory in France. There were still large stocks of the original white X-Wing at Palitoy, so both varieties were issued at the same time. The same airbrushed picture from the *Empire Strikes Back* packaging was used, with the text printed in English on one side and French on the other, which seems fitting for a Palitoy-Meccano product. There is also evidence that this new gray X-Wing was issued in the *Empire* packaging early in 1983.

Palitoy released two new vehicles in its own *Return of the Jedi*-branded packaging that had been part of the 1982 American range from *Empire*. The Scout Walker was a hugely exciting item, considering how it had been part of *Star Wars* marketing since 1980 and would be featured in *Return of the Jedi* (although the picture on the box depicted Hoth). The toy could be made to walk with the assistance of a child's hand, via a clever manually operated mechanism. The design had been based on the version seen in *Empire*, which had been intended to hold a single pilot (and even replicated the tiny gargoyle-like image on the side of the film prop). The second new release, the Rebel Transport was a mighty flagship for the Rebel's toy forces and doubled as a carry case for *Star Wars* figures.

"For my fourth birthday, I was given a maximum of £10 to spend at the Kind Thoughts toy shop in Ebbw Vale," says Grant Criddle. He continues,

> This was perfect, because it guaranteed an Action Man doll. Most of what happens next was recounted to me by my mother and babysitter at the time. Apparently, just before reaching the toy shop, I have a joy meltdown, running up to the shop window, yelling "AT-AT! AT-AT!" This was very uncharacteristic of me as I would be a shy child in public. I dashed into the shop before my mother and babysitter could catch me and actually began dismantling the shop window to reach the toy. Although an AT-AT was way outside our agreed birthday budget at £30.00, an agreement was made by my babysitter and mother to purchase one. The AT-AT needed some figures to go with it as well, so an AT-AT Commander and TIE Fighter Pilot were also purchased. Looking back, what surprises me is that I had not seen *The Empire Strikes Back*. Yet a child's mind, that had seen *Star Wars* for the first time a few months' prior, knew exactly what an AT-AT was. Lucasfilm and Palitoy had indeed found a way to bottle lightning.

The 1983 Airfix Modelers Manual was an exciting item for *Star Wars* fans. The futuristic looking cover featured an X-Wing Fighter and inside, there were three pages dedicated to *Star Wars*. All of the kits from the previous year were still available but there were some new additions including Boba Fett's Slave One spacecraft in 1:76 (HO) scale. The X-Wing Fighter was made available by Airfix too. The *Rebel Base* diorama was in the same scale as the *Battle on Hoth*, and contained identical Snowspeeders and figurines as its predecessor, along with a host of new items: miniature X-Wing Fighters, Y-Wing Fighters, the Millennium Falcon, a Rebel Transport ship and an array of equipment, along with a plastic diorama base to lay it all out on. This set had the same problems with the comparative scale of the figurines and vehicles as the *Battle on Hoth* diorama but this was of little concern to anyone but the most discerning modeler. Three new kits from *Return of the Jedi were* also included in the catalogue but **Top Secret** signs had been laid over the photographs. The Imperial Shuttle Tydirium, Speeder Bike and a "finely detailed replica" would be available alongside the new film.

I was a very glad recipient of the Rebel Base *diorama. I had bought the* Battle on Hoth *and combining the two sets was incredible. If I could pick out the best-ever products made*

for Star Wars, *the two miniature dioramas would be near the top. Being a very keen model maker and with a fishing box full of junk at my disposal, I constructed the main doors of the Rebel base. I also added the fins that stick out from behind the Y-Wings that were missing from the miniatures. Independent model shops often sold kits at knock-down prices (our local one must have been crazy) and I soon had a few of these sets and I believe Gary picked some up too. What better than to set up huge dioramas in miniature, complete with ground crew and equipment? If only the Imperial forces had been the focus of similar dioramas, it would have presented a perfect model making situation.*

The Jedi *Press Blitz*

In May, *Return of the Jedi* began to be featured in every area of the press, adding to the sense of excitement that the film had very nearly arrived. A one-sheet poster, painted by Tim Reamer, depicted a pair of hands holding aloft a lightsaber. Adverts began appearing in the press with an application form for booking tickets at the Dominion Tottenham Court Road and Odeon Marble Arch to see the film from June 2. The advert also stated that there was a *Return of the Jedi* display at the Harrods department store in London. The display was well worth seeing as it contained a life-sized Speeder Bike, pre-production paintings, model props and mannequins dressed in costumes used in the movie. H.C. Ford entered into *Return of the Jedi* merchandising early with new products. One was the Square Pencils that had been issued the previous year but displayed in a square plastic display box featuring Darth Vader from the *Return*

As part of an all-out promotional blitz, tickets for *Return of the Jedi* in London could be booked via the post.

of the Jedi teaser poster. Record Erasers were also released. Molded in gray, yellow, pink and blue, they looked exactly like miniature vinyl records. The display box also featured the teaser poster art. Advance merchandising such as this was extremely valuable to *Return of the Jedi*. All of the products that had been released by various companies in 1982 were still available.

The June issue of *Film Review* contained this statement:

> June 2 is a red letter day in the filmgoer's calendar. It marks the British launch of *Return of the Jedi*, the latest *Star Wars* film. Every moviegoer in the world testifies to the magnitude of *Star Wars* and *The Empire Strikes Back*, and now *Return of the Jedi* establishes the trilogy as a genuine and unique cinema culture. Just as the dwarf character Yoda was kept secret until *Empire* was released, so does a cloak of secrecy envelop a weird creature in *Jedi*—Jabba the Hutt—and for this reason we cannot picture him at this stage. Most of the new characters in *Jedi* are in the Creature category. An incredible array of barely conceivable intergalactic denizens populates the film.[12]

"I became aware of the *Return of the Jedi* publicity on hoardings around Wembley Stadium," says Joe Sales. "It was during the England vs. Scotland British Championship home international that May. The advertising around the pitch was for the film too." Much of the press coverage centered on Carrie Fisher, who was in London to promote *Jedi*'s opening. Her tabloid currency had increased yet further, due to her relationship with singer Paul Simon. Newspapers were just as interested in Fisher's celebrity lifestyle as they were about *Jedi*. A *Daily Mirror* article entitled "Princess Fantasy" interviewed Carrie Fisher, pictured dressed in a sailor's outfit, in the style of actor Cary Grant. Apparently the actor was Fisher's fantasy man "if only he was a few years younger," according to the reporter.[13] *The Sun* located a photograph of a new *Jedi* creature: Wicket the Ewok, which the newspaper claimed was a major exclusive. The article also included a photograph of Jabba the Hutt, with Princess Leia in a bikini-like costume. News stories highlighted the strange new creatures in *Jedi*, although few photographs emerged. A feature in the *Daily Mirror* focused on the character Bib Fortuna, under the title "*Star Wars* Nasty! The face of evil in the new space epic." The article pointed out that the film had been awarded a PG rating, meaning that children under 15 might need to be accompanied by an adult.

Jedi *Reading Matter*

As had been the case with its predecessors, *Return of the Jedi* was preceded by a novelization of the film. The book contained eight pages of color photographs, including images of the top-secret Ewoks and Jabba the Hutt. The novel was by James Kahn, whose connection to *Star Wars* came via Steven Spielberg's *E.T. the Extra-Terrestrial*. The film's production team had contacted the emergency room at St. John's Hospital in Santa Monica, California where Kahn was serving as a doctor. Initially advising on how an alien might be resurrected and contributing medical dialogue, Kahn and his colleagues were cast in the film as the medical team who attempt to revive E.T. Taking his chance, Kahn—already a published author—handed Spielberg one of his novels during the filming, and this resulted in him being commissioned to write the *Poltergeist* novelization. The *Return of the Jedi* novel followed, along with *Indiana Jones and the Temple of Doom*, *The Goonies* and *Poltergeist II*. Kahn has since written extensively for television, contributing to *St. Elsewhere, ER, Xena:*

Warrior Princess and many others. The *Return of the Jedi* novel contained significant information not included in the film. In their conversation on Dagobah, Ben Kenobi revealed to Luke that he had dueled with Anakin Skywalker and that he had fallen into a molten pit, so making official the Poster Monthly article written by John May in 1977. But the major revelation that Owen Lars was in fact Ben Kenobi's brother would not be cemented into Lucasfilm's *Star Wars* lore.

1987 saw the launch of the West End Games *Star Wars* role-playing game that replaced the expanded universe that I have described in this book. When I wrote to WEG to explain they had failed to include among other things in their new expanded universe, the connection between Ben Kenobi and Owen Lars, a senior representative wrote back asking me where I got this information. I found it astounding that even though almost every other *Star Wars* publication had been cast aside, the ROTJ novel had not remained sacrosanct. It was a new beginning but the core of the original EU remained. Elements such as Darth Vader's past, the central worlds of the universe, the Emperor's name Palpatine and Vader's *Executor* flagship had become dyed-in-the-wool, so in that respect its creators had left behind a legacy.

Personally speaking, the original Star Wars *Expanded Universe is the one that exists in my imagination (the comics I deem "official" are listed in Appendix II). Even though some LFL-endorsed guides to* Star Wars *attempted to retrospectively incorporate the older material, the fact that it had been ignored in the first instance did not make this process all that successful. I do not believe that it is necessary to form one single* Star Wars *universe and that there is room for alternative visions and time lines. The Expanded Universe 1977-1983 (and even stretching to the end of the comics in '85) works perfectly well in isolation but is not necessarily better or worse than the versions that followed. Every generation deserves something new, even though the die-hards may not always go along with it. It's difficult to see the* Star Wars *you love taken in a different direction but the stamp of "canon" does not affect the universe that you see in your mind.*

Another book timed with the release of *Return of the Jedi* was *Skywalking—The Life and Films of George Lucas* by Dale Pollock. It provided an even greater insight into Lucas' early life and the making of the *Star Wars* films, along with his other work including *Raiders of the Lost Ark*. The formative years of Lucas provided a great deal of the fresh material. It seemed that in a last-ditch push for *Return of the Jedi*, Lucas had added *himself* to the final assault on the public's consciousness. The May 22 *Sunday Express Supplement Magazine* (which was still running the *Star Wars* strip) contained a Lucas profile by Dale Pollock which was based on excerpts from *Skywalking*. "Driving home, George Lucas pushed his tiny Fiat's two-cylinder engine as fast as it would go, more than 60 miles an hour," said Pollock. "[T]he car flipped over four or five times before wrapping itself around a sturdy walnut tree. Recovering in hospital, George Lucas found his mind racing almost as fast as his Fiat had once had. 'I realized that I'd been living my life so close to the edge for so long. That's when I decided to go straight, to be a better student, to try to do something with myself.'" Pollock described how this incident had transformed Lucas from being a youth obsessed with cars and speed, to a serious-minded film student who soon proved that he had other talents apart from those on the race track. Pollock quoted Lucas saying, "I had the feeling that I should go to college and I did. I had the same feeling when I decided to make *Star Wars* when even my friends told me I was crazy."[14]

Lucas' story as told in the article and in *Skywalking* was of a hard-working, self-made family man, who had plowed everything into his personal vision and had achieved success far beyond an everyday person's dreams. That in itself provided just as much of a fantasy as the *Star Wars* films and had the benefit of being very much achievable.

In the June *Star Wars Monthly*, Mary Jo Duffy's story "The Stenax Shuffle" began with Luke, Lando, Chewbacca and R2-D2 traveling to the planet Stenax on the trail of the bounty hunter Bossk. A conversation between Luke and Lando showed flashback illustrations of Han Solo being frozen. On their approach to Stenax, Luke revealed to Lando that he had visited the planet before with the regular Rebel hero lineup before the events of *Empire Strikes Back*. The story went back to a time when Leia was dressed in her white gown and space buns, Luke was in his Tatooine garb and Han was his old, un-frozen self. The group was on Stenax to check on a Rebel base that was overdue reporting in. As they walked around the crumbling streets full of gargoyle-like warriors, they couldn't have felt less at home. There was no sign of any rebels at an ancient temple that had apparently been used as their base but three old colleagues of Han's had installed themselves there: a human gunslinger called Rik Duel; an alien girl of the Zelton race named Dani; and Chihdo, who was of the same creed as Greedo. Dani was instantly attracted to Luke, which seems (at least to this author) to be more to do with the tastes of Mary Jo Duffy than genuine character motivation! Han, Luke, Leia & Company agreed to help Rik Duel and his friends find Vol, a sacred statue which was said to be buried at the temple, without which the indigenous Stenax people would not take to the sky. The hope was that if the statue was found, the Stenax warriors would begin to fly once more and would be less accommodating to the local Imperial garrison. R2-D2 and C-3PO pinpointed the rough location of where the altar once sat by deciphering some ancient text on the temple walls. Luke soon dug up the head-sized statue with some jubilation but Rik Duel and Dani took it at gunpoint. As soon as they had made their exit, Chihdo arrived at the head of a squad of Stormtroopers. The Rebel heroes were saved by Stenax warriors who had sensed that *Vol* had been found and had finally given up their land-based lives. Rik Duel, Dani and Chihdo reached their spacecraft but found the local Imperial commander waiting at the head of a squad of the Empire's finest, and they were in no mood to take prisoners. The swarm of Stenax warriors descended on all of them and Rik Duel shook his fist angrily at the escaping Millennium Falcon as spears filled the air around him. With *Return of the Jedi* so close, "The Stenax Shuffle" neatly brought the plight of Han Solo to the forefront of the story and reminded readers of the events of *Empire Strikes Back*.

✳ ✳ ✳

This issue of the comic was an instant purchase for me. From then on, I did not miss a single issue until the comic folded many years later. More than ever before, I felt that the comic storyline was as real as the Star Wars *films.*

Time for Interviews

The May 23 edition of *Time* featured a fantastic cover painting of George Lucas surrounded by his famous *Star Wars* characters (a cover that he allegedly had wanted for the *Empire Strikes Back* edition but had lost out to Darth Vader). The article included brief quotes from a host of Lucasfilm-related sources, instead of an in-depth interview with a single individual. "I think *Jedi* is the best *Star Wars* movie ever made, and it is definitely going to be the most successful," said Steven Spielberg. "The effects in this film are more or less what I wanted them to be in *Star Wars*, but I didn't have the technology to carry them out," added Lucas. "The space battle is ten times more complicated than the one in *Star Wars*. If you went back and saw that one after seeing this one, it wouldn't be nearly as exciting as you remembered it."[15]

The tone of the article was upbeat, although there was room for criticism, too. "*Return of the Jedi* is a brilliant, imaginative piece of movie making", said Gerald Clarke. "But it does not diminish the accomplishment of Lucas and his youthful team to say that there are flaws nonetheless. The most obvious, ironically, is an overemphasis on effects and a too proud display of odd-looking creatures. Some otherwise breath-taking scenes, such as a visit to Jabba's lair, the hair-raising chases though the redwoods and the climactic space battle, are extended to the point of satiety. The other flaw is the ending: in all three films, Lucas has almost entirely avoided the rank sentimentality to which his story is vulnerable. In the final minutes of *Jedi*, he succumbs, however, and ends his trilogy with one of the corniest conclusions in recent years. On the other hand, the acting in *Jedi* is better than it was in the other two. Ford was always good as the likable, daredevil, cynic, but Fisher and, most importantly Hamill have broadened and matured their talents. In his final scenes with Vader, Hamill provides Luke with a hitherto unsuspected depth of personality. Despite its shortcomings, which are relatively minor in context, the film succeeds, passing the one test of all enduring fantasy: it casts a spell and envelops its audience in a magic all of its own."[16]

The June *Starburst* provided additional insights into *Return of the Jedi* via an interview with Richard Marquand:

> When I was first working on *Eye of the Needle*, I heard George Lucas was looking for a director, a new director for his next episode, and would I be interested in putting my name up. And I said, "There's no way in the world I'm going to be considered by George Lucas. Who the hell am I?" There are all these major directors looking for work. He could get anybody he wanted. They'd give their eyeteeth for a chance to direct it. But agents and other people like that, said, "What have you got to lose?" So I thought, let's go for it.

When Marquand subsequently became short-listed, Lucas set about researching the director's catalogue of work. "Documentaries I had shot at the BBC, little dramas I had done going way back. And he was doing that with other directors, both British and American. He was looking for someone who could work well, work fast, with an established cast, who was a fan of the series, who could think quickly because we had to keep the budget in check. They'd had problems with the budget on the previous film. It was about April or May of 1981. Then I got a phone call to hear I'd been chosen."

Marquand revealed that he sat down with Lucas and Laurence Kasdan to thrash out the plot of the film:

> I had a whole plan of how I wanted to present each character, each new character, to make it slightly different from the other ones, because *Empire* ends in a kind of explosion—everyone going off in dif-

ferent directions. All the characters are scattered on the four corners of the galaxy and then I could bring each one in a surprising way. And George liked that too. Larry [Kasdan] picked that up and turned it into something really terrific. Then I was talking about killing off one of the main characters. George wouldn't have that. I wanted to kill someone off—give it a kick—somewhere in the middle. No, no. He wouldn't do that.

Lawrence Kasdan was roped in as screenwriter, although he was in the middle of directing the film *Body Heat*. "[T]he three of us sat in a locked room for two, three weeks and really went through exactly what this film was and that we wanted to make."[17]

Return of the Sales Force

As the year progressed, it became clear that the *Return of the Jedi* marketing strategy was completely different from its predecessor. While *Empire* had been promoted in the traditional fashion of big Hollywood movies (sending the cast on a promotional tour, instigating Making of articles, blitzing the television schedules with content related to the film and organizing a glitzy premiere), *Return of the Jedi* had none of these things in Britain. Television coverage was blunted by an embargo on footage from the film, except for advertisements which began running in May. A selection of short clips were televised for the first time on June 2 edition of the ITV breakfast show *Good Morning Britain* and on *Film 83* on June 6. In the coming weeks, ITV's Saturday morning show *No. 73* (*Freeze Frame* in the southwest) and BBC2's *Entertainment USA* also provided brief glimpses. Carrie Fisher was the only American member of the cast or crew available in Britain for interviews during the buildup to the release of *Return of the Jedi*. Peter Mayhew and Anthony Daniels attended a regional press reception at the Manchester Odeon and also an autograph session at Harrods of London but it was hardly a drawn-out tour. Mayhew also appeared on the early morning children's program *No. 73* where he was interviewed by Sandi Toksvig. (Later in the episode, he joined in with the cast and studio audience in dancing to a live band, showing off surprisingly good dance moves.) Fisher appeared on the early morning BBC1 show *Saturday Superstore*, sitting in a circle of young people who fired questions at her. Another promotional stunt was Darth Vader accompanied by two red-robed Imperial Guards standing outside the BBC studio with signs saying "Vote Vader on the 2nd."

The May 28 *Screen International* focused on the *Jedi* promotional drive. The article revealed that the movie would enjoy a much more rapid distribution than its predecessors; all 300 prints were scheduled to be distributed by the end of July. "It's a picture designed for an immediate release," said Ascanio Branca. "You can't tell people in Liverpool they'll have to wait six months." 20th Century–Fox marketing director Colin Hankins added, "It's a much faster release pattern than the previous two, but we're so confident of this one that we don't feel we have to hold back. We've had some very important films this year, but this is definitely the biggest in terms of marketing for us. The target audience is massive—adults and children alike across the board, but the campaign is mainly geared towards the kids."[18] The article highlighted the huge merchandising drive for *Return of the Jedi*, Andrew Maconie and his office having set up a host of British companies to produce *Jedi*-related products. Private screenings at London cinemas had again been organized on behalf of licensees. There would be no repeat of the relative merchandise drought of *Empire Strikes Back*. School bags, stationery, lunch boxes, yogurt pots and transfer sets were far more valuable in spreading the news about *Return of the Jedi* than premieres and press interviews with the stars, which children were on the whole oblivious to. According to Carole Deighton,

> The anticipation generated at preview performances for *Return of the Jedi* certainly reached a peak. I guess it was because the film revealed much more about Darth Vader and his relationship to Luke and was genuinely edgy and exciting. The popularity of the toy range was still at a substantial level. And because by then, everyone was aware of the spin-off products, not just toys, it was possible to orchestrate the publicity campaign that much more effectively. We were also in the fortunate position of being able to arrange previews of *Return of the Jedi* for the press and other VIPs well before the film actually opened. There was always a policy of insuring we kept the currency of the tickets high by making guests aware they were like gold dust. I remember film reviewers begging us for tickets and Lucasfilm being adamant that they didn't want them to see it in advance of the official press screening dates as they might be tempted to run spoilers.

Promotional Pack Launch

A glossy *Return of the Jedi* promotional pack had been issued to interested parties earlier in the year, giving the impression of an extremely well-crafted campaign for *Return of the Jedi* that left nothing to chance. Printed on glossy paper, it included color text and was presented in an embossed white folder. It was a marked improvement to the very standard press packs for the previous films. The *Return of the Jedi* pack included a section on "Exploitation" which listed a number of ideas that could be used to make the most of the new film. Anthony Daniels would apparently be available for radio interviews in-character as C-3PO. A tape of an Ewok speaking would also be included, and C-3PO would translate. An interview by a radio host would however be restricted to a list of "appropriate" questions. There were the familiar templates for competitions, spot-the-difference quizzes and the like for magazines, shop owners and cinemas. An array of promotional aids were available for purchase including a set of four window stickers, a polystyrene-backed lightsaber/hands poster, a set of four 30 × 20" display posters featuring photographs against a white background and flyers (or "fan cards" as they were described) featuring Luke armed with a blaster. The "Quad" and "Feature Quad" posters and a set of "Color Theatre Stills" would be provided free of charge to cinemas. Also available was the *Return of the Jedi* trailer on video and other in other formats.

A huge amount of licensed merchandise was also listed in the promotional pack. One of the three major merchandising companies identified was Parker Brothers, which could boast of £500,000 worth of launch support for the two video games currently available and two more to be released in conjunction with the film. "Extensive advertising and promotional support" was slated for Airfix' 12 kits and an additional *Return of the Jedi* compendium kit. Palitoy would be spending £750,000 on year-round advertising at the cinema, press, comics and television.

The press pack listing the advertising of all of the major players was an innovation, and the decision by Lucasfilm to employ Andrew Maconie as a freelance promoting *Star Wars* had paid off handsomely. He and his team were used to working on the front line and had all of the key contacts at their fingertips. "Of course Palitoy remained the cornerstone licensee," says Maconie. "The company and its internal affiliates had established a broad range of licensed *Star Wars* merchandise. In addition, retail stores were given access to number of Darth Vader costumes with actors inside, which also helped to develop interest in sales of *Star Wars* merchandise."

The Menace of Darth Vader

Beginning in March, a major tour of "Darth Vader" at stores up and down the country was a very important element of *Jedi*'s promotional campaign. Appearances utilized the professional Vader costumes made by N.J. Farmer Associates that had been constructed for *The Empire Strikes Back* and were now managed by Munro/Deighton. "My agency organized nearly all of the Darth Vader in-store visits linked to the *Return of the Jedi* toy range," says Carole Deighton. She continues,

> It was such big business that [the agency] started another subsidiary company to handle all in-store appearances on behalf of our Palitoy client. Store venues were "awarded" the visits as part of their joint promotional package run by Palitoy Sales. The larger their turnover and profitability to Palitoy, the more visits and promotions they were entitled to. We also received direct requests from event organizers, cinema managers, even party planners. And if a costume was available and we felt the exposure was right (and they were prepared to pay!), we would arrange it. We combined the touring Darth Vader business with a publishing operation we ran for Palitoy for two consumer magazines supporting Airfix and Mainline Railways—and the business was profitable. As part of the package, we ran the local support publicity (TV, radio, press) for each Vader appearance plus providing promotional support material—posters, handouts, stickers, free gifts, Darth Vader autographs and, with the bigger events, coordinating local advertising in advance of the appearance, for which we would supply the main copy and all the artwork. We worked closely with Palitoy's marketing and sales teams and I'm certain they appreciated the enormous value to them of the highly successful p.r. and promotions campaign we implemented to support the toy range.
>
> There were several effective strategies in place to exploit the "live" visits of Darth Vader. We would aim to get the maximum pre-publicity to attract a good audience and then create the greatest impact for the appearance with an exciting buildup involving a special DV introduction at the location, autograph signing (even with him wearing his huge gloves!), plus general menacing behavior, all with the *Star Wars* theme music booming out in the background.

Darth Vader appearances were also being organized from Queens Gate Mews, using Nick Farmer-produced outfits. "We used to send out Dave Prowse to do costume appearances," recalls Jackie Ferguson. "The manager of one department store phoned me after one event and said, 'That was absolutely ghastly.' My mind was full of possibilities, such as people not having turned up. The man then explained that so many hundreds of people had wanted to see Darth Vader that they had completely wrecked that floor of his store in the crush!"

The Darth Vader appearances made a lasting impression on fans. "I met Darth Vader the other day," wrote Sonia Dibble from Berkshire, in a letter printed in *Star Wars Monthly*. "He was signing autographs and I finally got his signature. Also in the shop was a local DJ, who kept poking fun at him. Darth Vader silenced him by grabbing him by the throat. For a moment it seemed that Vader was going to silence him forever but the Dark Lord's attention was taken by some children wanting his autograph, so he let the man go."[19] Frank Mewes remembers that the Darth Vader he met was hardly an actor of the method school. "I was eight when my mother took me to a local toy shop where Darth Vader was making an appearance. As he strode past me, he stepped on my foot. Instead of telling me to get out of the way, he said 'sorry' in his best Darth Vader voice. I would have much preferred him to say something derogatory and threaten me, in my mind at that tender age anyway!"[20]

"I remember seeing Darth Vader in Bournemouth, right on the release of *Return of the Jedi*," says Ian Whitlock. "I had seen the trailer on the Jonathan King show, *Entertainment USA*, so was quite hyped-up about the film. I bought the storybook of the film and got

Vader to sign it. I never did compare it to the Vader autograph I got back in '77 but I can't see them matching at all." Robin Kennedy recalls,

I saw Darth Vader in early 1983 at the Scotch Corner Store in Kilmarnock. The appearance was advertised in the local newspaper for the area, the *Kilmarnock Standard*, a few days before the event. My dad took along myself, my little cousin Peter and my younger brother Alastair. The queue was extremely long and we had about a 45-minute wait just to get into the shop front door and then another 25 minutes to get to the upstairs toy section of the shop. My father took a photograph seconds before I actually shook the hand of Vader. I can't fathom why he didn't wait until I was in the actual picture! I remember being a little unnerved by the experience (I was quite a shy and nervous boy at the best of times) and that Vader's grip was really strong—but then again, I was a kid!

Seemingly every kid there was getting a toy or two bought for them by their parents in attendance and that Darth was then signing them, but it was no such luck for me or my brother. We didn't get even a single £1.49 figure. Our dad took us to see Darth in the flesh and then back home!

"Darth Vader came to the Debenhams toy department in Romford, shortly before *Return of the Jedi* opened at the local cinema," says Gary Harvey. He continued:

Darth Vader stalks the streets of Southend-on-Sea as part of the 1983 costume tour (*Southend Echo*).

I went to see him with Craig and his brother Paul. There was a huge crowd of children there (admittedly most of them much younger than us). We commented that Vader didn't seem very big but we were tall lads ourselves. I remember the trailer for the film being played on a loop on a TV set and there being a huge pile of advertising flyers on a table. Craig and I kept sneaking out with huge numbers of the flyers until we were spotted one time by the staff and told to put them back! We had assumed that the flyers were provided free of charge by the film company but I found out later that Debenhams had actually paid for them. A belated "sorry" to Debenhams!

Slightly older fans were not always swept up in the excitement of seeing Darth Vader. Jordan Royce recalls, "I saw him in Debenhams in Stockport. One of my friends got something signed but I was too embarrassed. I said, 'I'm 15. I'm not getting something signed by him.' Then there was an announcement over the store Tannoy [loudspeaker] Saying, 'Will the gentleman who has parked his TIE Fighter in front of the loading bay, registration T.I.E., please remove it.' Well, we all thought it was funny."

The Return of Palitoy

Palitoy's new range of *Return of the Jedi* action figures was made available shortly before the movie opened. Reflecting the diverse nature of the new characters featured in the film were Gamorrean Guard, Bib Fortuna, Emperor's Royal Guard, Admiral Ackbar, Chief Chirpa, Logray (Ewok Medicine Man), Klaatu, Princess Leia Organa (Boushh Disguise), Rebel Commando, Weequay, Squid Head, General Madine, Ree-Yees, Biker Scout, Nien Numb, Rebel Commando, Lando Calrissian (Skiff Guard Outfit) and Luke Skywalker (Jedi Knight Outfit). The quality of the figures had increased with more accurate likenesses of the characters and the further use of cloth clothing. Princess Leia Organa (Boushh Disguise) and Lando Calrissian (Skiff Guard Disguise) featured the innovation of removable helmets. Many of the character names had again been based on their nicknames during production, including Squid Head, Ree-Yees and Klaatu (Michael Rennie's character name in the film *The Day the Earth Stood Still*).

The reverse of the backing card depicted all of the 65 figures available, but with Chief Chirpa and Logray (Ewok Medicine Man) obscured by a black smudge to keep their image secret. "The obscuring of the new Ewok characters was a directive we received," says Geoff Maisey. "We were contractually allowed only to 'tease' the new characters ahead of the movie release." To keep shops supplied with main characters, the assortment of figures included Han Solo in Bespin Outfit, Chewbacca and Darth Vader in Jedi packaging.

The decision for Palitoy to package the figures at Coalville was not turning out as expected. "This proved to be a mistake," Maisey continues, "as the time taken to organize and execute Hong Kong and U.K. production meant that we were even worse off than before. Unfortunately we experienced some volume shortages. The problem always was that the expectations of the toy trade and the amount of stock they ordered were lower than the amount of sales they eventually encountered."

The Munro/Deighton Consultancy prepared to handle any negative publicity that the huge over-demand for the available *Jedi* stock would inevitably attract. "This became a major story for national TV news as well as in national newspapers but all it seemed to do was stoke demand and continue to build the enormous amount of publicity behind the toys," says Carole Deighton. She continues,

There was a particular in-depth report on *BBC Newsnight* in 1983 describing *Star Wars* toys as the biggest toy phenomenon in history and referring to Palitoy as "the gold mine on a coal mine." Film crews and news photographers were frequent visitors to Coalville to film the production line in the factory. As the shortage story broke, representatives from Palitoy gave carefully scripted interviews, as by then, Palitoy had been wrongly accused of making the shortages happen deliberately. They were able to prove this was not the case, and that most of these accusations were toy-trade instigated, with buyers understandably upset they couldn't get more stock, at a time when the products were literally flying off the shelves. Inevitably, certain *Star Wars* figures became more sought-after than others and a big swap mania started with fans. This also fed more and more stories to an eager media.

Jean Duwald, writing for the May 30 *Glasgow Herald*, highlighted the near cult status that *Star Wars* action figures had attained among children. "Instead of waiting for stamps to be sent from foreign climes, relatives and friends are supplied with lists of figures missing from collections. Foot-weary grandparents anxiously scan the neat rows of merchandising packs for Walrus Man or Hammerhead in the sure knowledge that supplying a missing link will guarantee a rapturous welcome on their next visit."[21] Retailers were on the whole oblivious to their customers' desire for the more unusual characters, according to Geoff Maisey. "Retailers still refused cartons of individual figures, apart from the key ones, so Palitoy had to continue providing assortment packs, otherwise the more minor characters would never have reached the high street. The assortments were always weighted towards the key characters, so the number and variety of minor characters was very limited."

This situation would have struck a chord with many fans, I'm sure. Personally, I found certain Star Wars *figures to be non-existent in the shops and there was not the option of logging on to the Internet to make an order. Gary and I set out on a regular patrol of local shops that the Royal Marines would have been proud of, including scouring many local towns reachable by bus. The Cantina characters, the background droids or the original Princess Leia? You could forget it. That being said, the eventual reward of locating a* Star Wars *figure was so much greater. After traveling miles and miles on my patrol, I eventually purchased a Hammerhead in my local Woolworths which was only a two-minute walk from my home!*

"Return to Stenos," featured in *Star Wars Monthly* #171, picked up the story after Luke's flashback tale of visiting the planet Stenos. Luke and Lando left their traveling companions Chewbacca and R2-D2 in the Millennium Falcon while they searched for leads to the whereabouts of Han Solo. After being split from Luke during a chase, Lando declared that he had actually found Han! Luke's thoughts instantly went into flashback, with the scene of Han being frozen in carbonite being shown once more. Lando excitedly led Luke to a group of men he had spotted, pushing a block of carbonite in a fashion which was very reminiscent of Han being transported to Boba Fett's ship in *The Empire Strikes Back*. The men moved the block into a warehouse, with Luke and Lando shadowing them. The situation was truly heart-quickening as Luke and Lando approached the carbonite block which had been stood on its end. The rebel pair found to their horror that *Chihdo* was the unfortunate occupant of the carbonite block and that they had walked into a trap set by Bounty Hunters IG-88 and Bossk. The story ended dramatically, as bounty hunters and dozens of hired guns surrounded Luke and Lando. In the magazine's Cosmic Correspondence section, fans continued to share what information they had heard about the new film. One fan described a new character called Bib Fortuna and said that he had heard that Han, Luke and Leia would die in the film. There was a full-page *Jedi* advertisement featuring the hands/lightsaber poster art, stating that the film would open on June 2 in London and at leading cinemas throughout the country. Issue #171 also included the news that starting with the next issue, the comic would be titled *Return of the Jedi Weekly*, would be in full color, and that the first issue would come with a free badge.

The Eve of the Jedi

The *Return of the Jedi* trailer was still being shown at cinemas and in shortened form on television. With the growing media coverage adding to the mix, there could have been no doubt that the cinemagoing public was aware that the film had arrived. 20th Century-Fox UK, Andrew Maconie and team, Munro/Deighton and Palitoy had focused every effort possible to promote it and the early signs seemed promising. Over 25,000 ticket applications had been received by the Odeon Marble Arch and the Dominion Tottenham Court Road since the advance box office opened on April 13, with over £100,000 taken in advance sales. The switchboard at 20th Century-Fox headquarters was jammed with callers. "It's incredible, it's become like royalty, seeing the film before anyone else,"[22] said Colin Hankins, expressing a similar sentiment to the young man who was first in line to see *Star Wars* at the Dominion in 1977. "The excitement was at the same level as when *The Empire Strikes Back* was released, or even greater," says Jordan Royce. He continues,

> Me and my friends wanted answers and we knew that we were going to have the resolution of the story in some way or another. A huge question surrounded whether Darth Vader was actually Luke Skywalker's father. That and the little scene where you saw the back of Darth Vader's head under the mask in *Empire* were big subjects for me and my friends. Images surfaced in *Starburst* and from other sources showing that Han Solo had survived being frozen but there were rumors that he was going to be killed off and all sorts of theories. We all just couldn't see *Return of the Jedi* quickly enough.

According to Declan McCafferty:

> Waiting for *Return of the Jedi* was an exciting time. I had my Admiral Ackbar mail-away action figure. I had the novel which, at the time, I couldn't really follow without a visual reference so I gave up on it. I studied the "eight pages of fabulous color," though. I had been buying Marvel's *Return of the Jedi Weekly* and I think it had serialized the film just up to the introduction of the Sarlacc just as the film got released. Which was a good place, as it hadn't spoiled too much of the plot. My best friend, Ian, came into school with a Biker Scout. "Wow," I thought. "This is the new Stormtrooper-y thing for this movie." And it was as cool as ever, so it boded extremely well. That Saturday, I persuaded my mum to take me into town to see the new figures. She got me four on the condition of no pocket money for a month. I got my own Biker Scout. And that new red guard—how could I not? I picked up the all-new black costumed Luke and I got Leia Boushh too. "They have removable headgear now? We've gone up in the world," I thought. My imagination ran riot wondering how they all fitted into the film.

On May 21, a *Return of the Jedi* press preview screening took place at the Odeon Marble Arch. The event was a light year away from the preview of *The Empire Strikes Back,* where the press was wined and dined along with the entire main cast and had gave the film negative reviews. If reviewers had not been impressed by the *Gone with the Wind*-esque nature of *Empire,* they were unlikely to be bowled over by *Return of the Jedi.*

On this occasion the reviewers would merely see the film (albeit on Europe's biggest screen) and not be offered even a sausage roll. *Star Wars* fan Shane Barry was lucky enough to attend with his brother Paul:

> On Capital Radio, they said that listeners might have a chance to review the film. All you had to do was write a letter saying why you liked *Star Wars*. If they liked your letter, you could see the film and talk about it on the radio. So I wrote to them the next morning and two weeks later we got a phone call from one of the DJs asking if I could be

A key part of the national promotions was *Return of the Jedi Weekly.*

at the Marble Arch cinema in London at about seven that evening. So my brother and I went to the cinema and there we were given tickets. Our seats were right at the front and in the middle of the first row. As yellow writing rolled up the screen, I couldn't believe my eyes.[23]

There was another preview screening at the same venue at 10:30 a.m. on the 22nd. (There was probably at least four screenings taking place on the 21st and 22nd at 10:30 and 7:30 each day.) *Return of the Jedi* was released in America on the 25th to a phenomenal reaction, earning a record-breaking $6.2 million on its opening day. The British press excitedly reported on the film's Stateside success.

The hopes and dreams of a generation in Britain were resting on two hours of celluloid. From Lucasfilm's perspective *Return of the Jedi* was a film that simply had to succeed, and to ape Yoda's way of speaking, look promising it did.

Chapter 11

Return of the Jedi

A special event took place on the evening of Wednesday, June 1, that had been arranged by 20th Century-Fox and the *Star Wars* Fan Club: a *Star Wars* triple bill at the Dominion Tottenham Court Road, Odeon Leicester Square Theatre and the Odeon Marble Arch. Fans arrived at the Leicester Square Theatre to find that the cinema had erected a huge hoarding above its entrance based on the British poster for *Return of the Jedi*, which included light effects. In addition to the main cast, the poster (created by UK artist Josh Kirby) depicted many characters including Bib Fortuna, Gamorrean Guard and Boba Fett. *Star Wars* began at 7:15, *The Empire Strikes Back* at 9:30 and *Return of the Jedi* at 11:44. The latter ended at two a.m. All of the cinemas were packed, with 4500 tickets sold. At the Dominion, Darth Vader strolled onto the stage before *Empire*. This was a fantastic event which incorporated the European premiere of *Return of the Jedi* and the world premiere of the *Star Wars* triple bill. "I was a member of the Official *Star Wars* Fan Club so I couldn't wait to book my tickets," says Sarah Baker-Saunders. "I remember the excitement as my ticket arrived on the mat at home. The event was a great evening. All three movies together. Darth Vader made an appearance across the stage in the interval between movies and a huge buzz when finally *Return of the Jedi* came on, all *Star Wars* fans together!" Laurie Calvert recalls, "I was there at the Dominion with some of my friends. It wasn't black tie. You could go in your ordinary clothes. The event had a real buzz to it. There were no guests there, no actors—it was just us fans."

Shaun Dawkins was there also. "It was great because all of the venues had sold out and they had sold out to *Star Wars* fans, which was brilliant. There was a genuine sense of electricity in the air." Jane High remembers:

> An incredible atmosphere had built up by the time we all sat down in our seats to see *Return of the Jedi*. We were about to have all of the questions answered after three years of waiting. Would Han and Leia end up together? Would the Empire be defeated? Would Luke become a Jedi? Was Darth Vader Luke's father? We could hardly contain ourselves as the curtains opened and the lights dimmed but then a reel of adverts was shown. Everyone booed at the top of their lungs in a deafening noise which seemed as if it would take the roof off! The adverts seemed to go on for ages and then the lights came back on. We waited a few minutes and then the lights dimmed and the curtains parted to reveal the certificate for *Return of the Jedi*. There was huge applause and then the film began.

Paul O'Donnell from Liverpool has vivid memories of the event. "I stumbled out of the cinema at 2:30 a.m. and spent the night on the Euston Station plaza with all the Scottish football fans who were down watching England vs. Scotland at Wembley."[1] Sid Ganis from Lucasfilm attended along with Colin Hankins, Ascanio Branca and 20th Century-Fox UK press and publicity manager Sue Blackmore. Ganis remembers Branca as "just zooming around and doing absolutely everything to make the premiere a perfect one

Top: **The queue at the Manchester Odeon for** *Return of the Jedi* **was a sign of the national phenomenon that was underway (Mirrorpix). Right: Anthony Daniels came to the Forbidden Planet shop for a signing session (courtesy Derek Dorking).**

and to make business perfect. He was a good man."[2]

Return of the Jedi opened to the public at the Leicester Square Theatre, Dominion Theatre Tottenham Court Road and Odeon Marble Arch on June 2. In that day's *Daily Mail*, Dermot Pergavie's America column stated, "Even in Hollywood where they invented boosterism, they cannot find enough superlatives to tag on to *Return of the Jedi.* They're saying that there's been nothing like it in the history of the cinema and you can see it today when the film opens in Britain."[3] Colin Hankins met for a celebratory champagne breakfast on the morning of June 2 with the manager of the Leicester Square Theatre David Pacey and the assistant managing director of 20th

Return of the Jedi widened its orbit across Britain.

Century-Fox Kevin Christie. The venue was Capital Radio's Capital Cruiser bus, parked in Leicester Square. The group was joined by Philip Pinnegar and David Taylor of Capital Radio. There was plenty to celebrate since *Jedi* had shattered the record for the first seven days in the U.S. and Canada with a gross of $45,311,004 for the two countries combined. There had been a caveat in that some theaters had increased ticket prices and put on round-the-clock showings. It did not matter how the figures were crunched, there was no doubt that the film was a runaway hit. The success of this latest chapter in the *Star Wars* saga Stateside continued to be the subject of numerous British press reports.

The film shattered the all-time records at all three theaters, the former two being held by *Star Wars*, taking ticket price inflation into consideration of course. Counting the triple bill night, the total gross for the first seven days was £245,728. Anthony Daniels publicized the film by appearing at the Forbidden Planet bookshop on Saturday, June 4. All of the key provincial cinemas listed in *Screen International* also broke house records the same week: the Odeon cinemas in Manchester, Glasgow, Liverpool, Southampton, Cardiff, Newcastle, Bristol, Bradford, Nottingham, Leeds and the Birmingham and Sheffield Gaumonts. The film was released in additional venues on Sunday, June 5, breaking the British seven-day record in the process with proceeds of £1,006,081. The queues at each were reminiscent of *Star Wars'* opening in January 1978.

It was a measure of how the reputation of the *Star Wars* brand had increased since 1980, that so many British venues had lined up to immediately show the film. Even the independents had fallen into line. The venues opening *Jedi* were the Aberdeen Odeon, Blackpool Odeon, Bournemouth Gaumont, Brighton Odeon, Bude Picture House, Carlisle Studio, Cromer Regal, Deal Classic, Dorchester Plaza, Douglas Picture House, Eastbourne Curzon, Edinburgh

Odeon, Exeter Odeon, Falmouth Grand, Folkestone Curzon, Great Yarmouth Cine, Grimsby ABC, Guernsey Gaumont, Hastings Classic, Herne Bay Classic, Jersey Odeon, King's Lynn Majestic, Lancaster Studio, Lowestoft Marina, Margate Dreamland, Morecambe Empire, Newport (IOW) Studio, Newquay Camelot, Norwich Odeon, Penzance Savoy, Plymouth Drake, Portsmouth Odeon, Ramsgate Classic, Redruth Regal, Ryde Commodore, St. Austell Film Center, St. Ives Royal, Sandown Queens, Southport Classic, Southsea Salon, Swansea Odeon, Taunton Classic, Torquay Odeon, Wadebridge Regal, Westgate-on-Sea Carlton, Weston-Super-Mare Odeon, Weymouth Classic, Worthing Odeon and the Yeovil Classic. The Bognor Picturedrome and Scarborough Odeon opened it on Thursday, June 9. The Bradford Odeon, Leicester Odeon and Southend Odeon opened it on Thursday the 16th.

All of the 13 listed key cinemas in *Screen International* saw a significant drop in admissions by the second week and this was repeated in the third. While it was not playing to full houses, *Jedi* remained far and above any other film on release at the time. A steady decline at that rate would be far from a disaster, as long as there was not a complete drop-off of business. *Jedi* needed to cling on in cinemas as long as possible, so the promotions battle had only just begun.

Reviewing the Jedi

With *Jedi*'s release came the newspaper reviews. Derek Malcolm of *The Guardian* said,

Star Wars freaks will probably be split down the middle as to whether this luxuriantly moral third dose of the fable is as good as the other two. Certainly it is a well-packaged effort with enough special effects to sink everything else this summer save the forthcoming *Octopussy*. What it lacks is the freshness and sense of fun of the original, adding a sense of importance instead. Thus Skywalker & Company are required to face a more detailed set of villains.... The best special effects as usual have to be seen to be believed.... [T]here's a modicum of wit around. But you can't beat the visuals unless you are Alec Guinness and he only appears, quite literally, as a shadow of his former self. Harrison Ford is there too, by the way. He hasn't a lot to do but since he is a vastly improved actor, does it with quiet panache. The rest is noisy panache which I was hardly bowled over by."[4]

Ian Christie, writing for the *Daily Express,* said, "[T]he eyeballs are constantly astonished by spaceships tearing through the sky, and high speed bikes without wheels roaring through the forests. The minions on the side of the nasties are splendidly odious, and the furry friends of the goodies are endearing. Personally I would have welcomed a little more verbal wit. But it would be a little churlish to carp at an adventure as good-natured and visually stimulating as this one, which Richard Marquand directs with enormous verve."[5] Tom Merrin of *The Daily Mirror* said, "The boundless imagination of George Lucas has ensured that fairy tales will never be the same again. It's an epic hunk of hokum in which a grotesque gaggle of intergalactic monsters and hundreds of special effects dazzle, excite and bewilder. At times the dialogue is difficult to follow, and there's a little too much of 'with one bound our hero was free' stuff. But the film will be a monster success."[6]

Jedi was the target of some truly negative reviews. Margaret Hinxman of *The Daily Mail* was unlikely to be impressed:

One hardly has to say that the film ... is a display of cinematic pyrotechnics.... Above all there is a glorification of ugliness in *Return of the Jedi* as there was in *The Dark Crystal*. It's not only a disturbing trend but a self-defeating one. When all of the creatures—even the cuddly bears—look like happenings in a nightmare, the nightmare ceases to be alarming. It's difficult for me to be objective about the *Star Wars* trilogy. I admire the extraordinary skill and talent that has been poured into them, while finding the concept behind these puerile video games in the sky mindlessly tedious."[7] Michael Strahan wrote in his *Rolling Stone* review, "Teddy bears on parade. In the third episode of the *Star Wars* saga the human characters are completely upstaged by a sort of intergalactic FAO Schwarz window display.... [T]he plot doesn't deepen the themes or the characterizations (as it did in Irvin Kershner's *Empire Strikes Back*), and the film has an awkward, bludgeoning quality. If *Star Wars* was like a toy symphony by Haydn, and *The Empire Strikes Back* had the manic-depressive beauty of Mahler, *Return of the Jedi* has all the sophistication of a high-school graduation march."[8]

The Fan Reaction

Star Wars fans were uninterested in reviews as they scrambled to see the film. Darren Slade couldn't wait to see it. "I saw the film on the opening day with a few friends at the Bournemouth Gaumont and thought it was amazing. We saw it at least six or seven times at least over the summer." James Simmonds says,

> I was on holiday again when I saw *Return of the Jedi*. It was on June 20 at the Bournemouth Gaumont. This time I was all geared up to see the film, having seen many photographs of it in *Bantha Tracks* and in the press. The morning before seeing the film really sticks in my mind for two reasons. Firstly, I purchased the Marvel/Piccolo version of the *Return of the Jedi* adaptation from W.H. Smith and secondly, I finally found the original Princess Leia figure after years of searching—in the same W.H. Smith! I held on to both purchases tightly as I sat in the cinema watching the film. I loved *Return of the Jedi* but I loved the display of Palitoy action figures that were pinned up on the wall in the foyer even more! It looked like just about every action figure released up until that year and I wish I could have bought them! As soon as I left the cinema, I wanted to buy a Biker Scout figure. We eventually found one in a hardware store in Boscombe that same week. I vividly remember picking the figure off a revolving display and thinking that it was weird that a shop which sold hammers had action figures in it. I guess it goes to show how popular *Star Wars* was back then.

Richard Harris was not going to miss out either. "I watched *Return of the Jedi* with my family at our familiar venue, the Odeon Queen St. Cardiff. In the lobby, I was bought the *Return of the Jedi Collector's Edition* book which contained the making of the film. I was hooked on *Jedi* because of this book and was fascinated how the film was made." Shaun Dawkins also recalls the time. "I took my grandmother to see the film when it opened locally at Folkestone. She said she loved it but I think she just liked the Ewoks. Both of my grandparents had seen *Star Wars* on television when it was first shown. I remember them thinking that they just had to see it because I had been going on about it forever. I think my grandfather was a bit bemused but my grandmother liked it." Gary Harvey remembers,

> My dad arranged for me and my mum to have what he described as a special meal in London. When we came out of the Tottenham Court Road underground station, there was the giant *Return of the Jedi* sign above the Dominion Theatre on the other side of the road. I was really excited and as we crossed the road, I asked if we could buy tickets and get one for Craig. The thing is, when we walked into the cinema it dawned on me that this was the real reason for our visit to London. I excitedly bought the *Making of Return of the Jedi* novel from a small kiosk selling merchandise in the foyer and we took our seats. I was completely blown away by the film. One of my strongest memories is of a man sitting by himself a few seats away who started crying when Darth Vader died. I couldn't believe it!

The first edition of Bunch Associates' *Official Return of the Jedi Poster Magazine* appeared but the writing team behind it was completely anonymous. The editorial stated,

"What could come after *Star Wars* and *The Empire Strikes Back*? For George Lucas only the amazing feats of *Return of the Jedi* were enough. He was determined to outdo everything he has done before." Opening the magazine, the reader encountered pictures of Wicket the Ewok and Jabba the Hutt. It was not surprising that Bunch wanted to make a splash with the two secret creations of the film. The first page continued in breathless fashion, "It's as if all of the energy and sheer class of *Star Wars* and *The Empire Strikes Back* had been compressed into one earth-shattering movie. And in a sense they have. For this is the culmination of all that has gone before in that galaxy far, far away."

The magazine contained the articles "Heroics on Location" and "ILM Storming the Quota," which took the reader from the claustrophobic confines of Elstree, to the location filming in California and finally to the complicated special effects sequences filmed by ILM. "*Return of the Jedi* breaks new ground for special effects grandeur, not least in sheer quantity. More than 3000 elements were shot for more than 500 special scenes, some of which flash onto the screen for only two or three seconds. This required a logistical effort worthy of a small army fighting a couple of wars at once."[9] Bunch Associates was seeking to put Making of articles at the center of its coverage and in this respect it had the jump on other publishers.

Pocket Money Palitoy

On June 3, the Palitoy range of *Star Wars* products was the focus of an item on ITV's *Central News*, in which Bharat Patel reported that Palitoy had doubled its workforce to keep up with demand. Viewers saw the production line where workers were assembling various *Star Wars* toys. Some of the new action figure accessory toys were small enough to be affordable by most parents. The Speeder Bike seemed tailor-made for pocket money budgets and with a spring-loaded exploding mechanism there was a lot of play value for the price. There were also new Mini-Rigs: AST-5 (Armored Sentinel Transport) and ISP-6 (Imperial Shuttle Pod). The Jabba the Hutt Action Playset consisted of a very faithful reproduction of the evil crime lord, his sidekick Salacious Crumb and a throne platform which could double as a prison for his unfortunate enemies. The Scout Walker was issued in an up-to-date Kenner box featuring Ewoks instead of Hoth that had featured on the Palitoy version. In fact the entire new range of products was supplied by Palitoy exclusively in Kenner packaging, as it was stock that had been imported, rather than manufactured by Palitoy. Kenner backing cards were evident with a great number of the action figures too. Pictured on the reverse was a C-3PO carry case that was destined never to be released in the shops in Britain and a Y-Wing Fighter which was due for a 1984 British release.

Also from Palitoy, there were three action figure accessories that had been featured in the *Star Wars* films, the Radar Laser Cannon, Tri-pod Laser Cannon and Vehicle Maintenance Energizer, which unusually for a Palitoy release did not use the English spelling (energiser). The packaging for these items, featuring English logos and text on one side and French on the other, would become known as Biologo and eventually encompass the majority of the range in the coming years. The 1983 Palitoy range included the Rebel Armoured Snowspeeder, Wampa, Tauntaun with Open Belly Feature, Slave I Boba Fett's Spaceship, AT-AT All Terrain Armoured Transport, Millennium Falcon Spaceship, Battle Damaged X-Wing and the Mini Rigs INT-4, Cap-2, MTV-7 and MLC, all of which were destined to become Bilogo (along with the Jabba the Hutt Action Playset, Scout Walker, Rebel Transport and Speederbike). Even though *Return of the Jedi* was the catchword, Darth Vader's Stardestroyer Playset continued to be issued in its packaging from *The Empire Strikes Back* and, remarkably, the Darth Vader TIE Fighter was manufactured in its box from *Star Wars*.

Despite all of the rebranding, many of the Kenner toys that had been released in America in 1983 would be part of Palitoy's line-up for the following year, including the Ewok Village Action Playset, Y-Wing Fighter and Battle Damaged TIE Fighter. "I was really disappointed at the range of toys for the new film," Bob Cole recalls. "I had already spied the Scout Walker and Rebel Transport in the shops but all I could find for *Return of the Jedi* was a Speeder Bike. I was unaware that items were being held back (as I have learned since), so I felt at the time that it was only Worcester that was being deprived." Jordan Royce was still collecting too. "For some reason I loved the Jabba the Hutt playset. I was of an age where I should have been starting to grow out of the toys but I just couldn't stop. I was 15 and I just couldn't stop buying these things. I was also spying things from the first movie, such as one shop having a Cantina playset."

I found my first Return of the Jedi *figure in a news agent's shop well ahead of the range appearing in the high street stores. I was proud to pick up General Madine on a Kenner backing card, although I had no idea of what his role in the film would be. I remember my heart leaping at the sight of an action figure Y-Wing and a C-3PO collector's case pictured on the backing card—it took my breath away. Then my eyes focused on the new selection of action figures on the card, most of which seemed exotic in the extreme. Considering the reputation the General Madine figure has acquired as being a boring action figure, I can well imagine that I had bought the last of the batch of* Return of the Jedi *toys that the shop had received. It did not matter to me, as I had my first action figure from the new* Star Wars *movie and an all-important reference to the new range.*

A new Palitoy television commercial for the Speeder Bike opened with a *Return of the Jedi* clip of Luke rocketing along on the vehicle. There was a very innovative camera shot of a pair of hands maneuvering the toys through a forest of table and chair legs at high speed. A new commercial for the Scout Walker also began with a clip of the actual machines in action in *Jedi*. A boy was shown moving the toy along, operating the leg mechanism in a realistic forest setting, while another boy made his Ewok action figures ready for battle. "The Scout Walker can fight his own battles, win his own wars, but will he?" said the narrator. The commercial finished with a freeze frame of a miniature swinging log about to smash into the toy. The *Jedi* adverts mirrored the table-top and garden play world of children, who created alien environments out of everything they could find. According to Ian Whitlock,

> I never owned any *Star Wars* playsets after the Death Star and the Cantina. I used to make my own in the garden using my father's bits of scrap wood and pipe fittings. I ended up making some quite elaborate Hoth scenes using plaster. It was always an extra bonus when the snow came as it was the perfect background setting for my scenes. I built a huge AT-AT out of cardboard. It wasn't really that good but it was probably three times the size of the Palitoy toy and I hooked up a string mechanism to raise Luke

up into its belly. The last set I remember making was Jabba's palace. Back then I never thought twice about building something that I couldn't afford to buy (which was most things). I'm not sure things are like that now but I hope that there are still children who are encouraged to do this. There's a lot of satisfaction from figuring things out and then standing back to admire your hard work.

Richard Harris also used his creative skills. "By the time *Return of the Jedi* came onto the screens, my younger brother was playing with my old figures and my parents were buying him a lot more besides. Now 13, I was too old for the figures, but using my artistic side I laid Han Solo inside the plastic box off the front of one of the action figure card backs and filled it with Plasticine and sprayed it silver. That was the carbonite freezing scene sorted!" To give the *Jedi* toy range a further boost, Palitoy commissioned N.J. Farmer and Associates to construct *Star Wars* figure display scenes which were loaned to selected major retail outlets. There had been a plan to install a special promotion called *The Return of the Jedi Command Satellite*, also by N.J. Farmer, in large department stores but the idea was shelved until the following year.

The Jedi Merchandising Blitz

The *Return of the Jedi* merchandise boom outside of the Palitoy stable recaptured the spirit of 1978 with a campaign of huge proportions, and practically every item a child could want. Existing license holder Icarus re-released its entire home ware product range, branded this time with the *Return of the Jedi* logo and incorporating new artwork. Andrew Skilleter had been called upon again, to create two compilations of *Jedi* images which were sold by Icarus as laminated mini-posters. Even though Ewoks were part of the design, there was not a concern over security as Skilleter explains: "I had Ewok photos to reference from but I don't recall that we were working ahead of the movie or of any secrecy." An additional placemat featuring Ewoks was added to the selection but it was not by Skilleter. "This was at the very end of my involvement with Icarus and it was around then that they found other, cheaper artists. It was someone else who did the Ewok placemat, aping my style a little, I recall! I can look at my involvement with *Star Wars* with satisfaction though. For a short while, I was part of something massive which I could respect and relate to and I did my best to come up with the best art I could at that time. I'm frankly amazed people still remember my pieces but they do!"

H.C. Ford joined the fray once more with its selection from the previous year rebranded with *Return of the Jedi* logo but the images on the products were mostly from the previous films. There were additions to the H.C. Ford range including an extensive selection of items to write on; the company's notebook, sketch pad, exercise book, scrapbook, logbook, mini memo, mini notebook, star log, pocket memo, and memo pads may have exhausted every writing eventuality. The extensive range included rulers, plastic pencil cases, individually bagged erasers, various pencil tops, a deluxe boxed set and random products vacuum-packed onto backing cards. Jackie Ferguson remembers that one product had been the source of some concern: "H.C. Ford did these scented erasers, fortunately before health and safety was an issue. I recall that some time later, there were some concerns over children eating the erasers in their other product lines believing they were edible." Frankel and Roth returned with new school bags and cloth pencil cases. Penshiel Ltd. released a range of pajamas and dressing gowns branded with the logos of *The Empire Strikes Back* and *Return of the Jedi* on the same garment. There was also a bed ware range from Hayjax Manufacturing.

A large range of transfer sets were released by Thomas Salter, with value packs sealed in cellophane and larger sets packaged in boxes. Although the sets were designed very much in the mold of the *Star Wars* Letraset Action Transfers, the backgrounds and transfers were more simplistic and it was almost impossible to assemble a satisfying scene. Waddingtons released a set of four jigsaws which were supplied with a free poster. There was also a plastic Darth Vader lunch box and insulated flask from Thermos Ltd. (the same one as the previous year), flashing badges from Starfire UK Ltd., stickers from Fun Products, T-shirts and sweatshirts from Union Sales Ltd. and digital watches by Zeon Ltd. A series of costumes from Acamas Toys gave children the opportunity to dress up as Darth Vader, Luke, Chewbacca, Gamorrean Guard, Yoda or C-3PO. This range, along with a floor mat from Sutcliffe Engineering Ltd., were the only products released at this time featuring the *Star Wars* logo instead of *Return of the Jedi*.

A major item missing from the *Return of the Jedi* range was a Super 8 version of the film because by 1983,

(courtesy Craig Spivey).

Top, right and opposite page: Return of the Jedi merchandise included transfer sets from Thomas Salter, mugs from Kiln Craft, yogurt from Bridge Farm Dairies and a new stationery from H.C. Ford.

video technology had almost completely replaced every film-based format in home viewing. And there was no *Return of the Jedi* wallpaper, which would have been the icing on the cake for fans. Toiletries from Beecham Proprietaries (with no connection to Robert Beecham) had been listed in the press pack but the products did not arrive. This may have been a significant blow to *Jedi* promotions considering how toiletries were a key merchandising area. Addis Ltd. was signed to produce a range of *Star Wars* toiletries but they were not destined to be produced until the following year.

Bridge Farm Dairies launched their yogurt range. "All of the national supermarket chains thought that the *Star Wars* yogurt was terrific," says Jackie Ferguson. "They couldn't wait to stock it, so Bridge Farm Dairies achieved what they had wanted to. The Worlds Apart kite range proved to be very popular too. It was their first license and Worlds Apart eventually grew into a huge company and are still in business today."

Airfix's new range of *Jedi* model kits was released, supported by leaflets, posters and full-page adverts in children's publications which stated that a full-color poster was included with each kit. This poster was well worth having, with Jabba the Hutt on one side and Han on Endor on the other. As for the actual kits, the Imperial Shuttle Tydirium, a finely detailed kit in 1:76 (HO) scale, featured a movable boarding ramp, positionable wings and even a miniature Darth Vader. The Speeder Bike was a larger scale model with a Biker Scout figurine crouched over the controls.

The finely crafted replica announced in the 1983 Airfix catalogue ended up being a diorama of Jabba's palace, which was incredibly well-made and frustratingly inept all in one. Built in 1:72 scale, the set featured a huge number of alien creatures, most of which looked very authentic. But the main cast of characters, including Jabba, were not so well achieved and really let the set down. Even so, when constructed and painted, the kit made a very dramatic diorama, set out on the movie-accurate plastic base. The compendium kit previously announced by Airfix consisted of four snapfix kits packaged in a gigantic presentation box, which was sold at a premium price in model shops. The box contained an X-Wing Fighter, TIE Interceptor, A-Wing Fighter and B-Wing which could be assembled without glue and set up on individual display stands. Two further snapfix kits made available in America by MPC, the AT-ST (Scout Walker) and Y-Wing Fighter, were not released by Airfix at this time but could be obtained from specialist model shops and comic fairs.

Return of the Records

The *Return of the Jedi* soundtrack was released by Polydor on a single vinyl disk, tape cassette and also a relatively new innovation, a compact disc (CD). This time the soundtrack was only a single disc. Despite being of the high quality expected of the London Symphony Orchestra, it was far from a comprehensive selection of the music from the film. The record spent five weeks on the national album chart and peaked at #85 on June 25. A version of the soundtrack was again released by Charles Gerhardt conducting the National Philharmonic Orchestra, and it filled in some of the gaps in the London Symphony Orchestra recording. "Heroic Ewok" and "Fight in the Dungeon" were exclusive tracks. A version of "Ewok Celebration" without vocals was a fine finale to the album. The Utah Symphony Orchestra conducted by Varujan Kojian released *The Star Wars Trilogy* which contained "Fight with TIE Fighters" and "Darth Vader's Death," two tunes also not on the London Symphony Orchestra album. If people wanted to go to the trouble, they could collect all of the albums and compile their own comprehensive soundtrack album on a cassette tape.

I must admit to doing this myself. It was an excellent way of connecting with fellow fans, in the days when you had to literally lend someone a cassette to share some music.

There was clearly an appetite for *Star Wars* music. John Williams and the Boston Pops released "Out of This World," which contained four *Jedi* tracks. Damont Records re-issued the London Philharmonic Orchestra *Star Wars* album and played it safe this time with a very generic-looking spacecraft on the cover. RCA reissued *Star Wars* by Charles Gerhardt and the National Philharmonic Orchestra. Also available on vinyl and cassette was "The Story of Return of the Jedi." Buena Vista International released a *Return of the Jedi* storybook and record/tape produced by Jymn Magon. Buoyed by American sales of 1,800,000 of *Star Wars* and 1,600,000 of *Empire*, Disney Music president Gary Krisel was confident enough in the *Star Wars* license to oversee an expansion in the range. Adaptations of the Marvel comics stories "Droid World" and "Planet of the Hoojibs" were released, along with "The Ewoks Join the Fight," based on the finale to *Return of the Jedi*. The album "The Rebel Mission to Ord Mantell," written by Brian Daley and produced by Jymn Magon, chronicled the events of a mission by the Rebel heroes which took place shortly before the events of *Empire Strikes Back*. 3,000,000 combined units of Buena Vista International *Star Wars* products had been produced for the American market and the products seemed to be everywhere in Britain too, although "The Rebel Mission to Ord Mantell" was difficult to find.

Star Wars was released again to hire on video in VHS and Betamax formats by CBS/Fox. There had been a merger between 20th Century-Fox Video and CBS Video Enterprises, which held the rights to the output of a number of major film studios and to BBC Video in America. The new release featured an almost identical cover to one the previous year but with the new CBS/Fox logo. An age classification was not included on the cover but after the 1984 Video Recordings Act, "U" stickers were added. The video contained a trailer for a medley of films including *The Empire Strikes Back,* although the title was not yet available to hire or purchase at that time. Video hire shops were becoming much more commonplace and with video equipment becoming more affordable, fans had more opportunity to view *Star Wars* at home. The film was still not available to buy in the shops but everyone had a "mate" who could supply a copy.

Return of the Jedi generated a large amount of printed material which fans could choose from, depending on their age and interests. A *Storybook* was published by Octopus Books in Britain on behalf of Marks and Spencer. The *Return of the Jedi* annual from Marvel/Grandreams sandwiched the comic adaptation of the film between a beautiful cover painting by Pennsylvania-born comic book artist Bill Sienkiewicz on the front and back covers. In common with its two predecessors that contained the film adaptation, this annual was intended as a souvenir of the film on sale during the release, rather than an autumn edition. A *Star Wars Special Edition* annual, produced exclusively for British Home Stores, contained the comic adaptations of *Empire* and *Jedi*. The gorgeous cover art montage was by Jonathan Higgins. Bunch Associates' *Return of the Jedi Collectors Edition* followed the familiar format of providing a digest of the film's storyline and interviews with the production team. John May was not responsible for the publication on this occasion, although Bunch regulars George Snow was credited as the designer and Chris Rowley was the researcher. Felix Dennis had transferred the production of Bunch Associates' *Return of the Jedi* publications to his newly formed Manhattan-based company Pilot Communications, which had Hoovered up many of the British staff members. Bunch also produced the large-format publication *Heroes, Villains, Creatures & Droids* which included some of the more obscure *Jedi* characters such as Hermi Odle, Nikto, 8D8, Ephant Mon, Elom and EV-9D9. The publication was extremely light on material and contained little more than the name and a photograph of each character. Another Bunch production, the *Jedi Compendium*, contained eight mini-posters. If fans wanted to be more creative, also available in the shops from Random House was a mask book, punch-out and make-it book, a coloring book, a *Monster Activity Book* and *How to Draw Heroes, Creatures, Spaceships, and Other Fantastic Things.* "Craig and I discovered a copy of the *Return of the Jedi Storybook* in a local department store well ahead of the film," says Gary Harvey. "But we didn't want to spoil our enjoyment of the film by learning too much before it was released in our area. We couldn't resist turning the first page, however, and encountered a photograph of the half-finished Death

Star. Not knowing what it depicted, we thought that it was the original Death Star that somehow escaped complete destruction in *Star Wars* and was being repaired!"

The Promotions Battle Continues

Return of the Jedi was covered heavily by the press well into July. The July *Film Review* stated, "So once again the Force is with us. In other words, another *Star Wars* adventure, *Return of the Jedi* is filling screens to overflowing with action." The article focused on its wealth of new creatures, including Jabba the Hutt, "who comes into his own and heads an army of bizarre characters especially created for the film. *Return of the Jedi,* in fact, has more monsters than the two earlier chapters of the *Star Wars* saga combined."[10]

In creating the embargo on images of Jabba the Hutt and the Ewoks, 20th Century–Fox had almost guaranteed that publications would feature *Return of the Jedi* the month following its release, because the images were now available and magazines naturally wanted to use them. Additional coverage of Carrie Fisher also appeared. *The Daily Mirror's* follow-up article on the actress, "*Star Wars* Princess's new sexy image," referred to her slave girl outfit. *Bantha Tracks* #20, dated May 1983, was sent out to members with a letter apologizing for the delay, which had occurred due to security concerns over the film's more secret creations. A page of photographs from the film included Wicket the Ewok and Jabba the Hutt's band (Max Rebo, Droopy McCool and Sy Snootles, who had not been named in the film). Also announced was the fan club Creativity Contest which was open for all members around the world.

Marvel released the first issue of *Return of the Jedi Weekly* (dated June 22), which had reverted back to #1. "We did it that way in order for it to appear more like a brand new title rather than the continuation of an existing one," Tim Hampson explains. "In that way, news agents may have been persuaded to take more copies, rather than just take enough to sell to existing customers." A free badge featuring Darth Vader was taped to the front cover. The comic followed the same format as its previous incarnation, with the friendly "Lift-Off!" Editorial, a Cosmic Correspondence page and a new page dedicated to readers' art. "Cosmic Correspondence" was given a higher priority with a plea for readers to send in their letters. "Reader participation was always seen as important," says Hampson. "So it was good that we had the opportunity to devote space to a dialogue with the readers." The adaptation of the *Return of the Jedi* story, printed in color, was written by Archie Goodwin with art by Al Williamson, Carlos Garzon, Tom Palmer and Robin Frenz. The result was a highly realistic representation of the film, although the color printing in the British comic left much to be desired.

The previous main storyline became the backup story, which was still depicting the events leading up to *Return of the Jedi*. The story "Fool's Bounty" carried on from the exciting cliffhanger of Luke and Lando being surrounded by bounty hunters. Rik Duel and Dani had been hiding behind Chihdo's carbonite block and emerged with their guns blazing. Luke and Rik Duel managed to escape the melee but Lando and Dani did not. Even though it had never worked for Luke before in the entire comics saga, he opted to simply attempt to sneak back in the building with Rik, unaware that at that very moment Chewbacca and R2-D2 were doing exactly the same thing. True to form, Luke and Rik were quickly captured and it seemed as if they were going to be frozen in carbonite when Chewbacca and R2-D2 arrived at the head of a huge storm of Stenax warriors. Bossk and IG-88 attempted to escape but Chewbacca laid them both out with a single enormous swing of his fist. The Rebel heroes were no nearer to finding Han Solo, however. As they took off in the Millennium Falcon, they found that Dani, still lovestruck over Luke, had come along for the journey. "Fool's Bounty" had all of the fast-moving action and humor of the *Star Wars* films, along with the carefully observed depictions of the characters that fans had come to expect from Mary Jo Duffy.

Issue 2 of the *Official Return of the Jedi Poster Magazine* focused on the film's creatures. The article "The Ewoks of Endor" explained the process by which the furry heroes had been brought to life. The article "Jabba the Hutt & his court" explained how the creature-making process had originated. Howard Kazanjian selected ILM stop-motion effects expert Phil Tippett to head a new team in Northern California which was charged with designing and producing new aliens for the film. This issue of the poster magazine was packed full of photographs of Ewoks and of Jabba the Hutt's court which fans waiting for the film's release in their area could only marvel at.

Also keeping fans occupied was the continuing comic strip saga in the *Sunday Express* supplement magazine. Archie Goodwin finally had the opportunity to chronicle the Rebels' escape from their Yavin IV base and their journey to Hoth, a situation that had been on perpetual hold at Marvel. In the story "Race for Survival," the entire Rebel Fleet attempted to break out of the Imperial blockade around the Yavin System, assisted by the Mon Calamari. Darth Vader's Executor flagship menaced the Rebels too. Vader's progress towards the Rebel Fleet and an almost guaranteed victory was thwarted by the ambitious Admiral Griff, who was so desperate to reach the Rebels first and secure a victory that his flotilla of Star Destroyers collided with the Executor. The Rebel Fleet escaped the blockade and jumped into hyperspace to the Hoth system.

On June 30, London's *Evening Standard* newspaper featured the front page headline "The Great Jedi Rip-off." According to the article, thousands of video copies of *Return of the Jedi* "are flooding the market despite a big security operation. Many of the pirate videos were made from a copy of the film stolen from a cinema in Hastings."[11] The June 26 *Screen International* reported, "A £5,000 reward is being offered by 20th Century-Fox, Lucasfilm and Classic Cinemas. An advertisement offering the reward is being placed in a number of national newspapers."[12] The story of the *Jedi* pirate copies ballooned in both in the press and on television. Also on June 26, a *Times* article by David Hewson brought a stark message from 20th Century-Fox: "What the public has to understand is that there are no legal copies of *Return of the Jedi* in existence anywhere in the world… [T]hese are imprisonable offences."[13]

Phil Heeks recalls how it was fashionable to own a pirate film. "There was a kudos in those days about having seen a bootleg video copy of a major movie during or well before its cinema release, despite the fact that they often looked terrible. 'Oh, this copy is great. You can almost see the actor's faces!'"[14] The publicity had the effect of keeping the film in the headlines weeks after its launch, perhaps leading to an extended run. As was the case with similar news stories surrounding the release of *E.T. the Extra-Terrestrial* the previous year, the fact that criminals were reportedly doing everything in their power to steal and make copies of *Jedi* seemed to elevate the film's status.

Another story hitting the headlines was that George Lucas and his wife Marcia were due to divorce after 15 years of marriage. On June 15, Sid Ganis issued a statement that the couple was splitting up. "The divorce will not affect the business of the company," he said,[15] although the financial implications to Lucas would prove to be extremely impactful and indeed affect the direction of Lucasfilm. A more pleasing story covered in the press was that Carrie Fisher married singer Paul Simon on August 16. Naturally, all of the headlines referred to Carrie as Princess.

The extra publicity could not have harmed the wider release of *Return of the Jedi* on July 14, to venues including the Ashton-Under-Lyne-Metro, Ayr Odeon, Basildon (Essex) Odeon, Barking Odeon, Barnet Odeon, Croydon Odeon, Birmingham Queensway Odeon, Bolton Odeon, Bridport Palace, Bromley Odeon, Burnage Concorde, Bury Classic, Buxton Spa Cinema, Cambridge Victoria, Canterbury Odeon, Cannock Classic, Cheltenham Odeon, Chester Odeon, Chichister Granada, Colchester Odeon, Enfield ABC, Finchley Gaumont, Gatley Tatton Luxury Cinema, Gloucester ABC, Greenock Gaumont, Guildford Odeon, Hanley Odeon (Stoke), Hyde Royal, Ilford Gants Hill Odeon, Jersey Odeon, Kingston Granada, Leamington Spa Regal, Lewisham Odeon, Macclesfield Majestic, Old-ham Odeon, Oxted Plaza, Oxford ABC, Perth Odeon, Purley Astoria, Quinton Classic, Redditch Classic, Rochdale ABC, Romford Odeon, Sale Odeon, Peterborough Odeon, St. Albans Odeon, St. Austell Film Center, Staines ABC, Streatham Odeon, Salford Carlton Twins, Scunthorpe Majestic, Stockport Classic, Sutton Coldfield Classic, Taunton Odeon, Twickenham Odeon, Urmston Curzon Mayfair, Walsall ABC, Watford Odeon, Westcliff-on-Sea Cannon Classic, Winchester Odeon 123, Wilmslow Rex, Wood Green Odeon, Wolverhampton ABC, Well Hall Odeon, Whitby Empire, Worcester Odeon, Woolwich Odeon and York Odeon. Focusing on the Manchester area reveals that all of the satellite venues (the Cheetham Temple Twins, Whitefield Major, Altrincham Studio 1 and the Cheetham Temple Twins) opened on the 14th, so there is every reason to believe that every other cinema that wished to, opened *Return of the Jedi* on the same day nationally.

"*Return of the Jedi* did really well when we opened at the Westcliff-on-Sea Classic," says Derek Dorking. "We were packing them in. It was one of the biggest summer releases we'd had. There was a lot of fuss in the press in the lead-up to the opening. One of the things the local paper did was to run a whole page of advertisements using photographs from the film. There was one of Princess Leia advertising a local hotel, with the tag line 'When you find your princess, bring her to…'"

"I went to see *Return of the Jedi* with my sister and mother at the Worcester Odeon and I was completely blown away by it," recalls Bob Cole. "Princess Leia's slave girl costume was an utter revelation. I had never imagined seeing her being portrayed as being so feminine. I wanted to tell all of my friends about it but nobody of my age at school was interested in *Star Wars*. Kids of today won't be able to appreciate that, with the ability to get online and meet people. Back in Worcester, it was just me and my sister who were fans. I was desperate. 'Please. Anyone. Can I please talk about *Star Wars* with someone?!'"

Craig Spivey also saw the film as soon as possible. "It had been a long wait to see if Han was okay. By 1983, I was 12 and only had one other friend in the village whose mum was cool enough to let him catch the bus and take the ten-mile trip to Scunthorpe, and we'd go together to watch all the latest releases at the Majestic. It was a tiny place and we'd often have to queue out of the door and out onto the street so I remember getting there extra early for *Return of the Jedi*."

"I just loved *Return of the Jedi* to bits," recalls Louise Turner. "And I think that the music had much to do with it. For years I'd tried to recall the Imperial March, then when it rang out through the cinema (in Dolby Stereo…), I had this moment of utter epiphany. After seeing the film, I also started buying the weekly comic, posters, soundtracks, whatever, with all the determination of a basking shark."

I saw Return of the Jedi *at the closest cinema to my home, the Romford Odeon, on Saturday, July 23. Gary had already seen the film and while he said it was fantastic, he didn't reveal anything about the story except that Vader's real name was "Anakin." It was obvious that Han Solo would emerge from his frozen state in the film, as photographs had shown him alive and well. I also knew about Leia and Lando being in disguise from the action figures that were on sale. I knew nothing else about the plot but from the trailer, I expected to see Jabba's lair, a Speeder Bike chase and a space battle, complete with Admiral Ackbar's line "It's a trap." It was quite busy at the cinema but there was no queue to get in. I took my seat with Paul and Gary and as the film unfolded, I was completely captivated. I thought even the Ewoks were fantastic as the humor and the action was so good. I thought the beat of the film was perfect, unlike the tawdry efforts at sci-fi from other filmmakers. It seemed to me to be a reward for waiting so long and we all left the cinema on a total high.*

Not every fan rushed to see the film. "I didn't see *Return of the Jedi* when it came out in the cinema," says Joe Sales. "I had an idea that I knew what was going to happen. I knew that the good guys were going to win. I knew that Luke was not going to marry Leia. So I suppose that the story was going down a path that I wasn't particularly excited about. I later learned via the comic adaptation of Luke's actual relationship with Leia—a clever get-around, I thought. Funnily enough, I later saw the film on video and it's ended up being my favorite of the trilogy."

Jedi Promotions

A number of promotional ideas were created for *Return of the Jedi* to support the local movie release and the ongoing national showings, with every effort made to keep the film (and toy range) in the public eye. "By then, we placed a great deal of emphasis on cost-effective national newspaper promotions," says Carole Deighton. "Powerfully branded competitions were negotiated in *The Sun, Daily Mirror, Daily Express* and others that involved winners going to screenings, meeting Darth Vader as well as receiving product prizes." Cinemas could, through 20th Century-Fox's marketing department, offer the substantial prize of a tour of Elstree Studios for competitions connected to the film. Many cinema managers responded to encouragement to organize *Return of the Jedi* floats at summer carnivals, such as the Deal Cannon Classic and Westcliff-on-Sea Classic which won two first and two second prizes. The Deal Cannon Classic took advantage of the exploitation templates in the *Return of the Jedi* promotional pack, organizing a painting competition which featured in the local press. The Cannon Classic Sittingbourne hosted a large group of pupils from Barrow Grove School who saw *Jedi* as an end-of-term treat. "I helped with a promotion organized between Keddies Department store, the Southend Odeon and the local newspaper in the lead-up to the release," says Derek Dorking. "The paper did a spot-the-difference competition and the little boy who won it collected his prize of a Palitoy Rebel Transport vehicle from the Southend Odeon. I supplied my Darth Vader costume and dressed up in my Tusken Raider outfit. I did a walk around the fore-court in costume with Julie and some of the other cinema staff on the day of the opening but by that time, I was so busy in my work as a projectionist, I wasn't going out as much doing costume appearances."

The Darth Vader Tour was continuing, with local newspapers extremely excited when the "authentic" Darth Vader visited their far-flung area, with Nick Farmer's costume being totally convincing. Many people even believed that it was actually David Prowse who had turned up. "We had a roster of 'actors' and 'minders' with a fleet of rented vehicles and the agency organized hundreds of 'character' visits all over the U.K.," says Carole Deighton. She continues:

Martin Woodgate felt the evil of Darth Vader at Allders department store in Croydon. At least he was allowed to keep the sign advertising the event! (courtesy Martin Woodgate).

Department stores, toy stores, film screenings, trade and consumer exhibitions and fairs and large consumer events were all part of the program. To find "actors" suitable to wear the Darth Vader costume, we relied on word-of-mouth and some targeted advertising. To fit the costume properly, they had to be at least 6'3", well-built and agile enough not to trip over the long cloak! The actors were driven to venues by a "minder" who was also hired by us. It was an extremely hot and uncomfortable costume to wear and regular breaks had to be organized to survive! Darth Vader's minder would hand out "autographed" *Star Wars*-Darth Vader fliers and these were in great demand. For very special appearances, suitable vehicles would be hired for Darth Vader to arrive in style but mainly, the actor changed into his outfit somewhere private at the location. The strict rule was that whoever wore the costume, they must not be seen without it by the audience, shoppers and kids who turned up specially to meet Darth Vader. Rather like Father Christmas!

Darth Vader made his presence felt at the Scotch Corner store in Kilmarnock (courtesy Robin Kennedy).

Barry Smith recalls Darth Vader turning up at the Spar shop in Longton, Lancashire: "It's a little village where nothing much happens so that was kind of a big thing back then … and a little bit weird."[16] Graham Ogle recalls the Dark Lord's visit to Stoke-on-Trent:

> One Saturday, Darth Vader appeared in our town's only toy shop, a little independent called Playland. Apart from being small, it wasn't even a proper toy shop. Ninety percent of what it sold was baby stuff, prams, pushchairs and the like. One small section held "older toys." I was in town with a friend and saw a small crowd outside Playland. Looking through the window, I saw Darth Vader, posing menacingly with children. My friend and I were amazed and confused. What was Darth Vader doing in our small semi-toyshop? Was it David Prowse? Was it the actual suit? We didn't make it inside the shop as it was too busy. There had been no advance publicity as far as I am aware but the next week our local newspaper ran a photo of Darth, tagged "*Star Wars* villain comes to town."

"I met Darth Vader in the Allders department store in Croydon on Thursday, July 28, 1983," Martin Woodgate recalls. He went on:

> My dad worked in the town so he came and met Mum and me. Appropriately enough, Vader signed a Darth Vader figure that Mum grabbed off the shelf and I got a photo with him in which I look terrified! Then we paid for the figure and asked the cashier if we could have one of the event shop display signs advertising the Darth Vader appearance (despite it being around three feet high) and he said yes as

Darth Vader attracted a huge crowd upon his visit to Hinckley, Leicestershire (Mirrorpix).

they couldn't reuse then since they were dated. I still have the shop sign and the autographed Darth Vader figure unopened in perfect condition, which must be a rarity."

Return of the Jedi Weekly #4 (cover date July 13) continued the comic adaptation of the film. The backup storyline was still leading up to the events of *Jedi*. In the latest story, "Lashbane" by Mary Jo Duffy, Luke, Lando, Chewbacca and R2-D2 joined forces with Leia and C-3PO to hunt for a missing rebel agent, Yom Argo, in a forested area of the planet Lashbane. The Rebel Alliance high command had pulled the Rebel heroes off of the trail of Han Solo and his captor Boba Fett because Yom Argo and his colleague Tay Vanis were supposedly in possession of the secret plans to the Empire's new super-weapon, which had been revealed in *Jedi* as being the new Death Star. Leia was especially unhappy to be diverted from the search for Han. It transpired that although Yom Argo had suffered a fatal crash in his X-Wing on the planet, he had left behind some tapes that Leia & Company retrieved.

The Making of the Jedi

With the veil of secrecy covering *Return of the Jedi* having been lifted, along with the moratorium on photographs of the film's secret creations, magazines fell over themselves to produce Making of features. The film's marvelous creature designs were the obvious place to start. The November *Fantastic Films* focused on the Ewoks—which, incidentally, had not been referred to as such in the film. But due to the power of marketing, *Ewok* was a term that had become very widely known. According to the article, the creatures had individual names (Wicket W. Warrick, Chief Chirpa, Paploo and Logray the medicine man) also not mentioned on film, although some of them had been revealed by the action figure range. The same *Fantastic Films* included an article on the creature effects:

> The menagerie of alien creatures created for the opening scenes in Jabba the Hutt's court and later peppered throughout the Rebel Fleet are some of the most delightfully bizarre bug-eyed monsters ever seen in the movies. Veteran Lucasfilm animator Phil Tippett found himself in charge of a newly formed division of the special effects department aptly dubbed The Monster Shop. In an attempt to recapture the fun and wonderment of the cantina sequence of the first film, his orders were to create a workshop full of creatures, both horrible and lovable, that would test the imagination of the most ardent *Star Wars* fan.[17]

Longer clips of the film were also made available to television. On October 26 at 4:40 p.m., the children's game show *Screen Test* showed considerable sections of the Speeder Bike chase and space battle, after which host Brian Trueman said, "Great stuff, marvelous."

Such coverage was exactly what the *Jedi* campaign required to keep the momentum going. The October–November issue of *Space Voyager* focused on *Jedi*'s visual effects, with which Industrial Light and Magic had reached even greater levels of complexity and sheer spectacle. Despite dazzling audiences with his work, Richard Edlund (who was credited on the film as simply as "Visual Effects") still sounded modest:

> Even the best effect may convince audiences today but appear dated tomorrow. But if a film is a classic, I think that quality adds to its charm. Watching the *Buck Rogers* serial today, it's obvious that the backgrounds were painted on drums and that the spaceships are hokey. But we have to realize that while it may seem phony to us, to the people for which it was made, it represented exotic, futuristic worlds. Ten years from now, new audiences may look back on *Return of the Jedi* and think it looks dated, but like in the original *King Kong* or *War of the Worlds*, it will still be a classic.[18]

In *Bantha Tracks* #21, Dennis Muren and Ken Ralston were interviewed on the subject of special effects. Muren explained how video technology had been utilized to assist in planning the effects sequences in what had been dubbed *videomatics*: "It involves shooting a sequence with a video camera for viewing on a TV monitor screen." A basic mock-up of the Endor forest was set up with *Star Wars* action figures taking the place of the cast. "It was an experiment that worked out really well and clarified our idea of the sequence. Actually, it looked surprisingly like the finished film."[19]

The mainstay of *Star Wars* effects coverage, *Starlog* covered the creature-making process in its September issue. In October, it profiled the man who had been largely responsible for the fantastic designs in the *Star Wars* saga, Ralph McQuarrie. The artist made it clear that not all had been well during the production of *Jedi*: He had left the production of the film before all of the design work had been concluded and had since left Lucasfilm altogether. "I felt that I had contributed all that I was going to contribute. I was welcome to continue, but it was time to go on.... I was well into it when I left, but the design work was essentially done." Despite his contribution to *Star Wars*, not all of his ideas chimed with Lucas'. McQuarrie described how he had envisioned Jabba the Hutt as an individual who was mobile and physically dangerous, but Lucas wanted a "super slob": "My vision wasn't where he was."

One of the aspects of *Jedi* that McQuarrie had put a great deal of effort into, but had ended up not being used, was the designs for the Imperial capital world. "[W]e worked on this Imperial City a long time, but it is *never* visited in the film. George decided just to have everything take place in space. It's elaborate and quite pretty. But I don't want to reveal what it looks like because George just might use it in the future."

Despite leaving the film's production, McQuarrie was employed as a freelancer to paint a series of images for promotional purposes and for release of the *Return of the Jedi Portfolio*. Looking back at his involvement in the *Star Wars* saga, he was upbeat. "It's really a nice feeling to go down the street and see, on the sidewalk, a bubble gum wrapper with Darth Vader's picture on it. And Darth's face on the cover of *Time*, too. It's interesting to have done something out in the world that everyone looks at all the time. You become part of the public happening."[20]

I don't have any information to confirm it but I suspect that George Lucas was anxious to make Jabba the Hutt a repulsive slug because, against expectations, children had sought to emulate both Darth Vader and Boba Fett despite their villainous personas. As a result, the story was tweaked in order to make Vader a father figure who redeemed himself and to provide Fett with an embarrassing end. Children would boo Jabba the Hutt and would buy the toy, badge and sticker but they would not want to actually be him. If this was the case, it did not work entirely because at least one fan wrote a letter to Return of the Jedi Weekly *under the alias of Jabba the Hutt!*

Issue #3 of *The Official Return of the Jedi Poster Magazine* focused on the Endor Speeder Bike sequence, revealing that many of the techniques had been distinctly low-tech. The side view of trees rushing past ended up being easy to capture, as Dennis Muren explained:

"We realized that we could shoot most of what we needed very simply. We could just put the camera out the side of a car and drive along the forest roads. As long as we kept the road itself out of shot and just had trees flying by." Regarding the front and rear point-of-view shots from on board the bikes, cameraman Gary Brown was called upon to walk the route using a Steadicam camera. "Gary walked the course with the camera shooting at one frame per second," said Muren. "The result looked like you were doing 150 miles an hour. It was a great example of taking an old technology and human skill and taking it to an extreme."

The movement of the Scout Walkers was a long ways from the often jerky traditional stop-motion techniques. Phil Tippett and his team had pioneered the "Go-Motion" process, which the effects man attempted to explain: "[It's] a computerized rod-puppet technique and we have video animation tape machines which build up a library of the model's movements. We build up movements on one axis at a time until we achieve the motion that we want to keep. Then we connect this motion to the computer's memory and build on it. In this way we can quickly build up movements we can use over and over again."[21] *Return of the Jedi* had utilized the very latest processes while at the same time keeping the production grounded with time-tested, traditional techniques.

Peecher's View

The Making of Return of the Jedi, edited by publicist John Philip Peecher, chronicled the production of the film from start to finish. Producer Howard Kazanjian, who had been little more than a name in the Making of coverage up until that time, was finally introduced to fans. His filmmaking beginnings, like George Lucas', could be traced back to the University of Southern California Film School where the men had first met. "I was at USC at a time when experimental filmmaking was fashionable," said Kazanjian. "There were only a couple of people in my class—George arrived a year later—who wanted to make Hollywood films. I wanted to make something with a beginning, middle and an end." After graduation, Kazanjian enrolled in a Directors Guild training. A series of assistant director jobs followed on various films (including *The Wild Bunch* and *The Hindenburg*) before Lucas asked him to produce *More American Graffiti.* The producer's role on *Raiders of the Lost Ark* followed, and then *Return of the Jedi.* Asked to sum up his role, Kazanjian replied, "An arbitrator, creator, negotiator, psychologist, psychiatrist, developer, budget manager."[22]

Another important production team member to be put under the spotlight was first assistant director David Tomblin who, before *Jedi* filming began, was described by Peecher thusly: "Always gruff, occasionally grumpy, he usually knows best, and will provide the strong right arm that director Richard Marquand will need. In his early fifties, with his thick, graying hair worn slightly long, David Tomblin is a solid-looking bear of a man (it is only later you find that he is an old softie inside)." After working with Irvin Kershner on *Return of a Man Called Horse,* the 30-year British film veteran proved himself to be essential to the Lucasfilm production team on *Empire Strikes Back, Raiders of the Lost Ark* and *Jedi.* Tomblin brought an extremely serious attitude to his work but he displayed a lighter side when he joked, "When in doubt—mumble; when in trouble—delegate."[23]

Bantha Tracks #22 featured an interview with model makers Lorne Peterson and Steve

Gawley. With many previous special effects features focusing on more glamorous aspects such as optical effects, and robot- and creature-making, the pair were unsung heroes. People with an interest in how the film had been made would also have been drawn towards *The Art of Return of the Jedi* from Ballantine Books. The film script was included this time but again it had been based on the completed film instead of a shooting script. Additional background information could also be gleaned: Jabba the Hutt was the monarch of the galactic underworld who spoke Huttese. The language spoken by Boushh was Ubese and the robot in charge of the robot torture chamber was EV-9D9. Illustrations of the Jabba's Court alien characters Yak Face, Elom, Ishi Tib, Tooth Face, Squid Head, Barada, Klaatu, Nikto, Pote Snitkin and Ree-Yees were included. The main rebel cruiser was identified as the Headquarters Frigate (although the photographs of the craft were of the second Mon Calamari ship *Liberty*) and the individuals traveling with the emperor were members of the Imperial Council. There were also sketches of the stilt-legged Yuzzem that were intended to be co-inhabitants of Endor with the Ewoks, but they were eventually dropped. The Ewoks were actually described in the script as teddy bears.

Fan-tastic Times

As the year progressed, many *Star Wars* fans were finding that their individual interests were reaching a higher level. Sarah Baker-Saunders had an opportunity to add even greater *Star Wars* rarities to her collection. "As a family, we visited Canada and I managed to pick up bubble gum cards and other small items not available in the U.K. I didn't know that there were extra sets of cards, so they ended up being pride of place in my collection." Louise Turner's musical interest was beginning to peak: "One of my most treasured memories from school is of being invited to play the horn with the band of the Argyll & Sutherland Highlanders for a stirring rendition of the *Return of the Jedi* suite. At the time, I found it kind of disturbing, because the score was arranged to a disco beat which the musical purist in me detested, but it was still an opportunity to play a piece of music by John Williams while in the company of a bunch of really talented musicians." James Simmonds remembers:

> I used to write my own *Star Wars* magazine with my younger brother during the school holidays. It was called *Jedi Journal* and was all handwritten and illustrated. It was the kind of thing that I really wanted to read but there wasn't anything around at the time. Sort of a combination of *Bantha Tracks* and the weekly comic. I even had classified ads on the back page despite the fact that that only my parents were ever going to read it! In my late teens, the *Star Wars* films inspired me at first to co-author the U.K.'s first collector guide for the saga, contribute to the American Official Price Guide, write for the fan-run *U.K. Star Wars Fan Club Magazine* and run my own fanzine that ran for eight years. In my early twenties, I completed a media course at college which led me to write professionally about *Star Wars* for magazines such as *SFX*.

Shaun Dawkins finally achieved his aim to visit Elstree Studios. "It turned out that one of the actors that I went to see from *Return of the Jedi* knew Robert Watts and I wrote a letter asking if I could meet him. From that, we actually got to meet Robert Watts at Elstree. It was post–*Return of the Jedi* by then and he was preparing *Indiana Jones and the Temple of Doom* but that in itself was simply amazing." At the same time, Ian Whitlock was increasing his interest in special effects:

The jaw-dropping effects of *Star Wars* were something that had always stuck with me and I created my own special effects book (albeit in a naïve fashion), producing illustrations and text on how to achieve such cinematic mysteries. Highlights included hanging model spaceships from fishing wire and making a land vehicle appear to float via a large pole coming out the back of it. All of these early experiments really got me interested in filmmaking but it was the Tauntaun and AT-AT Walker sequences in *The Empire Strikes Back* that really turned my eye towards animation. I finally had the chance to try my hand at real animation when my art teacher at school offered me the use of a 16mm Bolex camera. I could finally recreate those Hoth battle scenes for myself and find out how those guys at ILM felt… Well, maybe not quite! My early attempts at animation were fairly crude, but after finding out all I could about the subject, I managed to find my first employment in stop motion and it's still something that I do to this day. I've been lucky enough to work on all but one of the *Wallace and Gromit* shorts, starting as a prop and puppet maker and then moving on to animation, as well as animating on several high-profile stop-motion features. My job has taken me all around the world working at some fantastic studios with very talented people.

Laurie Calvert reached his goal of working in the special effects industry. "I had written lots of letters of inquiry and a woman at the BBC wrote back to me saying that while there were not any jobs there, she had photocopied me some pages of an industry guide to British special effects companies. I wrote to 50 of them and ended up being employed as a light scan cameraman at Filmfex, which was one of the biggest effects companies in the U.K."

Being only 13 in 1983, I was behind the curve of the slightly older fans. Even so, I had found that English was by far my favorite and strongest subject at school. At some point during the year, my English teacher gave everyone in class an assignment to produce a dossier as part of their course work on any subject they wished and of course I chose Star Wars. *I had a library of* Star Wars *publications at home to reference. I used my collection of the* Official Star Wars Poster Magazines *to provide an idea of how to structure my writing. I believe that I earned top marks for my effort. It was the first time that I had put down on paper all of my thoughts regarding* Star Wars *and I really haven't stopped since. My schooling in English put me in good stead when I embarked as editor of the fan-run U.K* Star Wars Fan Club Magazine.

The Future of the Star Wars *Comic Saga*

With the Marvel comic filling in the story leading up to *Return of the Jedi* and the comic strip chronicling the events leading to *The Empire Strikes Back*, there was an obvious question: What would happen when these storylines set in the *Star Wars* saga's *past* had been brought up to date? The Goodwin-Williamson comic strip was still running in the *Sunday Express* and in newspapers around the world but it could surely not last very much longer because the story had reached the stage where the Rebels had installed themselves at their base on Hoth. The storyline was due to end when it reached the events of *The Empire Strikes Back*. The Marvel storyline at the very least seemed to have a degree of longevity ahead. Mary Jo Duffy explained how the defeat of the Empire in *Return of the Jedi* had opened up the *Star Wars* storyline to a wider range of story ideas: "We've got this wonderful backdrop of political intrigue to play with. We can do individual, slice-of-life stories on different worlds. We can pick two, three, four, six members of our team and put them on a planet and let them have an adventure that maybe doesn't relate to the political struggle." Duffy was also revealed that the Marvel *Star Wars* universe was a place where many characters outside of the films had become beloved in their own right: "We've been very fortunate. I, and David Michelinie before me, going back through Archie Goodwin all the way back to Roy Thomas six years ago, have each been able to introduce a couple of recurring

Return of the Jedi Weekly did not make many errors but this could be counted as a large one.

characters who were created solely for the comic, who our readers like. They clamor to see them back and do new things and meet up with new combinations of the heroes."[24]

Duffy enjoyed a long stint as writer of the Marvel *Star Wars* title. As to how she got the job:

> The person who was due to take *Star Wars* over [from David Michelinie] simply never did it. It was his assignment and he wanted to do it but month after month the work wasn't coming in. So they ran one of my fill-ins, then another of my fill-ins. In the meantime, I had been the assistant and then the managing editor for Archie Goodwin, one of the superb writers of all time. So the time finally came when they said, "She's edited these comics, she's proofread these comics. She's worked on every other aspect of Lucasfilm-related stuff. So let's just let her come in as acting writer."[25]

Return of the Jedi Weekly #9 (August 17) included a free badge. It was common practice in comics to include a bonus gift, to help insure that readers continued buying a comic title after a change of format. In this case, it was the first issue after the *Return of the Jedi* adaptation had finished. There was a small setback, in that the text on the cover said " Free bagde." "I remember this very well," says Tim Hampson. "We did have a few red faces in the office (mine included). Of course by the time we saw it, it was far too late. The publisher probably huffed and puffed and moaned about the quality of the editorial staff. I still tell people about it and the importance of proofreading—especially the big letters at the top of a cover!" Since the adaptation of *Return of the Jedi* had been concluded in the previous issue, the storyline leading up to the events of the film became the comic's main feature. In the latest story in the cycle, "The Iskalon Effect," the rebel heroes were ordered by the Rebel High Command to travel to the watery world of Iskalon, which the missing Rebel pilot Tay Vanis had reportedly visited. The original adaptation of *Star Wars: A New Hope* became the "back-up" story, which was presented in color for the first time in a British comic.

The *Star Wars* saga was also continuing elsewhere, albeit in the past once more in a new Futura novel, *Lando Calrissian and the Mindharp of Sharu* by L. Neil Smith. Set at a time before the Han Solo novels, this book chronicled the period when Calrissian owned the Millennium Falcon. This book was not available in Britain except via specialist science fiction book shops. It was followed by two other books in quick succession, *Lando Calrissian and the Flamewind of Oseon* and *Lando Calrissian and the Starcave of Thonbocka*.

Also continuing the *Star Wars* backstory was the *Sunday Express* comic strip. On August 28, the story "The Paradise Detour" had Luke, Han, Chewbacca and the droids land the Millennium Falcon on a planet for repairs. The Rebel Fleet had presumably made the journey to Hoth but Han's ship was not going anywhere. The planet was a paradise and Luke even met an old flame of his there, but he found to his terror that she was an ancient mind witch in disguise, looking to drain his mental energies. The woman used her formidable telekinesis to attack Luke but she overstretched herself and expired. "The Paradise Detour" was one of the weaker Goodwin stories, and it seems to have simply served to add a little color to the otherwise dull situation of the Rebels reaching Hoth.

The Magnificent Triple Bill

Another very exciting event, the *Star Wars* triple bill began a nationwide run of one-day showings at 18 large venues, all of which were still showing *Return of the Jedi*. There could hardly have been a better boost for *Jedi's* publicity. The Hammersmith Odeon began its triple bill run with a full house on July 30, with the cinema reportedly having to turn 1000-plus people away. Glasgow Odeon followed on July 31, Liverpool Odeon on August 7, Leeds Odeon on August 10, Ashton Metro on August 12, Sheffield Gaumont on August 13, Stockport Davenport on August 14, Nottingham Odeon on August 16, Birmingham Odeon on August 18, Huddersfield Classic on August 20, Southampton Odeon on August 21, Cambridge Victoria on August 22, Brighton Odeon on August 24, Ambassador Dublin on August 26, Southend Odeon on August 27, Dominion Theatre Tottenham Court Road on August 29 Bank Holiday (two showings), Bradford Odeon on Sept 1, Edinburgh Odeon on September 3–4, Southport Classic on September 3, Southend Odeon on September 11, Liverpool Odeon also on the 11th and the Brighton Odeon & Southampton Odeon on September 18.

The Star Wars Fan Club sent out an update to its members, listing all of the known showings. The sitting took roughly seven hours with breaks but for fans, the time seemed to fly by as they immersed themselves completely in the *Star Wars* universe. "My first triple bill was at the Glasgow Odeon," recalls Louise Turner. "I remember some Glaswegian muppet shouting out, 'And all because the lady loves Milk Tray' when Luke Skywalker finally gets through the Speeder Bike chase, falls off, land on his feet and kills the biker scout. Of course, the place erupted into laughter!" Jordan Royce says, "Me and my friends did the triple bill twice, which at the time seemed insane. I had never seen three films together before back to back which had a narrative that hung together. It was something really special." Ian Whitlock recalls, "It was my first chance to see *Star Wars* and *The Empire Strikes Back* on the big screen since their release so it was a big day for me. The trouble was that the projectionist decided that right in the middle of the *Return of the Jedi* Speeder Bike chase was a good chance to take a break. Seeing a close-up of Luke on his bike suddenly screeching to a halt with the word 'Intermission' being superimposed over his face was not really a good way to add tension!"

Attending the show was often dependent on logistics of travel and the willingness of parents. According to Craig Spivey, "I saw the triple bills being advertised in the national papers but they were all in big cities. Major conurbations were a world away from my Tatooine-esque rural existence." Fans in Britain who managed to attend a showing could consider themselves fortunate because the *Star Wars* triple bill had not yet debuted in any other part of the world, including America.

The highlight of 1983 for me was traveling into London with my brother Paul, Gary and his dad to see the Star Wars *triple bill at the Dominion Theatre. When* Return of the Jedi *had finished and I exited from the cinema on a total high on to the brightly lit streets of London, I felt as if I had been part of a happening, something to be treasured for a lifetime.*

With the triple bill, those who had seen *Return of the Jedi* could view *The Empire Strikes Back* in an entirely different light. The more extreme aspects of the film were diluted by the audience knowing that everything would turn out okay in the end. The film could still entertain but very importantly it could no longer *shock*. Some viewers also began to form the opinion that *Empire* was actually the best film of the trilogy. *Empire's* release on video in 1984 enabled fans to re-evaluate it further, to the point where today it is generally regarded to be the favorite of fans. "Over the years, it has come to be regarded much higher than at the time it was released," says Jordan Royce. "It's not a popular thing to say because most people's view is: 'Obviously, that's the best one of the three,' as if it was always like that—everyone leaving the cinema saying that it was brilliant. It was not like that at all and it took a long time for people to recognize how deep the film was. It was a sleeper. A lot of films are a lot better ten years on. Like a fine wine, they improve with age."

Fans did not have to go to the cinema to see *Star Wars* again, as it was repeated on ITV on September 15 at 7:30 p.m. It was #4 in the weekly national television chart, with over 13 million viewers. It was bested only by *Coronation Street* and its repeat showing and the *Winds of War* miniseries.

New Merchandise Everywhere

Return of the Jedi Weekly #13 (September 14) included a special offer for the Chewbacca Bandolier Strap toy from Palitoy, which could be obtained for £3.50 (or 12 zillion Groteks as mentioned in the ad) and five names from *Star Wars* figure backing cards. Loosely based on Chewbacca's single item of clothing, the toy was designed so that *Star Wars* figures could be clipped onto it but whether image-conscious children would actually wear this bizarre item was another question entirely. On the 10th and 17th of September, Panini gave away *Return of the Jedi* sticker albums and packets of stickers in the comics *Eagle, Buster* and *2000AD*. News agents and other outlets such as Woolworths and W.H. Smith stocked the stickers displayed in eye-catching display boxes. Many fans struggled to fill their albums and chose to write to

The queue for the triple bill at the Bradford Odeon was huge on September 1, 1983 (SWNS).

Panini directly and request the missing numbers. The sticker set was just one example of the memorabilia which appeared on the heels of *Return of the Jedi*. Other items included "Smile Money Bag" change purses from Touchline, a coin sorter money box from J & L Randall Ltd., a set of greetings cards from Westbrook publications, toothbrushes from Oral B and badges

Above, below and opposite page: Merchandise arriving later in 1983 included Smile Money Bag purses from Touchline, biscuits from Burtons and party balloons from Ariel.

and key chains from Present Needs, all of which were produced with *Return of the Jedi* logos. Many companies chose to use the overarching title of the franchise, *Star Wars,* rather than the Jedi branding. A football from Vullierme, party balloons from Kiwi Products, mint-flavored biscuits from Burtons and silver-colored pencil cases from Frankel and Roth were branded with the *Star Wars* logo.

"Not all of the products were arranged before the release of *Return of the Jedi*," says Jackie Ferguson. "You have to take into consideration that back then, licensing was an unknown quantity. *Star Wars* was the first big merchandising license. These days, for a licensing program it is much better timed; you have products appearing six weeks before a movie and six weeks afterwards and perhaps there is some merchandising potential around the DVD-Blu-ray release."

A *Star Wars* product of sorts was the Atari arcade game that began to appear at seaside video game arcades. "I thought that the *Star Wars* video game was absolutely fantastic," says Gary Harvey. "I discovered it whilst on holiday in '83 and I just played it endlessly. Eventually I found out that there was no end to it. The game reached a certain difficulty level and kept repeating until the player gave up! It seemed to be a game changer because from then on, there were lots of movie tie-in arcade games, such as *Tron*."

Lucas Calls It a Day

Although *Star Wars* mania was still running high in Britain, it became apparent that the momentum would not be supported by additional *Star Wars* films, at least not for the foreseeable future. In an interview in the August issue of *Rolling Stone,* conducted two weeks before *Return of the Jedi* opened, George Lucas revealed that he was actually closing down the film production department of Lucasfilm:

> Indiana Jones is really done out of the English office. They will shut down after *Indiana Jones* [*and the Temple of Doom*], and right now the American office is shutting down *Jedi*. Lucasfilm is not a production company. We don't have a studio, we don't have production heads. We have a producer who produces a movie. And we have an office in London with a producer—Bob Watts—that puts together crews. So we're closing down the production department. That means that there are about seven people who are going to be assimilated into other parts of the company or go and do their own thing. The rest of Lucasfilm is really a series of companies; each one somehow grew out of the films or what we were doing. And now they're service organizations for other people who make movies.

Exhausted from the ten-year epic making of the *Star Wars* trilogy, Lucas seemed intent on taking a take a well-earned holiday. He said,

> *Jedi* killed everybody, every department, from costumes to building monsters to sophistication of the mechanics to the special effects. Everything was very, very hard on everybody. This one was grim for me, just as bad as *Star Wars*, just as bad as directing. I don't know how I got into it. It's the demands, the amount of time one has to spend, and the anxiety, the worrying: "Is this going to be good? Is this going to work? Why is everything going wrong all the time?" ...I've put up with *Star Wars* taking over and pushing itself into the first position for too long. I've been trying to shove it back. Every time I kick it down, it comes rearing its ugly head back up again. This time I've kicked it down for good, I think.

There were also practical matters to consider. Lucas continued: "The way things are going, I couldn't afford to make another one like *Jedi*. I couldn't take the risk. Inflation in films is astronomical. There's got to be a cheaper way. I think if we started on the next series, we would probably try to do all three of them back to back." He did however hold out a sliver of hope that the *Star Wars* saga would one day continue. "All of the prequel stories exist: Where Vader came from, the whole story about Darth Vader and Ben Kenobi, and it all takes place before Luke was born. The other one—what happens to Luke afterward—is much more ethereal. I have a tiny notebook full of notes on that. If I'm really ambitious, I could proceed to figure out what would have happened to Luke."[26]

The specialist science fiction press picked up on the story of Lucas taking a break from *Star Wars*, as did the national press. A *Daily Mirror* article appeared under the headline "*Star Wars* boss quits the space race." The subject of there being further films was tackled in *Return of the Jedi Weekly*. In response to a reader's letter, C.Y.R.I.L. answered, "I've heard rumors through my mulita-core cables that there is a film due in 1985. Possibly called *Journal of the Whills*."[27] Tim Hampson recalls that this information had not been derived from any official source. "It was probably wishful thinking on our part together with the perceived wisdom of the time."

∗ ✳ ∗

I remember reading this statement in the weekly comic and while I was given heart that the saga would continue, I was also aware that there was usually a three-year gap between the Star Wars *films. I also hadn't spotted any mention of a new film from other sources. Whatever the truth was, it was clear that 1985 wouldn't see the continuation of the trilogy.*

The Jedi Keep Returning

Return of the Jedi was still showing at cinemas in August. Despite it being well past its peak, according to the *Screen International* chart, all of the main regional venues were still earning an excellent £1000–2000 per week: the Odeons in Birmingham (transferred from the Gaumont), Manchester, Glasgow, Liverpool, Southampton, Cardiff, Newcastle, Bristol, Bradford, Leeds, Nottingham, Edinburgh and the Sheffield Gaumont. Undoubtedly long runs of *Return of the Jedi* were happening elsewhere, especially at large venues with multiple screens. The first of the big cinemas to drop the film was the Cardiff Odeon on August 13 after an 11-week run. The rest of the venues ploughed into September with returns staying at a constant level. The Birmingham Odeon Queensway closed *Jedi* on September 3. In Southampton, the film had transferred to the Gaumont 1 which stopped its showing on September 3, as did the Edinburgh Odeon 3 after 14 weeks. The Bristol Odeon, Manchester Odeon and Sheffield Gaumont followed the next week. The Brighton Odeon ended its 17-week run on September 24. The Leicester Square Theatre finally closed Jedi on September 17 after a 16-week run. The fact that it did not last until the end of the year as the two previous *Star Wars* films had done was probably down to the fact that *Jedi* had been released so soon nationally (including all of the cinemas in Greater London), so reducing the amount of people wanting to travel into the center of London to see it.

The three main standard bearers for *Jedi* became the Liverpool Odeon, Newcastle Odeon and Nottingham Odeon which were still seeing over £2,000 per week in ticket sales (even though it was showing in their second and third screens) and they were showing no signs of slowing down. *Variety* reported that by the second week in August, *Jedi* had made $209,656,205 in the U.S. Its nearest rival was *Flashdance* at $71,216,567.[28] *Jedi* was still pulling in cinemagoers at the Liverpool Odeon, Newcastle Odeon and Nottingham Odeon in October. The Newcastle ABC took over from the Odeon on October 9 for a single week, bringing that town's run to a close. The Liverpool and Nottingham Odeons blasted on through to November 12 when they finally finished their runs after an incredible 24 weeks. The Southampton Gaumont had re-shown the film from October 23 with a three-week run which had also closed on the 12th. In London, the ABC Shaftesbury Avenue ended a six-week run on November 19. It had been a titanic extended release for *Jedi* and the Christmas re-release season was just around the corner.

The Fans Have Their Say

Many a conversation between fans centered on the next trilogy of *Star Wars* films, which would reportedly focus on the Clone Wars. Various facts had already been revealed on the subject in the *Star Wars* novels, Marvel comic, the poster magazines and even the films themselves.

The debate over *Return of the Jedi* also raged on. The September *Starburst* was a hotbed of opinion and not just in the readers' letters section. Reviews from regular *Starburst* contributors Alan Jones, Phil Edwards and Richard Holliss gave the message that *Jedi*, while being spectacular entertainment, was lacking in areas that would have satisfied more mature cinemagoers. Jabba the Hutt and his minions seeming unrealistic was one such issue, as was the quality of the acting and the cuddliness of the Ewoks. Reviewer John Brosnan wrote,

> I've got to admit it—I was disappointed by *Return of the Jedi*. For all its marvels it left me, for the most part, unstirred and uninvolved. Some sequences *did* make my pulse quicken, like the anti-gravity barge in the desert, and the chase through the forest on Speeder Bikes, but in the main *Jedi* seemed to consist of a series of repeated highlights from the previous two movies. ...I've got to admit that Lucas has probably given the kids and the *Star Wars* fans everything they wanted and expected in the final part of the trilogy. It's just that for *me* the magic of seeing *Star Wars* for the first time was not recaptured by watching *Jedi*. But that's inevitable I guess.[29]

The November *Fantastic Films* continued the *Jedi* debate with the inclusion of a lengthy letter from Joan B. Shumsky, who seemed to approach *Star Wars* saga with an extremely serious mindset. "It's the day after the long-awaited release of *Jedi* and I still can't shake the feelings of betrayal and hollowness I experienced… [I]t was all there—the magic, the fast-paced action and the "happy" ending. These people had become "family" to us and we were prepared to like this film and we *should* have liked it. However, the most important ingredient missing from *Jedi* was the promise made in the first two films. The characters, George. You forgot about the characters!"[30] Issues such as the scant information provided by the film regarding Boba Fett and Luke and Leia's mother were highlighted in the letter, along with the portrayal of Han Solo, along with the unsatisfactory continuation, in Shumsky's opinion, of Han and Leia's romance.

The letter revealed the degree to which fans had grown up since the summer of 1977. People who had originally seen *Star Wars* in their youth were now at the ripe old age of 20-something. Perhaps in becoming more sophisticated filmgoers, they had outgrown the actual target audience for the *Star Wars* films.

"I think that a lot of the negativity towards *Return of the Jedi* was because people of my age had grown older," says Derek Dorking. "*Empire* had been so different and you had expected *Jedi* to follow the same lines. I liked the film in sections. The beginning at Jabba's palace. The first encounter between Luke and the emperor and the big lightsaber duel. It was the middle section I didn't enjoy so much. I can't say that I cared for the Ewoks although I came to accept them as time went on." Ian Whitlock recalls having reservations. "It was my friend's birthday treat, who was trying to decide if he wanted to see *Return of the Jedi* or *Octopussy*. He was quite into Bond and it was his birthday but I didn't feel too bad about persuading him to see *Jedi*… Well, maybe a little once those little Ewoks turned up! It was definitely my least favorite of the three and maybe this was because *Empire* is really a much superior film and I was getting older and out of my toy-playing phase." According to Graham Ogle, "I was 15 years old when I saw *Jedi* on a day trip to Blackpool with a friend. We were both a little disappointed. Things seemed different—C-3PO didn't look quite right and Vader's voice had changed I thought. I liked Jabba and the creatures in his palace but once our heroes landed on Endor I found it a little boring until the Death Star. And Luke being brother to Leia? A little convenient, I thought. Besides, didn't they have a passionate kiss in *Empire*?"

There were also fans from the 15-plus age group who warmed up to *Jedi*. Gerald Crotty says, "Although I had problems with the film (those Ewoks!), the major storyline of Luke and Vader had resolved itself more satisfactorily than I'd ever imagined and I was more than happy with that." Sarah Baker-Saunders was also positive. "I loved it. All of those questions left from the end of *Empire* were answered in a satisfying way. There were some silly explanations such as Ben Kenobi lying to Luke and Leia being 'the other hope.' There were also the Ewoks, but I still loved it. It was *Star Wars*, after all."

Laurie Calvert was content: "I liked how they echoed some of the scenes from *Star Wars*, such as the pilots reporting in their numbers, a reverse of Han and Leia's lines 'I love you, I know' and other beautiful touches like that. The things I was uncomfortable with were the portrayal of the emperor, which I thought was too theatrical, and the Ewoks, which seemed like a bid to sell teddy bears. I saw *Return of the Jedi* multiple times after that and it gradually improved as I began to appreciate what George Lucas had intended with the film." Darren Slade was sixteen when he saw *Jedi* "and although I loved it, there was part of me that acknowledged that it was slightly derivative of *Star Wars*. Also, the revelation of Leia being Luke's sister was a bit convenient in resolving the romantic triangle. The drama and tension of Luke confronting the emperor more than made up for that and Luke standing by the burning armor of Darth Vader." Shaun Dawkins wrote in *Return of the Jedi Weekly*,

> All those questions that we wanted an answer to are solved and by doing so the film is conferred with a unique ability to hold the audience's attention and draw them into the unfolding drama. Every credit must go to the legions of production crew and artists who made this part of the *Star Wars* saga possible. Without their dedication and expertise, the films that we have come to appreciate so much would still be growing ideas within the mind of one George Lucas. This film deserves every possible success, if only to act as a way that we can say a very big 'thank you' to the *Star Wars* cast and crew.[31]

Shaun is enthusiastic about the film today. "Looking back, the only downside to watching *Return of the Jedi* was the feeling that that saga had come to a close." Jordan Royce had similar feelings: "The film has a really upbeat ending with the celebration at the end but it was really quite tearful. To me and my friends, it felt like the end of an era. It was the triple bill when it really sank in."

On the whole, it was the under-15s audience who reacted most positively to *Jedi*. "I loved the movie and I was happy to see things resolved," says Craig Spivey. "Han was okay in the end. I got my head around Luke's parentage and Lando's motivations. I liked all the new characters too. Even the Ewoks. The 'proper sci-fi' side of things was noticeably more 'out there'—the Royal Guards were extra-cool and menacing, ships like the B-Wing more unconventional and characters like Jabba and Sy Snootles were a lot more, well … 'alien.'" Richard Harris says, "*Jedi* became my favorite *Star Wars* film and still is today. The fast-paced Biker scenes, the skiff battle in the desert and Jabba's palace were my favorite parts of the film."

"We went on a school night in the early evening to see *Return of the Jedi*," says Declan McCafferty. "I was overwhelmed by it the first time I saw it. It took a second visit to actually *see* it. I loved it to the extent that, at the time, I was declaring it to be the best one. My brother was 17 and too cool for it, really. He wasn't up for seeing it a second time. I got a bit of a teasing from him about it: 'Teddy bears in space,' 'It's just a toy catalogue,' all that stuff." According to Gary Harvey, "*Return of the Jedi* exceeded the expectations of my 14-year-old self. It was so exciting and full of visual wonders. The only downside to it was that none of my friends were interested, not even in my *Making of Return of the Jedi* book when I took it to school. They were saying, even at 13, 14, that they were too old for it."

Being 13 years old at the time, I was perhaps on the upper edge of the target age for the new Star Wars *film. My impression was that* The Empire Strikes Back *had been the disappointment and* Return of the Jedi *had undone the damage. As I grew older, however, I became aware of shortcomings of* Return of the Jedi *to adult eyes (much along the lines of the negative reviews) and I can appreciate fully the feelings of older fans who were disappointed with the film. Nothing however can undo the euphoria that I had felt upon seeing the film as a child in 1983 and in that respect, the film had succeeded spectacularly. A large part of why* Return of the Jedi *has not held up so well in the years since its release is because it is only on the first time around that the viewer has a feeling of suspense, not knowing how it will end. People do not realize how great a sense of excitement the film generated when it first arrived. Nowadays,*

when everyone knows that Vader is Luke's father, that the Rebels won and the Death Star was destroyed, Return of the Jedi *has lost its dramatic edge.*

Whatever their view of *Jedi* was, the more mature fans considered the third film to be the close of this chapter of the *Star Wars* saga. Lucas' decision to take a break from his greatest creation had become very well known. Anyone who read newspapers or science fiction magazines could hardly have missed it. Perhaps the film maker would return one day to his notebook of ideas about *Star Wars'* past but it would not be for many years hence. "I was 18 in 1983 and doing my A-Levels," says Shaun Dawkins. "I went on to study at University College London. I continued writing my star interviews for *Bantha Tracks* and contributed to fan magazines. The complexities of life, however, can impinge on hobbies and interests, so I decided to archive my passion for *Star Wars*."

Gerald Crotty says, "After *Return of the Jedi,* I felt that there was a sense of finality. It certainly felt like a chapter of my life was over. I thought I might just leave *Star Wars* behind at that point but I was still in contact with my pen pals in the States and that kept me going. I went on to write for and produce artwork for *Star Wars* fan publications all over the world." According to Ian Whitlock,

> I felt that this was the end of the saga. I had heard that it was going to be a nine-part saga and wondered if I'd ever see the others. At my age, it was kind of all over for me. Although I was tempted to, I didn't buy any more toys as I was getting a little too old for that by then. The end of the trilogy was, I think, the right time, with my playing days coming to a close. *Star Wars* had been a massive part of my childhood but it just sort of ended after *Return of the Jedi* and once I had completed my sticker album, I felt it was time to move on.

As for Graham Ogle:

> Nineteen eighty-three and the end of the *Star Wars* films sort of coincided with the end of my childhood. People often say that they saw *Star Wars* at a perfect age. Well, I was ten when I saw it and 15 when I saw *Jedi,* I would be leaving school the next year. *Star Wars* was put on the back burner, so to speak. I had read that George Lucas had intended to make nine films altogether but deep down I knew that this wouldn't happen, at least not for a good few years. Most of my toys went to the tip [trash] a few years later and *Star Wars* was gone but not forgotten. The *Star Wars* years 1978 to 1983 were some of the happiest days of my childhood and collecting the vintage toys today helps relive that excitement.

Jordan Royce has similar recollections: "*Return of the Jedi* coincided with me and my two friends being around 15. We were about to leave school, become adults and have the kind of responsibilities that would bring the party to an end. It really was the very last of our childhood days." Laurie Calvert says, "My impression at the time was that *Return of the Jedi* was going to be the last one. The films were increasingly difficult and expensive to make and it had taken it out of George Lucas. Although there were more chapters of the saga, that they were not going to be told would remain a backstory. Then again, I thought, if special effects became cheaper or easier, then who knows?"

"I hoped that it would go on," Louise Turner recalls. She continued:

> But it soon became apparent that George Lucas was leaving the playground. I remember reading about him talking about how the *Star Wars* universe felt like home to him but sooner or later you have to leave it. At the time I felt confused, a little fearful and disbelieving too. I carried on with my fandom, though, and had started to write my own *Star Wars* stories which would turn into independent, not-for-profit publications, and years later to writing a series of novels. What *Star Wars* did for me was to

grant me an opportunity to learn my trade, and to serve my apprenticeship as a writer. They say you have to write a million words before you can even think of calling yourself a writer, and if I didn't write that million on *Star Wars* fan literature, it was pretty close.

Darren Slade remembers, "I had read that the *Star Wars* saga would continue but hadn't learned of Lucas stating he was taking a break. It just goes to show in the pre–Internet days that news like that didn't exactly go all around the world. I had no doubt at the time, though, that *Return of the Jedi* was the end of this particular story and of these characters. I went to university and naturally got into other things and different kinds of films." Derek Dorking recalls, "I thought that the *Star Wars* saga had reached its conclusion, although I did hope for further films. My cinema certainly did, it was good business! I went on to make a career of being a projectionist and married Julie."

"I really hoped there would be more but I really thought that was it. George had said so," says Sarah Baker-Saunders. "I had been to college and started work, so adult life beckoned. Although I kept up my *Star Wars* fan club membership and a general interest in any news that came my way, *Star Wars* unfortunately took a back seat. My mum even now says my obsession was all her fault and that the ticket she bought me in 1978 was the worst birthday present she ever gave me. I on the other hand will forever be in her debt."

A Future for Star Wars?

The *Star Wars* brand would continue into 1984 but without further chapters of the film series to support it, only time would tell how far it would run. Some fans who had recently left school or who were attending college began to plan their own fan publications and to write and publish their own *Star Wars* stories as small press editions. This was a movement that was far more advanced in other countries such as Germany and America, beginning as early as 1978, but it was only just taking shape in Britain at this time. "There was not as much of a tradition of sci-fi conventions in Britain, so there was less chance for fans to meet each other," says Shaun Dawkins. "My star interviews continued to be printed in fan magazines in other places around the world, even including *Bantha Tracks*, but I wasn't aware of organized fan activity in this country at the close of 1983. The next few years would be another matter, however."

"I was seen as the biggest *Star Wars* expert at my school," says Jason Grant. "I clubbed together with some of the other children to form a group we called Dragon Busters, which later morphed into the Moons of Yavin *Star Wars* club which roped in pen friends across the U.K. We all had ranks within the club, with me as commander. It was all very official and meticulously organized. I was determined to do my bit and support *Star Wars* until a new film came along, no matter how long that would take to come about. The club continued building in strength through to my adult life."

The Moons of Yavin club became the conduit through which all of Star Wars *fandom flowed in Britain and without it I doubt if I would be sitting here writing a book about* Star Wars. *I could not have greater appreciation for Jason Grant, not least for his typically modest "cameo appearance" in this book. Sean Connery appearing at the finale of* Robin Hood Prince of Thieves *does not hold more gravity.*

School age kids who barely remembered seeing *Star Wars* (if they saw it at all) during its original release fueled the ongoing *Star Wars* enterprise with their pocket money, paper-round earnings and birthday and Christmas gift choices. At this time, there was not a significant adult collector market as there is today. A vast number of young fans had been introduced to the saga through *The Empire Strikes Back* and the *Star Wars* double bill, and even younger ones had their first viewing of *Star Wars* on television. The youngest age group had their first experience of Lucas' universe with *Return of the Jedi*. It was in this respect that it can be imagined how the decision was made to make the third chapter of the trilogy appeal to children.

Younger fans looked forward to the New Year with a huge sense of optimism, perhaps buoyed by assurances in *Return of the Jedi Weekly* that the film series would continue. *The Journal of the Whills* was a possible title touted by the comic. "I don't know where it came from, it might have been friends at school, or a newspaper speculation, but it was always going to be nine films," says Peter Davis. "That was what we clung to, in full expectation of the *Star Wars* saga continuing." James Simmonds had a similar mindset: "In 1983, I thought that *Star Wars* would continue forever. I'd read many times that the saga was outlined as a nine-part story."

"I wasn't aware that George Lucas was taking a break from *Star Wars*," says Richard Harris. "I thought back then that the saga would continue with episode seven. I was 13 at the time and I appreciated how the films were made. To me, they were beginning to be more than just films—they were a series of the best films ever created."

"I was such a big fan that I went with it at the end of 1983," recalls Craig Spivey. "I was a member of the *Star Wars* Fan Club and things like *Bantha Tracks* did a good job of keeping the flame burning. When I turned 13 the following January, I lost interest almost overnight. It was like someone flicked a switch and I was suddenly into music, clothes and girls. I still had a lot of affection for *Star Wars*, though, and was determined that, while other aspects of my childhood were discarded or sold off, my '*Star Wars* stuff' should be kept stored in my parents' attic."

"In 1983, I was as into *Star Wars* as I ever could be," says Declan McCafferty. "I was still very young and impressionable when I saw *Return of the Jedi*. I had convinced myself that we'd get *Episode One—Journal of the Whills* in 1986."

"I was still a massive *Star Wars* fan at the end of 1983," says Gary Harvey. "There was no doubt in my mind that more films were just around the corner. Craig and I were so much into our collecting, that we were going to continue unabated in '84. The comic, *Sunday Express* strip and the toys were still going so there seemed no reason to stop."

"I had read about George Lucas stating that there wouldn't be any more *Star Wars* films for quite a while," remembers Bob Cole. "I carried on my interest in *Star Wars* although it remained a very solitary passion. Eventually I got in touch with a club called The Moons of Yavin, which was my gateway to finding like-minded *Star Wars* people and founding friendships that have lasted until today. My interest in *Star Wars* led into a passion for all things NASA and astronomy. Today when I give a lecture at an astronomical society meeting, I'll often cite *Star Wars* as providing the original spark."

*   *   *

Personally speaking, my mind was buzzing with Star Wars *at the end of 1983. I can't explain why I kept going when others put it behind them. Perhaps it was because I was a couple of years younger, in the middle of secondary school (and let's face it, fans in the younger age bracket like me were unlikely to have read about Lucas' break from* Star Wars *in the press). It is certain however that* Return of the Jedi *had completed what I saw as the perfect science fiction universe. The adventure was still continuing in the comic and the* Sunday Express *comic strip. It was so full of excitement, wonderful characters and incredible technology—the possibilities for adventure seemed boundless. I had the perfect collecting partner in Gary and it was not long before we had amassed what seemed to us to be world-conquering collections. My brother Paul too was a huge fan and a collector, so I was hardly alone in being a* Star Wars *fan.*

No matter what fans thought about how *Star Wars* would develop at the cinema, there was no doubt that the people working in the UK franchise felt that the saga had a future. "I think at first, many of us thought that new films would follow pretty quickly over the next few years," says Carole Deighton. "There was a strong belief that *Star Wars* would continue as a best-selling toy line supported by the new film releases." Dave Barnacle says, "I did think *Star Wars* would last. The toys were very popular and there was talk of other films to come in the franchise."

Geoff Maisey recalls, "Palitoy recruited new sales people towards the end of 1983, when I left to take up a European role for General Mills. They were certainly of the opinion that they could sustain the *Star Wars* brand beyond the life of the movies." Andrew Maconie too felt that he was promoting an ongoing property. "George Lucas had always envisaged nine movies. *Return of the Jedi* was #6 in the series."

The Reflection of the Stars

Now that the trilogy had come to a close, the question remained of what the cast would be doing next. Anthony Daniels spoke to *Starlog* about his aspirations beyond the *Star Wars* saga: "My ambition is to go on acting in roles that, preferably, are different from previous ones. ...*Star Wars*, I imagine, will always be the highest pinnacle in terms of blockbusters for me. I'm quite content. The *Star Wars* films have become a sort of art subsidy for me. I can afford to do a role in a theater which doesn't pay very much because George has paid my rent for the next year."[32]

Mark Hamill also shared some of his reflections with *Starlog*:

> It seems as if *Star Wars* is the life and breath of my existence. As much as I love it, though, I don't want to feel that it's the *only* thing I can do. I would rather try to further my other career opportunities.... Everyone and their mother has seen *Star Wars* and *The Empire Strikes Back,* so I can't help but be stereotyped. My best hope is to have the chance to meet people so I can show them my own personality. If I don't, they may not realize I'm *acting* when I play Luke.... What's really frustrating is that I wanted to go out for such films as *Midnight Express, Breaking Away, Tribute, The Great Santini* and *Ordinary People,* but I wasn't even allowed to read for them... [I]f you haven't been given the chance to fail, you don't feel like you've had a fair shot. It wasn't until I did *The Elephant Man* and *Amadeus* that the theatrical community sat up and took notice of me.[33]

David Prowse said in the August issue of *Film Review*: "I'm very grateful for the *Star Wars* films and my involvement in them.... Obviously none of us realized what a success

Star Wars would turn out to be. With all of those special effects, it was a difficult production for the artists. But through it all, George Lucas never lost his cool once." Regarding playing Darth Vader in the next chapter in the saga: "[Lucas] is going back in time for the next *Star Wars* film to perhaps before Vader was born. Whether Darth Vader or I will figure in it is too early to say. George only makes the films every two or three years. But if and when he does the next one, I'm ready and willing and certainly hope I'll be asked to play him again"[34]

Carrie Fisher spoke to *Starburst* while she was in London in May. "It's difficult to find things you like to do that are a fun to be part of as these films are. You have to be careful, I think, because a film is a long time out of your life and to spend five months having a bad time, which I did on one job, is a mistake you don't want to make. I'll do *Laverne and Shirley* or *Saturday Night Live*, so there's always something. So long as I'm acting. But I would like to do another film, so I have to go back to the States and find one that I'd like to do." Regarding the continuation of the *Star Wars* saga: "George is real tired. He oversees all the miniatures, the editing, the mixing, the looping, everything. If he does another one, I don't know if he'll do it for some time and then, I think he'd do *1,2* and *3*, which will be a young Kenobi and a young Vader in a pub in space."[35]

Towards the end of 1983, Ballantine released the *Return of the Jedi* 1984 calendar which highlighted the film's most exciting scenes with a series of high-quality photographs. Marvel released a 1983–84 *Return of the Jedi Winter Special* containing color reprints of the stories "Crucible" and "The Hunter." Another collectible on fans' Christmas want-lists was Marvel/Grandreams' *1984 Return of the Jedi Annual* which sported a montage on the cover by Terry Paris. The annual contained color reproductions of three complete stories from the comic ("Chanteuse of the Stars," "The Big Con" and "Ellie") which finally brought the Marvel storyline up to the events of *Return of the Jedi*. This was a genuine exclusive in Britain as the latter two stories had not yet appeared in *Return of the Jedi Weekly*. They had only recently featured in issues #77 (November 1983), #79 (January 1984) and #80 (February 84) of the American comic, which were printed at least four months before the cover date. "Chanteuse of the Stars" took Luke Skywalker and Princess Leia a pleasure resort, the space station Kabray. Their superiors in the rebellion had learned that Han Solo, before being frozen, may have learned about the Empire's new super-weapon. While Lando and Chewbacca had gone off to search for Han (who was still not known to have been delivered by Boba Fett to Jabba the Hutt), Luke and Leia had ended up on Kabray, looking for Tay Vanis. Their only backup was Plif the Hoojib. The station was awash with Zeltron women, who all swooned over Luke while he attempted to avoid the Stormtroopers on patrol. He managed to find another tape left behind by Tay Vanis. Leia adopted the persona of a cabaret singer in an attempt to maintain her cover but ended up taking to the stage and putting on a performance that was hopefully better than the one she put on in *The Star Wars Holiday Special*. Leia's stage debut came at just the right time because her voice entranced a dangerous Huhk creature who had been on a rampage. Luke had found another clue to the whereabouts of Tay Vanis but he was concerned over what the lovestruck Huhk would do when Leia ran out of verses.

In "The Big Con," Lando Calrissian, with Chewbacca in tow, attempted to learn Han's current location from a gang of ruffians. Lando knew that Solo had been involved with the gang in the past and that they were searching for two valuable statues. The Minstrel and the Dancing Goddess were well-known artifacts but Lando's tactic of using the possibility of obtaining the precious objects as a lever for information backfired when he was plied with alcohol. After hearing the gang report that Han had been delivered to Jabba the Hutt, Lando told them that he had previously traveled to Tatooine in the company of Chewbacca and had discovered that Han was not there. Learning that Lando's furry companion was Chewbacca rather than another anonymous Wookiee, the gang drew their weapons, causing the rebel pair to make a hasty exit. A Landspeeder chase ensued and when Lando and Chewbacca crashed, a shining object was propelled by the impact and landed in the street. The Minstrel, which Lando had been carrying all along, was snatched up by a member of the gang, who then turned her gun on her companions in order to keep the prize for herself. Lando and Chewbacca escaped with the sure knowledge of where Han was located. In a final twist, Lando revealed to Chewbacca that he had been carrying the much more valuable Dancing Goddess.

The story "Ellie" began with Luke, Leia and C-3PO in the midst of infiltrating an Imperial base. They came across a "female" protocol droid LE914 which was in charge of the communications. A holographic image of Tay Vanis explained that he and his colleague Yom Argo had found the *Bothan Tapes* mentioned in *Return of the Jedi* and that they had both fled with the Imperials in pursuit. Argo had made for the Rebel Fleet to summon aid but had perished on Lashbane, while Vanis had planet-hopped in order to lose his pursuers. In case of capture, Vanis revealed that he had handed the Bothan Tapes to his droid—Ellie. Luke, Leia and C-3PO invaded the Imperial prison facility on the planet in a bid to rescue Tay Vanis but a hologram of Darth Vader appeared boasting that the Force had allowed him to foresee that Luke would be the one to finally track down Tay Vanis and that Vanis had actually been under lock and key for months. Vader's plan was to keep both the Rebels and certain "ambitious" members of his own forces busy in a fruitless search. He did not wish to leave Luke & Company empty-handed, so he revealed that he had left Tay Vanis in his cell, to be claimed by anyone who found him. Luke and Leia were shocked to find Vanis slumped, a mere shell of a man, his eyes staring and uncomprehending. Ellie opened a compartment in her chest to reveal the Bothan Tapes. The droid then embraced its master and self-destructed, saving Vanis from his plight. The final panel was of C-3PO standing in the rain with droplets rolling down his face plate—or was it tears?

"Ellie" was a fine finale to the Marvel saga that led up to *Return of the Jedi* and perhaps one of the best stories that Mary Jo Duffy wrote for the *Star Wars* comic. The droid Ellie was a very well thought-out character and "her" end along with Tay Vanis was genuinely moving. The pre–*Return of the Jedi* storyline having been concluded, Mary Jo Duffy finally had the opportunity to continue the adventures of the Rebel heroes in the present time period (albeit, a long time ago in a galaxy far, far away).

On December 4, the *Sunday Express* supplement magazine story "A New Beginning" started. Having finally arrived on Hoth via the paradise planet, the Millennium Falcon seemed to have been followed by another spacecraft. Han, Luke and Chewbacca intercepted the spacecraft but, following Luke's suggestion that the disappearance of a spaceship might be suspicious, Han agreed to allow the Falcon to be drawn inside the hold of the foreign ship. Hopes that they would be able to talk their way out of the situation faded when the opposing captain was revealed to be Raskar, one of Han's smuggling colleagues. Raskar was aware of the bounty offered by Jabba the Hutt for Han and, since he was short on funds, he had no qualms about turning him in. Luke added to the play by mentioning Han's reward from the rebels, gambling that Raskar would have heard of the treasure but would not have known that it had already been stolen. This point of the story was a satisfying link to the Marvel *Star Wars* storyline which, under Archie Goodwin's stewardship, had featured Crimson Jack stealing Han's reward in issue #13 of the weekly comic. Raskar demanded that Han lead him to the treasure that surely must have been hidden on Hoth, but once on the chilly surface, they encountered a subterranean haul of rare lumni-spice guarded by a gigantic dragon slug. Once the beast was slain, Raskar and his men left Hoth, content with their haul of spice. "A New Beginning" concluded in January 1984. It was followed by "Showdown" and "The Final Trap," which brought the story up to where *The Empire Strikes Back* began.

The Year of the Jedi Comes to a Close

A letter and a photograph from Shaun Dawkins, included in *Return of the Jedi Weekly* #26 (December 14), chronicled his meeting Jeremy Bulloch and Bib Fortuna actor Michael Carter for an interview. *Return of the Jedi Weekly* #28 (December 28) featured a fantastic Christmas cover by Bob Wakelin, which depicted Darth Vader dressed as Father Christmas and a smiling Luke and Han holding presents from "Dad" and "Uncle Darth." If the year had not been exciting enough for fans, there was yet another chance to see the *Star Wars* triple bill on December 27 at the Leicester Square Theatre (it ran for ten days). The date was particularly apt as *Star Wars* had been released in Britain on December 27, 1977. For fans who made it to the showings, there could not have been a better way to end the year. "I saw the triple bill with a friend several times during that season, including two in one day, which is a lot of *Star Wars*," says Laurie Calvert. "I had seen all of the *Star Wars* films multiple times but they always remained fresh. In a way, it's like seeing an old friend. You know it so well and there's something very special about seeing the film for the umpteenth time. I still feel the same way today. You come out on a real high every time."

Nineteen eighty-three had been a spectacular year for the *Star Wars* brand in Britain. Much of the negativity and doubts of the previous decade in Britain had been swept away by the time *Return of the Jedi* arrived. At least from a young person's perspective, Britain was on a high. Aspiration was everywhere and everything seemed possible. British bands were topping the charts in America and on home soil. British films were also successful and were sweeping up awards; *Chariots of Fire, Gandhi* and *Educating Rita* topped the list. The upbeat vibe surrounding *Return of the Jedi* added to the party. Palitoy's year had been phenomenal. Jenny Glew, writing for *The Guardian* on December 10, placed *Star Wars* figures at the #1 spot for the best-selling toys of the year. "There are now some 20 million *Star Wars* figures in the U.K.—half of which have been sold in 1983. One reason for their success is that the 'low' price (£1.50) puts them into the category of pocket-money toys."[36] Carole Deighton has her own take on the phenomenon:

> *Star Wars* entered the consumer marketing history books as the first fully fledged movie toy franchise to be launched generating full year-round sales; not restricted to that golden, but rather short-lived, pre–Christmas period. That's why the U.K. retailers welcomed the toy brand with open arms. First and foremost, it was exciting to be part of a fabulous success story and they recognized the toy range was so desirable and highly collectable for consumers of all ages and tremendously profitable for them. The

toy trade perceived the range as unique because, as far as they were concerned, not only did it have its own "free advertising" campaign with the toys in a starring role in all three films, it had a huge, unstoppable marketing and p.r. drive behind the movie, the spin-off toys and branded merchandise. They could see this was a genuine first and a shot in the arm for their industry.

The *Jedi* campaign must have met every expectation within 20th Century-Fox and Lucasfilm, with the film grossing $12,000,000 in Britain.[37] "*Return of the Jedi* certainly fulfilled its merchandising expectations, both in the U.K. and mainland Europe," recalls the man with his finger on the pulse, Andrew Maconie. "Lucasfilm was so pleased with our efforts that they invited us to Lucasfilm Ranch," says Jackie Ferguson. Marc Pevers was provided with a rare guided tour. "I met with Lucasfilm senior vice-president Sid Ganis and he was kind enough to say that I had made it all possible."

Jedi's success was vital for Lucasfilm, as it allowed the company to move forward with its various projects, the most important of which was its new headquarters Lucasfilm Ranch. The *Star Wars* saga as a whole had been placed on a very firm footing and not simply in financial terms. If *Jedi* had been a box office success but had left cinema audiences uninspired, the *Star Wars* brand may have faded from the collective consciousness. A good example of how to kill a movie franchise with lackluster sequels is the *Matrix* trilogy. But *Jedi* had left people buzzing and had guaranteed that the *Star Wars* saga would be recognized as one of the truly great movie series and perhaps one of the best film trilogies of all time. Much of the *Star Wars* spirit of 1977 and 1978 had been recaptured in Britain in 1983, the pioneering techniques employed to market the *Star Wars* trilogy having been fine-tuned by all of those involved. Establishing a merchandising arm or employing agents to build a product base in advance of the release of a film has since become an industry standard practice, as has augmenting the advertising campaigns of all of the merchandise companies involved and producing high-quality promotional packs. Earlier parts of a film series are routinely shown on television and released on a

Above and following page: **For the Christmas season,** *Return of the Jedi Weekly* **sported a special cover and the Leicester Square Theatre showed the** *Star Wars* **triple bill.**

viewable format before the latest edition is theatrically released. Establishing an ongoing storyline in a comic, book series or television program is also seen as being vital. Today, peripheral merchandise is as important as toys and games. Creating an evergreen product is seen as the ultimate by the toy industry. Just as it was with the *Jedi* campaign, the promoting of a film series in the 21st century demands that every possible angle is covered by dedicated front line marketing teams. All of these techniques would need to come into play to maintain *Star Wars* through 1984 and beyond. This was not a brand that was being wrapped up but one that was intended to continue for the foreseeable future.

Lucasfilm Ltd., 20th Century-Fox and their affiliated agencies could look back on their shared *Star Wars* experience with a large degree of satisfaction. On the whole, fandom had been maintained at a high level in between the film chapters. The merchandise had never gone out of fashion, with the Palitoy range enjoying an unprecedented degree of popularity. Cinematic and television challengers to the *Star Wars* crown have come and gone, and many are all but forgotten today.

Great Britain played a pivotal role in the *Star Wars* success story: Peter Beale and his staff at 20th Century-Fox UK who made the filming of *Star Wars* possible. The British technicians and stars who brought the saga to the screen. Bunch Associates' creation of the Official Poster Magazines and Collector's Edition publications which provided the basis of much of the *Star Wars* expanded universe. The exclusive material published by the British

comic which contributed to the *Star Wars* universe. The BBC's key involvement with the *Star Wars* radio drama, without which it may not have been made. The world premiere of both the double and triple bill presentations. British-produced memorabilia has become the envy of collectors the world over, with high-water marks represented by the transfer sets from Letraset, houseware from Icarus, the sumptuously decorated boxes from the Metal Box Company and the beautiful stationery items from Helix, Letraset and H.C. Ford. Although the action figure toy range had its genesis in America, Palitoy put its own unique spin on the concept by producing highly desirable

Available at Christmas were the 1984 *Return of the Jedi* annual, 1984 calendar and the Marvel Comics *Return of the Jedi Winter Special.*

items of its own design. The Brits have undoubtedly made their mark and *Star Wars* is all the stronger because of it.

The fans who put *Star Wars* behind them in 1983 could do so with an immense sense of satisfaction and were able to look back on a perfect addition to their childhood and adolescence. *Star Wars* had not been banished from their minds entirely and they would be enthusiastic purchasers of the trilogy on video and the odd piece of merchandise in the shops, and they would speak freely of their love for the trilogy. In contrast, the fans that continued at the close of 1983 could shut their eyes and still see the laser beams flashing. *Star Wars* would continue to be a large part of their lives. Collecting memorabilia, writing their own stories, producing fan publications, costume-making and running conventions would all be part of a movement united by one shared experience; the yearning for a new *Star Wars* film to be produced.

Without a continuation of the *Star Wars* saga at the cinema for many years, it would be the responsibility of Colin Hankins and his team at 20th Century-Fox, the Fan Club, the various arms of the Palitoy Company, Munro/Deighton, Tim Hampson and his team at Marvel comics, the talents of Andrew Maconie and Jackie Moore, and of course the dedication and enthusiasm of all the fans to insure that the saga continued in Britain. The coming year of 1984 would return the *Star Wars* saga to unknown territory but there had never been a film series that had enjoyed the support of so many dedicated people. The Force would be with them.

Appendix I

Palitoy Products

This is a list of all known Palitoy *Star Wars* products released up until 1983, excluding mail-away promotions. I have listed where the items were released by Palitoy in Kenner packaging.

1978

Masks. Darth Vader, Stormtrooper, C-3PO, Sand-people, Chewbacca (Palitoy display box).
Dip Dots painting set (Palitoy).
Keel Kite (Palitoy).
Poster Art Set–Playnts (Palitoy).
Play–Doh set (Palitoy).
Escape the Death Star game (Palitoy).
The Adventures of R2-D2 game (Palitoy).
Destroy the Death Star game (Palitoy).
Light Saber (Palitoy).
First wave action figures: Han Solo, Luke Sky-walker, Princess Leia Organa, Ben (Obi-Wan) Kenobi, Artoo-Detoo (R2-D2), See-Threepio (C-3PO), Darth Vader, Death Squad Commander, Jawa, Stormtrooper, Sand People (Palitoy).
Land Speeder (Palitoy).
TIE Fighter (Kenner with Palitoy sticker).
X-Wing Fighter (Palitoy).
Death Star (Palitoy).
Large Size Action Figures: Luke Skywalker and Princess Leia Organa (Palitoy).

1979

Masks. Darth Vader, Stormtrooper, C-3PO, Sand-people and Chewbacca (Palitoy display box).
3D Poster Art (Palitoy).
Dip Dots painting set (Palitoy).
Light Saber (Palitoy).
First wave action figures (Palitoy).
Second wave action figures: Hammerhead, Snaggletooth, Walrus Man, Greedo, Power Droid, Death Star Droid, R5-D4, Luke Sky-walker X-Wing Pilot (Palitoy).

Land Speeder (Palitoy).
TIE Fighter (Kenner with Palitoy sticker).
X-Wing Fighter (Palitoy).
Death Star (Palitoy).
First wave Large Size Action Figures.
Die-Cast first wave: X-Wing Fighter, TIE Fighter, Darth Vader TIE Fighter, Landspeeder (Pali-toy).
Die-Cast second wave: Imperial Cruiser, Mil-lennium Falcon, Y-Wing Fighter (Palitoy).
Blaster Pistol (Palitoy).
Three Position Laser Rifle (Palitoy).
Radio Controlled R2-D2 (Palitoy).
Talking R2-D2 (Palitoy).
Darth Vader TIE Fighter (Palitoy).
Cantina (Palitoy).
Land of the Jawas (Palitoy).
Droid Factory (Palitoy).
Imperial Troop Transporter (Palitoy).

1980

First wave action figures (Palitoy SW).
Second wave action figures (Palitoy SW).
Third wave action figures: Han Solo (Hoth Outfit), Luke Skywalker (Bespin Fatigues), Leia Organa (Bespin Gown), Lando Calrissian, Rebel Soldier (Hoth Battle Gear), Imperial Stormtrooper (Hoth Battle Gear), FX-7 (Medical Droid), IG-88 (Bounty Hunter), Bespin Security Guard, Bossk (Bounty Hunter), Boba Fett (Palitoy ESB).
Land Speeder (Palitoy SW).
TIE Fighter (Kenner SW box with Palitoy sticker).
Death Star (Palitoy SW).

First wave Large Size Action Figures (Palitoy SW).

Second wave Large Size Action Figures: Boba Fett. IG-88 not released (Kenner ESB Palitoy sticker).

Die-Cast first wave (Palitoy SW).

Die-Cast second wave (Palitoy SW).

Blaster Pistol (Palitoy ESB).

Three Position Laser Rifle (Palitoy SW).

Radio Controlled R2-D2 (Palitoy SW).

Talking R2-D2 (Palitoy SW).

Darth Vader TIE Fighter (Palitoy SW).

Cantina (Palitoy SW).

Land of the Jawas (Palitoy SW).

Droid Factory (Palitoy SW).

Imperial Troop Transporter (Palitoy SW).

Millennium Falcon Spaceship (Palitoy ESB).

Tauntaun (Palitoy ESB).

Rebel Armoured Snowspeeder (Palitoy ESB).

Twin Pod Cloud Car (Palitoy ESB).

X-Wing Fighter (Palitoy ESB).

The Force Lightsaber. Red and Yellow. (Sold loose).

Play–Doh set (Palitoy).

1981

First wave action figures. Death Squad Commander changed to Star Destroyer Commander (Palitoy ESB).

Second wave action figures (Palitoy ESB).

Third wave action figures: Dengar, Lobot, Yoda, Han Solo (Bespin Outfit), Ugnaught, 2–1B, AT-AT Driver, Imperial Commander, Rebel Commander, Leia (Hoth Outfit), Bespin Security Guard (Palitoy ESB).

TIE Fighter (Kenner SW with Palitoy sticker).

X-Wing Fighter (Palitoy ESB).

Second wave Large Size Action Figures. Boba Fett. IG-88 not released. (Kenner ESB Palitoy sticker).

Die-Cast first wave (Palitoy SW).

Die-Cast second wave (Palitoy SW).

Die-cast third wave: Twin-Pod, Slave One, Snowspeeder. TIE Bomber not Released (Kenner ESB).

Blaster Pistol (Palitoy ESB).

Three Position Laser Rifle (Palitoy SW).

Darth Vader TIE Fighter (Palitoy SW with Bounty Hunter offer).

Imperial Troop Transporter (Palitoy SW with Bounty Hunter offer).

Yoda Hand Puppet (Palitoy ESB).

Tauntaun (Palitoy ESB).

Rebel Armoured Snowspeeder (Palitoy ESB).

Twin Pod Cloud Car (Palitoy ESB).

Turret & Probot playset (Palitoy ESB).

Imperial Attack Base (Palitoy ESB).

The Force Lightsaber. Red and Yellow (Sold loose).

Figurines—Craft Master. Yoda. Luke Skywalker on Tauntaun (Palitoy ESB unconfirmed)

Glow Paint by Numbers—Craft Master Luke Skywalker, Darth Vader, Han Solo & Princess Leia (Palitoy ESB unconfirmed).

1982

First wave action figures. Minus Artoo-Detoo (R2-D2), See-Threepio (C-3PO). (Palitoy ESB).

Second wave action figures (Palitoy ESB).

Third wave action figures (Palitoy ESB).

Fourth wave action figures. Luke Skywalker (Hoth Battle Gear), AT-AT Commander, (Twin-Pod) Cloud Car Pilot, Bespin Security Guard, Imperial TIE Fighter Pilot, Artoo Detoo (R2-D2) (With Sensorscope), C-3PO (With Removable Limbs) 4-Lom, Zuckuss (Palitoy ESB).

TIE Fighter (Kenner SW with Palitoy sticker).

Battle-Damaged X-Wing Fighter white (Palitoy ESB).

Second Wave Large Size Action Figure (Kenner ESB).

Die-Cast first wave (Palitoy SW).

Die-Cast second wave (Palitoy SW).

Die-Cast third wave (Kenner ESB).

Blaster Pistol (Palitoy ESB).

Three Position Laser Rifle (Palitoy SW).

Darth Vader TIE Fighter (Palitoy SW with Bounty Hunter offer).

Imperial Troop Transporter (Palitoy SW with Bounty Hunter offer).

Yoda Hand Puppet (Palitoy ESB).

Tauntaun (Palitoy ESB).

Rebel Armoured Snowspeeder (Palitoy ESB).

Twin Pod Cloud Car (Palitoy ESB).

The Force Lightsaber. Red and Yellow. Sold loose.

Mini Rigs. INT-4 Interceptor. CAP-2 Captivator. MTV-7 Multi-Terrain Vehicle. MLC Mobile Laser Cannon. PDT-8 Personnel Deployment Transport (Palitoy ESB).

Tauntaun with Open Belly Rescue Feature (Palitoy ESB).

Slave 1 Boba Fett's Spaceship (Palitoy ESB).

Wampa (Palitoy ESB).

Dagobah Action Playset (Palitoy ESB).

AT-AT All Terrain Armoured Transport (Palitoy ESB)

Millennium Falcon Spaceship (Palitoy ESB).

Darth Vader's Star Destroyer Action Playset (Palitoy ESB).

1983

First wave action figures. Minus Artoo-Detoo (R2-D2), See-Threepio (C-3PO). (Palitoy ROTJ).

Second wave action figures (Palitoy ROTJ).

Third wave action figures (Palitoy ROTJ).

Fourth wave action figures (Palitoy ROTJ)

Fifth wave action figures: Gamorrean Guard, Bib Fortuna, Emperor's Royal Guard, Admiral Ackbar, Chief Chirpa, Logray (Ewok Medicine Man), Klaatu, Princess Leia Organa (Boushh Disguise), Rebel Commando, Weequay, General Madine, Ree-Yees, Biker Scout, Nien Numb, Rebel Commando, Lando Calrissian (Skiff Guard Outfit), Luke Skywalker (Jedi Knight Outfit), Squid Head (Palitoy ROTJ).

Rebel Armoured Snowspeeder (Bilogo).

Tauntaun with Open Belly Rescue Feature (Bilogo).

Darth Vader TIE Fighter (Palitoy SW with Bounty Hunter Offer).

Wampa (Bilogo).

Tauntaun with Open Belly Rescue Feature (Bilogo).

Slave 1 Boba Fett's Spaceship (Bilogo).

Darth Vader's Star Destroyer Action Playset (Palitoy ESB).

AT-AT All Terrain Armoured Transport (Bilogo).

Rebel Transport vehicle (Palitoy ROTJ).

Scout Walker vehicle (Palitoy ROTJ).

Battle Damaged X-Wing. Both white and grey (Bilogo).

Radar Laser Cannon, Tri-pod Laser Cannon, Vehicle Maintenance Energizer (Bilogo).

Mini Rigs: INT-4 Interceptor, CAP-2 Captivator, MTV-7 Multi-Terrain Vehicle, MLC-3 Mobile Laser Cannon (Bilogo).

Jabba the Hutt Action Playset (Kenner ROTJ).

Speeder Bike vehicle (Kenner ROTJ).

Mini Rigs: AST-5 Armoured Sentinel Transport Vehicle, ISP-6 Imperial Shuttle Pod Vehicle (Kenner ROTJ).

Appendix II

The *Star Wars* Comics Saga

This is my personal selection of the comic stories that make up the *Star Wars* saga which concludes with *Return of the Jedi*. There are many entertaining and well-written stories that I have excluded that probably do not deserve to be considered as *fill ins* but I have attempted to put together a list which forms a coherent storyline.

Please note, the individual British comics were not always titled in the same way as the American. All of the comic stories have been reprinted many times in individual publications and are fairly easy to find.

Way of the Wookiee. Marvel USA: Marvel Illustrated books # 1. Marvel U.K. 95–96.

Star Wars. Marvel USA 1. Marvel U.K. 1–2.

Star Wars. Marvel USA 2. Six Against the Galaxy. Marvel U.K. 3–4.

Star Wars. Marvel USA 3. Death Star! Marvel U.K. 5–6.

Star Wars. Marvel USA 4. In Battle with Darth Vader. Marvel U.K. 7–8.

Star Wars. Marvel USA 5. Lo, The Moons of Yavin. Marvel U.K. 9–10.

Star Wars. Marvel USA 6. Is this the Final Chapter? Marvel U.K. 11–12.

The Day After the Death Star! Marvel USA: Marvel Illustrated books # 1. Marvel U.K. 97–99.

New Planets, New Perils! Marvel USA 7. Marvel U.K. 13–14.

Eight for Aduba-3. Marvel USA 8. Marvel U.K. 15–16.

Showdown on a Wasteland World! Marvel USA 9. Marvel U.K. 17–18.

Behemoth From the World Below. Marvel USA 10. Marvel U.K. 19–20.

Star Search! Marvel USA 11. Marvel U.K. 21–22.

Doomworld! Marvel USA 12. Marvel U.K. 23–24.

Day of the Dragon Lords! Marvel USA 13. Marvel U.K. 25–26.

The Sound of Armageddon! Marvel USA 14. Marvel U.K. 27–28.

Star Duel! Marvel USA 15. Marvel U.K. 29–30.

Silent Drifting! Marvel USA 24. Marvel U.K. 43–44.

The Hunter! Marvel USA 16. Marvel U.K. 31–32.

Crucible! Marvel USA 17. Marvel U.K. 33–34.

The Empire Strikes! Marvel USA 18. Marvel U.K. 35–36.

The Ultimate Gamble! Marvel USA 19. Marvel U.K. 37–38.

Deathgame. Marvel USA 20. Marvel U.K. 39–40.

Shadow of a Dark Lord! Marvel USA 21. Marvel U.K. 41–42.

To the Last Gladiator! Marvel USA 22. Marvel U.K. 45–46.

Flight into Fury! Marvel USA 23. Marvel U.K. 51–52.

Siege at Yavin. Marvel USA 25. Marvel U.K. 53–54.

Doom Mission! Marvel USA 26. Marvel U.K. 55–56.

Return of the Hunter. Marvel USA 27. Marvel U.K. 61–63.

What Ever Happened to Jabba the Hut? Marvel USA 28. Marvel U.K. 64–66.

Dark Encounter. Marvel USA 29. Marvel U.K. 67–69.

A Princess Alone! Marvel USA 30. Marvel U.K. 70–72.

Return to Tatooine! Marvel USA 31. Marvel U.K. 73–75.

The Jawa Express. Marvel USA 32. Marvel U.K. 76–78.

Saber Clash! Marvel USA 33. Marvel U.K. 79–81.

Thunder in the Stars! Marvel USA 34. Marvel U.K. 82–84.

Dark Lord's Gambit. Marvel USA 35. Marvel U.K. 85–87.

Red Queen Rising! Marvel USA 36. Marvel U.K. 88–90.

In Mortal Combat! Marvel USA 37. Marvel U.K. 91–93.

The Weapons Master! Marvel USA: Marvel Illustrated Books # 1. Marvel U.K. 104–106.

World of Fire! Marvel USA: Marvel Illustrated Books # 2 World of Fire. Marvel U.K. 107–115.

The Bounty Hunter of Ord Mantell. USA: LA Times Syndicate 2/9/81–4/19/81.

Darth Vader Strikes. USA: LA Times Syndicate 4/20/81–7/26/81.

The Serpent Masters. USA: LA Times Syndicate 7/27/81–11/01/82.U.K.: 13/05/83–12/08/84.

Deadly Reunion. USA: LA Times Syndicate 11/02/81–01/03/82.U.K.:19/08/84–14/10/84.

Traitor's Gambit. USA: LA Times Syndicate 01/04/82–03/07/82.U.K.: 21/10/84–16/12/84.

The Night Beast. USA: LA Times Syndicate 03/08/82–05/16/82.U.K.: 06/01/85–17/03/85.

The Return of Ben Kenobi. USA: LA Times Syndicate 05/17/82–7/25/82.

The Power Gem. USA: LA Times Syndicate 07/26/82–10/03/82.

Iceworld. USA: LA Times Syndicate 10/04/82–11/14/82.

Revenge of the Jedi. USA: LA Times Syndicate 11/15/82–01/23/82.U.K.: 01/02/83–03/06/83.

Doom Mission: USA: LA Times Syndicate 01/24/82–04/17/82.U.K.: 03/13/83–29/05/83.

Race for Survival. USA: LA Times Syndicate 04/18/82–07/10/82.U.K.: 06/05/83–08/21/83.

The Paradise Detour. USA: LA Times Syndicate 07/11/82–10/02/82.U.K.: 08/28/83–11/13/83.

A New Beginning. USA: LA Times Syndicate 10/03/82–12/25/82.U.K.: 11/20/83–02/19/84.

Showdown. USA: LA Times Syndicate 12/26/82–02/05/84.U.K.: 02/26/84–04/01/84.

The Final Trap. USA: LA Times Syndicate 02/06/84–03/11/84.U.K.: 04/08/84–05/06/84.

The Empire Strikes Back. Marvel USA 39. Marvel U.K. 118–120.

The Empire Strikes Back. Marvel USA 40. Marvel U.K. 121–123.

The Empire Strikes Back. Imperial Pursuit. Marvel USA 41. Marvel U.K. 124–126.

The Empire Strikes Back. To Be a Jedi. Marvel USA 42. Marvel U.K. 127–129.

The Empire Strikes Back. Betrayal at Bespin. Marvel USA 43. Marvel U.K. 130–132.

The Empire Strikes Back. Duel a Dark Lord. Marvel USA 44. Marvel U.K. 133–135.

Crimson Forever. Marvel USA 50. Marvel U.K. 1981 Annual (The Empire Strikes Back Annual No 2).

Resurrection of Evil. Marvel USA 51. Marvel U.K. 147.

To Take the Tarkin. Marvel USA 52. Marvel U.K. 148.

Plif! Marvel USA 55. Marvel U.K. 152.

Coffin in the Clouds. Marvel USA 56. Marvel U.K. 154–155.

Hello, Bespin, good-bye! Marvel USA 57. Marvel U.K. 156–157.

Sundown! Marvel USA 58. Marvel U.K. 158.

Bazarre. Marvel USA 59. Marvel U.K. 159.

Shira's Story. Marvel USA 60. Marvel U.K. 160.

Screams in the Void. Marvel USA 61. Marvel U.K. 161.

Pariah! Marvel USA 62. Marvel U.K. 162.

The Mind Spider! Marvel USA 63. Marvel U.K. 163.

Golrath Never Forgets! Marvel USA 65. Marvel U.K. 165.

The Water Bandits! Marvel USA 66. Marvel U.K. 166.

The Darker. Marvel USA 67. Marvel U.K. 167.

The Search Begins. Marvel USA 68. Marvel U.K. 168.

Death in the City of Bone! Marvel USA 69. Marvel U.K. 169.

The Stenax Shuffle. Marvel USA 70. Marvel U.K. 170.

Return to Stenos. Marvel USA 71. Marvel U.K. 171.

Fool's Bounty. Marvel USA 72. Marvel U.K. ROTJ Weekly 1–3.

Lashbane. Marvel USA 73. Marvel U.K. ROTJ Weekly 4–6.

The Iskalon Effect. Marvel USA 74. Marvel U.K. ROTJ Weekly 7–9.

Tidal. Marvel USA 75. Marvel U.K. ROTJ Weekly 10–14.

Artoo-Detoo to the Rescue. Marvel USA 76. Marvel U.K. ROTJ Weekly 15–19.

Chanteuse of the Stars. Marvel USA 77. Marvel U.K. ROTJ Weekly 20–25.

The Big Con. Marvel USA 79. Marvel U.K. ROTJ Weekly 32–37.

Ellie. Marvel USA 80. Marvel U.K. ROTJ Weekly 38–43.

Return of the Jedi. In the Hands of Jabba the

Hutt. Marvel USA 1. Marvel U.K. ROTJ Weekly 1–2.

Return of the Jedi. The Emperor Commands. Marvel USA 2. Marvel U.K. ROTJ Weekly 3–4.

Return of the Jedi. Mission to Endor. Marvel USA 3. Marvel U.K. ROTJ Weekly 5–6

Return of the Jedi. The Final Duel. Marvel USA 4. Marvel U.K. ROTJ Weekly 7–9.

Chapter Notes

Chapter 1

1. *Variety.* 08/28/75.
2. *Variety.* 08/28/75.
3. *Screen International.* 07/24/76.
4. Leslie Hilton. *The Sun.* 06/28/77.
5. David Lewin. *Daily Mail.* 08/01/77.
6. John Austin. *Screen International.* 06/11/77.
7. Marc Pevers. "The Man Who Sold Star Wars." *Palm Springs Life.* 06/04/07.
8. Marc Pevers. "The Man Who Sold Star Wars." *Palm Springs Life.* 06/04/07.
9. Marc Pevers. "The Man Who Sold Star Wars." *Palm Springs Life.* 06/04/07.
10. Marc Pevers. "The Man Who Sold Star Wars." *Palm Springs Life.* 06/04/07.
11. "An Interview with Bernard Loomis." D. Martin Myatt. Rebelscum.com.
12. *Plastic Galaxy: The Story of Star Wars Toys.* 2014. Director/writer Brian Stillman.
13. *Plastic Galaxy: The Story of Star Wars Toys.* 2014. Director/writer Brian Stillman.
14. *Plastic Galaxy: The Story of Star Wars Toys.* 2014. Director/writer Brian Stillman.
15. "The Guru: Uncut. A Tribute to Stanley Bielecki." *BAFTA podcast.* 01/01/12.
16. "The Guru: Uncut. A Tribute to Stanley Bielecki." *BAFTA podcast.* 01/01/12.
17. Tony Crawley. "Logan's Done." *Starburst.* May 1978.
18. Dez Skinn website. Dezskinn.com.
19. *A Garret in Goodge St.* Mark Williams. Dennis Publishing Ltd. P.27.
20. *A Garret in Goodge St.* Mark Williams. Dennis Publishing Ltd. P.28.
21. *Empire Building.* Garry Jenkins. Simon & Schuster Ltd. P.155.
22. *Star Wars* promotional brochure. 20th Century-Fox 1977.
23. George Lucas. *Star Wars.* Color segment. Del Rey Books 1976.
24. Charles Gerhardt. Sleeve notes, *John Williams Star Wars Close Encounters of the Third Kind.* RCA Ltd.
25. *Movie Collector magazine.* November/December 1994.
26. "My Star Wars." Brian Muir. *Star Wars Insider* issue 44.
27. Alan Jones. *Starburst* issue 46.
28. *2000AD Summer Special 1977.* IPC Magazines. Fleetway Publications.
29. Michael Rogers. *Rolling Stone.* 07/28/77.
30. "Space for Swashbuckling." Richard Roud. *The Guardian.* 10/21/77.
31. "Mask Force." Bill Hagerty. *Daily Mirror.* 07/27/77.
32. *Starlog* June 1979.
33. *Screen International,* January 28, 1978.
34. *Star Wars Official Poster Monthly (USA edition)* issue 1. Bunch Associates.
35. *A Garrett in Goodge Street.* Mark Williams. Dennis Publishing. P.40
36. *A Garrett in Goodge Street.* Mark Williams. Dennis Publishing. P.28.
37. *A Garrett in Goodge Street.* Mark Williams. Dennis Publishing. P.27.
38. "The Force Behind George Lucas." Paul Scanlon. *Rolling Stone.* 08/25/77.
39. John Austin. *Photoplay.* September 1977.
40. *Variety.* 09/21/77.
41. *House of Hammer.* October 1977.
42. *Theforce.net.* "Jedi Council Interview with Meco Monardo." April 2000. Paul Davison.
43. *episodenothingblogspot.com. Star Wars in the 1970s.* Darren Slade.
44. Fred Wehner. *Daily Mail.* 11/10/77.
45. *Nashua Telegraph.* 11/17/77.
46. *Nashua Telegraph.* 11/11/77.
47. "Carrie Fisher Speaks to Pendennis." *The Observer* 10/02/77.
48. "The Space Hero Who Is Conquering the World." Judy Wade. *The Sun.* 10/27/77.
49. "Meet the Stars of the Biggest Movie Hit Ever Made." Judy Wade. *The Sun.* 10/14/77.
50. "The Wonderful Wizardry of Star Wars." Alexander Walker. *The Evening Standard.* 11/10/77.
51. *Variety.* 11/19/77.
52. *Dez Skinn. Dezskinn.com.*
53. *Screen International.* 07/22/78.
54. Philip Norman. *Sunday Times.* 11/13/77.
55. Keith Waterhouse. *Daily Mirror.* 12/22/77.
56. Philip Norman. *Sunday Times.* 11/13/77.
57. Suzy Menkes. *Daily Express.* 12/21/77.
58. "A Long Time Ago in a Playground Just Down the Road." *Empire.* September 2006.
59. "Super Star Wars." Judy Wade. *The Sun.* 12/13/77.
60. "The Galactic Cowboy Comes Down to Earth." Jenny Rees. *Daily Mail.* 12/16/77.
61. *Daily Mail.* 12/19/77.
62. John Coleman. *The New Statesman.* 12/19/77.
63. Derek Malcolm. *The Guardian.* 12/19/77.

64. Gordon Gow. *Films and Filming.* January 1978.

65. David Robinson. *The Times.* 12/12/77.

66. John Brosnan. *House of Hammer.* May 1978.

67. Michael Moorcock. *The New Statesman.* 12/14/77.

68. Jonathan Rosenbaum. *Sight and Sound.* November 1977.

69. Margaret Hinxman. *Daily Mail.* 12/13/77.

70. Roderick Gilchrist. *Daily Mail.* 12/13/77.

71. Barry Norman. *Film 77.* BBC1. 12/17/77.

72. *Parkinson.* BBC1. 12/17/77.

73. *Time.* 12/18/77.

74. *2000AD.* IPC Magazines. Fleetway Publications. 12/24/77.

75. *BBC 1 News.* 12/27/77.

76. *ITV News.* 12/27/77.

77. *2000AD.* IPC Magazines. Fleetway Publications. 12/24/77.

78. Foreword. *Once Upon a Galaxy: The Making of the Empire Strikes Back.* Alan Arnold. Del Rey. 1980.

79. S. Schoenbaum. *Times Literary Supplement.* 10/05/77.

80. *Empire of Dreams: The Story of the 'Star Wars' Trilogy* documentary. 2004. Directors Edith Becker, Kevin Burns. Writer Ed Singer.

81. *Empire of Dreams: The Story of the 'Star Wars' Trilogy* documentary. 2004. Directors Edith Becker, Kevin Burns. Writer Ed Singer.

82. George Lucas. *Star Wars.* Del Rey 1976. Photograph center pages.

83. IMDB.com.

Chapter 2

1. *Evening Standard.* 01/03/78.

2. *ATV Today.* 01/13/78.

3. Margaret Hinxman. *Daily Mail.* 02/07/78.

4. *The Official Star Wars Poster Monthly (U.K edition) #1.* Bunch Associates.

5. Harrison Ford interview. Richard Tippet. *Look-in.* No. 11.

6. "The Worlds of Gerry Anderson." *Look-in.* No 11.

7. Maurice Rotheroe. *Birmingham Evening Mail.* 01/18/78.

8. Silver Jet. thedigifaxwww

9. *Manchester Evening News.* 02/12/78.

10. John Brosnan. *House of Hammer.* 01/14/78.

11. Jon Trux. *Official Star Wars Poster Monthly #2.* Bunch Associates.

12. Dr. M.F Marten. *Official Star Wars Poster Monthly #2.* Bunch Associates.

13. John May. *Official Star Wars Poster Monthly #2.* Bunch Associates.

14. Tony Berry. *Gloucester Journal.* 02/25/78.

15. "Out of This World." John Jones. *Daily Express.* 02/16/78.

16. "One of Our Spaceships Is Missing." *Potter's Picture Palace.* BBC 1. 04/28/78. Credits: http://www.imdb.com/title/tt1597436/; review: http://www.imdb.com/title/tt0490744/reviews, "Pure Popcorn Entertainment." Description from ShadeGrenade from Ambrosia, July 24, 2010.

17. "May the Force of the Sales Pitch Be with You." Berry Ritchie. *Sunday Times* 02/12/78.

18. Phil Heeks. *Waiting for Star Wars.* Lulu.com. 03/08/16.

19. "Behind the Scenes of Star Wars." *Star Wars Weekly# 4.* Marvel UK.

20. dezskinn.com.

21. "Behind the Scenes of Star Wars." *Star Wars Weekly# 2.* Marvel UK.

22. *Star Wars Annual No. 1.* Brown Watson. 1978.

23. "Star Wars in the U.K. Star Wars Comic Book Annuals." Mark Newbold. *Starwars.com.* 09/15/13.

24. "May the Force of the Sales Pitch Be with You." Berry Ritchie. *Sunday Times.* 02/12/78.

25. John May. *Official Poster Monthly # 3.* Bunch Associates.

26. Silver Jet. thedigifax.com.

27. "Interview with Meco Monardo." Jussi Kantonen. Discostyle.com. 09/12/07.

28. *Focus. The Magazine of the Colchester & East Essex Co-operative Society Ltd. Volume V, Issue XVIII,* March 1978.

29. "Cosmic Correspondence." *Star Wars Weekly #25.* Marvel UK.

30. *Official Star Wars fan club newsletter #2.* Lucasfilm Ltd.

31. "A Long Time Ago in a Playground Just Down the Road." *Empire.* September 2006.

32. "Cosmic Correspondence." *Star Wars Weekly # 17.* Marvel UK.

33. John May. *Official Star Wars Poster Monthly # 4.* Bunch Associates.

34. *The Making of Star Wars.* 20th Century-Fox Television 1977.

35. *Official Star Wars fan club newsletter #3.* Lucasfilm Ltd.

36. Harrison Ford interviewed by Tony Crawley. *Starburst* May 1978.

37. Dr. M.F Marten. *Official Star Wars Poster Monthly #5.* Bunch Associates.

38. Dr. M.F Marten. *Official Star Wars Poster Monthly #6.* Bunch Associates.

39. Jon Trux. *Official Star Wars Poster Monthly #6.* Bunch Associates.

40. *Star Wars.* George Lucas. Del Rey 1976.

41. John May. *Official Star Wars Poster Monthly #7.* Bunch Associates.

42. Jon Trux. *Official Star Wars Poster Monthly #7.* Bunch Associates.

43. Roy Thomas. *Star Wars Weekly #37.* Marvel UK.

44. Roy Thomas. Star *Wars Weekly # 37.* Marvel UK.

45. Kurt Busiek. *Comics Feature.* January 1982.

46. "Star Wars in the Comics." J. Collier. *Amazing Heroes #13.* July 1982.

Chapter 3

1. Patrick Lay. *Daily Express.* 07/18/78.

2. IMDB.com.

3. *Darth Vader's TIE Fighter model kit instruction booklet.* MPC.

4. "The Force Was with Us: A Star Wars Echoes Special." 12/15/15. Darren Slade. *Bournemouthecho.co.uk.*

5. "A Long Time Ago in a Playground Just Down the Road." *Empire.* September 2006.

6. John May. *Official Star Wars Poster Monthly #8.* Bunch Associates.

7. Brian Shepherd. *Official Star Wars Poster Monthly #8*. Bunch Associates.

8. *The Making of Star Wars*. 20th Century–Fox Television. 1977.

9. Brian Shepherd. *Official Star Wars Poster Monthly #9*. Bunch Associates.

10. Dennis Barker. *The Guardian*. 11/26/77.

11. Letters page. *The Guardian*. Edited by Brain Chugg. 09/16/77.

12. Brian Shepherd. *Official Star Wars Poster Monthly #9*. Bunch Associates.

13. *Star Wars (film)*. George Lucas. 20th Century-Fox 1977.

14. John May. *Official Star Wars Poster Monthly #9*. Bunch Associates.

15. "Cosmic Correspondence." *Star Wars Weekly #25*. Marvel UK.

16. Zac Jones. *Official Star Wars Poster Monthly #11*. Bunch Associates.

17. Mark Newbold. "Mary Jo Duffy TeeKay-421 Interview." 01/28/11.

18. Michael Marten. *Official Star Wars Poster Monthly #12*. Bunch Associates.

19. John May. *Official Star Wars Poster Monthly # 14*. Bunch Associates.

20. "Lucas and Spielberg Beyond Star Wars and CE3K." Tony Crawley. *Starburst*. December 1978.

21. IMDB.com.

Chapter 4

1. Editorial. *Star Wars Weekly #50*. Marvel UK.

2. Dez Skinn. Dezskinn.com.

3. John May. *Official Star Wars Poster Monthly #15*. Bunch Associates.

4. "Luke Skywalker Is Alive and Well in The Empire Strikes Back." Joseph Kay. *Starlog* December 1977.

5. Greg Moody. *The Milwaukee Sentinel* 11/17/78.

6. "Star Wars on Ice." Joe Steeples. *The Sun* 03/12/79.

7. "Hop on a Star" Editorial. *Daily Express*. 03/12/79.

8. "The Guru: Uncut. A Tribute to Stanley Bielecki." *Bafta podcast*. 01/01/12.

9. Bart Mills. *The Guardian*. 12/18/78.

10. Thompson Prentice. *Daily Mail*. 05/03/78.

11. David Robinson. *The Times*. 07/06/78.

12. "WAMU's Derek McGinty Show." "Authors of the Expanded Universe: Brian Daley." Michael Kogge. *Star Wars insider #115*.

13. Brian Daley. *Han Solo at Star's End*. Del Rey. 1979.

14. Mark Hamill interviewed by Steve Swires. *Starlog*. April 1979.

Chapter 5

1. "Designing the Original Star Wars Figures." *Tomart's Action Figure Digest*. No 77. July 2000.

2. "Star Wars in the U.K: Read-Along Adventures." M ark Newbold. *Star Wars.com*. 09/22/13.

3. John Chesterman. *Official Star Wars Poster Monthly #17*. Bunch Associates.

4. John May. *Official Star Wars Poster Monthly #17*.

5. Kurt Busiek. *Comics Feature* magazine. January 1982.

6. *Bantha Tracks #5*. Lucasfilm Ltd.

7. David Prowse interview. David Hirsch. *Starlog*. June 1979.

8. John Chesterman. *Official Star Wars Poster Magazine #18*. Bunch Associates.

9. John May. *Official Star Wars Poster Magazine #18*. Bunch Associates.

10. *Bantha Tracks #6*. Lucasfilm Ltd.

11. *Star Wars Annual no.2*. Marvel/Grandreams.

12. B.J Franklin. *Screen International*. 15/12/79.

Chapter 6

1. *starwarsinterviews.blogspot.co.uk*.

2. Tom Merrin. *Daily Mirror*. 03/17/80.

3. Peter Durisch. *Daily Express*. 03/17/80.

4. Alan Frank. *Daily Star*. 04/21/80.

5. *Cinemas of Hertfordshire* by Allen Eyles. Hertfordshire Publications.

6. *Variety*. 02/27/80.

7. *Bantha Tracks #7*. Lucasfilm Ltd.

8. *Film Review*. June 1980.

9. Billy Dee Williams interview. Bob Woods. *Starlog*. June 1980.

10. Brian Johnson interview. David Hutchinson. *Starlog*. June 1980.

11. Gerald Clarke. *Time* 05/19/80.

12. "An afterword from George Lucas." *Mediascene #41*.

13. *Bantha Tracks #8*. Lucasfilm Ltd.

Chapter 7

1. Terry Mottram. *London Evening News*. 05/20/80.

2. Chris Kenworthy. *The Sun*. 05/20/80.

3. Nicholas Wapshott. *The Times*. 05/23/80.

4. William Hall. *The Evening News*. 05/22/80.

5. Andrew Rissik. *Films Illustrated*. September 1980.

6. Gerald Clarke. *Time*. 05/19/80.

7. Cecil Wilson. *Daily Mail*. 05/23/80.

8. Ian Christie. *Daily Express*. 05/21/80.

9. Arthur Thirkell. *Daily Mirror*. 05/23/80.

10. Madeline Harmsworth. *Sunday Mirror*. 05/25/80.

11. Brian Johnson. *Screen International*. 05/24/80, 483.

12. "The Guru: Uncut. A Tribute to Stanley Bielecki." *Bafta podcast*. 01/01/12.

13. *The Empire Strikes Back Official Poster Monthly #1*. Bunch Associates.

14. *The Empire Strikes Back Collectors Edition*. John May. Bunch Associates. P.49.

15. *Starwarsforum.co.uk*.

16. "The Story of Freddie Mercury Getting a Piggy Back Ride from Darth Vader." Annie Zaleski. avclub.com. 09/05/15.

17. *Freddie Mercury: A Kind of Magic*. Mark Blake. Backbeat Books 2016.

18. Laurence Kasdan interviewed. Blake Mitchell and James Ferguson. *Fantastic Films*. July 1980.

19. "The Making of the Empire Strikes Back." Tony Crawley. *Starburst*. May 1980.

20. *Screen International*. 06/28/80, p. 20.

21. Dave Badger. *Film Review*. August 1980.

22. "Slaves to the Empire." Timothy White. *Rolling Stone*. 07/24/80.

23. *The Empire Strikes Back Official Poster Monthly #4*. Bunch Associates.

24. "Cosmic Correspondence." *Return of the Jedi Weekly #3*. Marvel U.K.

25. *Starwarsforum.co.uk*.

26. *Once Upon a Galaxy: A Journal of the Making of the Empire Strikes Back*. Alan Arnold. Sphere 1980. P.156.

27. *Once Upon a Galaxy: A Journal of the Making of the Empire Strikes Back*. Alan Arnold. Sphere 1980. P.42.

28. *Once Upon a Galaxy: A Journal of the Making of the Empire Strikes Back*. Alan Arnold. Sphere 1980. P.93.

29. *Bantha Tracks #9*. Lucasfilm Ltd.

30. Dr. M. F. Marten. *The Official Empire Strikes Back Poster Magazine #5*. Bunch Associates.

31. jmdematteis.com.

32. Bill Hays. *Fantastic Films*. December 1980.

33. IMDB.com.

34. IMDB.com.

35. IMDB.com.

36. IMDB.com.

37. IMDB.com.

Chapter 8

1. *Screen International* 01/10/81.

2. freewebswww/mrpalitoy. Mr. Palitoy's Star Wars card back guide.

3. *Bantha Tracks #11*. Lucasfilm Ltd.

4. "Star Wars comes to Radio." Frank Brady. *Fantastic Films*. June 1981.

5. The Guardian 04/27/79.

6. "Star Wars comes to Radio." Frank Brady. *Fantastic Films*. June 1981.

7. "Airfix Toys go to General Mills." Rosemary Unsworth. *The Times*. 23/04/81.

8. "Star Wars in the Comics." J. Collier. *Amazing Heroes #13*. July 1982.

9. Kerry O'Quinn. *Starlog*. July 1981.

10. Howard Kazanjian. *Bantha Tracks #13*. Lucasfilm Ltd.

11. Joe Johnson. *Bantha Tracks #14*. Lucasfilm Ltd.

Chapter 9

1. "Things to Come." Tony Crawley. *Starburst #43*.

2. Stuart Tendler. *The Times* 03/31/80.

3. Tony Crawley. *Starburst #43*.

4. *Bantha Tracks #15*. Lucasfilm Ltd.

5. *Bantha Tracks #15*. Lucasfilm Ltd.

6. *Bantha Tracks #16*. Lucasfilm Ltd.

7. *Bantha Tracks #16*. Lucasfilm Ltd.

8. *Screen International*. 05/22/82.

9. "Cosmic Correspondence." *Return of the Jedi Weekly #3*.

10. *Screen International* 12/06/82.

11. "Behind the Scenes—Star Wars: The Empire Strikes Back." *gamestm.co.uk*.

12. *Variety*. 09/01/82.

13. "TV review." Margaret Hinxman *Daily Mail* 23/10/82.

14. Mark Hamill interview. Susan Adamo. *Starlog*. December 1982.

Chapter 10

1. "Lift Off." *Star Wars Monthly*. January 1981. Marvel UK.

2. "Star Wars in the Comics." J. Collier. *Amazing Heroes #13*. July 1982.

3. "R.I.P. Al Williamson." David Robertson. *fredeggcomics.blogspot.co.uk*. 06/16/10.

4. "Star Wars in the Comics." J. Collier. *Amazing Heroes #13*. July 1982.

5. *Bantha Tracks #17*. Lucasfilm Ltd.

6. "Revenge of the Jedi on Location." Dan Smith. Duncan Osborne. Elizabeth Hannan. *Yuma Daily Sun*. 05/02/82.

7. *Bantha Tracks #18*. Lucasfilm Ltd.

8. *Bantha Tracks #18*. Lucasfilm Ltd.

9. Anthony Daniels interview. Ed Naha. *Starlog*. April 1983.

10. Howard Kazanjian interview. Robert Greenberger. *Starlog*. April 1983.

11. Richard Marquand interview. Steranko. *Mediascene Preview*. June/July 1983.

12. *Film Review*. June 1980.

13. Carrie Fisher interview. Pauline McLeod. *Daily Mirror*. 06/06/83.

14. Dale Pollack. *Sunday Express Supplement Magazine*. 05/22/83.

15. "Great Galloping Galaxies!" Gerald Clarke. *Time*. 05/22/83.

16. "Great Galloping Galaxies!" Gerald Clarke. *Time*. 05/22/83.

17. Richard Marquand interview. Alan Murdoch. *Starburst*. June 1983.

18. "Fox Helps an Assured Blockbuster on Its Way." Alex Sutherland. *Screen International* 05/28/83.

19. "Cosmic Correspondence." *Star Wars Monthly #169*. Marvel U.K.

20. *Starwarsforum.co.uk*.

21. Jean Duwald. *Glasgow Herald*. 05/30/83.

22. *Screen International*. 05/28/83.

23. "Cosmic Correspondence." *Return of the Jedi Weekly #15*. Marvel UK.

Chapter 11

1. "A Long Time Ago in a Playground Just Down the Road." *Empire*. September 2006.

2. *The Making of Return of the Jedi*. J.W Rinzler. P.336.

3. "Dermot Pergavie's America." *Daily Mail*. 06/02/83.

4. Derek Malcolm. *The Guardian*. 06/02/83.

5. Ian Christie. *Daily Express*. 06/03/83.

6. Tom Merrin. *Daily Mirror*. 06/03/83.

7. Margaret Hinxman. *Daily Mail*. 07/01/83.

8. Michael Strahan. *Rolling Stone*. 07/07/83.

9. *Return of the Jedi Official Poster Monthly #1*. Bunch Associates.

10. *Film Review*. July 1983.

11. *Evening Standard*. 06/30/83.

12. *Screen International*. 06/25/83.

13. David Hewson. *The Times*. 06/21/83.

14. Phil Heeks. *Waiting for Star Wars*. Lulu.com. 03/08/16.

15. *The Citizen*, Ottawa. 06/16/83.

16. *Starwarsforum.co.uk.*

17. *Fantastic Films.* November 1983.

18. "SFX Secrets Revealed." Adam Eisenberg. *Space Voyager.* October/November 1983.

19. *Bantha Tracks #21.* Lucasfilm Ltd.

20. Sal Manna. *Starlog.* October 1983.

21. *Return of the Jedi Official Poster Monthly # 3.* Bunch Associates.

22. *The Making of Return of the Jedi.* Edited by John Philip Peecher. P.77.

23. *The Making of Return of the Jedi.* Edited by John Philip Peecher. P.17.

24. Mary Jo Duffy interview. *Marvel Age* #10.

25. Mark Newbold. "Mary Jo Duffy TeeKay-421 Interview." 01/28/11.

26. "George Lucas Wants to Play Guitar." Paul Scanlon. *Rolling Stone.* 07/21/83–08/04/83.

27. "Cosmic Correspondence." *Return of the Jedi Weekly #23.* Marvel UK.

28. IMDB.com.

29. John Brosnan. *Starburst.* September 1983.

30. Letters page. *Fantastic Films.* November 1983.

31. "Cosmic Correspondence." *Return of the Jedi Weekly #6.* Marvel UK.

32. Anthony Daniels interview. Ed Naha. *Starlog.* April 1983.

33. Mark Hamill interview. Steve Swires. *Starlog* August 1983.

34. Dave Prowse interview. Ian F. McAsh. *Film Review.* August 1983.

35. Carrie Fisher interview. Ed Team. *Starburst.* September 1983.

36. Jenny Glew. *The Guardian* 10/12/83.

37. In researching this book, I have been unable to find accurate figures of how much *Return of the Jedi* grossed in the U.K in 1983. The brochure for the relaunch of *Star Wars* in Great Britain in 1994 provides the figure of £12,300,00. Considering how rushed the document appears, it seems as if the dollar total was simply quoted in pounds sterling. If this is the case, the figure would match my own dollar estimate and be in line with the profits of other films released that year. *Octopussy* grossed $8,305,00 and *Superman III* $6,710,00 (IMDB). It would be impossible to calculate the gross of any film by studying individual cinema statistics but taking into consideration how much longer *Return of the Jedi* ran for in cinemas compared to *The Empire Strikes Back*, I can only conclude that the film was considered to be successful.

Bibliography

Arnold, Alan. *Once Upon a Galaxy: A Journal of the Making of The Empire Strikes Back*. Del Rey. 1980.

The Art of Return of the Jedi. Ballantine. 1983.

Byrne, Fergus. *More Lives Than One*. Ebury. 2015. [Felix Dennis Biography].

Bulluck, Vic, and Valerie Hoffman, ed. Deborah Call. *The Art of The Empire Strikes Back*. Ballantine. 1980.

Freewebs.com/mrpalitoy.

Gilbey, Ryan. *It Don't Worry Me*. Faber & Faber. 2003.

Star Wars, vols. 1–3. Russ Cochran. 1991. [Archie Goodwin and Al Williamson comic strip].

Heeks, Phillip. *Waiting for Star Wars*. Lulu.com. 2016.

Jenkins, Garry. *Empire Building: The Remarkable Real Life Story of Star Wars*. Simon & Schuster. 1997.

Officialcharts.com.

Peecher, John Philip. *The Making of Return of the Jedi*. Del Rey 1983.

Pollock, Dale. *Skywalking: The Life and Films of George Lucas*. Harmony. 1983.

Rinzler, J.W. *The Making of Return of the Jedi*. 2013.

Rinzler, J.W. *The Making of Star Wars*. Ebury. 2007.

Rinzler, J.W. *The Making of The Empire Strikes Back*. 2010.

Robb, Brian J. *A Brief Guide to Star Wars*. Running Book. 2012.

Sansweet, Steve, and Pete Vilmur. *The Star Wars Vault*. Simon & Schuster. 2007.

Shone, Tom. *Blockbuster*. Simon & Schuster. 2004.

Slavicsek, Bill. *A Guide to the Star Wars Universe*, 2d ed. Del Rey 1994.

Star Wars Year by Year: A Visual Chronicle. D.K. 2010.

Taylor, Chris. *How Star Wars Conquered the Universe*. Basic. 2014.

Titleman, Carol, ed. *The Art of Star Wars*. Ballantine, 1979.

Velasco, Raymond L. *A Guide to the Star Wars Universe*. Del Rey 1984.

Ward, Arthur. *The Boy's Book of Airfix*. Ebury. 2009.

Williams, Mark. *A Garret in Goodge Street*. Dennis. 2012.

Winder, Simon. *The Man Who Saved Great Britain*. Picador. 2006.

For Further Reading

Cerealoffers.com. An excellent resource for breakfast cereal collecting including *Star Wars*.

Episodenothing.blogspot.co.uk is Darren Slade's excellent commentary on all things British and *Star Wars*.

Forcecast.net. The official podcasting network of Theforce.net and Rebelscum.com.

Freewebs.com/mrpalitoy. Mr. Palitoy's *Star Wars* card back guide.

Hqinfo.blogspot.co.uk is the place to find John May's Generalist blog.

igrewupstarwars.com. Photos and memories of everyone who grew up with *Star Wars*.

Imperialgunnery.com. Vintage weapons and accessories guide.

Jedinews.co.uk is the main U.K based website.

Jeditemplearchives.com. Collectible news, reviews and archives.

Ralphmquarrie.com. The art of Ralph McQuarrie.

Rebelscum.com. "Philp Wise presents… *Star Wars* collecting news."

Star Wars FAQ. Mark Clark. Applause.

Starwars.com

Starwarscards.net. Resource for cards, stickers, pogs and similar items.

Starwarscollector.com. Collecting news and HD photo gallery.

Starwarsforum.co.uk is a home for discussion on collecting.

swtvrpodcast.podbean.com. The *Star Wars* Vintage Rebellion podcast.

Theforce.net. "Your daily dose of *Star Wars*."

Theswca.com. The collector's archive.

Trilogo.info. Dedicated to *Star Wars* trilogo collecting.

Vintagestarwarsdiecast.co.uk. Everything you need to know about the die cast toys.

Index